A MILTON ENCYCLOPEDIA

A MILTON ENCYCLOPEDIA

VOLUME 1 Ab–By

Edited by

William B. Hunter, Jr., *General Editor*

John T. Shawcross *and* John M. Steadman, *Co-Editors*

Purvis E. Boyette and Leonard Nathanson,
Associate Editors

Lewisburg
Bucknell University Press
London: Associated University Presses

© 1978 by Associated University Presses, Inc.

Associated University Presses, Inc.
Cranbury, New Jersey 08512

Associated University Presses
Magdalen House
136–148 Tooley Street
London SE1 2TT, England

A Milton encyclopedia.

Includes bibliographical references.
1. Milton, John, 1608–1674—Dictionaries, indexes, etc.
I. Hunter, William Bridges, 1915–
PR3580.M5   821'.4   75–21896
ISBN 0-8387-1834-5 (v. 1)

PRINTED IN THE UNITED STATES OF AMERICA

PREFACE

This compilation attempts to bring together all of the important information and opinion concerning the life and works of John Milton. Because he wrote in a variety of forms, because he was deeply involved in the public issues of his day, especially political and religious ones, and because of the controversies that have always swirled about his name, the Encyclopedia has in some ways grown to be a study of English civilization of Milton's time and a history of literary and political matters since then, offering quick but authoritative access to individual topics.

Organization of this large body of information is alphabetical. There is no index, but cross-referencing is achieved in two ways. First, a subject that appears as an entry in the main alphabet may refer to another entry under which that subject is treated. Second, when subjects that are also discussed in other entries are mentioned, they are marked with asterisks, with the exception of certain ones appearing too frequently for such treatment to be practical. Among these are the titles of all of Milton's works (each has a separate entry); the various named characters who appear in the works; and the names of Milton and his family including his wife Mary Powell and her family, and his sister Anne Phillips and her family.

Articles were submitted by the various contributors from the fall of 1969 through the fall of 1972. A few additions were written (mostly by the editors) as late as the summer of 1975, the terminal date for the entire compilation. Purvis Boyette conceived the work originally; he served as general editor from the beginning until September 1971. John T. Shawcross then followed him, but in January 1973 relinquished the general direction to William Hunter, who has read and finally edited the entire manuscript. All of the entries have been approved by at least two editors, who have on occasion shortened them or revised them to accord with the style of the whole. The entries were written for the general reader by specialists. In every case they are original and represent the point of view of the author to whom each is attributed.

With great regret the editors have had to omit all bibliographies, owing to the size of the work, although references within the text have been retained. To achieve further saving of space, titles of articles in periodicals have been removed, together with the date of publication, as have the places of publication of modern books. The titles of Milton's various works have been uniformly abbreviated in forms to be found in the front matter of each volume, as have references to the major modern editions and biographical works. All otherwise unidentified quotations of his writings are drawn from the complete edition published by the Columbia University Press (1931–1938).

The editors wish to thank all the contributors of the entries, who have freely shared their expertise and have patiently awaited the appearance of the Encyclopedia. In addition, special gratitude is owing to Tulane University, to the University of New Hampshire, and to the University of Houston for financial help with the editing. We are indebted to the University of Wisconsin Press for its original support of the project, to the Tennessee State University Press for its consideration of the completed manuscript, and to Associated University Presses, Inc., and their Editor in Chief, Mathilde E. Finch, for seeing the work through publication.

June 15, 1975

Purvis E. Boyette
William B. Hunter, Jr.
Leonard Nathanson
John T. Shawcross
John M. Steadman

SHORT FORMS USED IN THIS ENCYCLOPEDIA

AdP	Ad Patrem
Animad	Animadversions upon the Remonstrant's Defense
Apol	An Apology
Arc	Arcades
Areop	Areopagitica
BrM	Bridgewater Manuscript
BN	Brief Notes upon a Late Sermon
Brit	The History of Britain
Bucer	The Judgement of Martin Bucer
CarEl	Carmina Elegiaca
Carrier 1, 2	On the University Carrier; Another on the Same
CB	Commonplace Book
CharLP	Character of the Long Parliament
Circum	Upon the Circumcision
CD	De Doctrina Christiana
CM	*The Works of John Milton* (New York: Columbia University Press, 1931–1938). 18 vols. The so-called Columbia Milton.
Colas	Colasterion
CivP	A Treatise of Civil Power
DDD	The Doctrine and Discipline of Divorce
1Def	Pro Populo Anglicano Defensio
2Def	Defensio Secunda
3Def	Pro Se Defensio
Educ	Of Education
Eff	In Effigiei ejus Sculptorem
Eikon	Eikonoklastes
El	Elegia
EpDam	Epitaphium Damonis
Epistol	Epistolarum Familiarium
EpWin	Epitaph on the Marchioness of Winchester
FInf	On the Death of a Fair Infant

French, *Life Records*	J. Milton French. *The Life Records of John Milton* (New Brunswick, N.J.: Rutgers University Press, 1949–1958). 5 vols.
Hire	Considerations Touching the Likeliest Means to Remove Hirelings from the Church
Hor	The Fifth Ode of Horace
Idea	De Idea Platonica
IlP	Il Penseroso
L'Al	L'Allegro
Literae	Literae Pseudo-Senatûs Anglicani Cromwellii
Lyc	Lycidas
Logic	Artis Logicae
Mask	A Mask (Comus)
Masson, *Life*	David Masson. *The Life of John Milton* (London, 1859–1880). 6 vols. plus Index.
May	Song : On May Morning
Mosc	A Brief History of Moscovia
Nat	On the Morning of Christ's Nativity
Naturam	Naturam non pati senium
NewF	On the New Forcers of Conscience
Parker, *Milton*	William Riley Parker. *Milton: A Biography* (Oxford: Clarendon Press, 1968). 2 vols.
Peace	Articles of Peace
PL	Paradise Lost
PR	Paradise Regained
PrelE	Of Prelatical Episcopacy
PresM	The Present Means
Prol	Prolusion
Ps	Psalm
QNov	In Quintum Novembris
RCG	Reason of Church Government
Ref	Of Reformation
Rous	Ad Ioannem Rousium
SA	Samson Agonistes
Shak	On Shakespeare
SolMus	At a Solemn Music
Sonn	Sonnet
StateP	State Papers
Tenure	The Tenure of Kings and Magistrates
Tetra	Tetrachordon
Time	Of Time
TM	Trinity Manuscript
TR	Of True Religion
Vac	At a Vacation Exercise
Variorum Commentary	*A Variorum Commentary on the Poems of John Milton.* 3 vols. to date (New York : Columbia University Press, 1970–).
Way	The Ready and Easy Way to Establish a Free Commonwealth
Yale *Prose*	*Complete Prose Works of John Milton.* 6 vols. to date. (New Haven, Conn. : Yale University Press, 1953–).

Wherever a reference is given by volume and page but without any other identification, *CM* (Columbia Milton) as given above is intended. Thus (11 : 21) refers to page 21 of volume 11 of that edition.

ABDIEL, an angel* in *PL,* who alone of Satan's "myriads" rejects Satan's proposed rebellion as soon as he knows of it (5. 809ff.). The angelic host rejoices over his loyal, though superfluous, warning and God praises his lone "testimony of Truth" in whose cause he has borne the "Universal reproach, far worse to beare/Then violence" (6. 34–35) of Satan's followers. God foretells an "easier conquest" in the coming battle, in which Abdiel smites Satan (6. 189ff.) and blasts three lesser rebels. Here Abdiel speaks 120 lines of religious steadfastness in the face of obloquy and of militancy against apostates, often interpreted as Milton's personal views.

Abdiel appears in 1 Chronicles 5 :15 as the name of a man, but nowhere in the Bible as the name of an angel. As the name of an angel, it does appear in a cabalistic conjuring book, the *Sepher Raziel,* not printed before 1701. Most likely it derives from a Hebrew noun meaning "Servant of God," words by which God addresses Abdiel and which St. Paul applies to himself (Titus 1 :1), a fact that Milton may have had in mind.

Abdiel's speeches and conduct have led some critics to question his success as a literary character. Nathaniel Salmon asked ironically, "what Notion must we have of Angelic Perfection, to admit *Abdiel* could think himself alone" when myriads of loyal angels and Christ himself were surely on his side (*The History of Hertfordshire* [London, 1728], p. 185); A. J. A. Waldock thought that Abdiel put a more favorable face on God's treatment of deviant angels than it deserves, and thus that Abdiel's characterization is part of Milton's arbitrary management of the action to justify God (*Paradise Lost and its Critics,* pp. 72–73); and John Peter supposes that Abdiel's moral insight, singular among an army of angels whom we must suppose quite as knowledgeable as he, is entirely implausible and merely Milton's indulgence of a taste for writing about "a just man or angel defying the multitude" (*Critique of Paradise Lost,* p. 71). Nevertheless, most critics consider Milton successful in his depiction of Abdiel, for it is Raphael rather than the narrator who recounts these episodes; and he is partisan, rhetorical, selective, and even a trifle inventive. He does not, of course, explain in psychological detail why one creature (angel or man) wills salvation while myriads of others as favorably situated will damnation. Abdiel's crucial role was invented to show that one angel decided for himself and thus to imply that others did so too (Burden, *Logical Epic,* p. 38). In the original ten-book version of *PL* Abdiel is "at the centre of the poem" as an "exemplum both to Adam and the reader" of the "individual saving remnant in the midst of evil" (Summers, *Muse's Method,* pp. 112–13). "The truth is," George W. Whiting asserts, "that Abdiel is not only a faithful servant of God but *also a prophet."* To emphasize the fact, Milton adapted the name of the Old Testament prophet Abdias (Obadiah) (*Studies in Philology* 60 :214–15). Mason Tung's survey of opinion of the Abdiel episode concludes that Abdiel is "a concrete and dramatic example of the sufficiency and the freedom of the will*," and his trial a parallel to Adam and Eve's to affirm that though "Adam fell by his passion and Eve by her false dictating reason, neither her fall nor his was inevitable" (*Studies in Philology* 62 :595–609). Plainly Abdiel's role does significantly parallel Adam and Eve's, the prophet's, the poet's (particularly Milton's), Enoch's, and those of other lonely "just men." It is tightly and extensively woven into the fabric of *PL* and is a success for any reader who finds the character himself convincing. [RHW]

ACCADEMIA DEGLI SVOGLIATI

("Academy of the Disgusted"), a society of Florentine wits and intellectuals who met to discuss and to study classical and Tuscan literature, philology, and history. Throughout Italy, savants belonged to similar academies, designated by such fanciful names as the *Apatisti* ("Passionless") and the *Gelati* ("Frozens"). Sometimes individual members were known by fanciful pseudonyms; for example, Carlo Dati*, a friend of Milton's and member of the *Svogliati*, was known as *Smarrito* ("the Bewildered") in the *Accademia della Crusca* ("Academy of the Bran"). Founded by Jacopo Gaddi* (1602–1678), a Florentine patrician who was a poet and an art historian, the *Svogliati* usually met at his home in the Piazza Madonna. Its members composed and read Latin and Italian poetry and published collections of poetry and historical essays. Shortly after Milton's arrival in Florence, he was invited to attend their sessions, and in the minutes of September 16, 1638, it is recorded that he read an erudite Latin poem in hexameter verse. A member with whom Milton became friendly was the priest Benedetto Bonmatthei* (1581–1647), who was preparing a new grammar of the Tuscan dialect. Milton recommended that Bonmatthei include a section on pronunciation that would benefit foreigners and that he provide some background information on Tuscan authors, later repeating his advice in a long letter in Latin (*Epistol* 8), dated September 10, 1638. The grammar, *Della Lingua Toscana,* 1643, discussed pronunciation, but did not include information about Tuscan

authors. On his return to Florence in 1639, Milton attended three successive meetings of the *Svogliati,* on March 17, 24, and 31. During the first two he read Latin poetry; and probably during this second visit to Florence, he was presented with two encomia that celebrate his scholarly attainment : a Latin prose letter by Dati (*CM* 1 :164–67), and an Italian ode by Antonio Francini* (*CM* 1 : 157–65). These encomia are prefixed to the Latin poems of the 1645 edition of Milton's minor poems.

Though he did not again visit Florence, Milton later recalled his visit and, in particular, his association with the academies : see *RCG* (3 : 235–36); *2Def* (8 : 122–13); and a letter to Dati (*Epistol* 10), dated April 20, 1647, in which he requests Dati to convey his greetings to members of the academies. Dati's letters to Milton in turn convey greetings from and news about Milton's Florentine friends, with warmth and affection. [ACL]

ACCEDENCE COMMENC'T GRAMMAR, Milton's contribution to simplify the teaching of Latin grammar (*accidence* deals with the rudiments of a grammar, specifically inflection), which was published in June 1669 by Samuel Simmons*. Wood's* date of publication, 1661, is clearly an error. While in places Milton borrowed from the generally used grammar of the day, that by William Lily, he felt that he was being original in his blending of the rules of grammar and Latin prose together, and in his drastic shortening of the material to one quarter the length of that in Lily. Of 530 quotations, 330 are directly taken from Lily and 25 from other grammarians. Milton contributed 175 quotations from classical authors that are not found in other grammars. The work is divided into two parts : "right-wording, usually called etymology" and "right-joyning of words, or *Syntaxis,*" and was written in English. When Milton began the work is unknown, but Parker's conjecture of 1645 (*Milton,* p. 920), while Milton was tutoring, is likely. John Phil-

lips mentioned the fact that Milton resumed work on the grammar around 1655. [WM]

ACCOMMODATION, THEORY OF.

How can finite man understand an infinite God? The answer to this question provided one of the most commonplace and central ideas of the Renaissance. As Milton explains it in *CD*, "our safest way is to form in our minds such a conception of God, as shall correspond with his own delineation and representation of himself in the sacred writings. For granted that both in the literal and figurative descriptions of God, he is exhibited not as he really is, but in such manner as may be within the scope of our comprehension, yet we ought to maintain such a conception of him as he, in condescending to accommodate himself to our capacities, has shown that he desires we should conceive" (14:31, 33). And as Raphael explains to Adam, "what surmounts the reach / Of human sense, I shall delineate so, / By lik'ning spiritual to corporal forms" (*PL* 5. 571–73).

The *locus classicus* for this theory of accommodation is St. Augustine's* *City of God* (15. 25), in which Augustine says that the Scripture "cannot do without declining to our low capacities" and by means of figurative speaking (*figurata locutio*), as he also puts it in *The Christian Doctrine* (11:15). St. Thomas Aquinas* likewise said that "poetry uses metaphors to depict, since men naturally find pictures pleasing. But sacred doctrine uses them because they are necessary and useful," although one must distinguish between the historical (*sensus historicus*) and spiritual (*sensus spiritualis*) senses (*Summa Theologica* 1. 1. 9).

The scriptural authority for such metaphoric readings is found in Hebrews 9:23–24, where the author says that patterns of things in heaven, when symbolized by man, become "figures of the true," and its authority was augmented by Philo Judaeus*, who said that Moses' account of the Garden of Eden was "intended symbolically rather than literally"

(*Philo,* trans. F. H. Colson and G. H. Whitaker [1949], 1:123).

The idea was ubiquitous, shared by Catholic and Protestant alike. St. Hilary of Poitiers wrote that God "has so far tempered the language of His utterance as to enable the weakness of our nature to grasp and understand it" (*De Trinitate* 8. 43). John Calvin* asserted that our understanding of God was adapted to our capacities, for as human beings "we need symbols or mirrors to exhibit to us the appearance of spiritual and heavenly things in a kind of earthly way" (*Theological Treatises,* trans. and ed. J. K. S. Reid [1954], p. 131). And Thomas Wilson wrote in words strikingly like those of Milton that "because our dulnes to conceive the thinges of God is so great as wee cannot perceive them, but by comparisons drawne from the things of men, for this infirmity of our understanding, the scripture very often speaketh of invisible thinges by visible, and shadoweth spirituall, by corporall" (*Theological Rules* [1615], p. 23).

As Raphael's words to Adam in *PL* indicate (5. 571–73; cf. 6. 297–301; 7. 177–79; 6. 893–96), Milton freely adapted to his own purposes as a poet a conceptual theory originally intended as a means of understanding Scripture, making it possible to read *PL,* especially, as an extended metaphor. But the theory most applies to the War in Heaven and to Milton's conception of God, who appears not so much anthropomorphically as anthropopathetically, "after the manner of men," as C. A. Patrides suggests (*Texas Studies in Language and Literature* 5: 58–63). Whatever distinctions one cares to make, it seems clear that Milton recognized the conceptual limitations of Scripture—and of poetic language as well—but believed that such limitations were a part of divine intent and therefore suited to man's limited capacities. Like George Gifford, Milton seems to warn against "grosse and foolish allegories" (*Foure Sermons,* 1582), and he would certainly have condemned the heterodoxy of John Colet's claim that the account of creation in Genesis is *merely* "a high and holy fiction." Fiction Milton may allow it to be, but such as we are to take literally. [PEB]

AD IOANNEM ROUSIUM *Oxoniensis Academiae Bibliothecarium* (To John Rous, librarian of Oxford University), 87-line Latin poem first printed in the 1673 edition of Milton's poems. Milton prefaced his ode* with its date of composition, January 23, 1646/47, and a brief note on its origin. At the request of Rous*, chief librarian of the Bodleian, Milton had sent a copy of the 1645 edition of his poems along with copies of the prose pamphlets published up to that time. The prose arrived, but the book of poems was lost, and Rous wrote Milton asking for a replacement. Pleased with the request, Milton not only complied but composed an ode, now bound between the Latin and English poems of that second copy.

Milton addresses the ode to his book, thus placing it in a tradition at least as old as Ovid's* *Tristia*. The poem is lively, in spite of the numerous classical allusions with which it is embellished. Milton begins by recalling the carefree days in England and Italy when he wrote the "boyish" poems that make up the volume. He notes England's current unhappy state but hopes that it has sufficiently atoned for past sins and that happier days lie ahead. As for his own little book, it may escape oblivion since Rous will preserve it in the magnificent library of which he is custodian. He concludes with the hope that when the bitterness of the present is forgotten, a saner posterity may judge his work more fairly.

Appended to the poem are observations about its metrics. Its three strophes, three antistrophes, and an epode suggest that he was imitating Greek choral odes, but his divisions did not parallel each other as classical precedent dictated. In his note he indicated his awareness of this, but defended his divisions as aids to the reader's convenience even if they did not exactly reproduce the features of classical versification. Since his metrical practices are rather free in the ode, he

suggests that it might more aptly be called "monostrophic," a term that he again used to describe the choruses in *SA*. The similarities between these choruses and the ode may corroborate the conjecture that *SA* was composed in the late 1640s. In any case, in both ode and drama Milton's metrical practices were much influenced by his reading of Italian poets such as Tasso* and Guarini. [ERG]

AD PATREM (To His Father), 120-line Latin poem appearing in both the 1645 and 1673 editions of Milton's poems. Its relationship with Milton's decision to make poetry rather than the ministry his career has suggested dates of composition as early as 1631–32 and as late as 1645. Unfortunately, factual information as to when he made that decision is lacking. The more usual date assigned the poem is the end of the Horton* period, 1637 or early 1638. Most speculations are summarized by Ernest Sirluck in the *Journal of English and Germanic Philology* 60: 766–67, 784–85; but see Douglas Bush, in *Modern Philology* 61 : 204–8, and *Variorum Commentary*, 1 : 232–40, where Milton's last year at Cambridge, 1631–32, is advanced. Even the usual connection between the poem and his career has been challenged. To Parker, Milton's career as a clergyman is still assumed in the poem, which is accordingly only a plea that his father not condemn the pleasant avocation of writing poetry. Parker saw the poem as originating in a dispute in 1634 over Milton's composing *Mask*. His father, it is argued, associated masques with worldliness and frivolity and felt that such writing was inappropriate for his son's projected career as a minister (*Milton*, 1 : 125–28, 2 : 788–89). The verses do suggest some kind of dispute, for several lines allude to the father's real or pretended dislike of poetry. It is difficult to know, however, whether we are supposed to take seriously this alleged disapproval by Milton Senior. Milton himself does not give it much credence : his father does not loathe "the dainty Muses," he writes, because he did not insist on his son's going into the law, but on the contrary gave him the superb education that has led him to love poetry (*AdP* 67–76). Since Milton's tone here and throughout the poem is self-assured and even humorous, these allusions may be merely a part of his poetic strategy. This tone does not obscure the author's learning or the skill of his compliments to his father. Milton details the education that his father had given him, listing specifically the languages* studied—Latin, Greek, French, Italian and Hebrew (77–85). The father might well have taken pride in receiving such learned poetry, and Milton further honors him by referring to his great love of music*. Urging the closeness of music and poetry, Milton rounds out his compliment by observing that Apollo has divided himself equally between father and son (56–66). Often read for its autobiographical* significance, *AdP* tells us much about the younger Milton; but quite apart from that, it is a graceful performance in its own right. [ERG]

AD SALSILLUM *poetam Romanum aegrotantem* (To Salsilli, a Roman poet, being ill), 41-line Latin poem published in both the 1645 and 1673 editions of Milton's poems. Its headnote indicates the meter in which it is written ("scazons") and the occasion that inspired it. It is dated November (?) 1638, when Milton was in Florence. The scazontic, or "limping" meter is an iambic trimeter with a spondee or trochee as the last foot, thus producing a halting effect. Milton's poem has been severely criticized because it does not conform precisely to the rules of Latin prosody, although license is frequent in Greek scazons. The Roman poet whose illness occasioned Milton's work was an obscure writer. A member of the *Fantastici* ("Fantastics"), he contributed fifteen poems to a volume published by the academy in 1637. This and the little we gather from his relationship with Milton is the sum total of our knowledge concerning him. The lack of evidence led Masson to conjecture that he may have died early (*Life,* 1 : 806). Edward Phillips

included Salzilli among the modern Italian poets in his *Theatrum Poetarum* (1675), although he makes no mention of any connection with Milton.

Salzilli's importance lies in his brief contact with Milton, whom he exalted in an extravagantly phrased Latin quatrain as superior to Homer*, Virgil*, and Tasso*. Milton included it in the prefatory material to the 1645 edition of his Latin poems. Possibly he took it more seriously than Salzilli intended, but no doubt can exist that the Italian courtesy expressed in such praises as this significantly added to his self-confidence. A well-known passage in *RCG* tells us that the written encomia that the Italians bestowed upon his work strengthened his growing conviction that he "might perhaps leave something so written to aftertimes, as they should not willingly let it die." It is not surprising then that, when Salzilli fell ill, Milton sent him verses wishing him a speedy recovery and looking forward to the day when once again he would "soothe the neighboring meads with sweet song." [ERG]

ADAM, a central character in *PL* as the first created man. The literary problems posed by the presentation of Adam and his wife, Eve, are unlike those involved in any other characterization in Western literature. In the first place, their experience sets them radically and uniquely apart from all that we as readers have ever known about mankind, for they are created and at first exist in a state of total innocence and joy. Furthermore, they must be made representative of all humanity, in one sense a summation of all that is human, for their very names suggest their generic significance, Adam in Hebrew meaning "man" and Eve meaning "woman" or "life." In *PL*, Milton employs them as surrogates for the reader, and he invites the reader to accept through their experience a universal understanding of man's nature, experience, and destiny.

The primary Old Testament treatment of Adam is found in the first five chapters of Genesis; though the Hebrew word is used generically for man over five hundred times elsewhere in the Old Testament, the only other unambiguous use of the word as a proper name occurs in a genealogy in 1 Chronicles 1 : 1. Otherwise, the Old Testament develops little thought about Adam, but major developments occurred in the intertestamental period, which laid the groundwork for the New Testament emphasis upon Adam as the "old man" whose fall was canceled by the action of Christ as the "new man."

In *PL* Adam is created by the Son in total innocence and freedom with reason as his guide—as Eve puts it, "we live / Law to ourselves, our Reason is our Law" (9. 653–54). The two purposes of his existence are inextricably connected—God's glory and his own happiness—and he is supplied with all knowledge "which best may serve / To glorifie the Maker, and infer / Thee also happier," as Michael tells him (7. 115–17). He is made sovereign over all earthly creatures, and is given particular responsibility for the Garden, though not "to irksome toile, but to delight" (9. 242). God made "all things to mans delightful use," and established within him the capacity for continuing his perfect happiness : "Happiness in his power left free to will" (4. 692 and 5. 235). When Adam asks for a companion to make his happiness complete, the Son commends him for recognizing that he must seek completion outside himself, a recognition that expresses the "spirit within thee free, / My Image" (8. 440–41). Adam's love* thus extends upward to God, outward to humanity other than himself, and is marked within by "self esteem, grounded on just and right / Well manag'd" (8. 572–73). Love is the basic element, "hath his seat / In Reason," and "is the scale / By which to heav'nly Love thou maist ascend," and Adam recognizes that in "contemplation of created things / By steps we may ascend to God" (8. 589–94 and 5. 509–12, 469–79). Milton makes much of the fact that sexual love is present between Adam and Eve in Paradise*, and calls it "the Crown of all our bliss"

(4. 728). The Fall* is not directly involved with sex, which was enjoyed more perfectly before it than afterwards.

In his enticement of Eve, Satan minimizes the physical and proposes instead a new kind of spiritual reward. Satan promises that eating the forbidden fruit will enable men to "be henceforth among the Gods," "be as Gods," and "put on Gods" (5. 77, and 9. 708–14). This satanic appeal to Eve is echoed in her appeals to Adam (9. 866, 877), and in Adam's hope that he and she may "be Gods, or Angels Demi-gods," while God refers to the Fall as man's "Affecting God-head, and so loosing all" (9. 934, 937, and 3. 206). In this way, the Fall of man parallels that of his tempter, Satan, but in Adam's case other considerations are also involved. In effect, Adam takes Eve as his god, and finds in her his primary hope of happiness rather than in God (10. 145). Adam's sin* thus conforms precisely to the two primary understandings of sin within the Christian tradition, as a usurpation upon deity and as a preference for a created good over the Creator God. This inversion of the scale of value built into creation* is at once a repudiation of reason and a loss of liberty*, and is followed by a perversion of love and a loss of joy.

After both have eaten the fruit, Adam and Eve engage in a lustful orgy, which, unlike their earlier lovemaking, is a drunken exploitation of each other, and is followed by their first experience of shame and guilt. Sleep becomes unrest, love an agony, and "just confidence" is exchanged for inner torments (9. 1045–98, 1120–26). The earlier joyful harmony is shattered in each of its three major dimensions, and is replaced by alienation from God, from self, and from each other. Adam shuns God, condemns and scorns himself with contempt and a wish for annihilation, and turns viciously against Eve. The "Understanding rul'd not," conscience* becomes an inner terror, and Adam exists "in a troubl'd Sea of passion tost" from which he can "find no way, from deep to deeper plung'd" (9. 1127, and 10. 718, 844). Existing no longer in love, the two self-deified "Gods or Angels Demi-gods" have substituted an Olympus of bickering and "mutual accusation" for their earlier paradise, and "of thir vain contest appeer'd no end" (9. 1187–89). There "appeer'd no end" precisely because fallen man needs salvation from himself, from his own self-centeredness, and for this reason he cannot by himself save himself. The only hope for Adam and Eve is to "renounce / Thir own both righteous and unrighteous deeds," and, as the Father has said to the Son, "live in thee transplanted, and from thee / Receive new life" (3. 291–94).

At this point God provides the first couple that "Prevenient Grace"* which comes as prelude to release from their impasse (11. 3–4). Eve first admits guilt and then Adam, and each attempts to accept sole responsibility for what has been done (10. 935, 955). What had been merely attrition is now turned to true repentance, which the Son describes to the Father as "thy seed / Sow'n with contrition" (11. 26–27). Adam and Eve here differ radically from Satan, for they find it miserable "to be to others cause of misery," and each wishes to be able to bear it all (10. 981–85 and 819–20), whereas the spreading of misery is Satan's joy, "for onely in destroying I find ease" (9. 129). The first parents thus repent and seek forgiveness in what the Son, their mediator, interprets as a prayer for reconciliation and the restoration of community (11. 37–39). The answer to the prayer comes, as Adam says, through "perswasion in me" growing and "peace returnd," as he finds relationships with God and Eve reestablished, as well as his respect for himself returning (11. 141–61). The Son, who combines the offices of judge and redeemer, has at the same time condemned their sin and initiated their redemption.

The central *mythos** of *PL* is now completed. Adam—meaning man or everyman—as *representative* of all humanity has chosen a life of alienation from God, and though Adam *as penitent individual* has returned to his divine allegiance, the consequences of humanity's chosen fall are yet to be worked out. Michael is sent to instruct man in those consequences and to advise him how to live in a fallen condition where peace is seen to corrupt and war to waste, where evil men in "a World devote to universal rack" exalt their own destroyers, and events seem "to good malignant, to bad men benigne" (11. 784, 821, 676–97, and 12. 538). Throughout this history of hate and lust and tyranny, there are unpretentious just men, righteous before God, who continue a tradition of faithfulness and also serve as precursors of the promised Messiah, in whom the incarnate Son offers the ultimate sacrifice for sinful man and provides release and redemption to all who are willing to accept the gift. It is a mixed and balanced account of the life of men in history, in which particular historical events and persons are used to foreshadow perennial problems and opportunities. Instructed and corrected step by step, Adam advances in his understanding, until Michael promises the ultimate destruction of all Satan's perversions and the reconstitution by the Son of a new heaven and new earth in which the tried and purified saints will live forever in a community of love for God and for each other. That faith and hope in the Son's work of redemption and second creation makes possible the "paradise within thee, happier farr" on which the epic closes (12. 587). [RMF]

ADAPTATIONS. Milton's poems have been adapted as straight stage presentations and as musical works. Most frequent has been *PL,* first tagged by John Dryden* as *The State of Innocence;* the emphasis on the Fall is repeated almost constantly thereafter. It was written ca. 1674, published in 1677 (and frequently reprinted), and apparently not performed; the music, by an unknown composer, has been lost. Augustin Nadal's theatrical version, *Le paradis terrestre* (pub. 1738), only loosely based on books 4 and 8 of Dupré de Saint Maur's French prose translation of *PL* (1729), was performed in Poitiers, March 23, 1736, with a musical setting by Louis-Thomas Bourgeois. Francis Peck's* *Adam Unparadis'd,* published in his *New Memoirs of John Milton* (1740), is a summary of Milton's manuscript drafts for dramatic versions of *PL,* together with *PL* 10. 720–1104 presented in dialogue and stage directions to demonstrate that Milton's original plan could be carried out by transforming the epic into dramatic form. *Adam et Eve* (1742) by the composer Alexandre Tanevot, was fairly popular and frequently mentioned by contemporary writers. An anonymous and otherwise unreported manuscript in the University of Illinois Library and dated 1750 presents "The Fall, A Masque taken from Milton." A well-received musical version, called an oratorio, was written by J. C. Smith (music) and Benjamin Stillingfleet (libretto) in 1758–1760. It was performed and published twice in 1760. Another French musical version was Jean-Nicholas Servandoni's *La chute des anges rebelles* (1758); it is notable for its use of materials from *PL* that do not center on Adam and Eve. Reference is also found to *L'Origine du monde et la chute du premier homme* (1763) by one Josse. Richard Jago's *Adam: or, the Fatal Disobedience. Compiled from the Paradise Lost of Milton. And Adapted to Music* was performed in 1768 and published in his *Poems,* 1784. No music is known. Mrs. Mary Granville Delaney is reputed to have prepared a libretto on the epic for Handel. The best known as well as most frequently performed musical version of *PL* is Franz Josef Haydn's *Die Schoepfung; ein Oratorium* (completed 1798, performed 1799, and published in Vienna in 1800). The libretto of *The Creation* was prepared by a Mr. Lidley (or Lindley or Liddell) and revised by Baron van Swieten.

Nineteenth-century versions include Matthew P. King's *The Intercession* (1816), Peter Ritter's *Das verlorne Paradies* (1819), Sir Henry R. Bishop's *The Battle of the Angels* (1820), Pio Cianchettini's *Paradise Lost,* Johann C. Schneider's *Das verlorne Paradies* (1824), Bishop's *The Seventh Day* (1833–34), Charles Edward Horn's *The Remission of Sin* (1835), Bishop's *The Departure from Paradise,* Henry Wylde's *Paradise Lost* (1853), Anton Rubinstein and Julius Rodenberg's *Paradise Lost* (1855), Adolphe Philippe D'Ennery and Ferdinand Dugué's *Le paradis perdu* (1856), John Lodge Ellerton's *Paradise Lost* (1856–57), Walter Leigh's combined *Paradise Lost and Regained* (1868), and Theodore Dubois's *Le paradis perdu* (1878). The attraction of the text for the twentieth century has continued : Marco Enrico Bossi's *Paradise Lost* (1906), Sir Alexander C. McKenzie's *The Temptation* (1914). Igor Markevich's *Paradise Lost* (1935), Maximilian G. Walten's "Paradise Lost" (1952ff.; unpublished opera), and Franz Reizenstein's *Genesis* (1958). An opera-oratorio, *Paradise Lost,* by Phillip Rhodes (libretto by Richard and Louise Kain) was performed in 1972. *Milton's* Paradise Lost : *Screenplay for Cinema of the Mind* was created by John Collier and published by Knopf in 1973; however, no film has appeared, although the scenario suggests that it could be successful.

Next in popularity has been *A Mask,* adapted at times with music. Paolo Antonio Rolli's* *Sabrina* (1737) preceded the most popular and still currently performed version, John Dalton's* *Comus* (1738) with music by Thomas Arne.* This version caused a permanent renaming of Milton's poem. It interpolated lines from *L'Al* and introduced a new character, Euphrosyne. Dalton's adaptation was revised (basically simplified) by George Colman in 1773; Arne's music was still used. Sir Henry R. Bishop's "Euphrosyne" (1812), drawn loosely from *Comus,* was at times employed in stagings of *Mask.* He wrote new music for an 1815 Drury Lane production. Mme. Vestris did a French version in 1842; and William Macready's production from 1843 survives in his prompt books. Further versions are Charles E. Horsley's in 1874; Sir Frederick Bridge's *The Masque of Comus* in 1908; and Lucy Chater's in 1911. In 1904 C. N. Smith composed new music and arranged Henry

Lawes's* five songs.

As noted before, Walter Leigh combined *PR* with the long epic in 1868. Carl Barbandt had produced a musical version of the brief epic in 1756. The only adapted stage version of *SA* is George Frederick Handel's in 1742 with a text by Newburgh Hamilton. It interpolated lines from *Nat* and *SolMus*. The oratorio was performed at the Theatre Royal in Covent Garden and immediately published. There are three issues of the printed text and one of *Songs from Samson an oratorio. The Words taken from Milton set to Musick by Mr. Handel* (London : for I. Walsh, 1742), the words and music in score, with the original singers noted. Reprintings are numerous, and the work has been performed many times up to the present. It is available on records.

An Occasional Oratorio (written 1745–46) advertises itself as being "Selected from the most celebrated compositions" of Handel on the title page and drawn from Milton among others in the heading. The librettist was Thomas Morrell; there is some adaptation from the translations of Psalms 2, 3, 5–7, 81, 86, and 136.

William Jackson revised *Lyc* into a musical entertainment that was performed at the Theatre Royal in Covent Garden in 1767; the music has not survived. It seems to be a most inauspicious work. Two centos by David Garrick presented Shakespeare's* *A Midsummer Night's Dream* in "operatic" form. *The Fairies* (1755) had music by John Christopher Smith and employed three passages from *L'Al* and one each from *PL* and *Arc*. The second using Shakespeare's title is a revision of the first; it has appropriations from *L'Al*, *Mask*, and *PL*, and was given in 1763.

In addition to stage adaptations that employed music (such as play, opera, or oratorio), a number of Milton's poems or excerpts from them have been set by composers since 1728, when Johann Ernst Gaillard wrote "The Hymn of Adam and Eve," taken from *PL* 5. An edition of 1773, giving words and music, also published "The overture, accompanying &

choruses added by Benjn. Cooke Mus. D. Organist of Westminster Abbey." An edition of *All the Favourite Oratorios Set to Music by Mr. Handel* (London, 1790?) gives in part two the text of "The Hymn of Adam and Eve, taken from Milton's Paradise Lost," "The music of both / 'Daphnis and Amaryllis' / selected from the most celebrated Italian composers." The reference is uncertain. Not only was this passage frequently reprinted in periodicals, but Philip Hart produced "The Morning Hymn" around 1729, Johann F. Reichardt composed "Morgengesang" around 1800, and "Hail Universal Lord" (5. 205ff.) was set by Sir George Dyson in 1958.

The epic was also the source for other songs, some by major composers of England and America. Handel's *Alexander Balus* employs the "Hail Wedded Love" passage from Book 4; A. Herbert Brewer composed "A Song of Eden" in 1905; Eleanor E. Freer used 4. 268ff. in "The Eternal Spring" in 1905; "Hail, Holy Light" from the proem to Book 3 is a song by Alexander D. Kastalsky, from around 1918; "Evening" was drawn from Book 4 by J. Bertram Fox in 1919 and by Charles Ives in 1921. Alan Dudley Bush in "Voices of the Prophets" (1953), Franz Reizenstein in "Genesis" (1958), and Ross Lee Finney in "Still Are New Worlds" (1963), all derive material from the epic.

Excerpts from Lawes's and from Arne's *Comus* frequently appear in print, and in addition other composers tried their hands at individual songs. Samuel Wesley*, ca. 1785, wrote a fragment of a chorus for the mask, beginning "Away ! to Comus' Court repair." Around 1838 R. L. de Pearsall put music to Comus's "List, Lady, and Be Not Coy" (line 737), while Henry Farmer, ca. 1845, did "Welcome Joy and Feast" (line 102). The end of the Attendant Spirit's epilogue (lines 1019–23) supplied the text for Hugh Archibald Clarke's "Love Virtue" (ca. 1890). C. N. Smith in 1904 wrote music for the mask and included an arrangement of Lawes's five songs. "By Dimpled Brook" (line 119), was set by both Thomas F.

Dunhill in 1916 and Clarence Lucas in 1945.

Only Manoa's "Nothing Is Here For Tears" seems to have inspired separate songs from *SA* : Sidney Bett's composition is dated 1930; Ralph Vaughan-Williams's, 1938.

Michael C. Festing's "Song on May Morning," 1740, published in *A Miscellany of Lyric Poems, the Greatest Part Written for, and Performed in the Academy of Music, Held in the Apollo,* was perhaps popular in its day; it was merely the first of numerous versions of the poem. Carl Barbrandt's "Now the Bright Morning Star" appeared in 1759; an unpublished manuscript dated 1765 records Joseph Harris's "Milton's Ode to May"; "Milton's Bright Morning Star" was composed by William Carnaby in 1800; about 1801 Reginald Spofforth's "Come Bounteous May" and Robert Greville's "Song on May Morning" appeared; around 1840 James Battye wrote "Hail Bounteous May"; the title of Henry Hugh Pierson's version, ca. 1870, like Barbrandt's is the first line; and Mary Travers's rendering around 1890 also attests to the popularity of this poem.

Twentieth-century composers have also been taken by the lyric : there are Bruce H. D. Steane's "On May Morning," 1902; C. R. Ward's "Now the Bright Morning Star," 1902; A. Herbert Brewer's "Song on May Morning," 1907; Henry Leslie's "Now the Bright Morning Star," 1908; Basil Harwood's "Ode on May Morning," 1913; Sir Donald Tovey's "On May Morning," 1921; Ethel M. Boyce's "On May Morning," 1922; Michael Head's "Hail, Bounteous May," 1930; Sara Newell's "Now the Bright Morning Star," 1945; Ross Lee Finney's "On May Morning," 1948; R. Müller-Hartmann's "Song on May Morning," 1951; and Arnold Cooke's "Song on May Morning," 1967.

Perhaps the best known and most performed musical version of Milton's shorter poems is George Frederick Handel's *L'Allegro ed il Penseroso* (London, 1739), to which was added a non-Miltonic third part, entitled "Il Moderato." The text was adapted by Charles Jennens. The poetic text or individual songs from the full work were frequently reprinted, as well as the music. Handel (1685–1759) came to England first in 1710 to produce his opera *Rinaldo.* In 1719 he became director of the Royal Academy, his fortunes depending on popular attitudes toward Italian opera. After his financial bankruptcy in 1737 and ensuing ill health, Handel began the composition of the oratorios, which are usually considered his masterpieces. *L'Allegro ed il Penseroso* and *Samson* coincide with the beginning of this new major phase of his career. The last oratorio, *Jephtha,* 1751, with a text by Thomas Morrell, the librettist for *The Messiah,* employs a passage from the "Nativity Ode." By 1753 Handel was totally blind and work ceased.

An important composer in his own right, Samuel Arnold, a major editor of Handel's works, compiled *Redemption* in 1790 from various works by Handel, including excerpts from *Samson* and *L'Allegro ed il Penseroso.* He himself set "Haste thee, Nymph" from "L'Allegro," around 1770. Henry Lahee's "Hence Loathed Melancholy" is dated 1878. In descent from Handel is Sir Charles H. H. Parry's "L'Allegro ed il Penseroso," 1890. J. E. Tidnam's "Milton's L'Allegro," 1904, remains in manuscript. "Haste Thee, Haste Thee" (cf. "L'Allegro," lines 25ff.) was composed by Harold E. Watts in 1923, and Robert Foresman produced a dramatic characterization of "Euphrosyne" in 1928. "Il Penseroso" by F. J. Nettlefold is closely related to Milton's lyric.

Nat has been one of the most popular poems for musical version. William Carnaby wrote "This is the Month" ca. 1800; there is an unpublished manuscript of "Ode on the Nativity" by Edwin George Monk, 1848; John Knowles Paine's "The Nativity" dates from 1883; and James Lyon's version of 1895 is unpublished. The Hymn was set by Sir John Blackwood McEwen in 1901 (republished 1904). Gerard Veerman rendered "The Nativity, An Ode" in 1906, and William Henry

Harris's version was done in 1909. Ralph Vaughan-Williams's Christmas cantata, *Hodie* (1954), is a setting for seven stanzas from *Nat*. Other versions include Edmund Langford Guest's in 1913, Maurice G. Burgess's in 1915, David Stanley Smith's around 1925, Alexander Brent-Smith's in 1927, Cyril B. Rootham's in 1928, Mary Chandler's in 1953, and Cyril Scott's (n.d.). Stanza 4 was set by John Zundel ("No War Nor Battle's Sound") and Stanza 13 ("Ring Out, Ye Crystal Spheres") was the text for William G. Whittaker (1926), Harold E. Darke (ca. 1930), Ian A. Copley (1960), Clifford Fletcher (1960), Robert Smith (1962), and Francis E. Reeson (1963.)

The two English odes *Sol Mus* and *Time* frequently appear in musical versions. John Stafford Smith composed "Blest Pair of Sirens" in 1775, as did John Alcock in 1790 and Sir Charles H. H. Parry in 1887. Charles Wood called his work "Milton's Ode on Time" in 1898; and other versions are by Nicholas Gatty (1905), Sir Henry Walford Davies (1908, revised 1936), Sir Charles Villiers Stanford (1914), and Egon Wellesz (1950). Sonnet 1, "O Nightingale," inspired R. J. S. Stevens in 1784, Edward J. Loder around 1845, Robert P. Stewart around 1870, and William Edmonstoune Duncan in 1895. Gerald Finzi set two sonnets in 1936.

Jackson's "Lycidas" does not seem to have been performed after the mid-eighteenth century, and the elegy is the source for only a few other musical versions, those by Archibald W. Wilson (1894, unpublished), John E. Borland (1903, "An Elegy: Words from Milton's Lycidas"), and Edgar L. Bainton (1928). "Arcades" supplied "A Pastoral" by Henry Bromley Devry in 1913. Psalm 84 ("How Lovely Are Thy Dwellings Fair") attracted the genius of Louis Spohr around 1846–47, as well as Harold E. Darke in 1914. Psalms 8 and 82 have been set once each by Henry Cope Colles, 1904, and Chastey William G. Hector, 1913, respectively. But Psalm 136 (perhaps because of its refrain) has been especially popular: versions are by John Zundel, Sir Arthur S. Sullivan, John Antes, John Wilkes, F. T. O. Durrant, John Fawcett, Henry Leslie, Alan Ridout, and Benjamin Milgrove. Anonymous settings include one in the *Boy Scout Song Book,* 1820. [RS and JTS]

ADAPTATIONS, LITERARY. Distinctions between *adaptation* and *imitation* and between *adaptation* and *translation* are not always clear. Stage and musical adaptations are considered under separate entries. Here *adaptation* is used to mean a version of one of Milton's works, modified by omission, by paraphrase, or by changes in language or versification. *Imitation* stresses such alteration that Milton's text is not really reproduced; *imitation* evidences rather *influence. Translation* implies an attempt to render Milton's text into another language even though some omission or paraphrase or change in language or form may occur. While Armand Boisbeleare de La Chapelle's lines from Book 8 of *PL* are really a rhymed paraphrase of Adam's dream, they are offered as a version of Milton's lines (see *Le Babillard, ou Le Nouvelliste Philosophe* [Amsterdam, 1725], pp. 105–7), and should probably be considered a brief translation. Or, for example, the Russian translation of the epic by Petrov (1772ff.) might seem an adaptation because it is so nonliteral, yet this is quite different from *Le Paradis Terrestre, Poëme Imité de Milton, Par Madame D. B***** (London, 1748). Marie-Ann du Boccage adapted Milton's poem into six books (*chants*) of verse; it is not a translation, nor should it be called an imitation as, for example, Sir Richard Blackmore's *King Arthur* (1697) or William Mason's *Musaeus* (1747), which is influenced by *Lyc,* would be. Madame du Boccage's work appeared also in 1760, 1762, 1768. Other noteworthy adaptations of *PL* are:

Cotton Mather. *Magnalia Christi Americana or, The Ecclesiastical History of New-England, from Its First Planting in the Year 1620 unto the Year of Our Lord,*

1698 (1698). [Paraphrase of *PL* 6. 386-93, in 2:47, 50.]

John Hopkins. *Milton's Paradise Lost Imitated in Rhyme. In the Fourth Sixth and Ninth Books; Containing the Primitive Loves. The Battel of the Angels. The Fall of Man* (1699).

William Howard. *A Paraphrase in Verse, on Part of the First Book of Milton's Paradise Lost* (1738).

[Andrew Jackson?]. *Paradise Lost A Poem. Attempted in Rhime. Book I* (1740). [Argument and Book 1 in rhymed couplets.]

[George Smith Green], Gentleman of Oxford. *The State of Innocence, and Fall of Man* (London: Thomas Osborne, 1745). [In prose with St. Maur's notes. Further editions in 1746, 1755 (2), 1756, 1767, 1770 (3).]

[George Smith Green], Gentleman of Oxford. *A New Version of Paradise Lost. In which the measure and versification are corrected and harmonised; the obscurities elucidated; and the faults, which the author stands accused of by Addison and other of the criticks, are removed* (Oxford, 1756). [Book 1 only; omits "difficult" allusions and passages.]

Jean-Nicholas Servandoni. *La Chute des anges rebelles* (1758).

M. Josse. *L'Origine du monde et la chute du premier homme* (1763).

John Wesley. *Paradise Lost Improved* (1763). [Omits similes, allusions, passages offering difficulty for the common reader. Reprinted as *Extract from Milton's Paradise Lost, With Notes* in 1791.]

James Buchanan. *The First Six Books of Milton's Paradise Lost, Rendered into Grammatical Construction* (*Edinburgh*, 1773).

Félix José Reinoso. *La Inicencia perdida* (1799). [In Spanish.]

The only other poems of Milton's that show similar adaptation are *PR* and *SA*:

Jesus. A Poem. In Book Verse (1745).

M. Lancelin. *Le Triomphe de Jésus-Christ dans le désert* (1775). [In French verse.]

The Recovery of Man: Or, Milton's Paradise Regained. In Prose (1771). [Author may have been George Graham.]

L. R. Lafaye. *Le Paradis reconquis. Poëme, imité de Milton* (1789).

John Penn. "Preliminary Observations" in *Critical, Poetical, and Dramatic Works* (1798), vol. 2. [Adaptation of *SA* into scenes by frequent omissions of allegedly inartistic sections.]

The foregoing adaptations of the three major poems present them in "standard" forms or verse, or in versions more easily comprehended by the common reader—largely by omissions, by paraphrases, or by rendering in prose. The nineteenth and twentieth centuries have also produced young people's stories out of *PL*. In none of these is Milton's authorship of the original version denied or obscured. However, prose adaptations may be quite different. Some like J. B. Salaville's French translation and adaptation of *1Def* (1789ff.) and Mirabeau's* French "imitation" of *Areop* (1788ff.) may be considered nonliteral translations. But others may revamp Milton's text by omissions or compression and pass off the result as the work of someone else. Today we would label such unacknowledged appropriation plagiarism. A work that has often been alleged as strongly dependent on *Tenure* is *A Treatise of the Execution of Justice, Wherein is clearly proved, that the Execution of Judgement and Justice, is as well the Peoples as the Magistrates Duty; And that if Magistrates pervert Judgement, the People are bound by the Law of God to execute Judgement without them, and upon them* (1663?), possibly by John Twyn. A more certain adaptation is the anonymous *Tyranny no Magistracy, or A Modest and Compendious Enquirie into the Nature, and Boundaries of that Ordinance of Magistracy. With An Essay to Demonstrate It's Specifick Distinction from Tyranny. By an Enemy to Tyranny and Lover of True Magistracy* (1687), likewise deriving from *Tenure*. Another clever adaptation of *Tenure*, employed like the preceding in the succession controversy, appeared two years later as *Pro Populo Adversus Tyrannos: or, The Sovereign Right and Power of the People Over Tyrants, Clearly Stated, and Plainly Proved. With Some Reflections on the Late Posture of Affairs. By a True Protestant English-man, and well-wisher to Posterity.* In 1669 Simon Patrick employed passages from the 1650 *Eikon*, pp. 206-7, in *A Continuation of a Friendly Debate*, pp. 127-29 (see Kathleen A. Coleridge in *The Turnbull Library Record* [May 1972], pp. 28-31).

During the discussion over licensing,

Charles Blount compressed the argument of *Areop* into eighteen pages, published as *A Just Vindication of Learning or, An Humble Address to the High Court of Parliament in Behalf of the Liberty of The Press* (1679). It was reprinted in *The Harleian Miscellany* (1745), 6 : 71–79; (1810, ed. Robert Dutton), 8 : 290–300; (1810, ed. John White et al.), 6 : 77–86. There are notes in the latter by Thomas Park on p. 79 concerning Milton, but indebtedness is not stated. *A General Dictionary, Historical and Critical* (1775), 3 : 401n, also cited Milton in talking of this work. In 1681 William Denton adapted Milton's argument in an addendum to his *Jus Caesaris et Ecclesiae vere dictae. Or a Treatise of Independency, Presbytery, the Power of Kings, and of the Church*. He called it "An Apology for the Liberty of the Press," pp. 1–9 (new pagination). At the beginning of the work itself appears "The Summe of Mr. J. M. His Treatise [i.e., *CivP*]," pp. 1–4. Blount again drew upon *Areop* in *Reasons Humbly Offered for the Liberty of Un-licens'd Printing* (1693). Both of Blount's tracts were reprinted in *The Miscellaneous Works of Charles Blount, Esq* (1695).

Thomas Hunt employed *1Def* in *Mr. Hunt's Argument for the Bishops Right: With the Postscript* (1682); it has been demonstrated that the *Postscript*, pp. i–lvi and 1–111 (new pagination), translates long passages from Milton's work. The same tract was used by Samuel Johnson in *Julian the Apostate: Being a Short Account of his Life* (1682): see "The Preface to the Reader," pp. iii–xxix. Both recourses to plagiarism were pointed out by Thomas Long in *A Vindication of the Primitive Christians. In point of Obedience to their Prince, against the Calumnies of a Book intituled The Life of Julian* (1683); see especially "The Epistle Dedicatory," pp. [xv–xix]; "To the Reader," p. [xxvi]; "Reflections on the Behavior of Those Christians," pp. 180–86, 191–97; and "An Appendix, Containing a more full and particular Answer to Mr. Hunt's Preface and Postscript," pp. 291–347.

Two further unacknowledged adaptations were made at the end of the seventeenth century. In 1692 the author of *Ludlow no Lyar* (Joseph Wilson? Slingsby Bethell?) drew much from *Eikon,* especially in the Preface; and in 1698 Jodocus Crull used chapter 12 of *Mosc* for his chapter 4 of *The Antient and Present State of Muscovy.* [JTS]

ADDISON, JOSEPH (1672–1719), essayist, poet, and literary critic. He attended Queen's and Magdalen Colleges, Oxford, receiving a fellowship at the latter in 1698, which he held until 1711. He was noted for his knowledge of Latin poetry as well as for his own poems in Latin. Many of these poems appeared in *Examen Poeticum Duplex* (1698), which also included five of Milton's Latin poems; others, in *Musarum Anglicanarum Analecta* (Oxford, 1699). His political poem "The Campaign" (1704) on the victory at Blenheim brought him a post as undersecretary of state (1706), and his position as a Whig was asserted frequently in periodicals of the day (such as his *Whig Examiner* in 1710 and *The Freeholder* in 1715–16). He was a Member of Parliament from 1708 until his death. He had met Sir Richard Steele when both were students at the Charterhouse in the mid-1680s. He wrote a number of papers for Steele's *The Tatler* in 1709–10, and together they produced *The Spectator* in 1711–12 and *The Guardian* in 1713. Addison tried to revive *The Spectator* in 1714. He also wrote or collaborated on various plays, the most noted being *Cato* (1713). Addison befriended Milton's daughter Deborah, it should also be observed, when she was in financial straits in 1719. His position as a critic rests largely on his papers on *PL* in *The Spectator* and the series of eleven papers on "Pleasures of the Imagination" in the June and July 1712 issues of the same periodical.

The first statement from Addison concerning Milton is part of his poem "An Account of the Greatest English Poets," dated April 3, 1694, and first published in John Dryden's* *The Annual Miscellany:*

for the Year 1694. Being the Fourth Part of Miscellany Poems (1694), pp. 321–23. He praises PL for its verse and subject, especially the War in Heaven*, but then laments that Milton had "profan'd his pen, To vernish o'er the guilt of faithless men." Therefore Addison cannot praise Milton's other works; the image of regicide and antimonarchist gets in his way—a curious position in many ways for a man who became such an important spokesman for the Whigs.* Yet the ambivalent statement is typical of the eighteenth-century attitude toward Milton. The next volume in the series of miscellanies associated with Dryden came out in 1704 (Poetical Miscellanies: The Fifth Part. Containing a Collection of Original Poems. With Several New Translations. By the most eminent hands). It includes "Milton's Stile Imitated, in a Translation of a Story out of the Third Aeneid," pp. 109–17, and "Notes on Ovid," in which Addison quotes from PL for "Fabula V," p. 590, and "Fabula VI," p. 591. Another imitation is "Proelium inter Pygmaeos et Grues," in Examen Poeticum Duplex (1698); it was published in Thomas Newcomb's English translation, "The Battel of the Pygmies and the Cranes" in Addison's Poems on Several Occasions with a Dissertation upon the Roman Poets (1719), pp. 31–50, and in other collections. An even more Miltonic version of Addison's Latin was done by William Warburton; "In Imitation of Milton's Style" appears in Miscellaneous Translations, in Prose and Verse, from Roman Poets, Orators, and Historians (1724), and as "Pygmaio-Geranomachia, or, The Battle of the Cranes and Pigmies, in Imitation of Milton's Style" in Tracts by Warburton, ed. Samuel Parr (1789), pp. 56–62. A posthumous work, A Discourse on Ancient and Modern Learning (1739), pp. 17–18, discusses Milton's choice of Adam and Eve as his main characters.

Four of the papers in The Tatler refer to and quote from PL: nos. 102 (December 1–3, 1709), 114 (December 29–31, written with Steele), 218 (August 29–31, 1710), and 222 (September 8–10). The comments show appreciation of Milton's language and imagery and subtleties of characterization. Thirteen papers in The Spectator, exclusive of those which constitute the critique of PL, also discuss Milton: nos. 12 (March 14, 1711), 62 (May 11), 70 (May 21), 73 (May 24), 89 (June 12), 160 (September 3), 173 (September 18), 237 (December 1), 249 (December 15), 262 (December 31), 323 (March 11, 1712), 393 (May 31), 409 (June 19), 417 (June 28), 418 (June 30), 419 (July 1), 421 (July 3), 425 (July 8), and 463 (August 21). Again the concerns are PL, its source of knowledge, comparisons with the classics, its language, its imagery, and its characterizations, but additionally Addison notes (erroneously) that Milton's genius is above wit (no. 62); that Milton's genius has formed itself by rules and submitted his "natural Talents to the Corrections and Restraints of Art" (no. 160); that Milton "has given us a very poetical Figure of Laughter" (L'Al, 11–16, 25–40; no. 249); that Milton is "a perfect Master in all these Arts of working on the Imagination" (no. 417); and that there is great delight in the freshness of a cool, still evening (IlP, 61–72, 147–54; No. 425). The papers on imagination (nos. 417–19, 421) repeat some of the concepts developed in the critique of PL written a few months before. While Addison praises Milton and PL, he seems to feel that it "falls short of the Aeneid or Iliad" in working on the imagination because of the language in which it is written. For him the most sublime sections are the War in Heaven, the figure of the Son, and "the Stature and Behaviour of Satan and his Peers" (no. 417); the description of Paradise* is more charming than that of Hell* (no. 418); and Sin and Death seem to be the only "imaginary beings" in the poem (no. 419). The perfection of the imagination comes from what is great, what is beautiful, and what is new, and Milton is "very perfect in all three aspects" (no. 421). The revived Spectator has four papers with references to Milton, only the first of which is certainly by Addison:

nos. 565 (July 9, 1714), 577 (August 4), 630 (December 8), and 632 (December 13). In the last the comment gives a frequent and perhaps correct answer to a vexing question: "Several *Epic* Poets have religiously followed *Virgil** as to the Number of his Books; and even *Milton* is thought by many to have changed the Number of his Books from Ten to Twelve, for no other Reason." *The Guardian* has two papers by Addison with citations of *PL* and quotations (nos. 103, July 9, 1713, and 138, August 19), and *The Freeholder* one (no. 32, April 9, 1716).

The critique on *PL* appears as six general papers on various topics and twelve papers each devoted to one book of the epic. They appeared as nos. 267 (January 5, 1712), 273 (January 12), 279 (January 19), 285 (January 26), 291 (February 2), 297 (February 9), 303 (February 16), 309 (February 23), 315 (March 1), 321 (March 8), 327 (March 15), 333 (March 22), 339 (March 29), 345 (April 5), 351 (April 12), 357 (April 19), 363 (April 26), and 369 (May 3). The first paper discusses the poem's qualifications to be called an epic* in terms of Fable. Like many eighteenth-century critics, Addison accepts certain rules by which one may evaluate a work of art; thus he examines the poem in an orderly fashion under the headings of one action (unity), an entire action (completeness), and a great action (significance), and concludes "that it is capable of pleasing the most delicate Reader, without giving offence to the most scrupulous." The second paper considers the Actors (characters): Milton has achieved variety and chosen those whom all people may relate to. Addison, like most people, considers only Sin and Death to be of fictitious nature, and thus he adversely criticizes the allegory* since he "cannot think that Persons of such a chimerical Existence are proper Actors in an Epic Poem." They have about them an insufficient "Measure of Probability." The third paper considers Sentiments (thoughts and behavior), and the fourth, Language. Here sublimity is stressed. Addison finds only few blemishes in Mil-

ton under Sentiments, though, as he does with Homer* and Virgil, he objects to the punning (as in Book 6 on the invention of cannon). He likewise finds only few failings in style of language, although he seems to consider that style* as consistent. He admits, without pursuing the point further, that it is "in some places too much stiffened and obscured by the frequent use of those Methods, which *Aristotle** has prescribed for the raising of it." These first four papers evidence that Milton "excels, in general, under each of these Heads." The fifth paper deals with the critic and the sixth proceeds to defects in the poem. In addition to those already noted, and again mentioned, these are: 1) The change of fortune for Adam and Eve from good to bad is not proper for a heroic poem. 2) The hero is unsuccessful and no match for his enemies. There is not really an intended hero, but he is definitely not Satan as Dryden thought, and would more likely be the Son (whom Addison insists on calling the Messiah). 3) There are improbabilities in the poem such as the Limbo of Vanity and the allegory of Book 2. 4) There are too many digressions by the narrator for a successful structure, "tho' I must confess there is so great a Beauty in these very Digressions that I would not wish them out of his Poem." 5) Allusions to heathen fables are too frequent, and there is an unnecessary ostentation of learning. 6) The language is sometimes labored and obscure; sometimes it jingles; and sometimes it is too filled with terms of art. The remaining twelve papers detail the prior statements as they arise for each book of the epic, and particularly aim at taking notice of "such Beauties as appear to me more exquisite than the rest." Throughout, Addison compares Milton with Homer and Virgil, very often finding him superior to both and almost never inferior to either.

To a modern sensibility Addison seems blind to strategies in the poem and to the total poem in perspective. His approach seems insufficiently able to understand echoing and balance, and his penchant for fitting a creative work into a pre-conceived mold obviates appreciation of Milton's innovations. But this critique did more to bring the greatness of *PL* to generations of readers than any other single work of criticism. It remains provocative in both its insights and its prejudices. Addison's intent, stated toward the end of the last paper, was admirably achieved: "I have endeavoured to shew how some Passages are beautifull by being Sublime, others by being Soft, others by being Naturall; which of them are recommended by the Passion, which by the Moral, which by the Sentiment, and which by the Expression. I have likewise endeavoured to shew how the Genius of the Poet shines by a happy Invention, a distant Allusion, or a judicious Imitation; how he has copied or improved *Homer* or *Virgil,* and raised his own Imaginations by the Use which he has made of several Poetical Passages in Scripture." The Poet-laureate Lawrence Eusden's reaction "On Reading the Critique on Milton, in the *Spectator,*" is probably typical; he praises the "great Critick" and says Milton would "blush for Glories" since Addison excels even these. But John Dennis* put in a minority report; in *Letters on Milton and Wycherley* (1721) Dennis criticizes what he considers inconsistency in Addison's remarks about Milton's sublimity. For he feels that Addison stops short of expounding Milton's "godlike Genius," a fault he endeavors to correct in his own work.

The critique was first published separately as *Notes Upon the Twelve Books of Paradise Lost. Collected from The Spectator. Written by Mr. Addison* (1719), and in this same year it was included in the tenth edition of *PL*. It has frequently been reprinted in editions of the epic or the poetry, sometimes only in selections. It will also be found in William Dodd's *A Familiar Explanation of the Poetical Works of Milton* (1762), pp. 3–144, as well as various editions of the periodical and of Addison's works, and in nineteenth- and twentieth-century separate editions. It does not appear with editions of the poem in America until the nineteenth century. It was included with the first French

translation* of the poem in 1727, although the periodical had been translated in 1714–1718. (There were other translations produced for later translations of the poem, for example, by Louis Racine*.) Johann Jacob Bodmer* included his German translation of the critique in *Critische Abhandlung von dem Wunderbaren in der Poesie und dessen Verbindung mit dem Wahrscheinlein in einer Vertheidigung des Gedichtes Joh. Miltons von dem verlohrnen Paradiese; ist Joseph Addisons Abhandlung von dem Schönheiten in demselben Gedichte* (Zurich, 1740), pp. 223–434; he discussed Addison's criticism in the main part of the work. The papers were not added to editions of the poem until the nineteenth century. *The Spectator,* however, had appeared in German in 1721–1725, and Addison's criticism was often a focus in the controversy between Bodmer and Gottsched*. The 1740 Paris edition of Paolo Rolli's* complete translation of the poem into Italian gives the critique in volume 2. The Danish prose translation of the epic by Johan Henricus Schonhender (Copenhagen, 1790) disperses Addison's notes before each book; and José Amaro da Silva's Portuguese translation (Lisbon, 1792) likewise includes these papers. [JTS]

AESCHYLUS: *see* DRAMATISTS, GREEK.

AESTHETIC, MILTON'S. Aesthetics are constructed more often by critics than by poets, who rarely articulate the assumptions which move them. In this, as in so many things, Milton is the exception. Everywhere in his writings one finds statements that bear directly on the traditional questions of aesthetic theory. What is the relationship between art and morality? How is one to fulfill the double obligation of instructing and pleasing? What is the place of education and formal training in a poetic* of inspiration? What is the nature of the correspondence between differing styles* and either intention or effect? Unfortunately, Milton's many comments on these matters are scattered and contradictory, but the contradictions can be resolved if the larger principles of which they are only the surface manifestations are laid bare.

In the first book of *PR* the Son of God scorns Satan's words because they are "ambiguous" and have a "double sense" (1.435), and yet at the climax of the poem he himself delivers a line that is, as Lewalski has observed, "notably" (and perhaps triply) ambiguous (*Milton's Brief Epic,* p. 316) : "Tempt not the Lord thy God, he said." Earlier in Book 4, the Son, who is usually presumed to be the poet's spokesman, sweepingly rejects all classical learning, its rhetoric*, its philosophy*, its literature, and yet the moment of his triumph is celebrated by a series of references to classical myth.* "Enjoy your dear Wit and gay rhetoric," cries the Lady to Comus (*Mask* 790), dismissing with contempt the art that has enabled him to entrap her, and yet Milton's opponents in controversy are often faulted and even vilified because they have proved themselves ignorant of that very art. These are not isolated instances. The most cursory examination of the statements collected by Ida Langdon in *Milton's Theory of Poetry and Fine Art* or of the index to *CM* will reveal similar inconsistencies. On the evidence, Milton is for plainness, but also for eloquence; for the careful labors of art, but also for the unpremidated verse of inspiration*; for reasonableness, but also for the searing vehemence of satiric speech; for decorum, but also for the earthy rudeness that calls a spade a spade. What are we to make of these (and other) contradictions? The answer seems to lie in what Sheridan Blau has called "Milton's Salvational Aesthetic" (*Journal of Religion* 46 : 282–95), and it will be the purpose of this article to define that aesthetic and explore its implications.

We can begin with another excerpt from *PR* :

Think not but that I know these things; or
     think
I know them not; not therefore am I short
Of knowing what I aught: he who receives
Light from above, from the fountain of light,
No other doctrine needs, though granted true.
                    (4. 286–90)

These lines follow immediately upon Satan's offer of pagan wisdom and eloquence, and they are notable for the care Jesus takes *not* to specify the extent of his knowledge of "these things." The effect of the passage is to shift the focus of attention away from the materials of philosophy and art (with which Jesus may or may not be familiar) to a better source of wisdom and eloquence, "Light from above," a light which, when it shines within, issues *naturally* in truthful speech and a "majestic unaffected stile" (4. 359). The point is made even more explicitly in *Apol,* where Milton speaks in his own voice : "For me, Readers, although I cannot say that I am utterly untrain'd in those rules which best Rhetoricians have giv'n, or unacquainted with those examples which the prime authors of eloquence have written in any learned tongue, yet true eloquence I find to be none but the serious and hearty love of truth" (3 : 362).

Here too the rules of rhetoric and the recipes for eloquence are neither embraced nor condemned, but simply bypassed, for the ends for which they were presumably instituted are declared to be inseparable from the spiritual state of the speaker or poet. This statement has obvious sources in classical and contemporary authorities, in Cicero's* identification of the orator with the philosopher, in Quintilian's* characterization of the orator as a wise man "whose wisdom is revealed in every aspect of his behavior" (*Institutes* 12. 2. 7), in Minturno's* sixteenth-century reformulation of a traditional definition, *"Definitur poeta vir bonus dicendi"*—"a poet is defined as a good man in speaking" (*De Poeta,* [Venice, 1559], p. 79), and in Ben Jonson's* insistence on "the impossibility of any mans being the good *Poet* without first being a good *Man*" (*Dedicatory Epistle to Volpone*). Milton no doubt was familiar with these and other versions of this commonplace (he echoes Jonson earlier in *Apol*), but the spirit in which he appropriates it is more Christian than classical and closer to Augustine* than to either Quintilian or Jonson. In the fourth book of the *De doctrina christiana* Augustine concludes a lengthy and appreciative analysis of St. Paul's prose style with this comment: "For these words were not devised by human industry, but were poured forth from the divine mind both wisely and eloquently" (trans. D. W. Robertson [1958], p. 132). Here the achievement of eloquence is explicitly disjoined from human industry (*humana industria*), from the labors of art, and attributed solely to the spirit that fills the speaker. In effect, eloquence as something apart from character (*ethos*) ceases to exist and becomes simply the outer manifestation of an inner probity. Moreover, and this is what distinguishes the classical from the Augustinian version of the topos, that inner probity is identified with the possession of (and possession by) a specifically Christian vision. This possession is simultaneously confining and liberating. It is confining because, as Augustine points out, the Christian has not three ends, but one end to his persuasions, the promulgation and propagation of the truth to which he bears witness. It is liberating because the nature of that truth, its total and exclusive claims, frees him from the rules of rhetorical and poetic theory. Augustine refers directly to those rules when he recalls Cicero's formula for the relationship between style and subject matter—"he therefore will be eloquent who can speak of small things in the subdued manner, of moderate things in a temperate manner, and of grand things in a grand manner"—and its application to juridical and deliberative occasions; but he immediately declares it *in*applicable to the concerns of Christian rhetors, for since "everything we say . . . must be referred, not to the temporal welfare of man, but to his eternal welfare . . . everything we say is of great importance" (p. 143). Moreover, it is of great importance *wherever* it is said, "either before the people or in private, either with one or with several, either with friends or with enemies, either in extended speech or in conversation, either in treatises or in books, either in long letters or in short" (p. 145). What have been dismissed in all these passages

are all the distinctions that fill out the categories of a rhetoric or a poetic and, as the remainder of the book shows, this dismissal authorizes a completely flexible use of the three styles and of the other weapons in the rhetorician's arsenal.

In Milton's case it authorizes even more, as we can see by looking at some other passages from *Apol*. In response to the charge that his language is intemperate and even scurrilous, Milton replies first that "in the teaching of men diversly temper'd different wayes are to be try'd" (3 : 312), and second that in his vehemence he imitates "the method that God uses; *with the froward to be froward, and to throw scorne upon the scorner*" (p. 288). This is not a rhetorical, but a religious defense "which make[s] use only of such reasons and authorities, as religion cannot except against" (p. 312), and it is a defense that precludes any criticism based on formal criteria. That is to say, by allying himself with the God in whose service he writes, Milton justifies (in both the moral and the theological senses) whatever means that service prompts him to employ. Joan Webber has suggested that for Milton "good style is a sign of grace" (*The Eloquent "I"*, p. 210), but his position is more radically anti-literary: the presence of grace* *makes* the style good, no matter what its formal properties. Obscurity, vehemence, vituperation, even obscenity (for "God himselfe uses the phrase, I will cut off . . . *him that pisseth against the wall*") are not only permitted, they are "pure" (p. 316), and they are pure by virtue (in the Renaissance sense) of the purity of the intention from which they issue. The "majestic unaffected style" that characterizes those who receive "Light from above" is thus inclusively rather than exclusively majestic. It is not decorous in the limited sense of *rhetorical* decorums, for it respects neither internal coherence nor the coherence of verbal formulae with the details of external reality. Rather it respects only its end—the "dear charity" of Christian teaching—which is in turn validated only by its source—in a regenerate spirit—and it is therefore a style that can properly include *anything*. If "to the pure all things are pure," to the pure poet all things are allowable, even those things for which he criticizes others. Everything depends on the position one occupies in relation to the saving and justifying truth. "There may be a sanctifi'd bitternesse," Milton insists, "against the enemies of truth" (*Apol* 3 : 314), and we are evidently meant to take "sanctified" literally. As Thomas Kranidas declares in *The Fierce Equation*, "Milton is accused of being improper. . . . Milton accuses his enemies of being *wrong*" (p. 101).

They are wrong even when their words are mild and their sentences "well order'd," for this "outside" decency is a mask for inner corruption. King Charles* may profess and speak fairly, but "he who from . . . any . . . verbal Devotion, without the pledge and earnest of sutable deeds, can be perswaded of a zeale and true righteousness in the person, hath much yet to learn; and knows not that the deepest policy of a Tyrant hath bin ever to counterfet Religious" (*Eikon* 5 : 84). The important word here is *counterfet*, because the judgment is not on the language, but on the sincerity. What Milton's opponents call decency and good order, in ceremony and ceremonious language, he calls hypocrisy, and the decorum to which they are faithful is, in the context of Christian duty, often *in*decorous. Thus Hall* is scorned because he writes "toothlesse Satyr[s]" (*Animad* 3 : 114), and a "spruce fastidious oratory" when the occasion calls for a more vehement strain (although Milton will later attack him for writing vehemently and thus indecorously against God's servant). Throughout his career Milton vigorously opposes "formalists," those who avail themselves of ready-made verbal formulae in order to evade the responsibility of Christian teaching or (what is worse) to disguise a foul intention with fair words. In either case, the inner man and the outer expression are disjoined rather than unified, and the resulting language is appliqué work, which stands in sharp contrast to "those free and unimpos'd expressions which from a sincere heart unbidden come into the outward gesture" (*Apol* 3 : 355). Everything else is a "devis'd bravery," "*a faire shew in the flesh*," and is therefore, whatever its observable properties, "nothing but a deformed uglinesse." In short, the opposite of a "majestic unaffected style" is a majestic *affected* style, which, because it is affected, is not truly majestic even though it may superficially resemble the style of one who speaks from an inward prompting. Milton thus has it both ways : his "bad" language becomes, because of his intention, good, while the "good" language of his opponents becomes, because of their intention, bad. His aesthetic is characterized by a wonderful and terrible consistency, which refuses to value formal features apart from the spirit that appropriates them.

The presence or absence of that spirit is also crucial to what happens at the other end of the communicative process. In *PR,* the true eloquence of the "majestic unaffected style" is preferred only by those of "true tastes" : "Sion's songs, to all true tasts excelling" (4. 347). And in *Apol,* the identification of the "truly eloquent" with the "regenerate" is followed almost immediately by a reference to those who are the "only fit persons to be taught" (3 : 287f.). The spirit that informs a speaker and sanctifies his utterance also informs the reader or hearer and sanctifies his response. Two pure intentions, one of the teacher and one of the pupil, meet over words that they jointly justify. The requirement that the poet be "withall a good man" (3 287), a "true Poem" (3 : 303), is extended to his audience, and the result is a unified aesthetic that depends on a circuit of intention. Just as the unregenerate speaker is incapable of a truly majestic style, so is the unregenerate audience incapable of responding to its excellence of having a "true taste." Milton characteristically addresses two audiences, the "fit audience . . . though few" (*PL* 7. 31) who like him are disposed toward the truth and its propagation, and the "rest" who, for whatever reason, are unamenable to instruction. Sometimes Milton's characterization of this latter (and larger) group is social; they are the "vulgar" or the "rabble" and he disdains both their applause and their criticism. "I would be heard only," he declares in *RCG,* "by the elegant and learned reader" (3 : 234). More often, though, the deficiencies of this "meaner sort" are moral and religious; they cannot be taught because they prefer the productions of their own imaginations to the word of God : "as for the proud, the obstinate and false Doctors of mens devices, be taught they will not, but discover'd and laid open they must be" (*Apol* 3 : 288). What "discovers" them is the inadequacy of their response to the revealed word, whether it proceed from the Scriptures or from the writings of those who are illuminated by the Holy Spirit* (a distinction that is finally without a difference). Not only do the obstinate and the proud resist the instruction of the word, but they make literary judgments on it (and on those who preach it) that directly reflect the absence in them of an answerability to the truly majestic style. They complain, for example, of obscurity, a complaint that Milton turns against them : "The very essence of Truth is plainnesse, and brightnes; the darknes and crookednesse is our own. . . . If we will but purge with sovrain eyesalve that intellectual ray which *God* hath planted in us, then we would beleeve the Scriptures protesting their own plainnes, and perspicuity" (*Ref* 3 : 33). Once again we see Milton shifting the burden of aesthetic evaluation from formal to intentional criteria, in this case to the intentional "set" or disposition of an audience. Plainness, which is in classical terms a condition of the language and definable in formally descriptive terms, is here a condition of the understanding, an index not of literary but of *spiritual* discerning ("by the spirit discerning that which is good"). The point is made even more forcefully in *RCG,* where Milton is himself the illuminated audience for whom the Scriptures are answerably plain: "Let others therefore dread and shun the

Scriptures for their darknesse, I shall wish I may deserve to be reckon'd among those who admire and dwell upon them for their clearnesse" (3 : 184). Their clearness is his clearness because the spirit that informs them fills him too and also fills those of his readers who agree with him.

It must be admitted that this aspect of Milton's aesthetic is complicated by what he says elsewhere in *RCG* about the abilities and obligations of the poet : "These abilities, wheresoever they be found, are the inspired guift of God rarely bestow'd, but yet to some . . . and are of power . . . to inbreed and cherish in a great people the seeds of vertu . . . to allay the perturbations of the mind, and set the affections in right tune" (3 : 238). Here there seem to be no limits on the number or nature of those who may be reached and changed by the inspired poet, and in the same paragraph Milton speaks of the necessity of using his gifts to teach those "who will not so much as look upon Truth herselfe, unlesse they see her elegantly drest" (3 : 239). The contradiction between this and other statements in the prose and poetry is obvious, and it is not resolved. Throughout his career Milton wavers between believing that the man who is a true poet can speak only to readers similarly constituted, and believing that such a man can raise readers to the level of fitness and illumination that he himself enjoys. It may be that his position on this question varied with the rise and fall of his hopes for the establishing of a community of saints for whom he would be the spokesman and the prophet (see Michael Fixler, *Milton and the Kingdoms of God*), but it is a question he never settles and we can see him wrestling with it in the controversial pamphlets and in the autobiographical passages of *PL.*

Nevertheless, Milton's wavering on this one point does not compromise the distinctive feature of his aesthetic, its dependence, for both description and evaluation, on standards of intention and effect. (To Milton's acknowledged heresies* we should add the modern heresies of the intentional and affective fallacies.) For even when he assumes the stance of the teacher who numbers among his pupils all men of whatever kind, his "literary" vocabulary has reference to nonformal properties. When plainness is not already an attribute of the clear-eyed audience, it is an attribute of the prose or poetry that seeks to create that audience, and thus a Miltonic plain style can include deliberate obscurity (as the parables are obscure), involuted and convoluted constructions (which like some parts of Scripture exercise and purge the mind of the reader) and even downright deception (which after the manner of Christ teaches by "entangling" [*Tetra*, Yale *Prose* 2 : 642]). That is to say, a Miltonic plain style need not be formally plain (although it can be), for the measure of its clarity is the clarity of the understanding it produces. If Milton is a formalist in any sense, he is a formalist not of physical configurations but of effects, and indeed his very definition of "form" is couched in affective terms : "The form or very ground of an art is not so much the methodical disposition of its rules as it is the teaching of something useful; for an art is what it is rather because of what it teaches rather than because of the manner or arrangement of its teaching" (*Logic* 11 : 8; trans. SEF). In other words, it is not the materials of an art or their disposition, but their end that is of the essence, and what makes the end good is not a technical facility or a mastery of precepts and rules, but the goodness of the intention that desires it. "Faith," writes Milton in *CD* (17 : 7) "is the essential form of good works" and it is the possession of faith and the "fervent desire" to infuse it into others that makes good, that is, true, poems.

Does this mean then that Milton would advise would-be poets to have nothing to do with rhetorical and literary training? Not at all. His example alone would militate against such a conclusion, and curiously enough his "salvational aesthetic" confers a higher value on "human industry" than the more conventional aesthetics of classical and Elizabethan decorums. The reason for this is the relationship between "human industry" and the achieving of the regenerate spirit from which good poems (and speeches and pamphlets) naturally flow. In *RCG*, the "knowing reader" is promised a future work, one that will be "obtain'd" not "by the invocation of Dame Memory and her Siren daughters," that is, of the Muses*, "but by devout prayer to that eternall Spirit who can enrich with all utterance and knowledge" (3 : 241). Here "all" is unqualified and there would seem to be little room or need for any other avenue of knowledge; but then this declaration is immediately followed by another and the arts over which the Muses preside are reinstated : "to this must be added industrious and select reading, steddy observation, insight into all seemly and generous arts and affaires" (3 : 241). The order of these statements prevents us from arranging them in any simple sequence of cause and effect. Rather, the suggestion is of some measure of cooperation between the "eternall Spirit" who enriches in answer to prayer and the industrious (and secular) efforts of the petitioning poet. Neither the form nor the portions of this cooperation are specified, nor should they be, since to specify them too exactly would be to court the danger of "appoint[ing] heavenly disposition" (*SA* 373). What is important is that the poet is allowed some area of responsibility for perfecting the gifts that God has given him; and since those gifts, if they are nurtured, finally flower in the unaffected majestic style of God's prophet, the education of the poet is exactly equivalent, in means and end, to the education of the Puritan Saint. Milton resolves the tension between art and inspiration (that is, between works and grace) by making the latter the goal of the former. The labors of art are (like everything else) directed toward a regeneration of the spirit, one sign of which is the immediate and natural possession of the eloquence for which art has labored. Although the words that pour forth are not *now* devised by human industry, human industry is at least partly responsible for the perfection from which they issue.

Thus, despite his tendency to devalue human endeavor, Milton manages to find an honorable (and even necessary) place in his aesthetic for the arts of poetry and rhetoric, but this place is forfeited if those arts are pursued apart from their salvational end. "Language," we read in *Educ*, "is but the instrument conveying to us things useful to be known" (4 : 277), and it is possible that Milton here recalls Augustine's distinction in *On Christian Doctrine* between those things which are to be enjoyed and those things which are to be used (pp. 9–10). It is for this reason that the glories of pagan philosophy and literature are rejected in *PR*, not because they are intrinsically evil, but because Satan offers their sweetness as a *substitute* for the sweetness that would make us blessed. ("He who receives / Light from above, from the fountain of light, / No other doctrine needs, though granted true.") In another context, when they are no longer in this particular configuration of choice, the same materials can be pressed into the service of the truth of which they (and everything else) are refractions. And so it is that in the same poem (463–75) the words of pagan mythographers are used to celebrate the triumph of the living word.

What is true of pagan myth is true of poetry in general : it is to be used rather than to be enjoyed for its own sake. J. B. Broadbent once remarked that Milton "always had a sense that poetry does not matter" (*Modern Philology* 56 : 224–42). This is a half truth. What Milton *knew* was that poetry did not *ultimately* matter, but he also knew that in our present situation the ultimate is not immediately available. In short, we must do the best with what we have, and in the category of what we have, poetry is preeminent, not as a self-sustaining value, but as the best of the vehicles that sustain us as we move toward blessedness. "In this body," Milton explains, "our understanding cannot found it self but on sensible things, nor arrive so clearly to the knowledge of God and things invisible, as by orderly conning over the visible and inferior creature" (*Educ* 4 : 277). It is because poetry too is founded on sensible things that it is uniquely able to touch us and so move us in the direction of knowledge of God. There are of course other means, but poetry is finally "precedent" because it is "more simple, sensuous and passionate" (*Educ* 4 : 286), that is, more in touch with our infirmities and thus better able to play a part in the repairing of them. [SEF]

AETHELWEARD: *see* SAVILLE, SIR HENRY.

AFER, JOHN LEO, author of *Descriptio Africae,* an account of his travels in Africa in the late fifteenth century. Milton, using the Leyden 1632 edition and the material on Afer in Purchas, cited Afer in the "Poetry" entry of *CB* concerning a native chief who heard poetry recited at his meals. Although Milton never again referred to him, some of Afer's information about Africa may lie back of the references to Araby in *PL* (4. 163) and Fez (11. 403). [WBH]

AGAR, THOMAS (1597?–1673), Milton's second brother-in-law. Information relating to Thomas Agar and his family is frequently uncertain, and areas needing investigation are many. Apparently the Agar family became friends and relatives of the Miltons through Edward Phillips, Milton's first brother-in-law, although they may have been part of the family living in the parish of All Hallows, Bread Street, during the 1630s. (A Thomas Agar was buried there on November 23, 1637.) Phillips was Deputy Clerk of the Crown in the Court of Chancery when he died in August 1631. An "intimate friend" of Phillips, Agar, who had also been a clerk in Chancery, succeeded to the vacant position. At this time he was married to Mary, the only daughter of the prominent London physician Dr. Thomas Rugeley (the name also appears as Ridgeley), who was buried on June 24, 1656, in St. Botolph's without Aldersgate. Her brother was Dr. Luke Rugeley (1615?–1697), also an important London physician; he was a student at Christ's College* from 1633 to 1638. This is shortly after Milton and his brother Christopher left. The Rugeleys were politically connected and community leaders; they lived in the parish of St. Michael Bassishaw at this time. A genealogical chart made around 1633 for a visitation indicates that Mary and Thomas Agar had one daughter, who may have been the "Mrs. Anna Eager" who was buried from St. Martin in the Fields on November 13, 1633. The note in the chart implies that Mary Agar had previously died.

Agar married Milton's widowed sister Anne on January 5, 1632, at St. Dunstan in the East, becoming step-father to Edward and John Phillips. Anne and Thomas had two daughters, Mary, baptized on October 10, 1632, in Kensington, her parents then residing in Brompton, and Anne. Mary died young. If Agar's daughter Anne by Mary Rugeley died in 1633, Milton's niece Anne was probably born after that date; according to the age given on her marriage license in 1662, she was born around 1636. The date of Milton's sister's death is unknown. Speculation has suggested that she died while Milton was abroad in 1638 or 1639, possibly in childbirth of Anne, but also that she was still alive on December 29, 1639. The daughter Anne was licensed to marry David Moore of Sayes House, Chertsey, Surrey, on December 29, 1662. He died on January 12, 1694, leaving Anne and their son Thomas, who was knighted in 1715 and died in 1735.

Thomas Agar and his brother John drew up a will for a Thomas Harding in 1630. John was living in Kensington in the early 30s, while the Miltons were in nearby Hammersmith*, and Thomas and Anne Agar were in nearby Brompton. John may have been admitted to the Inner Temple on May 27, 1636. If so, he may

also have been the attorney in Common Pleas who died about May 1671 and was buried in Barnes, Surrey. This John Agar was mayor of Barnes, not far from Sayes House, Chertsey, where the Moore family resided. On March 10, 1637, a writ addressed to Thomas and John Agar was drawn up for Sir Thomas Cotton, who was bringing action against John Milton, Senior, and his former partner, Thomas Bower, over moneys that they had managed for his late granduncle John Cotton. Milton, Senior, was required to answer the writ, which he did on April 13, 1637; his answer is signed by the Agars. A delay in answering had been sought by Christopher Milton on April 1 on the basis of family concerns; Milton's mother died on April 3 and was buried on April 6.

Agar was removed from his post as Deputy Clerk during the Interregnum, regaining it with the Restoration. He became Clerk of Appeals in July 1660. During the Interregnum he lived in Lincolnshire, clearly a Royalist by persuasion, but by 1662 he was in the parish of St. Sepulchre. He died on November 1, 1673; his monument was erected in Temple Church. His will, proved on November 5, 1673, was executed by his brother John's son Thomas, who had entered Gray's Inn on February 26, 1658, and the Middle Temple on June 30, 1658. He was called to the bar in 1663. As a widower (his first wife being unknown) he was licensed to marry Mary Bolles, daughter of the Royalist landowner Sir Richard Bolles, on June 8, 1674. The will left £200 to Edward Phillips, referred to his brother-in-law Dr. Luke Rugeley, and bequeathed funds to his daughter Anne and grandson Thomas. Phillips, however, was required to use the money under the executor's advice, and the bequest would have been voided had Phillips been appointed to the Deputy Clerk's office in the Court of Chancery. Instead Thomas Milton, eldest living son of Christopher, became Deputy Clerk of the Crown Office. There is no mention of John Phillips or the Miltons in the will. [JTS]

AITZEMA, LIEUWE VAN (1600–1669), a Dutch (or better, Frisian) nobleman, son of Meinardus van Aitzema, Burgomaster of Dokkum and Secretary of the Admiralty. A man of letters who devoted his career to statesmanship and history, Aitzema matriculated in liberal arts at Franeker Academy, publishing his *Poemata juvenilia* at the age of sixteen. After taking a doctorate of Law at Orleans, he returned to his homeland and began to practice. At the request of the City of Magdeburg, he was recognized by the States General in 1627 as the Agent for Madgeburg at The Hague, and two years later the Hanseatic League, then consisting of Hamburg, Bremen, and Lübeck, named him the Hanse Resident, a post he held until his death. In this capacity he enjoyed a kind of diplomatic immunity as well as influential connections at The Hague. Reputedly a master of modern tongues, he visited England in 1636 and 1652 on behalf of the Hanse towns. During his second embassy, lasting from February 25 to the end of August 1652, his handling of his mission won an especially good character from Parliament, and on more than one occasion he visited Milton, then Secretary* for Foreign Tongues. Aitzema, whose attitudes toward religion and tolerance are suggestive of Hugo Grotius*, reported to his superiors on English policies in religious questions, taking special note of the Racovian catechism* which, as he undoubtedly knew, Milton licensed against the wishes of the authorities. Perhaps respect for the Secretary's unorthodox views is evident in Aitzema's letter to Milton of January 29, 1655, informing him of his plans to publish a Dutch translation of his views on divorce* and inquiring whether the Englishman wished to change anything. No Dutch translation of any of the divorce tracts has come to light, however, and perhaps Milton's disapproval of the project—he preferred a Latin translation—was honored.

What Anglo-American commentators on Milton (and even some on Cromwell's intelligence services) fail to note is that besides his legitimate diplomatic activities, Aitzema also ran a "spy service" in Holland—not one that gathered information, but one that sold intelligence on a subscription basis to foreigners about the civil, diplomatic, and military strategy of the United Provinces, even in wartime. In the difficulties following the beheading of Charles I*, what the English had to know was whether their European neighbors were for or against the new government, whether they intended neutrality, and how seriously they were divided on the issue. *Accurate* information of exactly this sort was what Aitzema's organization specialized in. John Thurloe*, Cromwell's Secretary of State, is known to have paid out as much as fl. 1,000 quarterly for Aitzema's services under the Protectorate, and Dutch historians have thought that such relations had begun during Milton's secretaryship, or even earlier. The fact that Aitzema was searched and robbed by a Dutch Agent from Zeeland on his return from Britain in August 1652 suggests that he was then already suspect, and Edward Phillips's remark about governmental "Industry and good Intelligence" during Milton's tenure in office seems to confirm this. Certainly the procurement of the official instructions to the emissary of the States General on the eve of the first Dutch war, and Milton's answer to them before the emissary could arrive in London, implies an information service like Aitzema's, and it is perhaps no coincidence that Aitzema himself was present in London at a time when state letters by Milton claim that the English had outmaneuvered the Dutch. That the Parliament held him in esteem and that he obtained ready access to Milton, when people such as Hermann Mylius* could not, is thus understandable.

Aitzema's practices yielded one of the finest histories of the age. Though cynical about mankind, Aitzema respected truth and care in reporting, and out of the many documents that he accumulated for his irregular profession, he fashioned his monumental *Historie of verhael van saken van staet en oorlogh* (1657–1668). Because of its detail and the use of primary sources, this work is indispensable for studying the years 1621–1667; indeed, the incorporation of documents and frank evaluation of persons and actions caused the States of Friesland to ban the second edition (1669–1672). (Milton is discussed in 6 [1662] : 205.) After Aitzema's death, his clerks were arrested and his private papers confiscated by the States-General at The Hague, where they remain an important though neglected source of history of the seventeenth century. [PRS]

ALCHEMY: *see* HERMETICISM.

ALFRED THE GREAT. Among the subjects for "British Tragedies" jotted down shortly after his return to England from Italy and Switzerland and still preserved in *TM*, Milton included an entry on Alfred as the protagonist of a possible epic or drama : "Alfred in disguise of a minstrel discovers the danes negligence sets on with a mightie slaughter about the same tyme the devonshire men rout Hubba & slay him." Then follows the further suggestion that this phase of the king's career may be suitable for epic development : "A Heroicall Poem may be founded somewhere in Alfreds reigne. especially at his issuing out of Edelingsey on the Danes. whose actions are wel like those of Ulysses" (18 : 243).

After this brief allusion, we hear nothing more of Alfred as a subject for either dramatic plan* or epic* treatment. In *RCG* (1641), Milton was still seeking a king or knight before the Norman conquest who might serve as the protagonist of a patriotic epic and as an example of Christian heroism.

Since Alfred's attack on the Danes is the only specifically English subject that Milton mentions as a potential epic argument (with the possible exception of later allusions to the heroic role of the anti-Royalist forces in the Puritan revolution), this entry has inevitably invited comparison with Milton's earlier references

to British themes in *Mansus* and *EpDam*. Francis Peck asserted that Milton intended to write a long heroic poem entitled *Alfred* in imitation of the *Odyssey*, paralleling his imitation of the *Iliad* in an *Arthuriad**. David Masson observed that "under the jotting of Alfred as a subject there is proof that, though the dramatic form was chiefly in favour with him for the time," Milton "had not entirely committed himself to that form against the epic." E. M. W. Tillyard regarded Milton's entry on Alfred as "proof that even if Milton still contemplated an *Arthuriad,* Arthur was not the only possible subject. . . . I think it probable that Milton, now definitely under the influence of Parliamentary thought, has abandoned the legendary and Royalist Arthur for the historical and constitutional Alfred, and that more generally he has yielded" to the century's growing "demand for scientific truth." Thus "it is possible not only that he has now turned from Arthur as a subject but that he is beginning to dislike the whole romantic matter of the Renaissance epic and to seek a stricter imitation of the classics."

Though Tillyard further suggests that Milton's comparison between Alfred and Ulysses recalls the poet's "early Odyssean ambitions in the *Vacation Exercise* and his account of epic poetry in *Elegia Sexta*," the primary basis of this comparison is the well established classical image of Odysseus as a master of strategic deception and tactical ruse. More specifically, Milton is alluding to Odysseus's frequent resort to ignoble disguises on espionage missions and other perilous ventures in hostile territory. Both Euripides* and Homer* had alluded to his entering Troy disguised as a beggar; and it was likewise in a beggar's disguise that he returned to his palace on Ithaca to wreak vengeance on the suitors. Though Milton would never develop the analogy between Alfred and Odysseus further, this allusion indicates his early awareness of the epic potentialities of a hero who penetrates an enemy citadel in an ignoble disguise—a motif that would reappear in his treatment of Satan in *PL* and (with variations) in his exploitation of the disguise-and-discovery motif in *PR,* where Satan's initial use of the ignoble disguise counterpoints the partial concealment of the Messiah's identity by his human nature and form. In a sense the divine hero of *PR,* like the infernal pseudo-hero of *PL,* can be regarded as a variant of the pattern Milton perceived in Alfred and Odysseus; for the former, no less than the latter, achieves victory through entering hostile territory in humble disguise.

In *Brit,* Milton would subsequently return to the adventure that had attracted him earlier as possessing dramatic or epic potentialities : "*Malmsbury* writes, that in this time of his recess, to go as a spy into the *Danish* camp, he took upon him with one Servant the habit of a Fidler; by this means gaining access to the Kings Table, and sometimes to his Bed-Chamber, got knowledge of their secrets, their careless encamping, and thereby this opportunity of assailing them on a sudden" (10 : 214). An additional parallel with Ulysses, moreover, could be found in the fact that both royal heroes temporarily took refuge with a swineherd : "*Alfred* . . . for some time all alone, as *Florent* saith, sojourn'd with *Dunwulf* a Swine-heard . . ." (10 : 213).

Milton's allusions to Alfred in *CB, Brit,* and other works emphasize the king's union of active and contemplative virtues*, his excellence in the administration of justice and in the dissemination of learning, and his mastery of the arts of peace and war. *CB* not only praises his erudition and justice (18 : 137, 139, 143) but especially commends his turning "the old laws" into English. "I would," Milton adds, "he liv'd now to rid us of this norman gibbrish, the laws of Molmutius" (18 : 166). Two of Milton's prose tracts summon Alfred for aid in the controversy over the relative authority of King and Parliament. *Eikon* cites him as authority for the king's subjection to the laws of the realm : "Nay *Alfred* the most worthy King, and by some accounted first absolute Monarch of the Saxons heer, so ordain'd : as is cited out of an ancient Law Book . . . , where it is complain'd on, *As the sovran abuse of all,* that *the King should be deem'd above the Law, whereas he ought be subject to it by his Oath . . .*" (5 : 299). *1Def* observes that Alfred promulgated laws "from an assemblage of his wisest men" (7 : 439). The history notes his "great desire of learning," his thirst "after all liberal knowledge," his "conning of *Saxon* Poems day and night," and his "translating Books out of Latin into English." From "the time of his undertaking regal charge, no man [was] more patient in hearing causes . . . , more exact in doing justice, and providing good Laws, which are yet extant; more severe in punishing unjust judges or obstinate offenders. . . ." Alfred's "noble mind . . . rendered him the mirror of Princes"; in spite of illness he was not "disinabl'd to sustain those many glorious labours of his life both in peace and war" (10 : 220–23). [JMS]

ALL HALLOWS, BREAD STREET: *see* BIOGRAPHY.

ALLEGORY, a rhetorical figure defined as the "description of a subject under the guise of some other subject of aptly suggestive resemblance" (OED); its developed form is the personification allegory, in which characters representing abstractions move in a plot of general human significance (e.g., *Everyman*). Although Cicero* was the first to use the rhetorical term, the practice of allegorical interpretation goes back to several Greek philosophers who looked upon Homer's* tales as allegories of philosophical teachings. Plato's* objections notwithstanding, it was frequently assumed that whatever poetry was not educationally useful must have been intended figuratively. On that assumption, Philo* (d. ca. A.D. 50), a Jewish philosopher living in Alexandria, maintained the dignity of Moses by reading the biblical books attributed to the prophet as a Neoplatonic* treatise. The medieval practice of allegorizing Virgil* and Ovid* has therefore a long and respectable ancestry.

To the allegory of poets the Middle Ages added the allegory of theologians, also known as the doctrine of the manifold sense of Scripture. Origen* of Alexandria (ca. 185–255) explained that every biblical detail expresses simultaneously a literal, moral, and spiritual truth. Origen's method of explication was passed on, through the Church Fathers, to Pope Gregory the Great (ca. 540–604), who promulgated the view that Scripture has a fourfold sense : historical, allegorical, moral, and anagogic. For instance, the historical Temple of Jerusalem is allegorically the Church on earth; morally it is the individual believer, and anagogically (or mystically) it is the final communion of saints in heaven. The second of these levels, which the theologians called the allegorical sense, is what one now calls the figural or typological* meaning. The allegory of theologians upon the Bible differs from that of poets in the treatment accorded to the surface subject. In the allegory of poets the written text is merely a disguise for some other subject, whereas the theologians must respect the historical truth of the biblical narrative. Examples of sustained four-level interpretation are rare in medieval literature. Although rigid in theory, the allegory of theologians was in practice a discursive and explanatory method of literary analysis not unlike the modern analysis of imagery. The method of biblical exegesis, the memory of the ancient belief in the allegory of poets, together with the scholastic devotion to the study of universals in metaphysics, stimulated the medieval taste for allegorical reading and writing, a taste that only gradually declined during the next age. Petrarch* and Boccaccio* still thought of allegory as the very justification of poetry, and the finest instance of sustained personification allegory belongs to the Renaissance : Spenser's* The Faerie Queene. Satan's encounter with Sin and Death (PL 2. 629–889) is Milton's only fully developed example in Spenser's genre.

The humanists of the Renaissance and Reformation introduced the study of philology and, with it, a more scholarly regard for the historical character of a literary text. The study of the time, place, occasion, and intention of a work began to check the allegorizing fancy. The Protestant Reformers held that Scripture had no other than a literal meaning. However, since that meaning must be the one intended by God, their definition of literal included the second of the four medieval senses (the figural or typological meaning, a development from St. Paul) as being part of the divine intention. This is also Milton's view. Although Protestants put strict limits on biblical allegorizing in support of dogma and doctrine, the traditional moral and anagogic readings of scriptural passages continued to appear in Anglican homiletic and devotional writings (e.g., in Donne's* Sermons and Herbert's The Temple); the Puritans and Milton scorned the use of these interpretations (see H. R. MacCallum, "Milton and Sacred History," Essays in English Literature from the Renaissance to the Victorian Age, ed. Millar Maclure and F. W. Watt [1964], pp. 149–68).

Respect for historicity also lessened the interest in the allegory of poets, but the lessening was gradual : Donne understood Ovid as a pagan and libertine poet, but George Sandys supplied a lengthy allegorizing commentary to his translation of the Metamorphoses (1632). Unwilling to surrender any part of their classical patrimony, and yet desiring to find a didactic purpose in every part of it, Renaissance minds continued to allegorize the strange and the fabulous. Francis Bacon* was not sure whether mythological* tales had been allegorically intended, but he did not hesitate to promote such "worthy contemplations"; in his Wisdom of the Ancients (1609), the genealogy of Cupid is an allegory of the natural motion of the atom, and the myth of Orpheus* a description of the history of universal philosophy. The Attendant Spirit in Milton's Mask subscribes to the commonplace that the poetic imagination is never without serious purpose :

Ile tell ye, tis not vain or fabulous,
(Though so esteem'd by shallow ignorance)
What the sage Poets taught by th'heav'nly
    Muse,
Storied of old in high immortal vers
Of dire *Chimeras* and inchanted Iles,
And rifted Rocks whose entrance leads to
    Hell,
For such there be, but unbelief is blind.
                                    (512–18)

If Bacon interpreted strange fables as ethical or scientific allegories, the Renaissance Neoplatonists, especially Ficino, read them as mystic, that is, as allegories of the soul's quest for union with the One. According to Sears Jayne, *Mask* is the Miltonic example of Neoplatonist allegorizing.

Although *Mask* and the infernal trinity of Satan, Sin, and Death are the only conspicuous examples of Milton's use of allegory as a rhetorical device, his debt to the allegorical tradition is extensive for the reason that allegory was so large a part of his inheritance. Orpheus became a type of Christ in *Lyc* because he had long been an allegory of immortality; the Comus-Circe myth was a moral allegory before Milton spun from it a "divine philosophy"; the birth of Sin (*PL* 2. 747–58) is a gruesome inversion of the birth of Athena, goddess of wisdom; Milton's allusion to Proserpine and Ceres (*PL* 4. 268–72) is a reference to a traditional allegory of death and rebirth. These are a few examples of Milton's frequent practice. *PL* is not an allegory—Adam and Eve are real in a way that Spenser's Knights and Ladies are not—but to appreciate its art, the reader must attend to the allegorical burden of many of its details. [JRM]

ALLEN, DON CAMERON (1903–1973), American scholar. He took his bachelor's and doctor's degrees at the University of Illinois. After a few minor appointments he moved to Washington State College, now University, where during the Depression years 1932–1938 he spent a sizable library budget to build up so remarkable a collection of Renaissance holdings that it is the only one in the Northwest to be listed in Wing's Short Title Catalogue. From there he moved to Duke and then in 1942 to the Johns Hopkins University, where in 1950 he was named to the Sir William Osler chair. Aside from his many publications, he helped edit *Modern Language Notes* and *ELH: A Journal of English Literary History*. Under his lead as chairman, Johns Hopkins retained its preeminence in English literary studies. Before his retirement he served as vice-president of the Modern Language Association (1966–67) and published a commissioned book (1968) that examined the traditional requirements for the English doctorate, arguing that a new definition of the degree was needed. This report has had great influence.

As Renaissance scholar, Allen published on a great variety of subjects. His most important Milton contributions are contained in *The Harmonious Vision* (1954), but Milton also figures largely in his study of Renassance religious issues, *Doubt's Boundless Sea* (1964); of its metaphorical traditions, *Image and Meaning* (1960); and of its allegorical interpretations of various traditions, *Mysteriously Meant* (1970). [WBH]

ALLUSIONS TO MILTON. Through 1700, references to Milton or his works fall into two categories : incidental allusions found in letters, printed works, newspapers, and the like (as well as in publishers' listings), and more extended arguments or discussions, biographical notices, and some imitations. Most of these references were at first political, though also concerned with religious and sociological positions, and later increasingly literary or concerned with Milton the poet. The earliest allusions and more extended discussions (1641–1648) are generally negative, in opposition to Milton's antiprelatical views or to his position on divorce*. Milton is not always cited by name, nor is the work that has evoked reaction. The earliest allusion recorded is in the anonymous *A Compendious Discourse, Proving Episcopacy To Be Of Apostolicall, And Consequently Of Divine Institution* ([May] 1641), p. [3] : "The late unworthy Authour of a booke intituled, *Of Reformation*, &c. hath found some quarrell against him [Irenaeus] : but *Fevardentius*, in his apologeticall preface (in the defence of Irenaeus) hath well answered such exceptions." The first full-scale argument against Milton is the anonymous *A Modest Confusion of a Slanderous and Scurrilous Libell, Entituled, Animadversions Upon the Remonstrants Defense Against Smectymnuus* (1642); it is sometimes ascribed to Bishop Joseph Hall* and/or his son Robert. The earliest manuscript allusion known is also the first commendatory reference. In his diary, *Ephemerides,* for 1643 Samuel Hartlib* wrote that "Mr. Milton in Aldersgate Street hase written many good books a great traveller and full of proiects and inventions." The earliest poetical imitations with verbal appropriations were written about April 1647. In his *Erotopaignion* [Greek characters]. *Or, the Cyprian Academy*, Robert Baron echoes Milton's 1645 *Poems* often (see, e.g., Book 1, pp. 54, 55, and Book 2, pp. 3, 28, 34, 43, 45). The poems echoed in these citations are *Nat, May, L'Al, IlP*, and *Lyc*. The earliest definite reference to Milton in a newspaper seems to be in John Hakluyt's pro-Commonwealth *The Metropolitan Nuncio*, no. 3 (June 6–13, 1649), last page : "An Answer is comming forth unto those Idolized *Meditations* of the late King, with Marginall Notes upon them, no doubt but they will be good because of some good Tenents which the Author holds, whereof this is one, that a man may put away his wife for lesser faults then fornication . . ." (dated June 11). The first notice in a book published outside the British Isles is found in Christopher Wasse's *Electra of Sophocles: Presented to Her Highnesse the Lady Elizabeth; With an Epilogue, Shewing the Parallel in Two Poems, The Return, and the Restauration,* published at The Hague for Samuel Brown in 1649. "Whilst like

the froward Miltonist, / We our old Nuptiall knot untwist" are two lines from "The Return," p. [E8r] (p. 3 of new pagination). The first non-English notices occur in 1651 after the publication of *1Def.*

From 1649 through 1660 references to Milton are generally concerned with the political issues of *Eikon*, the three *Defenses*, and the pamphlets of 1659–60. The years in which the most numerous allusions or longer notices occur are 1651 continuing through 1652 and 1660, the first because of Milton's attack on Salmasius* and his defense of the Commonwealth and the latter because of the changing atmosphere in England. Some allusions are praiseworthy, though usually only when their author is an antagonist of Salmasius* or More*, or an adherent of republicanism; most continue to be negative. Milton and his antimonarchial work became part of the subject of a series of German dissertations by Caspar Ziegler (who does not cite Milton), Jacob Schaller, Erhard Kieffer, and Christopher Güntzer on the English regicides during the 1650s. The first publication of Ziegler's dissertation, *Circa Regicidium Anglorum Exercitationes,* was in Leipzig in 1652, and this was reprinted with Schaller's examination of Milton's part in the controversy in 1653 in Leyden. Kieffer's defense of Schaller's dissertation was published in Strasbourg in 1652; Güntzer's further defense was published in Strasbourg in 1657; and Schaller's, Kieffer's, and Güntzer's were reprinted together in the latter place and year.

With removal from public life and with the Restoration, Milton was less frequently referred to from 1661 until his death in 1674. At times his relationship with the Cromwellian government is recalled (as in Henry Foulis's *The History of the Wicked Plots and Conspiracies of Our Pretended Saints* [1662], pp. 4, 24) or his involvement in the controversy over Charles I* and *Eikon Basilike* (as in Henry King's *A Sermon Preached the 30th of January at White-Hall, 1664. Being the Anniversary Commemoration of*

K. Charls the I, Martyr'd on that Day [1665], p. 34). One other attack on Milton during this period should be mentioned. To discredit Andrew Marvell*, the author (Richard Leigh?) of *The Transproser Rehears'd* (1673) criticized *PL* and its blank verse. The author opposed Milton's political and religious views, but chose to demean the man and his poetic work. This strategy was to become common in the eighteenth century. Or an author (like Joseph Addison* in "An Account of the Greatest English Poets") would praise the poetry and lament Milton's political aberrations. Other poetical imitations or appropriations during Milton's lifetime are found in Robert Baron's *Pocula Castalia* (1650), a number of Marvell's poems, Joshua Poole's *The English Parnassus* (1657), Thomas Flatman's *Poems and Songs* (1674), and of course Dryden's* *The State of Innocence.* (*See also* ADAPTATIONS, LITERARY.)

During his lifetime Milton was primarily known through the controversies* in which he figured. There is little allusion of any other significance during this period. Works such as *PL, Educ,* and *Areop,* which today are perhaps the most widely known, read, and reprinted, received very few notices. Some works like *RCG* (omitting publishers' notices) are never alluded to. The allusion book compiled by William R. Parker in *Milton's Contemporary Reputation* (1940) lists 113 references printed during Milton's lifetime. Nineteen of these are advertisements and sixteen are brief notices. Only fourteen of the remainder are favorable to Milton. Parker's list has been supplemented in French's *Life Records* and in Parker's *Milton,* both of which include manuscript allusions. (See also John T. Shawcross's introduction to *Milton: The Critical Heritage* [1970].)

The period of 1675–1699 saw the rise of an interest in Milton and his works that was both scholarly and critical. There were still political notices, particularly in connection with the authorship of *Eikon Basilike* and Pamela's prayer, and an undercurrent among the Whigs made

Milton the representative of a lost cause. (*See* WHIGS, MILTON AND THE, and ADAPTATIONS, LITERARY.) But the dominant view seen in allusions of the last quarter of the century cast Milton as the chief representative of the heroic tradition in England. He was compared favorably with Homer* and Virgil*; he became the sublimest of poets; and he increasingly is the model for poetic excursions into epic and into blank verse*. For example, Edward Ecclestone's *Noah's Flood, Or, the Destruction of the World* (1679) is influenced by Dryden's *The State of Innocence* most directly, though Milton's "original" is also recalled, and Sir Richard Blackmore's *Prince Arthur, An Heroick Poem in Ten Books* (1695) and *King Arthur. An Heroick Poem. In Twelve Books* (1697) show close imitations throughout. While there were those like Wentworth Dillon, Earl of Roscommon (1685), who praised *PL* in blank verse, there were also those like Dryden who damned while praising because of different criteria or because of a lack of real understanding of the epic. Or there were those like Thomas Rymer (1678) who deplored the verse and others like Charles Leslie (1698) who criticized the epic on theological grounds. On the other hand, Richard Bentley* employed two quotations from the poem to prove his points in *A Confutation of Atheism From the Origin and Frame of the World. The Third and Last Part* (1693), p. 40. Almost all literary attention was directed toward *PL,* part of the impetus deriving from the success of the fourth edition of 1688.

During this period also Milton became an authority on early British history, an evaluation that was to carry well into the eighteenth century. See, for example, Aylett Sammes's *Britannia Antiqua Illustrata* (1676), pp. 48, 50, 83, 387, 476–77, 559, and James Tyrrell's *The General History of England, Both Ecclesiastical and Civil,* 1 (1697): vi, viii, 17, 20, 136, and 116 (second pagination). He also became a spokesman again for freedom of the press through the adaptations of Charles Blount and William Denton. His name appears repeatedly in literary discussions or in poetic imitations in periodicals, such as *The Athenian Gazette: Or Casuistical Mercury* (also known as *The Athenian Mercury*), 1691 onward. He is alluded to or quoted from in sermons; for example, John Moore quotes twice from *CharLP* and once from *Eikon* in *A Sermon Preach'd Before the House of Lords, in the Abby-Church at Westminster, Upon Monday, January 31. 1697* (1697), pp. 27, 33. Similar allusions to those already noted appear on the Continent; for example, in Daniel Georg Morhof's *Polyhistor sive de notitia auctorem et rerum commentarii* (Lübeck, 1688), pp. 304–5, and *Unterricht under teutschen Sprache und Poesie* (Lübeck and Frankfurt, 1700), pp. 183, 212, 231, 515, 672.

With the rise of formalized biography and biographical dictionaries, Milton's name and works were further popularized. Among these are the following : William Winstanley's notice in *The Lives of the Most Famous English Poets* (1687), p. 195, is well known for its antagonism (he also alludes to Milton under "John Phillips," p. 210). Sir Thomas Pope Blount primarily reproduced lengthy statements by Dryden and from *The Athenian Mercury* in *De Re Publica: Or, Remarks Upon Poetry With Characters and Censures of the Most Considerable Poets, Whether Ancient or Modern. Extracted Out of the Best and Choicest Criticks* (1694), pp. 135–38, with allusions on pp. 1, 105, 215. Pierre Bayle's first rather brief notice, to be amply expanded in later editions of *The Dictionary Historical and Critical,* appeared in 1697. Edward Phillips's "Life" of his uncle, introducing his translation of *Letters of State* (1694), and John Toland's* "Life," prefacing the first volume of *A Complete Collection* (1698), reprinted separately the next year, establish "fact" or interpretation concerning the man and his work, as well as biographical direction, for future biographers.

The allusions and more extended references to Milton become quite numerous by the end of the seventeenth century. Unfortunately, no full listing of these notices is available at present, the most complete citations being given in Parker's and French's books previously referred to. [JTS]

ALMONI, PELONI : *see* ANTAGONISTS.

AMANUENSES. Even before his government service (1649) and his blindness (1652), Milton employed others to do various writing and textual chores for him. Texts for publication may have been prepared by scribes, who sometimes at least may have been one of his nephews, Edward and John Phillips. After his blindness, texts were probably written down and readied for publication by a variety of amanuenses. A few scribal emendations occur in the *TM* copy of *Mask,* which were probably made when the text for the first edition (1637–38) was prepared. This unknown hand is not found in any other material. The treatment of text of the 1645 *Poems* when compared with the copies in *TM* and of second editions of *Tenure* and *Eikon* likewise suggests that someone other than Milton prepared copy.

John Phillips served his uncle often as scribe up to the time he left his uncle's home in 1652, when he became twenty-one. *Sonn* 8, 16, 17, *NewF,* and a note alongside *Sonn* 15 in *TM* are in his hand. An additional sonnet was transcribed by him in Milton's copy of Giovanni della Casa's* *Rime e Prose* (in the New York Public Library), p. 28. The manuscript of *Rous* sent to John Rous* is likewise in his hand (with a one-word correction by Milton), as are the two translations of letters from Princess Sophie to Prince Maurice and to Prince Rupert* (1649) (with corrections by Milton in the letter to Maurice). Phillips wrote the inscription in the album of Christopher Arnold*, to which Milton affixed his signature, on November 19, 1651. He penned letters to Hermann Mylius*, dated November 7, 1651; December 31, 1651 (with a correction of date by Milton); February 10, 1652; and February 21, 1652. He affixed the ending and signature to letters to

Mylius, dated January 8, 1652, and January 20, 1652, and added a note to the Safeguard for Oldenburg*, dated February 17, 1652. Further, he wrote down the letter to Whitelocke*, dated February 12, 1652; the entries from Machiavelli's* *Discorsi* (except the entry by Edward Phillips) in the *CB*, pp. 148, 185, 195 (2), 198 (2), 242 (3), 243 (2), 245, and 246, and entries from Berni*, pp. 71, 187, and Boiardo*, pp. 77, 187, plus the headings and index entries for pp. 77, 148, 198. These entries from Berni and Boiardo are assigned to Amanuensis A by Hanford. John Phillips also completed Milton's entry concerning the birth of Deborah in the family Bible* (British Museum, Additional MS 32310), ca. May 1652. Most of his work can be dated 1642, 1647, 1649–1652.

Edward Phillips probably checked over the text of *PL* as it was being developed, as he reports in his *Life* of his uncle, and may have acted as preparer or corrector (proofreader) of various works including *PL*. His hand is seen in some corrections to the manuscript of Book 1 of *PL*. In addition he wrote down a letter to Mylius, dated February 13, 1652, and two citations from Machiavelli on p. 197 of *CB* as well as a note concerning the Index Theologicus* and the heading and index entry for that page. He is designated Amanuensis B by Hanford. What evidence of his hand exists can be dated 1650–1652, 1665(?).

An unidentified, careless, and rather ignorant amanuensis worked for Milton around early 1653 when the familiar letter to John Bradshaw was written. His hand is seen also in the *TM* making changes in *Sonn* 13 (second draft, title), 12, 16, 17, and *NewF*, and recopying *Sonn* 11, 12, 13, and 14 into the quarto sheets. The texts of these sonnets (and probably of *NewF*), which were finally published in 1673), owe some erroneous accidentals and spelling to this unreliable scribe.

A scribe called by Hanford Amanuensis E entered a note from Buchanan* in the *CB* (p. 198). It is very badly written and spelled; was the scribe one of Milton's

students? If so, and since it is dated after entries from Machiavelli (1651–52?), may it have been Richard Jones, later Viscount Ranelagh*, who became Milton's pupil ca. 1653? Another unidentified scribe, Hanford's Amanuensis F, made entries in the *CB* from Signonius* (pp. 19, 181), and Costanzo* (pp. 5, 248), and wrote a note on page 185 and the heading and index entry for page 248. The scribe's work would seem to date after the Machiavelli entries also. Amanuensis F may also have made at least one marginal addition to *CD* (p. 647), and if so, it suggests his employment by Milton over a few years during the 1650s or an earlier dating for *CD* than now generally accepted.

The amanuensis of the extant manuscript of Book 1 of *PL,* which is dated ca. 1665, entered two items in the *CB,* one from Dante's *Purgatorio* (p. 197 and dated after Edward Phillips's Machiavelli notes), and one from Nicetas Acominates* (dated after 1647 and perhaps before 1658). He also wrote the heading and index entry for page 249. The dating of the work of Amanuensis D, as Hanford labeled this scribe, raises a number of questions, which might be solved if he is ever identified: did he work for Milton over a fairly long period (1652?–1665?)? was Milton still using the *CB* for only one or two entries after 1652 and as late as 1665 (a similar question arises over Picard's work in the *CB*)? have we erred in dating the finished *PL*?

Jeremy Picard's* datable association with Milton is 1658–1660. He affixed Milton's procurational signature on a document dated January 14, 1658, and on a conveyance of a bond to Cyriac Skinner*, dated May 5, 1660. The further items that he wrote out for Milton have thus been dated within this period. But Picard produced an audit concerning the Piedmont massacre for Sir Samuel Morland* in mid-1655 (Public Record Office, SP 46/112, f. 63–63v), and it is possible that Milton came to employ him at that time, or it is possible that he was in Milton's employ prior to that date and came to work for the government through Milton.

Possibly he was one of Milton's students as Parker has suggested, and may be identical with the "Mr. Packer, who was his Scholar," with whom Aubrey spoke and from whom he learned that Milton had written an "Idioma Linguae Latinae." He may be the "Jeremiah Pickard" admitted to Bethlehem Hospital on September 7, 1700, and discharged on November 4. A German traveler, Adam Ebert, reported that he had seen "a secretary of the well-known Milton" in Bethlehem Hospital in 1678.

Picard wrote at the same time the two last entries in Milton's family Bible, listing the deaths of his first wife and son John and of his second wife and their daughter, after March 17, 1658; a note in the Bible opposite Romans 15 : 6, probably around the same time; the transcription of *Sonn* 23 and a directional note placed before *Sonn* 10 in *TM*; the manuscript of *CD*; and two entries in the *CB*. The entire manuscript of *CD* must have been in his hand before Daniel Skinner* recopied the first part. Picard's work now appears only on pp. 197–308a, 309–548, 553–71, 575–735 (i.e., 745), plus corrections. Hanford discussed Picard as Amanuensis C. The entries are from Rivet*, p. 188, which probably dates after 1651, and Augustine*, p. 195, which dates after the Machiavelli notes. Considered should be the possibility that Picard was Milton's student and that these entries may be dated earlier (*c.* 1652). In turn the transcription (and date) of *Sonn* 23 would not then necessarily be limited to 1658–1660. One further item may be the handwriting of Picard : Milton's procurational signature on the contract with Samuel Simmons* for *PL,* dated August 27, 1667. If this prove true, various new problems of dating arise.

Cyriac Skinner recorded the two sonnets addressed to him (Nos. 21 and 22) in *TM* in 1655; Thomas Ellwood* wrote out the receipt for payment of £5 from Samuel Simmons for *PL,* dated April 26, 1669; and Daniel Skinner retranscribed the first 196 pages of *CD* as well as pp. 308 and 571–74 plus corrections (ca. 1674).

Probably around the same time he copied (with Milton's authorization) state letters into what is now known as the Skinner MS*. There are at least five other hands than Picard's and Skinner's discernible in the manuscript of *CD*; most of these correct or add material, but one produced pp. 549–52. Three to five hands beyond Amanuensis D's and Edward Phillips's are distinguished in the manuscript of Book 1 of *PL*. In addition, the original state papers that have been discovered are in various hands, most, however, undoubtedly being official scribes. Unassigned manuscript material includes a signature on a salary receipt, February 13, 1655 (British Museum, Stowe MS 142, f. 61), a letter possibly to Christopher Milton and possibly dated January 1658, and signatures on three documents connected with Thomas Maundy and Jeremy Hamey, all dated June 7, 1665 (two in the Rosenbach Collection, Philadelphia, one in the Folger Shakespeare Library, MS 960.1), as well as the motto given in John Zollikofer's album, September 16, 1656, which Milton signed himself. *CM* assigned the letter and Hamey acquittance to Picard. No complete study of the manuscripts, signatures, and the like has been published; possibly such a study could solve problems associated with Milton's amanuenses and suggest which amanuensis may have prepared a particular text for publication. [JTS]

AMBROSE, ST. (ca. 339–397), Bishop of Milan, a jealous upholder of orthodoxy, who maintained the independence of the Church against civil power, and championed morality. His most notable work, *De Officiis Ministrorum,* is a treatise on Christian ethics*, based on Cicero*, with special reference to the clergy. With Jerome*, Augustine*, and Gregory the Great, Ambrose is one of the four traditional Doctors of the Latin Church.

Milton's reference to Ambrose is erratic—in one breath complimentary, in another condemnatory. In pleading for the deliverance of England from the tyranny of bishops in *Ref,* Milton speaks of the terrorizing power of Ambrose, who placed "the most Christian Emperor" Theodosius "under excommunication above eight moneths together" and subjected the emperor to a most humiliating and tyrannical madness; Milton asks his readers, "thinke yee then our Bishops will forgoe the power of excommunication on whomsoever?" In *1Def.* Milton is appalled that Ambrose, who zealously argued for separation of Church and State, surrendered his conviction of independence of civil affairs from church power in his dealings with Theodosius. Ambrose's teaching that all men are to be subject to the emperor is for Milton a blatant example of prelatical tyranny and hypocrisy, since Ambrose, deviously enough, according to Milton, wanted to enthrall the emperor to himself. But in the same work, Milton, in exonerating the new government that resisted the power of the Church and executed Charles I* for his tyranny, reminds his readers that even Ambrose, who insisted that all men are to be subject to the commands of the emperor, lived by the rule that free men must resist tyrants. This inference Milton draws from Ambrose's refusal to obey Valentinian the younger's command.

In the divorce* tracts, Milton regards Ambrose more favorably and invokes him more consistently. In *Bucer* Milton cites Ambrose's interpretation of 1 Corinthians 7 : 15 as a reason for divorce: "Matrimony is not ratify'd without devotion to God" and "the dishonour of the Creator dissolvs the right of Matrimony." In *Tetra* Milton strengthens his views on divorce by adducing Ambrose's commentary on Luke 16 to the effect that "all wedloc is not Gods joyning" and with Ambrose's commentary on the Septuagint, namely, that "a wife is fitted by the Lord, and temper'd to a kind of harmony; and where that harmony is there God joyns; where it is not, there dissension reigns, which is not from God, for God is love." Thus Milton concludes that, if there is no harmony, the marrying of pagan with Christian can be no marriage at all and that divorce would be without sin. Further-

more, Milton states that Ambrose assigns other causes for divorce than disharmony and dishonor of the Creator, such as adultery and apostasy. [PAF]

AMES, WILLIAM (1576–1633), puritan theologian and "one of the most acute controversial writers of his age," was born at Ipswich (Suffolk) and educated at Christ's College*, Cambridge, where he became a Fellow. His tutor, puritan William Perkins*, died in 1602 and Ames fell into dispute with Valentine Cory, Master of Christ's College. In a sermon preached on Saint Thomas's Day (1609), Ames vigorously condemned the practice of selecting a "lord of misrule" in the colleges, and the playing of cards and dice. For this and other indiscretions he was suspended by the Vice-Chancellor. Denied the pastorship at Colchester, Ames removed to the Netherlands (Leiden, then Rotterdam), where he wrote against the Arminians* (Remonstrants), engaging in particular controversy with Nicholas Grevinckhaven; participated in the Synod of Dort (1618–1619), out of which came his *Coronis ad collationem Hagiensem*; and published numerous theological works. Ames became chaplain to Sir Horace Vere, English magistrate at Brill, having succeeded to that post after marrying the daughter of the previous chaplain. Later in life Ames married a second time and became father of a son and daughter. For more than ten years he was at Franeker (Friesland), beginning in 1622; he occupied the chair of divinity and eventually became rector (1626). Seeking a more healthful climate, he transferred to Rotterdam to become pastor (with Hugh Peters) of the English church, but he died (November 1633) soon after the move.

Ames was consistently Calvinistic and an opponent of Arminianism; he desired to preach but seems to have done his most outstanding work as professor and controversialist. His chief works are *Medulla Theologiae* (an outline of Calvinism), *Fresh Suit Against Ceremonies,* and *De Conscientia, et eius jure, vel Casibus Libri Quinque* (definitions of specific points of Christian morality). Other of his titles are *Bellarminus Enervatus, Manuductio Logica, Analysis on the Book of Psalms,* and *Notes on the First and Second Epistles of Peter.* Nethenus collected and published Ames's Latin works (with a biographical preface) in five volumes at Amsterdam (1658).

Edward Phillips identifies "Amesius" as one of "the ablest of divines," from whom Milton collected material for "A perfect System of Divinity." Milton's indebtedness to the *Medulla* has been examined by Maurice Kelley (pp. 35–44 in *Th' Upright Heart and Pure,* 1967) and by W. R. Parker, *Milton* (1968). *Medulla Theologica* was first printed in Latin in Amsterdam in 1623 and was widely circulated; it was available in English translation by 1638. Milton may have owned a copy of *Conscientia* (Amsterdam, 1635).

In *Tetra,* Milton reproduces Ames's definition of marriage, and proceeds to object to the order in which Ames lists the elements of marriages, declaring that Ames's arrangement "perverts the order of God." In *CD* (2 : vii) Milton (calling Ames "our countryman") quotes and comments on a passage from *Medulla Theologiae.* [JWH]

ANABAPTISTS and BAPTISTS *Anabaptist* (compare German *Wiedertäufer,* Dutch *Wederdooper;* also Zwingli's* use of simple *Täufer* in 1525 and *Katabaptist* in 1527; also modern *Mennonite*) is a Greek word meaning "rebaptizer." It was not used by the Anabaptists to identify themselves, for it had been applied to them (contemptuously) by their foes and generally connoted heretical and unlawful practices.

Early Anabaptists (prior to the Reformation) advocated rebaptism of those whose first baptism had been by a priest later considered unqualified, and it was against this form of Anabaptism that the penalty of death was decreed (Justinian Code). Anabaptists of the Reformation period insisted that baptism should be performed only after confession (that is, at an age of accountability) and so

considered infant baptism to be unscriptural and ineffective as practiced in both Catholic and Protestant congregations; therefore they favored rebaptism of those who had been baptized as infants. These later Anabaptists felt their practice to be distinguishable from the earlier form and the penalty of death no longer just : the quality of "anabaptism" had changed, and so the judgment of the Church toward Anabaptists should be changed.

During the Reformation the word *Anabaptist* was used carelessly to include all groups that opposed infant baptism (for whatever reason), and in modern times it is still applied ambiguously in the same way.

Attempts have been made to associate the Anabaptist movement with some of the medieval sects (such as Franciscans or Waldenses*), but Anabaptist groups did not make this claim and their basic doctrines probably originated from renewed individual perusal of Scripture.

The Anabaptist movement (of the Reformation) began in Zurich (1523), spread into Augsburg, and gained strength in Austria and Moravia under the zealous leadership of men such as Jakob Hutter. Other divisions of Anabaptists devolved under the direction of Melchior Hoffman (in Strasbourg and the Netherlands), John of Leiden (in Munster), Menno Simons, Caspar Schwenckfeld, and others. In Italy, Anabaptist tendencies were circulated by Servetus; and in Poland and Lithuania by Petrus Gonesius and others. Several of these groups, and at various times, espoused Anti-Trinitarianism, Unitarianism, pacifism, communal living, freeing of serfs, polygamy, millennialism, refusal to take oaths, immersion (instead of sprinkling), and other "radical" ideologies. Some Reformation theologians, including all such views under the label of *Anabaptist,* bitterly denounced the Anabaptists, identifying them as the radical and fanatic fringe. Many Anabaptists considered their task to be not the reformation of the medieval Church but the restoration of the primitive, New Testament church.

Sympathetic scholars credit the Anabaptists with the development of certain doctrines widely held by modern Protestant denominations: adult baptism, separation of church and state, salvation by faith, authority of Scripture, "priesthood" of the believer, and so on.

In *DDD* Milton referred to "Anabaptism, Familism, Antinomianism, and other fanatick dreams"; but, more sympathetically, in *TR* he examines the Anabaptist position and concludes that they must not be classified as "heretics" from a Roman Catholic point of view. In the same work, he defends the right of Anabaptist books to circulate. W. R. Parker calls these passages an "explicit plea" for toleration of Anabaptists. He concludes that "probably before 1658 . . . Milton was a unique combination of semi-Arian, Arminian*, Anabaptist, anti-Sabbatarian, Mortalist*, semi-Quaker*, 'Divorcer,' and polygamist*" (*Milton*, 1:496). The early biographer, John Toland*, records: "In his middle years he was best pleas'd with the *Independents* and *Anabaptists*, as allowing of more Liberty than others, and coming nearest in his opinion to the primitive practice."

According to Masson (*Life* 5:15), Anabaptists were widely condemned in the England of 1644, but accepted into significant positions in Cromwell's government by 1654; and Baptist pastors were allowed in the Established Church of the Protectorate.

Baptists, clearly Calvinistic and congregationalist in their beginnings, developed into distinct denominations in seventeenth-century England—"General Baptists," emerging from an Arminian-oriented group who tended to separate themselves from the Anglican Church; and "Particular Baptists," who maintained independence within the established church. Anabaptist influence on Baptists is generally considered to be small at most points, although traditional Baptist doctrine parallels many elements of Anabaptist doctrine. It was from the use of immersion by some of the Anabaptist groups that the English General Baptists took over the practice. Masson suggests that about 1632 there were only "few scores of Baptists, in London, in Norwich, and elsewhere" (1:342). By 1644 "they counted seven leading congregations in London, and forty-seven in the rest of England" (3:147).

Among Baptist groups there was no agreement on the proper manner of "baptism"—the matter of immersion being left an open question, practice varying. The Baptists did gain the reputation, however, of favoring immersion over sprinkling. Milton's comments (see *CD*) are consistently opposed to infant baptism and consistently in favor of immersion (in the baptism of adults). [JWH]

ANDREINI, GIOVANNI BATTISTA (1579?–1654), the author of a comedy on the Fall* called *L'Adamo,* published in Milan in 1613. In the 1732 French version of *An Essay on Epic Poetry* (*Essai sur la poésie épique*), Voltaire* contended that Milton had seen a performance of *L'Adamo* in Florence (in 1638), which led him to conceive a tragedy on the same subject. Later, while sojourning in Milan, Milton is supposed to have composed an act and a half. In the earlier version (published in *Essay upon the Civil Wars of France, and also upon the Epick Poetry of the European Nations, from Homer to Milton* [London, 1727]), Voltaire said nothing about Milton's decision or first attempts to write a tragedy. He wrote only that "*Milton* pierc'd through the Absurdity of that Performance to the hidden Majesty of the Subject, which being altogether unfit for the Stage, yet might be (for the Genius of *Milton,* and for his only) the Foundation of an *Epick* Poem" (p. 103). This example of being able to conceive greatness out of inferior work was employed to illustrate Voltaire's contention that the great poetry achieved by a nation like England was due to its authors' rejection of slavish imitation of classical rules. The revised version of the essay, and thus the more specific charge therein, grew from Voltaire's desire to modify his extravagant praise of *PL* in the first version.

Paolo Rolli* was the first to take Voltaire to task for his allegation; see *Remarks upon M. Voltaire's Essay on the Epick Poetry of the European Nations* (London, 1728). Alexander Pope*, according to Joseph Spence, professed, "I can't think that he ever intended to have made a tragedy of his Fall of Man; at least I have Andreino's, and I don't find that he has taken any thing from him" (*Observations, Anecdotes and Characters, of Books and Men* [London, 1820], p. 95). Samuel Johnson* noted that Voltaire offered no proof; see his Preface to William Lauder's* *An Essay on Milton's Use and Imitation of the Moderns in His Paradise Lost* (London, 1750). Giuseppi Baretti (1719–1789) rejected Voltaire's argument in *A Dissertation upon the Italian Poetry in which are interspersed some remarks on Mr. Voltaire's 'Essay on Epic Poets'* (London, 1753). He knew neither the play nor the author, and even suggested that Voltaire may have been lying. The basis for his rejection of the allegation is that it is ridiculous to think that "Milton could have raked among the rubbish of Andreino . . . so bright a jewel as the *Paradise Lost.*" But William Hayley* revived the controversy in *The Life of Milton, in Three Parts. To which are added, Conjectures on the Origin of Paradise Lost: With an Appendix* (London, 1796), printing a number of extracts from *L'Adamo* in Italian and facing English. Influenced by Hayley, William Cowper* accepted the source relationship between the two works, but Henry John Todd* dismissed it in his 1798 edition of *Comus, A Mask.*

During the nineteenth and twentieth centuries the charge has sometimes been raised by those wishing to discredit Milton or those wishing to elicit all the "sources" of the epic. But the subject matter of Andreini's play and Milton's epic, deriving from the basic Genesis story, is the only point of tangency between the two. [JTS]

ANDREWES, LANCELOT (1555–1626), bishop of Winchester and most eminent churchman of his age. Born in All Hallows, Barking, he attended Coopers' Free Grammar School, Merchant Taylors' school and Pembroke Hall, Cambridge, where he became a fellow, later a catechist, and eventually a master. He was also a fellow of Jesus College, Oxford; pastor of St. Giles, Cripplegate (where Milton would be buried); prebendary of St. Paul's and Southwell; dean of Westminster; bishop of Chichester, Ely, and Winchester; dean of the Chapel Royal; privy councillor; participant in the Hampton Court conference; and the first divine on the list of those appointed to translate the Bible for King James*. In Elizabeth's reign he had refused two bishoprics in opposition to proposed alienation of their revenues. Outstanding in piety, generosity, and learning, though overly deferential to royal authority, he was as significant as Hooker in the development of the Anglican church, through his opposition to both Roman Catholicism and Puritanism and his emphasis on patristic theology. According to T. S. Eliot*, his sermons with their subtle conceits rank with the finest English prose; and his *Manual of Private Devotions* has been widely used. Between his death on September 25, 1626, and the end of the year, Milton, then seventeen, composed a sad tribute to his "mournful funeral pyre" (1. 255), which is referred to in the opening lines of another similar poem on the Bishop of Ely. *El* 3 laments above all the ravages of plague and war the death of the "most worthy Bishop, once the crowning glory of the Winchester [he] loved" (1. 179), whom he imagines apotheosized in a final vision of heaven. A very different tone prevails in the *RCG*, which refutes the arguments for prelacy offered in *Certaine Brief Treatises* by Ussher* and Andrewes, "for their learning . . . reputed the best able to say what may be said in this opinion" (3. 196). Andrewes's *Summarie View*, frankly presented as a posthumous culling of "rude draughts," is attacked as "rude draughts indeed" (3. 201), "a marvellous piece of divinity . . . well worth . . . six thousand pounds a year" (3. 207), "shallow reasonings . . . [from] a man so much bruited for learning" (3. 201), who would "winde into any figment or phantasme to save [his] Miter" (3. 204). Milton sees the dangers of pope and mass as implicit in Andrewes's inconsistent attempt to ground episcopacy in the Jewish priesthood of the tribe of Levi as well as in the apostolic ordination of bishops. Another reference to Andrewes occurs in *CB*, where Milton notes Rivet's* defense of usury citing Andrewes and Calvin*. [ETM]

ANGELS. Angels are important in Milton's poetry chiefly as characters in *PL* and *PR*, although the Attendant Spirit in *Mask* and the heathen Gods in *Nat* also are angelic beings. In *SA* Samson mentions an angel who twice foretold his birth, and some other works (*Sonn* 19, for instance) allude to angels. Milton's only important prose treatment is in *CD*, especially 1 : vii, viii.

Eighteenth-century critics of *PL* noticed difficulties with angels : angels filled up the cast of characters and they became persons, though at the same time their nonhuman characteristics allowed them to function as "machines," the supernatural agents that admirers of classical works thought necessary in an epic* poem. Generally the critics had no objection on principle to angels as characters, though Dryden* had thought that they could be machines only. They were, he held, surely the best of machines, since nearly everybody believed in them. Still, Milton had too many in proportion to the human characters ("A Discourse Concerning the Original and Progress of Satire" in *Essays of John Dryden*, ed. W. P. Ker, 2 : 34). Voltaire* voiced a much-repeated criticism when he wondered why the good angels were ineffective against the evil ones (*Milton: The Critical Heritage*, ed. John T. Shawcross, p. 256, and entries below on GABRIEL, MICHAEL, and RAPHAEL). These critics were chiefly concerned with literary values, whereas much seventeenth-century comment was upon Milton's management of angelology, especially his elaboration of scriptural accounts as orthodox authorities had interpreted them. Angels use weapons and armor,

even partake of earthly food as though they were material, and, more daringly, make love* among themselves. Milton embraced a severe Puritan belief in angels, supplemented rather freely from well-known works to meet the requirements of the epic of "scientific and Protestant didacticism" that he was writing (E. M. W. Tillyard, *The Miltonic Setting*, pp. 172–73).

Orthodox medieval theology, established in its dominant form by Aquinas*, held that angels were created on the first day as purely intelligential beings who were superior to man as closer in nature than he to God but inferior to man in history, since Christ died for man and not for the one-third of heaven's host that had revolted. Angels had a ninefold order among themselves, both of grace* and of nature*, which persisted in the nature of the fallen. Angels praised God and served him for His glory as messengers and as managers of material nature, especially of the stars in their courses. Angels could manifest themselves to men in assumed bodies, usually made of air, though they only managed these bodies and could perform no vital function in them. Their knowledge was intuitive by God's implantation of forms at their creation, and they knew much that man could not know except by revelation, both of holy mysteries and of the future. To every man was assigned a guardian, and angels had the power to convey both truth and illusion directly into a man's mind, but not to control his will. The will of angels themselves was rigid in moral choice once a decision was made, so that the fallen had no power to repent nor the elect to sin.

These commonplaces appear in sermons and treatises of Milton's time, and Milton believed some, used many in *PL*, and flouted a few by introducing several borrowings from Platonistic and Protestant sources and at least one stubborn notion that seems unique to him. In suiting angels to his story, Milton had one of the same troubles that he had with Adam and Eve : he needed to enhance and embellish considerably the skeletal account in Genesis, which, although it says that the Lord set cherubim to keep Adam and Eve from the Garden, tells nothing about the nature or history of angels and provides no angels' names. The canonical books of the Bible, in fact, name only two good angels (Michael and Gabriel) and the Apocrypha* only Raphael. Milton had, then, to rely on tradition and invention. He used both extensively, though with some effort, the evidence suggests, to stay free of offense to all readers. Thus of the four major disagreements between Protestant and Catholic angelologists, Milton makes a positive Protestant declaration only on angelic substance and manifestation. Following the tradition of Augustine* (which owes much to Neoplatonism*), he indicates that angels are in some sense bodily and can make their true selves sensible to men. When Raphael appears to Adam it is in his "proper shape" (5. 276), and when they eat together it is not "seemingly / The Angel, nor in mist, the common gloss / Of Theologians" (5. 434–35) but the true angelic being.

On the other chief controversies between Protestants and Catholics, PL shows striking reserve. Although in CD (17. 147) Milton says flatly that Papists err in worship paid to angels, he is unexplicit on the matter in PL. In CD (15. 101) he seems of the Protestant opinion that angels are not individually deputed as guardians, but again in PL (and in Mask) he maintains reserve. Most strikingly, he seems to take pains not to offend the Catholic liking for Dionysian orders, but uses the terms of angelic rank so flexibly and ambiguously that Protestants and Catholics alike can be content.

In a few matters Milton sides in both CD and PL against most Christian orthodoxy. He holds, for instance, with some Greek fathers, that the angels were created long before the Six Days and that hell* is a local place outside the physical universe. He agrees with Arminius*, too, that elect angels stand by their own strength, not by a compulsive grace*, and

that their wills are not fixed; they may fall at any time. In at least one matter he agrees with Catholics rather than Protestants: the name Michael signifies not Christ but the first of the angels.

In some ways especially serviceable to his story, Milton depends in PL on Platonistic ideas that pious Christians of all sorts were inclined to think "curious" because they go beyond Scripture in their confidence and detail. Thus in 1. 423–32, Milton explains that spirits can contract or dilate their substance as they please and shape it to their ends. For this passage he depends unmistakably on Michael Psellus*, an eleventh-century Byzantine Platonist widely quoted by angelologists. In 6. 327–30 and 344–53, Milton again uses Psellus in explaining how Michael's sword passes through Satan's "Ethereal substance" and pains him, though the substance closes behind the blade without harm because spirits are simple, not compound. CD does not even hint at any of this.

Finally, Milton insists in PL on two points of angelology so unusual as to bear the stamp of heresy* : angels may both consume and be nourished by human food, and they make love physically with each other. Only one writer on angels before Milton is known to assert their ability to digest earthly food, and none at all to assert their amorous activity with each other. Yet Milton is explicit that Raphael eats with "real hunger, and concoctive heate / To transubstantiate" (5. 437–38) and gives Raphael a long expository speech (5. 469–505) to explain this ability to Adam. Later (8. 615–29) Raphael responds to Adam's question on whether angels express their love by "immediate touch" with what most commentators take to be a blush and the admission that angels enjoy "in eminence" whatever men enjoy in the body and "obstacle find none / Of membrane, joint, or limb."

These "heresies" have won both praise and blame from critics. Early critics disliked the liberties Milton took with orthodox angelology in having Raphael truly eat, and they thought the passage on love-making an impious contradiction of Matthew 22 : 30. Some later critics have held Raphael's "smile that glow'd / Celestial rosie red, loves proper hue" (8. 618–19) to be in poor literary taste. (See Northrop Frye, *The Return of Eden,* pp. 61–62; John Peter, *A Critique of Paradise Lost,* pp. 108–9). Barbara Lewalski, however, replies that red is a seraph's proper hue as well as love's; Raphael is not blushing like a schoolgirl but smiling in friendship upon Adam and his question ("Innocence and Experience in Milton's Eden," *New Essays on Paradise Lost,* ed. Thomas Kranidas, p. 115). William Empson seems to feel that Raphael's blush is a humanizing touch; it is to Milton's "eternal credit" (*Milton's God,* p. 105).

The predominant twentieth-century view of the passages on eating and loving is that Milton had literary and philosophical reasons for them that far transcended whatever regard he could have had for angelology as such. He "could afford to be pretty free with angelic lore in general," says Frank Kermode, ". . . but not to hint at any discontinuity between body and spirit. This was more important to Milton than any other single belief . . ." ("Adam Unparadised," *The Living Milton,* ed. Frank Kermode, p. 91). Dennis H. Burden thinks rather that Milton's reason was simply to establish a parallel between angels and Eve : let Raphael hunger and eat to show "that a creature's hunger affects neither its freedom nor its virtue; that Eve's hunger at noon argues no improvidence on God's part. . . ." She does not "have to eat of that particular tree." Similarly, "Raphael's blush . . . is, like Eve's, the blush of innocent modesty, of pure and private sexuality" (*The Logical Epic,* pp. 136, 158).

Though *PL* says that good angels make love with each other, it denies that they are libidinous toward women (4. 446–50). Eroticism is, nevertheless, basically the same in the angelic species as in the human; this is clear from Satan's lust for Eve (*PL* 4. 503–6) and from his

speech in *PR* about Belial's "lusty Crew / False titl'd Sons of God" (2. 178–79), who coupled with women and begot a race. Presumably this coupling had much in common with Adam and Eve's lustful one after the Fall*.

The idea that men and angels have a common nature and that a man may rise to a rarer substance if he will and an angel may fall is a superb one, says J. B. Broadbent, and "in spite of its Pauline basis and Thomist affinities, Milton concocted it for himself." Angels are "Not ti'd or manacl'd with joynt or limb" (*PL* 1. 426) but "live throughout Vital in every part" (6. 344). These Psellian lines Broadbent takes as a rejection of "the Platonic separation of soul from body" (*Some Graver Subject,* p. 209). Milton did indeed deny that either angel or man was dichotomous, though few commentators have thought his passages from Psellus a signpost of it.

Modern critics can view the angelological heresies with complete equanimity, but some of them are not able to do the same about the levies on Psellus; and some, unlike Broadbent, think poorly of Milton's stress on the materiality of all creation. A. J. A. Waldock finds the passages on angels' plasticity awkward and literarily damaging and supposes that "seventeenth-century [angelological] science can do better than this." Waldock revives and reinforces Samuel Johnson's* objections to Milton's practical applications of his Psellian borrowings, chiefly in the battle in heaven. For instance, he finds it "treating us very nearly as morons" to say first that Satan's substance closes unharmed behind the shearing blade of Michael and then that "Moloch threatens to bind Gabriel and drag him at his chariot wheels" (*Paradise Lost and its Critics,* pp. 109–11). John Peter calls the first Psellian passage "unnecessarily startling . . . and . . . not very easy to reconcile with the dignified conception of angels we had expected" (p. 10). Later he decides that Milton's borrowing from Psellus is inappropriate and refractory. Far from allowing that the great teleological concept of transcendable body redeems or at least excuses it, Peter finds that "at the root of this refractoriness lies Milton's doctrine of the materiality of all creation*." Though he allows Raphael's setting forth of that doctrine to be acceptable, he thinks that by and large Milton abused the idea to the disadvantage of his whole picture of angels (p. 22).

Waldock's strictures have been taxed as somewhat literal-minded, and both his and Peter's assume, perhaps presumptuously, that the adaptation of angelology to epic narrative was more convenient than anyone in Milton's time or before had found it to be. Lawrence Babb aptly makes the point that Raphael "tells Adam the story of the war in Heaven in accommodated language. To represent an angel as a warrior in armor is not completely to express the nature of the angel, but at least it suggests something of the embattled angelic character" (*The Moral Cosmos of Paradise Lost,* 1970, p. 7). Milton's treatment of angels certainly requires some charity at the places where the "science" of them and the poetry of them join. Most of the time it is a charity not hard to allow. [RHW]

ANGELS, FALLEN: *see* BEELZEBUB.

ANGLO-SAXON PERIOD, Milton's knowledge of. Throughout Milton's lifetime, the study of Anglo-Saxon antiquities was pursued by a number of prominent scholars. Some, like William Camden* and Sir Robert Cotton, were disinterested antiquarians, but most were seeking historical precedents to use in current controversies. Sir Henry Spelman* and James Ussher*, following the example of Archbishop Parker, devoted themselves to ecclesiastical history and law. John Selden* and Sir Edward Coke* studied political history in an effort to defend Parliamentary right and Common Law against the absolutism of the Stuart kings. These men, and others, encouraged the publication of Anglo-Saxon texts and created a general intellectual awareness of the Anglo-Saxon past. Although he did not read Anglo-Saxon himself, Milton was influenced by their work in several interesting ways.

He seems first to have seriously encountered the Anglo-Saxon past in the years 1639 to 1642, when he undertook systematic reading in English history. There are a great many entries from various authorities on this subject in *CB* —none, however, in Old English. His literary concerns for the period are best evidenced by the series of thirty-three numbered subjects entered in *TM* under "British Troy," and five more, not numbered but including Macbeth material (without any suggestion of Shakespeare) entered three pages later under "Scotch stories or rather brittish of the north parts."

His study of the standard historians of his day, Speed*, Holinshed*, and Stow*, must have convinced him that he could perform a real service for his countrymen by providing an accurate and coherent national history. The standard accounts were especially weak for the Anglo-Saxon period, yet, if Milton had wished to begin work on a history in 1642, he would have been unable to find reliable editions of Anglo-Saxon source materials. In 1643, however, the situation changed. Abraham Wheloc*, first holder of a Cambridge lectureship in Anglo-Saxon founded by Spelman, published in a single volume a new and competent edition of Bede's* *Ecclesiastical History* and the first printed edition of the *Anglo-Saxon Chronicle,* accompanied by a Latin translation. Wheloc's work was reissued in 1644 with the addition of the *Archaionomia,* a collection of Anglo-Saxon laws edited and translated into Latin by William Lambarde. By providing three essential sources for the Anglo-Saxon period, Wheloc may well have given Milton the final impetus to undertake his *Brit,* which he began writing before 1648.

Brit is noteworthy for its citations of original sources, many of which had been edited by seventeenth-century English scholars. For the Anglo-Saxon period

(Books 3–6), Milton relies on, in addition to Wheloc's texts, Camden's 1603 edition of Asser's* *Life of Alfred*; Sir Henry Savile's* 1601 edition of the chronicle of Aethelward; and Sir Roger Twysden's* 1652 edition of Simeon of Durham's *Historia Regum,* a twelfth-century compendium of materials from Bede, Asser, and the *Anglo-Saxon Chronicle*, and from the lives of Dunstan, Osward, and Aethelwald. While Milton's method in using Anglo-Saxon sources is certainly praiseworthy, his portrayal of the Anglo-Saxon period is far from enlightened. It has been argued that, as a result of the association of Arthurian legend with the Stuart monarchy, Milton is anti-British and pro-Saxon in *Brit;* but he tends to regard both Britons and Saxons as little more than sinful barbarians. He writes as a man disillusioned with the entire English past, often expressing contempt for both his subject and those very sources he so arduously perused. He even has a churlish remark for the Venerable Bede. In view of this attitude, it is not surprising that, with the exception of an important reference to the "crown-oath of Alfred" in *Eikon,* there is little later use of materials from English history in Milton's other works.

Milton's attitude toward the Anglo-Saxons might have been different if he had had the opportunity to know more of their literature. English Saxonists of the first half of the seventeenth century, embroiled in the controversies of the day, had concentrated on texts of a theological, legal, or historical nature, while the *Beowulf* MS lay undiscovered and unedited in Cotton's library. Not until 1655 was an Anglo-Saxon text of purely literary interest published, and that was the famous edition of the Caedmon MS by Francis Junius*. This manuscript, which Junius acquired from Ussher in 1651, contains several poems, including a version of Genesis long thought to be the work of Caedmon. The Genesis poem published by Junius has been subsequently shown to be a conflation of two poems: *Genesis A,* a long, rather dull paraphrase of Genesis through 22:13; and *Genesis B,* a vigorous, highly dramatic account of Satan's fall and the Fall of Man. Commentators have noted similarities between *Genesis B* and *PL* and debated the question of whether Milton knew, and was influenced by, the Anglo-Saxon poem.

The problem of how Milton could have known of the poem is considerable. There is no evidence that he ever made use of the published edition. He would have needed an expert Saxonist to translate it for him, since the syntax of the poem is unusually difficult, but no candidate for this role has ever been suggested. But in terms of the characterization of Satan after his fall, *Genesis B* and *PL* are remarkably similar. Like Milton's Satan, the Anglo-Saxon Satan is still defiant. He stands on his "injur'd merit" and claims that his punishment is unjust. Although chained hand and foot to the floor of hell, he is still "Vaunting aloud" about what he would do if, for one brief hour, he had control of his hands. In contemplating the temptation* of Man, he is clearly motivated by the traditional motive of envy, yet he takes equal pleasure in the prospect of angering God and perverting His plans. Both Man and God are the objects of his revenge. In such respects *Genesis B* is closer to *PL* than any other literary analogue adduced to date, although this correspondence may be a simple coincidence.

Aside from the similarities between the two Satans, there are few, if any, striking parallels between *Genesis B* and Milton's poem. Eve's demonic vision in *Genesis B* and her demonic dream* in *PL* both combine features found only separately in all other literary versions of the story: the idea of a diabolical vision and the idea that the Tempter masqueraded as an angel. The Temptation scenes in the two poems differ, however, in many details and in fundamental conception. The sympathy of the Anglo-Saxon poet is all on the side of Adam and Eve, whom he views, not as sinners, but as innocent victims of deception. He can make no theological sense out of the Temptation at all, and openly questions why God ever allowed it to happen. Nothing could be more un-Miltonic than that! [TAC]

ANIMADVERSIONS UPON THE REMONSTRANT'S DEFENCE, AGAINST SMECTYMNUUS, Milton's third antiprelatical tract. Printed in July(?) 1641 by Richard Oulton and Gregory Dexter for Thomas Underhill, it is a section-by-section lampoon of arguments raised by Joseph Hall* in *Defence of the Humble Remonstrance against the frivolous and false exceptions of Smectymnuus,* registered on April 12, 1641, and published twice within the year. There is a cancel in Milton's tract of pp. 45–48, which would have corresponded to Sections 6–12 of the *Defence.* The reason for the cancel has not been explained. The satire of *Animad* often tends to vehemence and derives largely from verbatim quotations out of context, which are ridiculed through pointing out alleged lapses of logic, poor grammar, careless writing, and personal inadequacies. The few longer, serious sections seem oddly out of place, but by contrastive reversal they point up Milton's opinion of Hall's arguments against the Smectymnuan* position. Milton makes clear Hall's dependence on authority and tradition rather than on objective evaluation of any issue, and he shows a desire on his own part for simplicity and rationality in church organization. In answer came *A Modest Confutation of a Slanderous and Scurrilous Libell, entitled, Animadversions upon the Remonstrant's Defence against Smectymnuus,* published sometime after March 25, 1642. It is anonymous, as was *Animad,* although Hall and his son Robert have been mentioned as its authors. It attacks the author of *Animad* through its inferences from the text as to the character of the author of that scurrility. It provoked Milton's fourth antiprelatical tract, *Apol,* published within two weeks. [JTS]

ANNESLEY, ARTHUR, born in 1614, and created first Earl of Anglesey on April 20, 1661. He was a friend of Milton's and a frequent visitor to the poet after the Restoration. It was to him, Phillips reports, that Milton gave the section (or sections) of *Brit* that was not licensed in 1670. The most frequent conjecture is that this section became *CharLP* in 1681, and the remarks of the preface lead to such a conclusion. However, why *CharLP* should be objected to in 1670 but not in 1681 is unclear, and the suggestion that Milton himself decided not to include the digression on the Long Parliament in the published history opposes the conjecture. Besides, Phillips does not mention *CharLP* or include it in his bibliography of Milton's works, which might be specifically expected if it were the "unlicensed papers." Similarly, Toland* repeats Phillips's statement, but the 1698 collection of prose omits *CharLP.* It has been further conjectured that Annesley was the member of the House of Lords who consulted with Milton ca. March 1670 in connection with the Roos* affair.

Annesley died on April 16, 1686, and his library was auctioned off by Edward Millington on November 16. Among the items in the effects was a memorandum concerning the authorship of *Eikon Basilike*.* It noted that in 1675 Charles II* and the Duke of York (later James II) had both said that the book was not their father's but was written by John Gauden*. The memorandum was published on an unsigned leaf of *Eikon* (Amsterdam, 1690) under the heading, "An Advertisement." (It is not found in all copies of this edition.) British Museum, Additional MS 4816, f. 35, has a note by Annesley indicating his knowledge of the forgery. There had been some attention paid to the authorship of the book over the previous four decades, but the memorandum and the edition of *Eikon* set in motion a widespread controversy, involving also Milton's allegation concerning Pamela's prayer, which continued throughout the 1690s and which has frequently been reprised in later years. [JTS]

ANONYMOUS BIOGRAPHER: see SKINNER, CYRIAC.

ANOTHER ON THE SAME. The second of Milton's poems on the death of Thomas Hobson* appeared in both the 1645 and 1673 editions of his poetry, in *Wit Restor'd*, in two editions of a similar collection, *A Banquet of Jests* (1640; 1657), and in non-Miltonic manuscripts now located in the Bodleian and Huntington libraries. The text in Milton's editions of his *Poems* differs in a number of ways from the other copies of the poem, a fact that led W. R. Parker to conclude that these copies "probably reflect . . . a version of the poem earlier than the text which Milton printed. . . ." If this is so, it is significant in that it opens up the possibility that Milton did "last-minute revision of other poems in 1645" (*Milton*, 2 : 766).

Like the first of Milton's Hobson poems, it is written in rhyming couplets of iambic pentameter. Thirty-four lines long, it suggests, as does the first, that enforced idleness was the cause of Hobson's death; but it does so in a much wittier way, relying heavily upon pun, paradox, and wordplay. The wit, unfortunately, has not aged well. Lines such as "Too long vacation hastned on his term" are still faintly amusing, but the poem on the whole is a dated specimen of topical verse. Still, judging from the number of times that it appeared, it must have appealed to Milton's contemporaries; and it is pleasant to note that Milton could succeed, when he chose, in the writing of such verse. [ERG]

ANSELM, ST., (ca. 1033–1109), Archbishop of Canterbury and one of the earliest of the Scholastics. His *Cur Deus Homo* proved the most considerable contribution in the Middle Ages to the theology of the Atonement.* It interpreted the doctrine in terms of the satisfaction due to the outraged majesty of God and strongly repudiated the notion that the devil had rights over fallen man.

In *RCG* Milton makes the unfair statement that Anselm "to uphold the points of his Prelatisme made himselfe a traytor to his country" by not granting openly, as did Jerome*, that custom only was the mate of prelaty—a fact he knew only too well from his understanding of the Epistles to Titus and the Philippians. In *CB* Milton remarks that Anselm forbade priests in England to marry and that he was condemned for this by Henry Huntington. [PAF]

ANSWER TO A BOOK ENTITLED, THE DOCTRINE AND DISCIPLINE OF DIVORCE, AN: *see* ANTAGONISTS.

ANTAGONISTS. Separate entries are given for a number of Milton's antagonists : Peter Du Moulin, Thomas Edwards, Joseph Hall, Sir Roger L'Estrange, Alexander More, William Prynne, and Salmasius. Other published works that at least alluded to opposed positions to Milton's in the antiprelatical, divorce, and monarchic controversies are noticed here.

Ref drew forth criticism from the anonymous author of *A Compendious Discourse, Proving Episcopacy to be of Apostolicall, and Consequently Divine Institution* (May 1641), who used the name Peloni Almoni (that is, "Anonymous"). The point of contention was remarks on Irenaeus. John Bramhall (1594–1663), Archbishop of Armagh after the Restoration, objected to Milton's disrespect for Protestant martyrs in *Ref* in *The Serpent Salve* (1643). He was erroneously alleged to be the author of *Eikon Aklastos* and *Pro Rege et Populo Anglicano Apologia* (and was so treated by John Phillips in his *Responsio*). In a letter to his son on May 9/19, 1654, he denies his authorship of *Apologia*, refers to Milton's difficulties with William Chappell* at Christ's College*, and alludes to some unpleasant and unacceptable aspect of Milton's personality. He says he has communicated his feelings to Milton "long since"; the reference for "it," which was communicated, seems not to be about the authorship but rather about this aspect of Milton's personality. (Parker, *Milton*, pp. 420–21, misreads or obfuscates; cf. p. 729 n20.)

Robert Baillie (1599–1662) castigated Milton as a divorcer in *A Dissuasive from the Errours of the Time* (1645) and quoted from *DDD*; he is the "Scotch what-d'ye-call" of *NewF*. He refers to Milton in a letter dated January 31, 1661. An anonymous work incensed by Milton's divorce* views was *An Answer to a Book* (1644), a full-length attack by a "former serving-man turned solicitor" and, Milton believed, Joseph Caryl* (1602–1673), its licenser. The work is generally feeble in argument and reacts to the first edition of *DDD*, although the second edition had already appeared. Milton's rebuttal was the humorous and scurrilous *Colasterion: a Reply to a nameless answer against The Doctrine and Discipline of Divorce. Wherein the trivial Author of that Answer is discover'd, the Licenser conferr'd with, and the Opinion which they traduced defended* (1645).

Daniel Featly (1583–1645), rector of All Hallows, Bread Street, during 1626–27, noted "a Tractate of Divorce" but not the author in *The Dippers Dipt* (1645), a frequently republished work. Milton may have been including him in *New Forcers of Conscience* as one who named and printed as heretics those of learning, faith, and pure intent. *Heresiography* (1645 and frequently reprinted) by Ephraim Pagitt (1575?–1647) likewise called Milton a heretic* for his views. The "divorcer" constituted a new religious sect. The allusions to Milton increased in succeeding editions. This kind of listing for Milton continued in such volumes as John Wilkins's *Ecclesiastes* (1646 and frequently reprinted); Wilkins (1614–1672) was Bishop of Chester. The Puritan divine Herbert Palmer (1601–1647) preached a sermon before both Houses of Parliament on August 13, 1644, against liberty of conscience, and specifically damned Milton for *DDD*. The immediate reaction was a formal inquiry into such pamphlets by the House of Commons, although its results are vague. The sermon was printed in 1644 as *The Glasse of Gods Providence*. Milton rebuked Palmer in *Tetra* (1645).

Milton's two governmentally com-missioned antimonarchic works, *Eikon* and *1Def,* created anathema that lasted a long time and often overshadowed any positive reaction there may have been for his poetry. Joseph Jane (d. 1660?) tried to counter the first with *Eikon Aklastos* (April 1651; reissued in 1660 with the misleading title *Salmasius His Dissertation and Confutation of the Diabolical Rebel Milton*). Jane says nothing about Milton himself, apparently not knowing the author, although he is horrified by the "libeller" of the beloved late king. The pamphlet is a point-by-point answer to *Eikon* that does not achieve refutation. John Durel (1625–1683) planned to translate the work into French, but abandoned it as "weak and obscure in many places." Jane was the brother-in-law of Sir Edward Nicholas and an M.P. for Liskeard, Cornwall. Typical of the antagonism directed toward Milton for his stand against the king from 1649 to 1693 (*Eikon* was republished in 1690) are the allusions by the Royalist minister Richard Perrinchief (1621?–1673) in "The Life of King Charles I" in his edition of *Basilike. The Workes of King Charles the Martyr* (1662, 1687) and *The Royal Martyr* (1676ff.). George Bate (1608–1669), Charles's physician, published *Elenchi Motuum Nuperorum in Anglia* in 1650; there is no mention of Milton for *Eikon* or *Tenure*. But the second edition in 1661 chastises him for his antimonarchical views, his satire and libel against the king. *Elenchi* served as a source for Claude Barthelemy Morisot's defense of the royal martyr, *Carolus I., Britanniarum Rex. A securi et calamo Miltonii vindicatus* (Dublin [i.e., Dijon], 1652). Morisot also refers to Milton's argument for divorce and tries to rebut his ideas in *1Def*.

The Tenure of Kings and Magistrates was attacked by Clement Walker (using the pseudonym Theodorus Verax) in the second part of *Anarchia Anglicana: or, The History of Independency* (August 1649); Milton's divorce views clearly showed him to be a libertine. On October 24, 1649, Milton was ordered to examine Walker's books and papers because of his activities to deflect the verdict passed on the king. He was arrested and, on November 13, remanded to the Tower for high treason. Walker died in 1651.

As to be expected, many joined with Salmasius in condemning *1Def*. The author of *Pro Rege et Populo Anglicano, contra Johannis Polypragmatici (alias Miltoni Angli) Defensionem* (Antwerp, 1651), was John Rowland (1606–1660), although others had been conjectured. Rowland admitted his authorship in *Polemica, sive supplementum ad Apologiam Anonymam pro Rege et Populo Anglicano* (1653). *Pro Rege* is tedious, full of quotation from Milton, and merely adulatory of Salmasius. Perhaps family difficulties caused Milton not to refute Rowland, or perhaps he felt that it was too inferior a work for him to take so seriously. Rather, his nephew, John Phillips, was called upon to supply the attack, apparently with extensive help from Milton. *Joannis Philippi Angli Responsio* appeared in December 1651, although dated 1652. Rowland's *Polemica* is a subdued reaction to the *Responsio*.

Sir Robert Filmer (d. 1653) wrote *Observations concerning the Originall of Government, upon . . . Mr. Milton against Salmasius . . .* (February 1652); it was reprinted in 1679ff. as controversy over republicanism again arose. As author of the then unpublished *Patriarcha*, Filmer argued intelligently and calmly that *Tenure* and *1Def* did not offer a system of government that answered some fundamental problems in the relationship between constituent groups. In contrast, his own full-scale thesis offered a government based on patriarchal principles, relationships, and morality.

With the Restoration and Milton's 1659–60 tracts, other opponents arose to challenge his ideas. *The Censure of the Rota upon Mr Miltons Book* (1660) attacks *The Ready and Easy Way* with satire and burlesque and incisiveness. The author pretends to be James Harrington* (1611–1677), author of *The Rota* (1660), and cleverly criticizes the views of both Milton and Harrington. An often-quoted

epitome of Milton's prose style indicates the kind of thrust in *The Censure*: "You fight always with the flat of your hand like a rhetorician, and never contract the logical fist." *The Dignity of Kingship Asserted* (reissued as *Monarchy Triumphing over Traiterous Republicans,* 1660) also opposes *The Ready and Easy Way,* and in the course of discussion refutes ideas in *1Def*. It is not very effective, but it is a polite exposition of Milton's wrong thinking, elegant style, and misinterpretations. It was written by George Starkey (1628?–1665), who turned out two further books in 1660, both with less polite allusions to Milton: *Britains Triumph* and *Royal and Other Innocent Bloud*.

Insults abound in *The Transproser Rehears'd* (Oxford, 1673), probably written by Richard Leigh (b. 1649). The tract attacks Andrew Marvell* in his *The Rehearsal Transpros'd* (1672) for his attack on Samuel Parker*, Archdeacon of Canterbury and a former friend of Milton. Since Milton and Marvell were friends, Leigh turned on Milton for such inappropriate matters as blank verse*, sneered at his blindness*, and was contemptuous toward many of Milton's pamphlets. Marvell thought the author was Parker, who had begun the controversy by a strong diatribe against nonconformists. The controversy continued for a year or two with other pens joining in. Edward Phillips says that his uncle had prepared "an answer to some little scribing quack in London, who had written a scurrilous libel against him." William R. Parker (pp. 629–30) interprets this to mean that Milton had written a pamphlet against the author of *The Transproser Rehears'd*; no such work was published or has been found. [JTS]

ANTHROPOMORPHISM. Milton freely assigned human attributes to his vision of God and the divine hierarchy. About how one is to imagine God, he is assured that "Our safest way is to form in our minds such a conception of God, as shall correspond with his own delineation and representation of himself in the sacred writings" (14. 31). Milton recognized, however, that God was not literally the character represented in Scripture, because He had "accommodated* himself to our capacities," which meant that our imaginations were expressly limited by the images and manner of representation in Scripture. As the word of God, the Scripture not only prescribed how one was to conceive of the divine attributes but also cautioned against trying to imagine God in any other way. It has been argued that Milton's anthropomorphism led him to a theologically misjudged characterization of God in *PL* (cf. William Empson's *Milton's God*), and that the epic is flawed by his attempt to dramatize (sometimes with nonscriptural invention) the thoughts, words, and actions of the Deity. [PEB]

ANTICHRIST. The term *Antichrist* represents Christ's direct opponent in history, at various times identified as Antiochus IV, Pompey, Herod the Great, Caligula, Nero, the Roman Empire, the Papacy, and Martin Luther*. The word was first used in the Epistles of John, but it reaches back to Jewish Apocalyptic Literature and Persian eschatology, and is rooted in the myth* of the battle of God versus Satan at the end of the world.

Milton usually identifies Antichrist with the Pope or the Roman Catholic Church as a whole. But any corruption linked with wealth and promotion "will hatch an Antichrist wheresoever," even in the Church of England, for "Antichrist is Mammons Son" (*Ref* 3 : 54); and the first manifestation of Antichrist was brought about by Constantine's* wealth, which nourished "golden Chalices and woodden Preists" (3 : 25). Furthermore, because of its "fleshly supportments," carnal ceremonies, and secular power, prelaty in the English Church is "more Antichristian than Antichrist himselfe" (3 : 268–69).

The Pope had been identified as Antichrist at the end of the twelfth century by those Franciscans who had remained true to their vows of poverty,

and later by Wyclif, Hus, Luther, and a host of Renaissance apologists. In *CivP,* Milton explained that "all true protestants" account the Pope Antichrist because he assumes infallibility over both the conscience and the Scripture (6 : 8); and in *Animad* he asserted that only those churchmen not ashamed of "the ensigne and banner of Antichrist" would assume the powers of the temporal magistrate (3 : 158). The two arms of Antichrist are force and fining (6 : 10).

In *CD,* Milton refers to the following Scriptures concerning Antichrist : 2 Thessalonians 2 : 3, 5 : 8; 1 John 2 : 18ff., 4 : 3; 2 John 7; Revelation 13ff. (16 : 315). Like Nicholas Byfield and many others, Milton believed that the Antichrist would arise from within the church, and regarded his revealing as one of the signs of Christ's coming (16 : 315, 343). Milton's poetry does not mention Antichrist by name, but there are several allusions (e.g., "In Proditionem Bombardicam"; *PL* 12. 508–39). Ultimately, of course, Milton's Satan embodies all the "sphere of atrocity and horror" that Calvin* defined as Antichrist. [VRM]

APHORISMS OF STATE: *see* Cabinet-Council, The.

APOCALYPSE. The Apocalypse, or Revelation of St. John, is the last book of the New Testament and of the canon of Scripture. Milton referred to it as "that mysterious book of Revelation," and likened it to "some eye-brightening electuary of knowledge, and foresight." It is almost impenetrably obscure, but of its obscurities he wrote that it soared to a "Prophetick pitch in types, and Allegories*." With its fulgurant, complex symbolism the work has traditionally been of greater significance for the faith and emotion it has inspired than for its narrative or doctrinal intelligibility. For all its difficulties (or perhaps because of them) Revelation has unarguably helped to shape the Western mind. Northrop Frye sees the apocalyptic world of which it is in some measure the archetypal document, as presenting "the categories of reality in the forms of human desire." Frank Kermode suggests that the power of the Apocalypse and its influence on the literary imagination derives from its character as a model for all "fictions of the end," wherein the beginnings and ends of things are made commensurable. The relevance of the Apocalypse to Milton's work in-includes both of these possibilities of interpretation and others as well, and may perhaps be best approached by considering how many ways the term *apocalyptic* applies to the things he wrote and the views he defended.

In general usage the term *apocalyptic* refers to communal and individual negative forebodings of an ending to civilization in some holocaust of complete destruction, or to a positive anticipation within a traditional Christian perspective of a millennial* consummation, including the Last Judgment and the glorification of the saints in a new earth and a new heaven*. In the latter sense particularly, as an adjectival qualification for moods of social and political excitement such as animated many Puritans, including Milton, in various phases of the Puritan Revolution, the term means much the same thing as "millenarian," "chiliastic," and "messianic." In this aspect it was an important conditioner of Milton's thinking on many of the issues that drew him into public polemic and debate between 1641 and 1660. (*See also* ECCLESIOLOGY, MILTON'S MILLENNIALISM; and POLITICS, MILTON'S.) There is, however, another set of related positive meanings of *apocalyptic* that has made the term useful as a literary category for the study of Milton's poetry. Because the apocalyptic aspects of Milton's prose writings are elsewhere described, what follows mainly deals with the Apocalypse as it relates to his poetry.

The word *apocalypse* itself originally meant "revelation," the communication of a knowledge of divine things unknowable to human beings except through the intermediary of an inspired visionary. These matters are distinguishable in essentially three ways: as they concern the very beginning and ultimate end of things, as they foreshadow prophetically the historical future of the people of God up to the Last Judgment, and as they pertain to the glories of the heavens and the torments of hell*. It is the second category that concerned Milton particularly during his early involvement in the highly aroused Puritan hopes for reformation in England. The relevance, however, of the first and third categories of apocalyptic to Milton's poetry should be immediately apparent. *PL*, for example, deals with the celestial and infernal beginnings of things, and allusively or prophetically with their ends as well, not as history, but as poetically refashioned visionary revelation. There is, moreover, an underlying congruence between these apocalyptic aspects of the poem and its inner form or structural pattern, which is apparently derived from Milton's intricate adaptation to his poem of the structural and thematic development of the biblical Apocalypse itself. The third category, the apocalyptic vision of heavenly things, is also the basis for the transcendental perspective of the poem, as well as for Milton's techniques, identified partially by the Archangel Michael's method of explaining things to Adam, of accommodating* heavenly knowledge's ineffably transcendental visary character to human understanding.

And there is above all a sustained particular interest, evident throughout the whole of Milton's poetic development, in a very special feature of the Apocalypse, the heavenly worship that marks each distinct phase of St. John's visions. In an impressively variable approach Milton continually recurs, from adolescence to late age, to the vision of saintly beatitude linked in his faith and imagination (his "high-rais'd phantasie") with participation in the adoration of the angels around the throne of God,

That undisturbed Song of pure content,
Ay sung before the saphire-colour'd throne
To him that sits theron
With Saintly shout, and solemn Jubily.
(*SolMus* 6–9)

So persistently do such images recur, and

so closely identified are they thematically with the most intense moments of apocalypticism recorded in his prose, the prayers climaxing *Ref* and arresting *Animad,* that the theme may safely be taken as the key to Milton's overall susceptibility to apocalyptic ways of thought. And by virtue of its relationship to the spirit of Puritan worship, this theme may be as well an index of the experiential basis for the very general Puritan disposition to apocalyptic imaginings.

There was in Puritanism a way of living in the world that derived much of its remarkable energy from its otherworldly roots, as in Milton's confidence, for example, that all his life was to be, as ever, in his "great task Masters eye." (*Sonn* 7). In another sense this assurance is reflected in the terms of contemporary logic that could be made to bring the ideal object or end of religion itself into primary relationship with every particular endeavor as its first and efficient cause, much as Milton in *Educ* defined the whole of his educational program as a consequence of assuming that the ultimate object of all human aspiration was to recover the unfallen state of Adam and Eve. For Milton this meant not only to learn "to know God aright," but as well how to be like him, which knowledge in *PL* is the essence of Adam's magnanimity, his ability

> to correspond with Heav'n
>   whence his good
> Descends, thither with heart and voice and
>   eyes
> Directed in Devotion, to adore
> And worship God Supream.
>   (7.511–15)

Worship was the purest bridge fallen man had to his original nature. In their special understanding of the church, Puritans tended to emphasize the peculiar nature of the brotherhood or fellowship of visible saints joined together for edification and worship on the basis of their individual conviction of being each in some measure regenerated and endowed again with elements of mankind's unfallen nature. They were members of the universal church of true saints and of that Kingdom of Glory which existed at the beginning as it would be revealed at the end, and in which the saints and angels worshiped, as Milton so lovingly phrased it, "in supereminence of *beatifick Vision* progressing the *datelesse* and *irrevoluble* Circle of *Eternity*" clasping "inseparable Hands with *joy,* and *blisse* in over measure for ever" (*Ref* 3 : 79). When Puritans prayed together, especially since they relied intently on immediate inspiration, they often imagined this ultimate consummation not only as their reward but as the very type toward which the character of their fellowship and worship aspired. Their worship, in short, had a remarkably powerful underlying apocalyptic component.

In Milton's work the apocalyptic element appears as a signal aspect of his tendency to use his poetry, whenever possible, as a special form of worship. The most obvious example of his fusion of poetry and worship in celebrating an apocalyptic theme is *SolMus,* already cited, where the immediate experience of choral worship inspired in him an imaginative identification with heavenly worship as the recovery of that lost correspondence with heaven which unfallen Man originally enjoyed in common worship with all creatures, and which then swept him forward in prayer to anticipate the renewed concordance of the saints in the final beatific worship celebrated around the throne of God. The poem's movement explicitly encompasses the whole of the apocalyptic paradigm, the relationship of heaven to earth and of the beginning to the end of things. Just as explicit and far more ambitious is *Nat,* which is again poetically an act of formal worship. Through the conceit of his heavenly Muse* the young poet joined his voice "unto the Angel Quire," thence celebrating the Nativity in sweeping apocalyptic perspectives, up and down between heaven and earth, forward and back from the beginning to the end of time. What is striking is that every stage in those movements is an evocation of a different moment and kind of worship, all of them dominated by the concordance of the celestial worship at the Nativity with the universal worship of all creation* at the beginning and end of things. And Milton's role in the poem was to anticipate the whole consummation in his own devotion, linked to heaven himself by the kindling of his Muse's inspiration with the seraphic fire of God's altar.

In other contexts Milton tended to use the apocalyptic moment of beatific worship climactically, with the poem becoming thereby a vehicle for the imaginative ascent to the consummation of faith* indicated in the image of beatific worship, as in *Lyc*; or as an allusive focal point suggesting that such an ascent is or should be the poem's proper orientation, as in *Vac, Time,* and *AdP*. Of all the early poems, *Lyc* most effectively makes use of the apocalyptic image of beatified worship as the natural and inevitable climax of the Christian consolation for grief over the meaninglessness of human death and the spiritual uncertainties with which such grief disquiets faith. As the poem moves through stages of greater or ascending spiritual insights, the final consolation is a species of revelation based on the dual nature of the visions in the Apocalypse, which at the last make clear enough that divine wrath and divine love* are complementary elements. In the poem the wrath of the two-handed engine thus precedes the apotheosis of Lycidas among the worshiping saints of heaven. The parallel moment after a somewhat different development in the *EpDam,* Milton's lament for the dead Charles Diodati*, is in the climactic vision of Damon (Diodati), with his head haloed in glory, singing eternally in the ecstasy of worship at the apocalyptic Marriage Supper of the Lamb of God and his saints, the revelry growing ever wilder under the touch of "the thyrsus of Zion."

The allusive function of the apocalyptic theme as an oblique index to what should be poetry's proper orientation or animating vision is illustrated by the lines in *Vac,* where the young Milton invoked the "graver subject" on which he would have preferred to write : "Such where the deep transported mind may soare / Above the wheeling poles, and at Heav'ns dore / Look in"; or in listening to "what unshorn Apollo sings" to the assembled gods "before the thunderous throne." The image is allegorical* in Milton's sense of the term, as is the similar image of the Muses who "in a ring / Ay round about Jove's Altar sing" in *IlP*. A variant on both of them that illustrates the ease with which Milton could think himself into heaven is *AdP*'s image of Milton mythologized* in an Olympian heaven, crowned and circling in bliss, singing a metrical hymn of his own composition concordantly with heaven's worship (*AdP* 30–34).

Even more direct and certainly of greater weight is Milton's setting of himself into the first and most important chorus of *PL,* where he joins the angels celebrating the original offer of grace after the judgment of Man by the Father and the offer of redemption by the Son (3. 410–15). This moment in the poem, where Milton pointedly rededicates himself to the unvarying and perpetual worship of God through the Son, corresponds to and is based on the moment in the Apocalypse when the Lamb of God is worshiped in heaven for taking up the seven-sealed book of judgment, and when every creature in heaven and earth is heard concordantly worshiping God on his throne and giving praise "unto the Lamb forever and ever" (Rev. 5. 13). *PR* presents the earthly analogue of that moment in Christ's glorification by the angels after his triumph on the pinnacle of the Temple, when he is transported to the paradisial fields and waters of life (the same that in the Apocalypse are the rewards of those who overcome all evil), and there a hymn of heavenly praise is sung to him (4. 586–635). In the apocalyptic prayer with which Milton concluded *Ref,* the most enthusiastic moment he ever put on record, the reward he asked or expected above all for himself was to participate in some measure on earth as he would in heaven in that same eternal worship. [MF]

APOCRYPHA AND PSEUDEPIGRA-PHA.

The apocryphal books of the Old Testament, called deuterocanonical by Roman Catholics, are those which occur in the Septuagint and Vulgate versions but are not included in the Jewish canon: I and II Esdras, Tobit, Judith, Esther 10–16, Wisdom of Solomon, Ecclesiasticus, Baruch, additions to Daniel (The Song of the Three Holy Children, Susanna, Bel and the Dragon), The Prayer of Manasses, and I and II Maccabees. In addition there are the pseudepigraphal books, called apocryphal by Roman Catholics, including The Life of Adam and Eve, The Gospel of Jesus' Youth, the Books of Enoch, and various Apocalypses* and Acts. Because Milton was a Protestant and used the Apocrypha either in the Authorized Version of 1611 or in the Junius-Tremellius (Protestant) Latin version (*see* BIBLES), it is best for Miltonists to utilize Protestant definitions of the Apocrypha and Pseudepigrapha.

Milton valued his Hebraic sources in the following order: by far the most important, because he regarded it as God's word, the canonical Scriptures; then, as the words of men, in descending order of authority, the Apocrypha; the Pseudepigraphs and the older midrashim; and the later Jewish legends and commentaries, such as the cabalistic *Zohar* or the *Pseudo-Josephus*. It is wise to bear these Miltonic priorities in mind to avoid overemphasis on peripheral sources, especially remembering that the majority of Renaissance commonplaces turn out to be either canonical or apocryphal.

The 1640 edition of the Geneva Bible, printed by Thomas Stafford in Amsterdam and representing the severest Calvinistic attitude toward the Apocrypha, agrees with Milton's own estimate of the apocryphal books: they are "by no means of equal authority with the canonical, neither can they be adduced as evidence in matters of faith" (*CD* 16:249–51). Yet the Geneva admonition lists among others the following apocryphal "contradictions" of the canon, all of which are Miltonic concepts: mortalism*, freedom* of the will, divorce* for reasons other than adultery, lying when justified by expediency, and the creation of the Wisdom of God, which "gainsayeth and makes of no force . . . the Eternity of the Son* of God." True to his own evaluations, Milton does not base any of his doctrines on apocryphal proof-texts, but he does cite the Apocrypha as reinforcement of doctrines he feels he has already proved from canonical texts, as in his use of Ecclesiasticus 13:16, 37:27, and 25:26 in his divorce tracts to underline the concept of divorce for incompatibility. Similarly, *CD* lists Wisdom of Solomon 11:17 and 2 Maccabees 7:28 to back up Hebrews 11:3 as proof of creation* from pre-existent matter as opposed to creation from nothing (15:19).

In *Eikon* Milton gives a detailed summary of 1 Esdras 3 and 4, molding the story of the three noble guardsmen and the primacy of truth into a powerful political weapon. And like that of other Renaissance figures, Milton's emphasis on right reason*, describing faith* in predominantly rational terms, is apocryphal in tone: cf. Wisdom of Solomon 9:17–10:3, which asserts that men are "saved through wisdom"; the book of Ecclesiasticus, which assumes the identification of virtue with knowledge; and Wisdom of Solomon 1:4–5, which establishes godliness as a prerequisite to wisdom. Milton's depiction of right reason is carefully governed by his concept of man's Fall* and need for redemption*, using Platonic imagery of gradual spiritualization to describe the prelapsarian state and the postregenerative state, never the state of unregenerate man. Much of the Platonism in *Mask* and *PL* seems to have come to him by way of the Apocrypha, with its peculiar combination of Hebraic morality and Platonic expression.

The apocryphal concept of Wisdom influenced the character of Milton's Muse and the Muselike Attendant Spirit of *Mask*. Like the Hebraic concept of Wisdom, the Attendant Spirit descends from the presence of God (Wisdom of Solomon 9:4, 9–10) and enters only into "holy souls" (7:27). He refers to earth as a "dim spot" (cf. "the shadow of the world,"

2 Esdras 2 : 36, 39) and regards earthly living as an oppressive confinement (cf. Wisdom of Solomon 9 : 15–16). The "crown that vertue gives/After this mortal change to her true servants" is an allusion to Wisdom of Solomon 4 : 1–2 (virtue "weareth a crown . . . having gotten the victory") and to 2 Esdras 2 : 45 ("These be they that have put off the mortal clothing, and put on the immortal . . . now are they crowned"). The latter passage apparently was influential on Paul's more familiar version in 1 Corinthians 15 : 51–53. And the "due steps" by which the just aspire to open "the Palace of Eternity" are outlined in Wisdom of Solomon 6 : 17–20 (cf. the Platonic step imagery in *PL* 3. 502–5, 5. 469–72, 478–79).

Milton's idea that, before the Fall, access to God was relatively easy, "a passage wide, / Wider by far then that of after-times" (*PL* 3. 528–9), may derive from 2 Esdras 7 : 11–15 : "When Adam transgressed my statutes . . . Then were the entrances to this world made narrow, full of sorrow and travail. . . . For the entrances of the older world were wide and sure, and brought immortal fruit." This passage obviously influenced Matthew's more famous contrast between the postlapsarian narrow road to life and the broad road to destruction, and hence *Pilgrim's Progress* and many other works.

Milton alludes to the book of Tobit throughout his career, but especially in *PL* 3–6. In 3. 505, the description of the gate of heaven* shows the influence of Tobit 13 : 16 as well as Revelation 21; in 3 : 651 the description of the angelic messengers is based on Tobit 12 : 15 as well as several canonical passages. More important is the web of allusion in *PL* 4 and 5 by which Milton identifies Satan with the evil spirit Asmodeus and Adam and Eve with young Tobias and his wife Sara, allowing Raphael to play a role similar to his role in the Apocrypha. In 4. 168–71, Satan's approach to the garden utilizes an overt reference to Asmodeus and "the fishie fume" that drove him from the marriage chamber "with a ven-

geance"; thus, even as Satan approaches the scene of his triumph, we are reminded of his ultimate defeat. In 4. 720, Adam and Eve's prayer before retiring is reminiscent of the bedtime prayer of Tobias and Sara (Tob. 8 : 5–8); Adam's contrast between "adulterous lust" and "domestic sweets" parallels the contrast between Asmodeus and Raphael and harmonizes with the concept of Tobit 8 : 7; and the couple's happy sleep in the presence of danger is paralleled in Tobit 8 : 9. *PL* 5. 221–23 returns to direct allusion, identifying Raphael as "the sociable Spirit, that deign'd / To travel with *Tobias,* and secur'd / His marriage with the seaven-times-wedded Maid." In 5. 433–38 Milton painstakingly contradicts the statement of Tobit 12 : 19 that Raphael did not actually eat but only seemed to do so; characteristically, Milton here follows the canon rather than the Apocrypha (ref. Gen. 18 : 5–8, 19 : 3). In 6. 365 the parallel to the Tobit story is rounded out when, on the first day of the Heavenly war, Asmodeus is quelled by Raphael in single combat. And in *PR* 2. 151, Belial is identified as the most dissolute and sensual of fallen angels, as a fleshly incubus second only to Asmodai (Tob. 3 : 8, 6 : 14). Thus there can be no doubt that the book of Tobit informed Milton's imaginative handling of the relations between Satan, Eve, Adam, and Raphael.

Milton drew upon the Apocrypha for other details concerning angels, darkness, and demons—for instance, the lordly Uriel from 2 Esdras, and certain details concerning hell* from the Wisdom of Solomon's powerful account of the Egyptian plague of darkness (chap. 17). Satan's metamorphosis into a "monstrous Serpent . . . punisht in the shape he sin'd" (10. 514ff.) reflects Wisdom of Solomon 11 : 15–16; and Satan's description of the Maccabees in *PR* 3. 163–70, when read against the apocryphal 1 and 2 Maccabees, reveals the satanic character by his projection of his own selfish motives and methods onto other, purer beings.

Milton's treatment of the *de casibus virorum* theme in *SA* 164–75 is illuminated by comparison to Ecclesiasticus 11 : 1–6 ("Wisdom lifteth up the head of him that is of low degree. . . . Many mighty men have been mightily disgraced"). Samson's fall came about not by chance, but because of a loss of "vertue" or Wisdom. And this sort of fall, says the Chorus, is the mirror of mankind's "fickle state."

A dissertation by Virginia Mollenkott (*Milton and the Apocrypha,* N.Y.U., 1964) provides a 28-page listing of apocryphal allusions in Milton's poetry and prose.

In the pseudepigraphal books of 1 and 2 Enoch, Milton found such details as the attacks of Michael, Raphael, and Gabriel on their fallen peers, Azazel as a leader among the fallen angels, and Raphael's warning to humanity. Both Enoch and *PL* locate hell inside a chaos beyond heaven and earth; both display a preponderance of angelic revelation and dream vision; and both end in the promise that God and the Messiah will dwell with man.

The pseudepigraphal Books of Adam and Eve contain a disconsolate dialogue between the fallen couple after their expulsion from Eden (similar dialogue in *PL* occurs before the judgment and expulsion); a description of Satan's fall through refusal to worship the newly created Adam (transmuted by Milton to a refusal to worship the newly-created Son of God); Eve's dream foretelling the murder of Abel (transmuted by Milton to a dream foretelling her own sin); Adam's plea to be permitted to stay in Paradise after the fall (expanded by Milton to individual pleas by both Adam and Eve); and the vision of mankind's future that Michael gives to Adam (changed by Milton from just before Adam's death to just before the expulsion from Eden). [VRM]

APOLLODORUS, Greek scholar of the second century B.C. to whom was attributed *The Library,* one of the many sources of Renaissance mythology*. It has been suggested as a possible origin of many of the mythological allusions in Milton's early works, especially the *Prol.* For instance, the first paragraph of *Prol 4* mentions Typhon, Ephialtes, Antaeus, and the Harpies, all of whom are discussed by Apollodorus. But because of the commonplace nature of such subject matter, it is difficult to demonstrate any individual source. [WBH]

APOLOGUS DE RUSTICO ET HERO ("A Fable about a Countryman and his Master"). Found only in *Poems* (1673), this brief Latin poem has generally been attached to Milton's grammar-school period, an attachment that W. R. Parker accepts though noting the bare possibility "that this 12-line fable against greed was composed in Italy, to be read to one of the academies" (*Milton,* p. 720). Masson dated the poem even later, finding "a touch of political significance in it, belonging to a time when Milton's thoughts had become steeped in politics" (*The Poetical Works,* 1 : 272). A twentieth-century reader, however, has difficulty in finding any political significance. It relates the story of a landlord who transplanted a particularly desirable apple tree from the country to his city gardens. His hope was to get all the tree's fruit for himself, but the tree withered as a result of the move. Thus the story makes the same point as the more familiar one of the goose that laid the golden eggs and has many analogues in fable literature.

Milton's source was Giovanni Battista Spagnuoli, or Mantuan as he was commonly called. A Carmelite monk of Mantua who became general of his order, Mantuan (1448–1516) was a prolific neo-Latin writer whose works were standard texts in English grammar schools during the Renaissance. It is problematic whether he was included in the curriculum of St. Paul's School* while Milton was there, but he may have been. Certainly Milton's poem can be most easily assimilated to Mantuan's in the light of then prevalent grammar-school practices of translation and paraphrase. Students translated Latin poetry into English, then later translated their English back into Latin. By comparing their Latin with its original, they learned about the choice and placing of words. Sometimes they were provided with previously prepared English versions, thus skipping the first step in the process. Two such versions of Mantuan's poem—one prose, one verse—are found in William Bullokar's *Aesop's Fables in True Orthography* (1585). Harris F. Fletcher discovered the original from which Milton paraphrased in the 1513 edition of Mantuan's *Primum Opera* (*Journal of English and Germanic Phililogy* 55 : 250–53). A comparison of Milton's poem and Mantuan's reveals close verbal parallels and suggests that Milton's may well have originated in school exercises such as those sketched above. [ERG]

APOLOGY AGAINST A PAMPHLET

Call'd A Modest Confutation of the Animadversions upon the Remonstrant against Smectymnuus, An. Milton's fifth and last antiprelatical tract was published soon after April 8, 1642, by John Rothwell. The date is that of the news given in Parliament of James Butler, Earl of Ormond's defeat of the Irish rebels at Kilrush on March 15 (see 3 : 340). It was printed by Edward Griffin, shows an erratum, and has variant states. It did not sell well, for in 1654 Rothwell reissued it and *The Reason of Church-Government* with a new title page : *An Apology for Smectymnuus. With The Reason of Church-Government. By John Meltom, Gent.* It was edited, in facsimile with introduction and notes, by Milford C. Jochums in 1950, and in the Yale *Prose* by Frederick L. Taft in 1953.

The tract answers *A Modest Confutation of a Slanderous and Scurrilous Libel, Entitled, Animadversions,* published in late March, which itself was answering Milton's third tract of July 1641. The author or authors are unknown, although Bishop Joseph Hall* and/or his son (usually Robert) have most often been cited. *A Modest Confutation* vilifies Milton as a person and his morals. Milton's aim in *Apol* is thus to rebut such slanderous and scurrilous (to use the confuter's terms) fabrications, and therefore his tract is extremely important as a source of biography, particularly a kind of spiritual autobiography* of his hopes for himself and of the truths that guide his life. Milton protests that his opponent's work is far from "modest," that his own *Animad* is not scurrilous, and that the alleged author's (Hall's) other books are hardly without censure. The latter part of *Apol* analyzes *A Modest Confutation* section by section, countering remarks on both his own book and on the ideas of the Smectymnuans*. Milton justifies his own vehement language by the arguments that like demands like and that there should be distinction between common usage and stylistic decorum.

Apol shows a great variety of rhetorical style, appropriate to one who was being forced to present himself in praiseworthy terms and as a poetic spirit. Milton is satiric, humorous, ironic, logically serious, aloof and personal, critical and informative, and the writing demonstrates a complex structure. The first twenty pages (first third) are devoted to general discussion of his attacker and of his own life. The pamphlet then proceeds in the last two thirds (pp. 20–59) to take the author of *A Modest Confutation* to task for those matters in which Milton himself is superior : sincerity, logic*, laughter, ideals, writing ability, learning*, and the like, without specifically discussing himself. Milton's remarks are a demonstration of his own worth and at the same time a put-down of the confuter. The sections complement each other and allow Milton to conclude punningly that the prelates' "great Oracle . . . will soon be dumbe, and the *Divine right of Episcopacy* [Hall had written *Episcopacie by Divine Right*] forthwith expiring," the people will no more be troubled "with tedious antiquities and disputes." Milton's audience would remember that it was the birth of Jesus and the true religion that grew out of that event that supposedly stilled the pagan oracles. The author of laudable things (and his work), like Christ and his work, must be a true poem, Milton says, a composition and pattern of the best and most honorable things (p. 16). To oppose this self-asserted "modest" confuter, Milton took an avowedly immodest stance and produced a patterned composition, with the ironic result that his readers understand more clearly the primacy of God and His agency on earth. Just as the confuter's work illustrates the falseness of episcopal claims, so Milton's *apologia pro sua vita* demonstrates the truth represented by the Smectymnuan view.

The tract may have contributed to a decision on Milton's part to return resolutely to his private studies and writing, and not be detoured into such controversy. His next essay into public writing did not occur until August 1643 with *DDD*. [JTS]

APPEARANCE, PERSONAL. Milton's personal appearance is inferred from portraits* (which are not necessarily reliable), statements in his own works, and remarks by relatives and associates. Throughout his life Milton seems to have given the impression of being younger than he was, primarily because of delicate features, a fair complexion with high color, and pleasant, alert eyes. His hair was auburn, though later brown (sometimes worn long, sometimes short), according to his daughter Deborah, and his eyes were brown. He was of medium height and not particularly lean. His youthful expression showed him to be "very merry" to his servants* at the time of his death, Elizabeth and Mary Fisher. His pictures did not look like him, Aubrey* reports from his widow, and perhaps what was meant was the sternness usually reflected in the face. Deborah, upon seeing William Faithorne's* painting, is supposed to have exclaimed, " 'Tis my father!", for this portrait shows a softer and more serene face. Such an appearance, coupled with carefulness of dress and speech, may have contributed to Milton's being called the Lady of Christ's, as Elizabeth Milton told Aubrey. But undoubtedly the epithet was also suggested by his high academic seriousness and his moral attitudes toward

activities popular with his fellow undergraduates. Milton's attire seems to have become (after the early 1640s?) fairly drab and plain with little variation.

Blindness* had little effect on his outward appearance as he relates in *2Def* and *Sonn*22. There was no injury to the eyes; they remained unclouded to external view; and they seemed to retain their brightness. [JTS]

APPETITE. *Appetite,* from the Latin *appetere,* "to strive after," means a constant disposition toward an object deemed suitable in itself and, conversely, a retreat from what is regarded as undesirable. In present-day usage, the term is normally restricted to the physical appetites of food, drink, and sex, but traditional psychology uses "rational appetite" as a synonym for the will*. Just as man's sensory knowledge directs him in the choice of physical goods, so his reason* directs his will in the realm of moral good and evil*; both involve striving or avoiding, and differ only in their respective objects.

In *PL* the term is used in both senses. At times physical appetite alone is intended (5. 85; 7. 49; 8. 308; 10. 565; 11. 517), but elsewhere the usage is more complex. After the creation of man, the Father bids Adam enjoy the fruits of the earth with the exception of that on the Tree of Knowledge* of Good and Evil. If he eats of this tree, he shall die: "Death is the penaltie impos'd, beware, / And govern well thy appetite, least sin / Surprise thee, and her black attendant Death" (7. 545–47). The symbolic nature of this prohibition is clarified when Raphael reminds Adam of his obligation to obedience, advising him that "Knowledge is as food, and needs no less / Her Temperance over Appetite, to know / In measure what the mind may well contain" (7. 126–28). At other times, there is a note of ambiguity. Gluttony* plays a part in the fall of Eve: as the hour of noon approaches, there is aroused in her "An eager appetite, rais'd by the smell / So savorie of that Fruit . . . sollicited her longing eye" (9. 740–43). But in the context of Satan's argument that precedes (9. 679–732) and Eve's acceptance of its premises (9. 745–79), there is clearly present an inordinate appetite for knowledge as well as for food. Adam recognizes this fact when, after he has eaten, he plays upon the word "savour" (9. 1019) with its double meaning of "to taste" and "to know." Milton then explains the effect of this eating : "For Understanding rul'd not, and the Will / Heard not her lore, both in subjection now / To sensual Appetite" (9. 1127–29). The rational appetite has rejected its directive norm, and the physical appetite has likewise rebelled against both. [RF]

APULEIUS, philosopher and writer of the second century A.D., best known for his story of the adventure of its hero, Lucius, who was transformed into an ass: *The Golden Ass.* Milton disparaged his florid style in comparison with Cicero's* (*Apol* 3 : 347). The most famous episode of Apuleius's novel is the account of the love affair between Cupid and Psyche, to which Milton alludes in some cryptic lines near the end of *Mask* :

> far above in spangled sheen
> Celestial *Cupid* her [Venus's] fam'd son advanc't
> Holds his dear *Psyche* sweet entranc't,
> (1002–4)

who will be the mother of Youth and Joy.

Also in *Mask* Milton may owe some kind of debt to Apuleius's *God of Socrates,* an account of the *daemon* that directed that philosopher's life. Though the idea became a Renaissance commonplace, either here or in Augustine's* redaction of the work in the *City of God* 8–10, Milton may have found the statements about "certain divine powers of a middle nature, situate in this interval of the air, between the highest ether and the earth below," which he developed into the depiction of the Attendant Spirit or Daemon Thyrsis. [WBH]

AQUINAS, ST. THOMAS (ca. 1225–74), Doctor of the Church, Doctor Angelicus, philosopher and theologian. His philos-

ophy received its characteristic shape under the influence of the metaphysical writings of Aristotle*. Although he abandoned much traditional Platonic teaching, at a deeper level Aquinas continued to uphold many fundamental Platonic doctrines that had come down from St. Augustine*. He held a sharp distinction between reason* and faith* but felt that such truths as the existence of God can be discovered by the natural reason altogether apart from revelation. He accepted the Aristotelian distinction between potency and act. At the top of the metaphysical scale is pure act, namely, God, since in him every possible perfection is wholly realized. At the bottom is pure potency without act, which is a self-evident impossibility. Intermediate in the scale are creatures, natural or angelic, composed of act and potency. Closely related is the other Aristotelian distinction between matter* and form. Matter is the principle of individuation. While all the individuals in the same species have the same form, the matter is proper to each individual. Less original, but no less thoroughly elaborated, was Aquinas's theology. The Incarnation* and the Sacraments* claimed his special interest. He held that the seven sacraments were instituted by Christ, that the Eucharist is the highest of them, and that the priesthood is the highest of the seven orders; for the elaboration of the doctrine of transubstantiation, he employed the Aristotelian concept of substance and accidents. His *Summa Theologica,* the highest achievement of medieval theological systemazation and until recently the accepted basis of Roman Catholic theology, was his last work, left unfinished at his death.

In *Areop* Milton, attacking those who legislate to suppress the publication of books in order to preserve virtue, insists that good and evil* exist in the world together and that the knowledge of good is so involved and interwoven with the knowledge of evil that such knowledge is inseparable. It is for this reason then that Milton cannot praise "cloister'd vertue";

the true wayfaring Christian for Milton is the man who can expose himself to vice, who can apprehend and consider its pleasures, yet abstain, distinguishing and preferring that which is truly better. To support his argument, Milton cites Spenser*, "a better teacher than Scotus* or Aquinas," who allows true temperance* under the person of Guyon to go through the cave of Mammon, and the "bowr of earthly blisse that he might see and know, and yet abstain" (4:311). (Like Valvasone, who held that the uneducated might learn more about theology from pious poets than from Scotus or Aquinas, so too Milton suggests that the Christian might be better taught the way to virtuous living by reading Guyon's journey in *Faerie Queene* than by reading Aquinas.)

In *Prol* 5 where Milton writes about the controversy over unicity and plurality of substantial forms, he reveals considerable familiarity with Aquinas's teaching on the subject, agreeing with him in theory. Milton here is dealing with the opposition: that "when a part of an animal has been cut off it remains in act after the separation, not through the form of the whole, . . . nor through the form recently acquired, since there is no agent, no perceptible action, and no previous alteration; therefore it exists in act through the proper form which it had before, while it still formed a part of the whole." Aquinas, in his teaching about the unity of substantial form, opposes the view of plurality of forms, maintaining that the higher form always contained within itself the functions of the lower. In a substance, therefore, there was but one substantial form. In man, for example, this is the rational soul which, when united with matter, makes a man, simultaneously, exist in space and perform all the functions of vegetation, sensation, and intellection. Although Milton is limiting himself in this prolusion to a consideration of animals, he argues that "if there is a plurality of partial forms in every part, of a man for example, from them there will certainly arise one complete form distinct from the rational soul; hence

this form will be the form either of an inanimate thing or corporeity, or of a mixture (which in fact is most unlikely to exist in man in addition to the soul); or else it will be a sensitive or vegetative soul" (trans. from 12:198–200; cf. *CD* 1:vii). He totally rejects this conclusion and subscribes to Thomistic teaching when he maintains "the fact that we can perceive manifold operations in an animal is not due to distinct partial forms but to the preponderance of the total soul, which is of equal importance with the forms distinct in appearance."

In *Prol* 7 when Milton treats of the relationship between Virtue and Learning, he introduces a discussion of intellect versus will, where he subscribes to the Thomistic position. St. Thomas held that, since the will engenders a desire for the good apprehended in the intellect, it is dependent upon the intellect to make the judgment of what is good. Conversely, the will can move the intellect, because it is the power that has the highest end, good itself. Thus they supplement each other —the will as an agent moving the intellect, and the intellect as an end moving the will, since the will is unable to function unless the intellect provides a motive. In other words, an act of the will is not likely to be made independently of the intellect in view of the fact that a judgment of some kind has to be made by the intellect before the will has sufficient reason to act. In this prolusion Milton subscribes to this teaching and applies it to his distinction between learning and virtue. He says, "I believe, an established maxim of philosophy that the cognisance of every art and science appertains to the Intellect only and that the home and sanctuary of virtue and uprightness is the Will. But all agree that while the human Intellect shines forth as the lord and governor of all the other faculties, it guides and illuminates with its radiance the Will also, which would else be blind, and the Will shines with a borrowed light, even as the moon does." In transferring this teaching to his discussion of virtue and learning, he says,

"Virtue without Learning is more conducive to happiness than Learning without Virtue, yet when these two are once wedded in happy union as they surely ought to be, and often are, then indeed Knowledge raises her head aloft and shows herself far superior, and shining forth takes her seat on high beside the king and governor, Intellect, and gazes upon the doings of the Will below as upon some object lying far beneath her feet" (trans. from 12 : 260). [PAF]

ARATUS OF SOLI (third century B.C.), author of the *Phaenomena,* a poem in Greek on astronomy, and of *Diosemia,* one on meteorology that is probably part of the former. Milton purchased a copy in 1631 (the Paris 1559 edition), which survives with his annotations in the British Museum. They show that he read the book carefully, comparing its text with other editions, and that he was a competent Greek scholar. He taught it to his nephews and recommended it in *Educ* along with such authors as Orpheus*, Hesiod*, and Theocritus*. The *Phaenomena* is quoted by St. Paul (Acts 17), a passage to which Milton recurs several times (*PL, Areop*); he also shows the influence of Aratus perhaps more directly in *PL* as an authority for such astronomical information as that of 10. 668ff., surveying the positioning of the sun in the signs of the zodiac. [WBH]

ARCADES. First published in 1645, this entertainment by Milton, which appears in *TM*, is a lyrical, 109-line theatrical work consisting of a song, then a single speech in pentameter couplets, and finally two more songs. The slight invention and incidental action of the entertainment concerns nymphs and shepherds of Arcady who, led by the "Genius of the Wood," approach and pay homage to an enthroned rural queen. Designed for outdoor performance on the grounds of Countess Alice Spencer's* country estate in Middlesex, *Arc* is described in the 1645 edition as "Part of an Entertainment presented to the Countess Dowager of *Derby* at

Harefield, by some Noble persons of her Family, who appear on the Scene in pastoral habit, moving toward the seat of State. . . ." Although the rest of the entertainment, whether written by Milton or another author, has been lost, the surviving work is complete in itself and has a clearly defined structure.

In the opening song the nymphs and shepherds express excitement and surprise as they make a sudden discovery of the rural queen on her "shining throne" :

> This this is she
> To whom our vows and wishes bend,
> Heer our solemn search hath end.
>
> (5–7)

The main action of the entertainment is revealed in the central, 57-line speech by the Genius of the Wood, who appears before the nymphs and shepherds, halts their advance toward the seated Lady, and explains that he serves the queen by tending the plants in her domain. He then offers to conduct the noble performers to the rural queen, thus introducing the climactic presentation segment of the entertainment :

I will assay, her worth to celebrate,
And so attend ye toward her glittering state;
Where ye may all that are of noble stemm
Approach, and kiss her sacred vestures hemm.
(80–83)

As the nymphs and shepherds move forward to kiss the garments of the rural queen, the Genius sings a presentation song :

> O'er the smooth enamel'd green
> Where no print of step hath been,
> Follow me as I sing.
>
> (84–86)

Pastoral dances by the nymphs and shepherds evidently followed, for the final song by the Genius begins with the words "Nymphs and Shepherds dance no more" (96). The Genius concludes the performance by inviting his charges to remain on this "better soil" (101) in a region where "greater grace" may be enjoyed :

> Here ye shall have greater grace,
> To serve the Lady of this place.
> Though *Syrinx* your *Pans* Mistress were,

Yet *Syrinx* well might wait on her.
   Such a rural Queen
All *Arcadia* hath not seen.
                 (104–9)

Internal references in the text, together with the limited external evidence available, suggest that *Arc* was performed after dark on the elm-lined green leading to the entrance of Harefield House, probably on May 4, 1634, in celebration of the Countess's seventy-fifth birthday. She was a distant relative of poet Edmund Spenser*. She would have played the rural queen simply by occupying a commanding position on the chair of state. The identities of the persons who approached her across the "smooth enamel'd green" are unknown, but included among the "noble persons of her family" were her stepson, John Egerton, Earl of Bridgewater, and his children, three of whom were later to appear in *Mask*. The court musician Henry Lawes*, music teacher to the Egerton* family and a collaborator with Milton on *Mask*, would have been well suited to the role of the Genius of the Wood; however, proof that he performed in the entertainment is lacking.

Scholars and critics have offered general praise of Milton's light and gracious creation; yet, in comparison with the poet's other writings, relatively few complexities in theme, imagery, symbolism, and thought have been uncovered. Tension has been noted in the work between the forces of good and evil. The nymphs and shepherds observe that Envy can be found in the land undoing the praise of the rural queen offered by Fame (8–13), and the virtuous Genius must work to protect plants in the queen's wood from various "harms" : the attacks of "noisom winds," "blasting vapours," and the "hurt-full Worm" (49–53). Moreover, Platonic* elements are present in a statement by the Genius about the role of the Fates and the harmonious music* of the spheres (61–73).

The few close critical readings available tend to focus upon what may be symbolized by the discovery of the rural queen. Cleanth Brooks and John Edward Hardy claim that the queen represents the spirit of English pastoral* poetry. In their view the nymphs and shepherds are poets who are coming from Greece to England to create a new and better form of pastoral verse. J. M. Wallace, arguing that the symbolism of the work can be found in the dramatic event and in the social fame of the persons addressed, insists that the countess in life was eulogized by poets for her wisdom. Sapience is then said to be the main theme of the work. J. G. Demaray centers attention upon traditional elements in Milton's entertainment, pointing out how the pagan disguising reflects an actual social event.

Entertainments such as *Arc* were presented in various indoor and outdoor locations and were given structure and content to accord with the requirements of a particular occasion : a banquet, visit, progress, or entrance into a city. Unlike the more elaborately staged court masques*, these less ambitious works did not serve as an introduction to an indoor masked ball in which the audience participated. Entertainments, as a form of social art, were created with the aim of complimenting one or more noble guests through dialogue, song, and sometimes dance. The guests, and at times the aristocratic performers as well, were often depicted in a double-focus vision as figures whose influence brings harmony both to the pagan realm of the disguising and to the real social world. Thus passages in Milton's work deftly hint that the nymphs, shepherds, and rural queen, beneath their pagan trappings, are important members of an existing social establishment.

Arc in a general way resembles other entertainments, though no single work has been cited as its primary source. Lines praising Queen Anne in Ben Jonson's* "An Entertainment at Althorpe" (1603) appear to be echoed in the opening song of Milton's work; character-types in *Arc* are comparable to those in Thomas Campion's "The Entertainment Given by Lord Knowles" (1613) and Ben Jonson's "The Entertainment at Highgate" (1604);

and Milton's work was no doubt staged in a manner similar to that of the anonymous "The Entertainment of Queen Elizabeth at Harefield" (1602). [JGD]

AREOPAGITICA, published November 23, 1644, to protest Parliament's Licensing Order of June 16, 1643, and perhaps the most eloquent and certainly the best known of Milton's pamphlets. The Licensing Order was designed to control what could be published in England. Since at least 1530, "prior censorship" had existed in the form of royal prerogative, but Milton treats it as a recent import based on Roman Catholic example.

In 1637, King Charles's Court of Star Chamber had published a decree concerning printing. This decree required that both new books and reprintings be licensed*; it controlled the number of printers and presses, and distribution of printed matter; and it empowered the Stationer's Company to search for illegal printers. Though not the first, this was the fullest statement of royal censorship in English history. When the Star Chamber was abolished in July 1641, there were no governmental controls of printing. On January 29, 1642, Commons published an order requiring the author's consent to publication of his work, and publication of the author's name as well as the printer's on the title page. Evidence within two subsequent orders, of August 1642 and March 1643, shows clearly that all three were interim measures before Commons could establish a full policy on printing. Nonetheless, Milton assumes that the first order was Parliament's original intent, he ignores the other two, and treats the full licensing order of June 1643 as a throwback to the tyrannical policies of Charles* and an imitation of Catholic tyranny. According to Ernest Sirluck (Yale *Prose* 2:163), "The immediate object of the *Areopagitica* (the first work devoted primarily to freedom of the press) is to achieve 'Liberty of Unlicenc'd Printing' by obtaining the repeal of the Licensing Order and a 'return' to what Milton saw fit to think the policy under-

lying the Signature Order [of January 1642]." Milton favored corrective regulation, with printer and author responsible for the publication of anything illegal, but he thoroughly rejected preventive censorship.

Milton was unsuccessful in his immediate objective. *Areop* had no effect on the licensing order; in fact, under a similar two-year order of 1649, Milton himself served as licenser of the journal *Mercurius Politicus**. But as an important document in the history of English civil liberty*, it probably has had a real if intangible effect. In effect, *Areop* meant one thing to Milton and another to its many readers after 1738, when it first became popular.

For Milton, *Areop* was occasional. Its occasion was not only the public event of the licensing order, but Milton's own personal circumstances and developing thought about liberty. For over a year preceding *Areop,* he had tried to engage clergy and Parliament in a serious discussion of divorce* (*DDD,* August 1643 and February 1644; *Bucer,* July 15, 1644). *DDD* was unlicensed (as of course was *Areop* itself) and it seemed clear that despite the licensing of *Bucer,* any further arguments on this subject, and perhaps others, would encounter hostile licensers rather than open debate. In fact, *Tetra* and *Colas* (March 4, 1645), Milton's further works on divorce, were unlicensed. Milton, whose publications had in the past served the Parliamentary and Presbyterian causes, was now being treated as a fool at best, at worst a heretic, and he had reason to object. In addition, he had begun to see his own humanist belief in learning and reason countered by the dogmatic authority of the Presbyterians*. *Areop* is, among other things, a sign of Milton's coming break with the Presbyterians and his alliance with the Independents* and tolerationists*.

If it failed in its immediate objective, *Areop* has nonetheless become the standard of eloquence in defense of freedom of printing. Its second edition (apart from its inclusion in the prose collections of

1697 and 1698) appeared in 1738, with a preface by the poet James Thomson. Its publication was evidently in response to a fear that strict licensing of the press was about to be renewed. Since then, *Areop* has been the most popular and most often republished of Milton's prose works. It became a document of the eighteenth-century enlightenment, and had a place in the oratory of the American and French revolutions. Mirabeau's* powerful French adaptation, *Sur la liberté de la presse, imité de l'Anglois de Milton* (1788) has had a political and literary history of its own.

W. R. Parker provides an extensive list of editions of *Areop* (*Milton* 2 : 1224); Sirluck gives an account of the best editions, along with a collation of the text (Yale *Prose* 2 : 480–83). The following editions are among the best : T. Holt White's of 1819 provides the basis for much subsequent scholarship. It gives *Areop*'s bibliographical history prior to 1819 and sets a high standard for annotation and explication. It also includes Mirabeau's adaptation. John W. Hales's Oxford edition, first printed in 1866 and reissued often until 1939, provides excellent notes on *Areop*'s classical and biblical background. Edward Arber's edition in *The English Reprints* Series (1868) provides an accurate text and reprints the Star Chamber decree and the Parliamentary orders of January 1642 and March and June 1643. The editions by Merritt Y. Hughes in *John Milton: Prose Selections* (1947) and *John Milton: Complete Poems and Major Prose* (1957) offer fine notes. The most thorough and useful edition is Sirluck's, which gives text, notes, background, and analysis.

Areop's continued popularity depends in part on the ideas it expresses, or at least on the interpretation given those ideas by subsequent libertarian societies. The tercentenary of its publication, for example, was marked by a wartime conference of international writers and thinkers, gathering in London to discuss the implication of *Areop* in the twentieth century. The talks are published as *Freedom of Expression, A Symposium* (ed. Hermon Ould, 1944), in which the literary critic B. Ifor Evans rejects the importance of *Areop*'s style in favor of its ideas ("Milton and the Modern Press," pp. 26–29). Herbert Read, on the other hand, demands respect for *Areop*'s literary style, but also summarizes its position as a work of ideological importance : "The *Areopagitica* is Milton's greatest prose work, and this rank is given to it on account of its inherent qualities of fervour and style : but it is great also because of its wisdom, its logic and the universal application of its argument. Every newly established tyranny brings its pages to life again : there is no encroachment on 'the liberty to know, to utter and to argue freely' which it does not anticipate and oppose with unanswerable reason" (*Freedom of Expression*, p. 122).

That Milton's arguments are not "unanswerable" is clear from the controversy surrounding censorship in printing (see, e.g., F. S. Siebert, *Freedom of the Press in England, 1476–1776* [1952]). It is also hard to see how a pamphlet that explicitly excludes Roman Catholics from publishing, as *Areop* does, could be seen as a perfect model for twentieth-century freedom. But, as George F. Sensabaugh shows, Milton-as-liberal has long been interpreted to provide the spirit, if not the letter, for particular libertarian movements (*That Grand Whig Milton* [1952]; see also *Milton in Early America* [1964]).

Arthur Barker portrays *Areop* as a document that bridges the political and the literary, a Renaissance humanist plea for enlightened learning and the rights of learned men (*Milton and the Puritan Dilemma, 1641–1660* [1942, 1956], pp. 74–100). As a speech meant to persuade, *Aerop* cannot be separated from its political purpose. Though it did not achieve its immediate goal, it has become one of the finest examples of the art of persuasion, employed on a subject of immense importance to literary and learned men, and it has developed into a major political document. Its ultimate importance, then, derives from the staying power of its artistry, which in turn depends on its tone, strategy, and the enduring effect of its statement.

Milton's oration, as Sirluck notes, is loosely classical in structure (Yale *Prose* 2 : 170–71). Milton begins with the exordium (4 : 293–96); he proceeds with his proposition that Parliament should reconsider "that order which ye have ordain'd to regulate Printing" (4 : 296–97); he continues his confirmation with a fourpart argument against licensing, in which narration and confutation are interspersed (4 : 297–346); and concludes with the peroration (4 : 346–54).

The tone is established in the exordium. The initial and stated audience, Parliament, is a high court of equals, a great government, but a government elected by free men who need not apologize for addressing it. Those who do address Parliament will naturally feel strong emotion in so weighty a task. But Milton, a learned man who has proved himself a friend, supporter, and a kind of peer, is launching into a subject that he can discuss on the basis of common principles and mutual trust (4 : 293–95). Milton calls on the model of ancient Greece, where Isocrates could write an oration to "the *Parliament* of Athens" on the subject of the Greek high court, the Areopagus, with freedom to "admonish" the state. (For Milton's use of Isocrates, see Sirluck, Yale *Prose* 2 : 486 n1 and 489 n12; see also Joseph A. Wittreich's suggestion of a double irony in Milton's choice of Isocrates, in *Milton Studies* 4 [1973]). It is customary to use flattery in an exordium, but Milton's flattery is based on his assurance that he is free to differ with his audience, and free to persuade them to reform. Milton, from early in the essay, uses both sound and rhythm to suggest parallels even as they carry his statement forward : for example, "when complaints are freely heard, deeply considered and speedily reform'd, then is the utmost bound of civill liberty attain'd, that wise men look for" (4 : 293). The effect is of a style that is simple, generally paratactic, but tense with an eloquent energy that is likely to (and does) break forth when the logic of an argument reaches its passionate core.

Sirluck suggests that Milton's real audience is "much broader" than Parliament alone : "As a printed pamphlet the speech is addressed also to the general public. In addition, two official organizations were intensely interested in the double issue [of freedom of the press and religious liberty] treated in *Areop* : the Westminster Assembly and the Parliamentary army" (Yale *Prose* 2 : 173). Sirluck goes on to suggest that Milton's tone is an attempt to appeal to the tolerationists and Independents in Parliament, and especially the Erastians*, at the expense of the Westminster Assembly* of Presbyterian and nonseparationist clergy. In the background of his appeal is the largely independent army. This seems reasonable. Throughout *Areop* Milton assumes that blame for the Licensing Order falls on the Presbyterian clergy. And in the exordium and proposition, Milton's voice takes on its own priestly character. He announces his intention to "admonish" Parliament (4 : 296), a clerical function, by means of a "Homily" (4 : 297). But whatever the tactical purpose of the tone, Milton here reveals his belief in the priestly function of the learned man, a belief that anticipates, if it is not parallel to, the priestly function of the poet in *PL*.

In the introductory tone, then, Milton not only establishes his good will toward his audience, but implies the divine importance of what he has to say. Freedom of the press and religious liberty become inextricably interwoven, since man's right to learn is given (and even demanded) by God, and the duty of the learned man to teach and "to admonish" is a religious duty. With all these implications lurking very close to the surface, Milton begins his formal argument.

The "Homily" is based on a four-part argument, first stated in the proposition and developed in the confirmation. Milton asks Parliament to consider "first, [that] the inventors of [licensing] . . . bee those whom ye will be loath to own; next what is to be thought in generall of reading, what ever sort the Books be; and that this Order avails nothing to the suppressing of scandalous, seditious, and libellous Books, which were mainly intended to be supprest. Last, that it will be primely to the discouragement of all learning, and the stop of Truth, not only by disexercising and blunting our abilities in what we know already, but by hindring and cropping the discovery that might bee yet further made both in religious and civill Wisdome" (4 : 297).

From here Milton proceeds to establish further the tone of the divinity of learning : "As good almost kill a Man as kill a good Book; who kills a man kills a reasonable creature, Gods Image; but hee who destroys a good Booke, kills reason it selfe, kills the Image of God, as it were in the eye" (4 : 298).

The bulk of Milton's subsequent argument, in the confirmation, relies on reason rather than authority, though he will use authorities to serve his logic. In the first part of his four-part discussion, Milton blames "some of our Presbyters" for advocating a practice (censorship) that is both un-English and un-Christian. Censorship is a development of the papacy, and has been used by the Roman Catholic Church to support "tyranny and superstition." The implication is that the presbyters, following the hated footsteps of the English bishops, wanted to resurrect censorship in order to deny religious freedom and the pursuit of truth.

He then turns to his second argument —that all books, good and bad, serve the cause of truth. "Bad" books may "serve in many respects to discover, to confute, to forewarn, and to illustrate" (4 : 309). That this is true is the result of the human condition. "It was from out the rinde of one apple tasted, that the knowledge of good* and evil* as two twins cleaving together leapt forth into the World. And perhaps this is that doom which Adam fell into of knowing good and evill, that is to say of knowing good by evill. . . . I cannot praise a fugitive and cloister'd vertue . . ." (4 : 310–11).

Even if licensing had a moral purpose, it is unsuccessful : "Suppose we could expell sin* by this means; . . . so much we expell of vertue : for the matter of them both is the same; remove that, and ye remove them both alike" (4 : 320).

And, finally, licensing can do no good, but it can cause "manifest hurt . . . in being first the greatest discouragement and affront that can be offer'd to learning and to learned men" (4 : 323). The thrust of the attack is against the unlearned censoring the learned, to the glorification of ignorance and the demeaning of all learned men. The triumph of ignorance is not only foolish, but dangerous to both true religion and good government. By implication, the unlearned include the Presbyterian clergy. Milton builds on his tone of comradeship with Parliament to argue against the interference of the Westminster Assembly, though the Assembly is not mentioned by name. Clergy in general, and presbyters in particular, come in for heavy disapproval.

Licensing, then, may "prove a nursing mother to sects" and general divisiveness, but it is definitly a "step-dame to Truth." Truth must be exercised; "A man may be a heretick in the truth" (4 : 333) if he is told what to believe, but does not understand the truth he professes. Such automatic and untested belief also leads to sloth and ignorance in the clergy. Finally, licensing may inhibit the discovery of new or fuller truth. "Truth indeed came once into the world with her divine Master" (4 : 337), but after the departure of Christ and his apostles, "the virgin truth" was torn into a thousand pieces; man must now seek her and reassemble her to as much wholeness as he possibly can. It is England's special responsibility to gather, guard, and give witness to truth. It is again the clergy who are not to be trusted; they suppressed Wycliff and so made England late in Reformation instead of first, as it seemed called to be. Now once again God has put England in the forefront of true Reformation. What the clergy call sect and schism are really a sign of the "earnest and zealous thirst after knowledge and understanding which God hath stirr'd up in this City" (4 : 341). The confirmation moves toward its conclusion, and here is Milton's famous passage on England's reawakening, typical of the burst of eloquence that Milton can produce when he seeks to transcend his logic* with his passion : "Methinks I see in my mind a noble and puissant Nation rousing herself like a strong man after sleep and shaking her invincible locks. . . ." (4 : 344). It is England's zeal for learning that gives her a place in God's great Reformation. Therefore, "give me the liberty to know, to utter, and to argue freely according to conscience, above all liberties" (4 : 346).

In the concluding peroration, Milton is a tolerationist, allowing for large areas of indifference. All religious practice should be allowed that "need not interrupt *the unity of Spirit,* if we could but find among us *the bond of peace*" (4 : 349–50). Roman Catholics are not to be tolerated on the theory that the suppression of freedom is a principal tenet of the papacy; and seditious and libelous matter ought to be prosecuted once it is published (see Sirluck on "The Limits of Toleration," Yale *Prose* 2 : 178–81). *Areop* is nonetheless a strong and eloquent plea for free thought and communication, with an underlying faith in learning as redemptive, and the learned and literate man as one of God's chosen.

So *Areop* has long been loved by learned and literate men. A greater tribute to its artistry is its ability, for at least the past 200 years, to inspire almost all people to a sense of the sanctity of free expression. What were struggling, though not original, ideas in Milton's time are now the assumptions of much of the English-speaking world. Milton's statement, with all its personal and topical focus, probably remains the greatest expression in English of ideas that have, in the main, prevailed. [SW]

ARIANISM. When *CD* was published in 1825, readers had for the first time unquestionable proof that according to

Milton's Christology the Son* is subordinate to the Father*, generated at the beginning of creation* from the divine substance (14 : 193), but neither coessential, coequal, nor coeternal with the Father. If the Son were of the same whole essence as the Father, they "would be one person" (14 : 187); and God could not beget "a co-equal Deity, because unity and infinity are two of his essential attributes" (14 : 311). The Father and the Son are one only because "they speak and act with unanimity" and "in love" (14 : 211, 213); and the Holy Spirit is inferior to both of them (14 : 377). The Son is divine "by the will of the one God" (14 : 255).

There has been much discussion concerning whether these views should properly be termed Arian (Masson, C. S. Lewis, Kelley, Conklin), Semi-Arian (theologians Philip Schaff and F. J. Foakes-Jackson), Anti-Trinitarian (Sewell, Robins), or Subordinationist (Hunter, Adamson, R. M. Frye, Patrides).

Arius (d. A.D. 336), combating Sabellianism, which denied any distinctions among the persons of the Trinity*, maintained a total distinction of substance between the Father and the Son, and the subordination of the latter. But the doctrine of subordination was common to many ante-Nicene Fathers, including Tertullian*, Hippolytus, and Origen*. According to theologian H. D. A. Major, the text of Scripture plainly teaches the subordination and obedience of the Son; but the Arians associated Christ's obedience with inferiority in His divine nature. In reaction against Arianism, however, many theologians espoused a view that accords with Milton's whole philosophy of obedience* : "Subordination in the form of voluntary and rational obedience, so far from being a mark of inferiority of nature, is the mark of identity with the divine nature" (*Encyclopedia of Religion and Ethics,* ed. Hastings, 11 : 910).

Milton's references to Arius and Arianism are never flattering. His most favorable reference occurs in *TR,* where he argues that the books of Arians as well as those of Arminians*, Anabaptists*, and Socinians* should be freely sold and read, because "all controversies being permitted, falshood will appear more false, and truth the more true" (6 : 178). In the same work he discusses Arian doctrine as espoused by certain of his contemporaries: "The Arian and Socinian are charg'd to dispute against the Trinity : they affirm to believe the Father, Son, and Holy Ghost, according to Scripture, and the Apostolic Creed; as for terms of Trinity, Triniunity, Coessentiality, Tripersonality, and the like, they reject them as Scholastic Notions, not to be found in Scripture. . . . They dispute the satisfaction of Christ, or rather the word *Satisfaction,* as not Scriptural : but they acknowledge him both God and their Saviour" (6 : 169). Here Milton's sympathetic tone is in keeping with his whole argument : although various groups may have fallen into error, "misunderstanding the Scripture after all sincere endeavours to understand it rightly," they are not heretics unless they have chosen "profestly against Scripture" (6 : 168). Of several things, then, we may be sure : Milton would not at this time have proclaimed Arius a heretic, although he had done so earlier, in *Eikon* (5 : 224); nor would he appreciate the application of the term *heresy** to his own concepts. But it is perhaps significant that he uses the pronoun *they* concerning the Arians, rather than *we.* Milton is not known for lacking the courage of his convictions; and since in 1611 two Englishmen had been burned to death for "obstinate Arianism," it is hard to imagine that Milton would have embraced Arianism without being aware that he had done so. Clearly he thought he was returning to the true doctrine of the Trinity as implied in Scripture, understood by the early Church Fathers, and revived in the Renaissance by Cambridge Platonists* like Henry More and Ralph Cudworth.

The chief point of Arian doctrine anathematized at the Council of Nicaea was the creation of the Son from nothing rather than from the substance of God. Philo* and many of the Church Fathers had accepted a two-stage theory of the Word (first, eternal as a property of God and then created as an external entity), and the implied inequality or subordination of this theory was never banned. That the substance of the Son was the crux of the matter is indicated by John Bidle, who about 1653 defended Eusebius* against charges of Arianism: "For whereas *Arius* held that God before he began to make the world created of nothing a certain Spirit, called his Son, which was afterward incarnated; . . . *Eusebius* . . . affirmed that God, before he made the world, did in an ineffable manner generate out of his own substance a Son, who afterward assumed a humane nature" (*Testimonies of Irenaeus* . . . [1653], pp. 75–76). Since Milton viewed both Son and Spirit as deriving from the divine substance (14 : 403), he would not have regarded himself as Arian, nor would his seventeenth-century readers have assumed that he saw the Logos as a mere creature in any modern sense. It therefore seems wise to refer to Milton as Subordinationistic rather than Arian, semi-Arian, or anti-Trinitarian.

Milton avoids the term *three persons*; he affirms that there is one *substantia,* or divine substratum, but three *essentiae,* or *hypostaseis,* or essences. The Father, Son, and Holy Spirit each has the *essentia* proper to Himself, and these are not equal (14 : 401; cf. 43, 221, 311). But the difference from Arianism is crucial : by denying that the Son is similar to the Father in any way, extreme Arians had denied the historical basis of Christianity and eviscerated the doctrine of the Incarnation. Conversely, by asserting that the Son was created from the substance of God and indeed was Himself God, Milton asserted also the central Christian tradition.

Maurice Kelley has claimed that *PL,* like *CD,* is an Arian document, citing especially *PL* 3. 243–44, 305–7, and 317–19 as anti-Trinitarian statements. Yet Sewell gives orthodox interpretations for these passages, and Patrides maintains that even the subordinationism of *CD* is not present in *PL*. Not only does the Son fully reflect the Father's glory and love*, but He is the image of God in all things (*PL* 3. 139, 225; 5. 720; 6. 720, 736; 7. 196; 10. 66). As soon as the Council in Heaven is over, the distinction between Father and Son is dropped, so that Christ is called God as He creates and is termed "the Lord God" as He judges the fallen Adam and Eve (10. 163).

Milton's avoidance of any inescapably subordinationist passages in his poetry may be explained by reference to dates of composition and changing attitudes, as Sewell urges; but perhaps an explanation is suggested by a Latin quotation in *CB* that approves of Constantine's* instructions to Alexander and Arius to "bury in silence" those "fundamental questions about God which the human reason finds it difficult to interpret or solve . . . lest they should become known to the common people and thus afford material for schisms" (18 : 138). [VRM]

ARIOSTO, LUDOVICO (1474–1533). A sequel to Boiardo's* *Orlando Innamorato* ("Orlando in Love"), Ariosto's romance-epic *Orlando Furioso* ("Orlando Insane") first appeared in 1516 and was republished in a revised and expanded version in 1532. Like Boiardo before him and Tasso* after him, Ariosto belonged to the entourage of the dukes of Ferrara (his patron was Cardinal Ippolito d'Este) and glorified the Este family in his romance. Milton's early familiarity with Ariosto's poem is indicated by references in his ecclesiastical treatises and his *CB*, and by marginalia* in a copy of the 1591 edition of Sir John Harington's translation. A note in the Harington volume (dated September 21, 1642, and attributed to Milton) declares that he had read "questo libro" (i.e., canto 46 or possibly the entire poem) twice. In *CB* Milton cites canto 34 on the subject of "alms given after death." In *Ref* he describes Ariosto as "equall in fame" to Dante* and Petrarch* and quotes excerpts from two stanzas in this canto—one quoted directly from Harington, the other apparently translated by Milton himself

from the Italian original. In a biographical passage in *RCG,* he asserts that he had "apply'd my selfe to that resolution which *Ariosto* follow'd against the perswasions of *Bembo,* to fix all the industry and art I could unto the adorning of my native tongue. . . ." A parallel passage occurs (as Haug points out) in Harington's essay "The Life of Ariosto" as well as in Pigna's biography of Ariosto in *I Romanzi* (Venice, 1554) : *Modern Language Quarterly* 4 : 291.

Milton's early interest in the *Orlando Furioso* reflects the youthful taste he expressed in several works (*Apol, IlP, Mask*) for allegorical* fable and romance; and it is significant that he regarded the order of nature* as a possible model for epic* construction (*RCG*). Nevertheless, when he came to write *PL,* he had (as Shumaker observes) rejected the irregular and episodic plot of the Italian romance-epic, the paraphernalia of magic, and its "ruling interests" : valor, honor, romantic love.

Though Milton was obviously fond of the *Orlando Furioso* in his youth, nevertheless in his later poetry it is sometimes difficult to distinguish Ariosto's influence from Spenser's* (Spenser, had, in fact, acknowledged Ariosto as his original in the *Faerie Queene*). Possible borrowings from or allusions to *Orlando Furioso* have been noted by many critics. The phrase "Things unattempted yet in Prose or Rhyme" may echo Harington's "A tale in prose ne verse yet sung or said" (*OF* 1. 1. 10). References to Montalban and Damascus (*PL* 1. 583–84), to "fabl'd Knights In Battels feign'd" (*PL* 9. 29–31), to Agrican's siege of Albracca to win the fair Angelica (*PR* 3. 338–42) allude indirectly to Ariosto's epic as well as to other Renaissance romances. The periodic metamorphosis of Satan and his angels into serpents (*PL* 10. 572–77) has been compared to the lot of the fairy Manto in *OF*. Milton's account of the diabolical origin of artillery (*PL* 6. 484–89) involves a Renaissance commonplace that Ariosto also exploits. Milton's Limbo of Vanity may be indebted to Ariosto's lunar limbo of "things that on earth were lost, or were abus'd" : but scholars disagree as to the extent of Milton's indebtedness. In *PR* 4. 541–42, there is an explicit allusion to the "wing of Hippogrif," the flying steed of *OF*; and a simile earlier in the same book (4. 10–20) has been regarded as an echo of Ariosto's comparison of a Moorish attack to the swarming of flies around grapes.

If *OF* actually influenced *PL* to any significant degree, its influence was more subtle than the theft of a phrase or incident. Milton may have profited from Ariosto's use of irony, his skill in describing the marvelous, or his subtlety in portraying the character and sensibility of his heroines. [RCF]

ARISTOTLE: *see* POETICS, MILTON'S.

ARISTOTLE AND MILTON. Milton's knowledge and use of Aristotle have strangely escaped the sort of book-length investigations represented by Herbert Agar's *Milton and Plato* (rpt. 1965) and Irene Samuel's *Plato and Milton* (1947). Whereas these and many shorter studies make a convincing case for Milton's Platonism* or Neoplatonism*, it seems that critics are reluctant to mention Aristotle in their titles, as careful inspection of Calvin Huckabay's *John Milton: An Annotated Bibliography* (1969) surprisingly reveals, even though many studies —long and short—either devote intensive attention to Aristotelian elements in Milton, as in the case of T. R. Hartmann's "Milton's *Prolusions:* A Study" (dissertation, New York University, 1962), or convey by few or cursory references the impression that the reader should already be aware of the nature and extent of Aristotle's influence and may be reminded thereof by the mere mention of his name.

By patient use of the indexes to *CM* and to Yale *Prose,* in addition to footnotes in the better textbook editions, it is easy to establish such early examples as *Vac,* in which Milton assumes the role of absolute being—the Aristotelian concept of *Ens,* and *Idea,* to which scholars favoring

Milton's Platonism point as an instance of his preference, just as in *Prol* 2 he refers to Aristotle as "the envious and perpetual calumniator of Pythagoras* and Plato." In reference to Milton's rhetoric*, in *Plato and Milton* Samuel gives a general insight that provides a simple mirror— ". . . poetry is own sister to rhetoric in enchantment. Aristotle, Horace*, and the rest will explain how the art succeeds or fails in casting the spell, but Plato tells what spell is to be cast" (pp. 66–67)— to be held up to Aristotelian references as diverse as those to be found in the introduction to the Second Book of *RCG,* the treatise on *Educ,* the title page and epistolary preface of *SA, DDD, Ref, Logic, Prol* 4 and 6, and, of course, *CD* and *CB,* to mention but a few.

Commentators on Milton long ago directed attention to Milton's concern with Aristotle, however accurately or inaccurately according to modern interpretations. Two examples will suffice. John Dennis*, in his "The Grounds of Criticism in Poetry" (1704), observes that in his desire to write an epic poem Milton ". . . resolv'd at the same time to break thro' the Rules of *Aristotle*. Not that he was ignorant of them, or contemn'd them. On the contrary, no Man knew them better, or esteemed them more, because no Man had an Understanding that was more able to comprehend the necessity of them. . . . But at the same time he had discernment enough to see, that if he wrote a Poem which was within the compass of them, he would be subjected to the same Fate which has attended all who have wrote Epick Poems ever since the time of Homer" (rpt. J. T. Shawcross, *Milton: The Critical Heritage* [1970], p. 128). Joseph Addison*, who as in *Spectator* nos. 267 and 297 praises Milton's "Action of an Epic Poem" and faults *PL* for the "several Defects which appear in the Fable, the Characters, the Sentiments and the Language," does so partially by reference to Aristotle (rpt. Shawcross, esp. pp. 149, 165). What Dennis says turns out to be, in limited ways, surprisingly contemporary.

Of far more importance than most such references and allusions is that knowledge of Aristotle that scholars increasingly have revealed as related to Milton's own thought and as expressed in both his content and literary practices in his poetry and prose. It is here that a thorough and comprehensive study is needed in order to demonstrate what use Milton makes of Aristotle in areas or on topics such as astronomy, catharsis*, cosmology*, epic*, ethics*, logic*, metaphysics*, ontology*, philosophy*, physics, poetics*, politics*, psychology*, Ramus*, rhetoric*, science*, tragedy*—but to begin a list. Reiteration of what may be covered in full and detailed treatment under these headings would be uneconomical here. What follows is intended to be neither minute coverage nor a mere sampling of pertinent research but rather "imaginations thus display'd."

To venture the premise that Milton's utilization of Aristotelian concepts was often a process of modification, adjustment, or transformation, based upon a thorough plumbing of most of Aristotle's treatises, suggests that repetition may be avoided by judicious selection of instances that illustrate what is often referred to as Milton's eclecticism, but here within the boundaries of Aristotelianism. As a case in point, Addison's previously cited concern with "the Fable, the Characters, the Sentiments," is more precisely dealt with by the distinctions made by John M. Steadman (*Milton's Epic Characters* [1968], p. x): "In Fable, Character, and Thought alike, Milton conforms, on the whole, to neo-Aristotelian principles; it is chiefly in their relative importance that he seems to diverge. His basic orientation is decidedly in the direction of Aristotelian rationalism, and the result is a poem more logical, more tightly conceived and articulated, than any of the epics or tragedies lauded in the *Poetics*." By providing one of the more sustained explorations of Aristotelian elements in Milton, Steadman tends to clarify statements by Platonic advocates such as Samuel's "Milton recognized . . . that the writings of master and pupil disagree far less than those of the militant Platonists and Aristotelians of later generations. On Milton's page the two often appear together in support of the same doctrine, and this agreement is not forced. The emphasis is right; in general, Aristotle does 'rather distinguish than deny' Platonic teachings. And where Aristotle 'distinguished,' Milton often accepted the refinement" (Samuel, p. 34). Steadman advances another step by demonstrating that in his emphasis upon "Character and Thought in relation to the Fable," Milton's "predominantly logical approach to these problems" may go beyond Aristotle (p. ix).

In a similar vein, Steadman succinctly reviews one kind of situation with which Milton had to cope: "Just as it [Renaissance poetic theory] tended to approach the heroic poem in terms of Aristotle's *Poetics,* so it usually interpreted the *Poetics* in terms of the *Nicomachean Ethics* and *Politics.* The result was to emphasize the intellectual element in poetry, to rationalize the relationship between Character and Action, to underline the importance of probability and necessity in Plot and Character alike, and to stress the logical or rhetorical method of the speeches by the various *personae.* *Mythós, Ethos, Dianoia* (Fable, Character, and Thought)—Aristotle had rationalized all three; and in theory, if not always in practice, Renaissance poets found it difficult to escape the limitations of this philosophical attitude toward the problems of literary composition" (p. ix). He concludes with a partial echo concerning *PL* that "The tight logical structure of Milton's epic and the prominence he assigns to the analysis of the causes and effects of the central action reflect this rationalistic approach to the epic plot" (p. ix). Such comments also reflect, in part, typical Miltonic modifications or qualifications of Aristotle. In point of *PL*, Milton's challenge was not unique. As B. K. Lewalski points out concerning late-sixteenth century Italian criticism affecting biblical epics, "Much of this criticism implicitly challenged the epic claims of many if not all biblical poems, but some treatises —commentaries on Dante*, on the Italian romances, on Plato, and even some on Aristotle's *Poetics*—offered formulations which could accommodate the biblical epic kind" (*Milton's Brief Epic* [1966], p. 71). Obviously, Lewalski's comment is more concerned with *PR* than *PL*, but the implications apply to both.

It is in the Introduction to Book 2 of *RCG* that Milton wonders "whether that Epick form whereof the two poems of *Homer*, and those other two of *Virgil* and *Tasso* are a diffuse, and the book of *Job* a brief model : or whethet the rules of *Aristotle* herein are strictly to be kept, or nature to be follow'd which in them that know art, and use judgement is no transgression, but an inriching of art" (3 : 237). Allan H. Gilbert has noted touching this passage that Milton is "perhaps echoing Aristotle's 'watery' and 'short,' though it seems without suggestion of censure" (*Literary Criticism, Plato to Dryden* [1967], p. 114 n204). Even so, in the composition of both *PL* and *PR*, Milton's detailed knowledge of Aristotle did little to discourage him from making modifications as he saw fit. See further POETICS, MILTON'S.

Some of the more important recent contributions to an understanding of just how thoroughly Milton knew Aristotle have to do with quite specific matters. Although acknowledging that Merritt Y. Hughes has found a kinship between the Christ of *PR* and Aristotle's magnanimous man (*Studies in Philology* 35 [1938]: 254–77), Lewalski reads *PR* 2. 457–83 in terms of Milton's definition in *CD*, "Magnanimity is shown, when in the seeking or avoiding, the acceptance or refusal of riches, advantages, or honours, we are actuated by a regard to our own dignity, rightly understood" (17 : 241), and argues that the definition "is obviously derived (with some modification) from Aristotle, and the Christ of the poem displays some of the qualities Aristotle enumerates," except, of course, Aristotle's attitude toward worldly goods (Lewalski, p. 244). She concludes, ". . . Aristotle's magnanimous man seeks

'honour in accordance with his deserts,' whereas Milton's Christ does not seek his own glory, 'but his / Who sent me'" (*PR* 3. 106–7; Lewalski, p. 244). M. B. McNamee's chapter "Magnanimity in Milton" in *Honor and the Epic Hero* ([1960], pp. 160–78) also stresses the modifications Milton made to the concept as described by Aristotle.

Another valuable line of investigation contributing to an understanding of specific ideas and concepts common to Aristotle and Milton may be found in the carefully formulated insights in several studies by W. B. Hunter, Jr., of which a few must be mentioned. In order to elucidate Milton's treatment of the Son* of God and his relationship to the Father*, Hunter examines in "Milton's Theological Vocabulary" (*Bright Essence* [1971], pp. 15–25) the detailed history of terms such as *substance, subsistence, essence,* and *hypostasis,* to support the thesis that "Milton has often not followed the interpretations of these words usually held in Christianity; rather, he has adopted meanings which were very early associated with them but which lost currency centuries ago . . ." (p. 15). The sharp distinctions Milton makes in *CD* between *essence* and *substance* are traced back to Aristotle's "two aspects of *ousia*" according to the *Metaphysics* (7) and the *Categories* (5). By using Aristotle's "primary sense of the word" as representing "particular individual beings," Milton can assert "the separate reality of each of the persons of the Trinity" (p. 19). By additional such analysis, distinguishing between the Latin and Greek history of such words, Hunter is able to conclude that for Milton "the Persons were distinguished as three hypostases or as three essences, both words being understood in the sense of the Aristotelian first *ousia*" (p. 25). Milton's knowledge of Aristotle in these matters serves to support Hunter's argument ("Milton's Arianism Reconsidered," *Bright Essence,* pp. 29–51) that Milton was "no Arian."

With reference to the Incarnation*, Hunter bases similar arguments upon Aristotle's terms, especially *essence*, in his discussion of Christ's divine and human roles ("Milton on the Incarnation," *Bright Essence*, pp. 131–48) to show how "Milton vindicated Christ's free human will by accepting the theological dangers inherent in the concept of his personality. Its clearest exercise would be found in its free choice when confronted by evil, the subject of *Paradise Regained*. Even before the Incarnation, the Son had possessed the same complete freedom . . ." (p. 148). On a somewhat different topic, the reasoning power of animals, Hunter suggests in "A Note on *Lycidas*" (*Modern Language Notes* 65 : 544) that Milton may have had Aristotle in mind, whatever other traditions may have been available.

Still an additional illustration of the value of a close examination of Milton's knowledge of Aristotle as a way of better reading Milton is Hunter on "Milton's Power of Matter" (*Journal of the History of Ideas* 13:551–62). In part disagreeing with W. C. Curry's "Milton's Scale of Nature" (rpt. in *Milton's Ontology, Cosmogony, and Physics* [1957], pp. 158–82), where the stress is partly upon Neoplatonism, Hunter (although not discarding the possibility of Augustinian* elements), in developing reasons for doubting that Milton's "power of matter" in *CD* (15 : 49, 53) is the same as "Augustinian seminal reasons," points out that Milton, having referred to the theory of *potentia materiae*, assumes it "is widely known and generally accepted," being "inherited from Aristotle by the Middle Ages and the Renaissance" (p. 551), and provides supportive evidence from Aristotle's *De Anima, Metaphysics*, and *Physics*. The extent is examined to which Aristotle's "theories of the matter-form relationship" imply "the idea of a continuous scale of nature" and may be said to be "consistent with the poet's argument that matter works up through various levels to spirit" (pp. 561–62). Here again is evidence of Milton's grasp of Aristotelianism and of subsequent traditions. (For a partial dissent from Hunter's argument see John Reesing, "Milton's Philosophical View of Nature," Harvard diss., 1954.)

Rhetoric is another of the practiced talents attributed to Milton. Deliberative rhetoric, as treated in detail in a chapter by Steadman entitled " 'Semblance of Worth' : Pandaemonium and Deliberative Oratory," typifies the kind of careful research that remains possible in the discovery of Aristotelian elements in Milton. Largely concerned with the Council in Hell (*PL* 2), the chapter early relates Milton's method to Aristotle's precepts: "The subject of the 'Consultation'— 'whether another Battel be to be hazarded for the recovery of Heaven' and 'by what best way, Whether of open Warr or covert guile'—is a standard object of deliberative rhetoric : '. . . for nearly all the questions on which men deliberate, and on which the deliberative orator harangues, those at least of the highest concernment, are in number *five*; and these are questions of *finance*, or *war and peace* and again respecting *imports and exports*, and also respecting *legislature*' " (*Epic Characters*, p. 243; *Rhetoric*, trans. T. Buckley [1851], p. 29). However, "The conditions of Hell are incompatible with the usual objects of deliberative rhetoric. . . . The critics who find the devil's arguments absurd are, therefore, partly correct, for the conventional objects of deliberative rhetoric—the concepts of happiness and the greater good—are ends not only inaccessible to the fallen angels, but indeed diametrically opposed to the subject of debate" (p. 245). Milton is not unaware of the rhetorical contributions of Cicero* and Quintilian*, drawing from them when Aristotle does not suffice, but Steadman's careful analysis demonstrates that the Aristotelian rhetorical principles seem to predominate (pp. 252–53). Even for the observation that "in its progressive discrimination between the practical and the impractical, the Stygian council exemplifies the principles of deliberative oratory" (p. 256), Steadman finds a parallel in the *Rhetoric* (trans. Buckley, p. 263). Thus, as Milton weaves the argument, the rhetoric of the "devilish participants" is "essentially an art of pretense" (p. 257). Therefore, the council scene and its rhetoric contribute to the plot of *PL* : "Aristotle had maintained that actions should seem 'probable' or 'necessary'—the logical or plausible consequences of prior actions or of Character and Thought" (p. 261). It follows that "the oratory of Pandaemonium is cut from the same cloth as that of the temptation scene. The same type of eloquence displays itself in the inception of the infernal enterprise and in its execution. The structure of Milton's epic hinges on a perverted rhetoric" (p. 259). Milton, then, adapts the techniques of deliberative rhetoric to his own purposes.

It is not a great leap from rhetoric to logic, another topic subsequently to be treated separately, nor should assertions such as that of Walter J. Ong, saying "in logic Milton was a follower of Peter Ramus* . . . in the very patent sense that his *Artis logicae plenior institutio* . . . is an edition, with commentary worked in, of Ramus' *Dialectic* or *Logic*" ("Logic and the Epic Muse," *Achievements of the Left Hand*, ed. M. Lieb and J. T. Shawcross [1974], p. 244), forbid attempts to identify Aristotelian elements in Milton, whether in his *Logic* or other writings. Milton does not always agree with Ramus, and since "Ramus' mind was not a speculative mind" (Ong, p. 246), and Milton's undoubtedly was, his strong attraction to a system of logic based upon "ultimate closure" (Ong, p. 265), however apparent in his *Logic* and in *PL*, should not forbid his reaching back to Aristotle when Ramist method becomes too restrictive. Or, as R. M. Adams has phrased it, ". . . his position, halfway between Ramist intuitionism and Aristotelian reliance on the syllogism . . . , may be construed as an expression of his need for intellectual elbowroom" (*Milton and the Modern Critics* [1966], p. 174).

To take a different tack, by way of an illustrative exemplum, Aristotelian references may be followed through a single work, *CD*. Milton writes, ". . . it appears that God cannot rightly be called Actus Purus, or pure actuality, as is customary in Aristotle, for thus he could do nothing except what he does do, and he would do that of necessity, although in fact he is omnipotent and utterly free in his actions"

(*CD* 1 : ii). Maurice Kelley refers the reader to Aristotle's *Metaphysics* 9. 6–7, and further notes that "*Actus purus* . . . denoted 'a being from whom potentiality is excluded and is consequently pure actuality and perfection'" (Yale *Prose* 6: 145–46). Here and in a good many other places, it is apparently left to the diligent reader to make the proper leap from Peripatetic philosophy to, in this instance, Christian concepts of God. In a discussion of angels* leading to the problem of "motion" and "time*," *CD* 1 : vii records: "There is certainly no reason why we should conform to the popular belief that motion and time, which is the measure of motion, could not, according to our concepts of 'before' and 'after,' have existed before this world was made. For Aristotle, who taught that motion and time are inherent only in this world, asserted, nevertheless, that this world was eternal." In this case Kelley makes a cross-reference to *PL* 5. 580–82, and mentions Aristotle's *Physics* 4. xii, 221a–22a, and 8. i, 250b–52a, "if Milton consulted them" (Yale *Prose* 6 : 314). Shortly thereafter, Milton questions "by what sort of law could we make a soul* answerable for a crime which Adam committed . . .?" He continues : "Add to this Aristotle's argument . . . that if the soul is wholly contained in all the body and wholly in any given part of that body, how can the human seed, that intimate and most noble part of the body, be imagined destitute and devoid of the soul of the parents, or at least of the father, when communicated to the son in the act of generation? Nearly everyone agrees that all form—and the human soul is a kind of form—is produced by the power of matter" (*CD* 1 : vii). The Aristotle passage is credited to *De Anima* 2. 412a–b (Yale *Prose* 6 : 321); on the "power of matter," see the comments by Hunter, above, and TRADUCIANISM. Similar to the point in *CD* 1 : vii, Milton asks, "And what about the theory that there is no time without motion? Aristotle illustrates this (*Phys.* 4. 11) by the story of those men who were said to have gone to sleep in the temple of the heroes and who, on waking, thought that they had gone to sleep one moment and woken up the next, and were not aware of any interim. It is even more likely that, for those who have died, all intervening time will be as nothing . . ." (*CD* 1 : xiii). An allusion shortly thereafter (*CD* 1 : xiv) to Aristotle's *Metaphysics* (5. 4. 7) touching the words *nature, person,* and *hypostasis* has been previously mentioned. Much later in *CD,* in the definitions of *elegance* (2 : ix), Milton says "Opposed to this is luxury." Kelley notes, "The definitions of *lautitia* (elegance) and its opposite *luxus* (luxury) derive ultimately from Aristotle, *Nicomachean Ethics* 4. i" (Yale *Prose* 6 : 733). Among further definitions, *faint-heartedness* is opposed to *high-mindedness* (*CD* 2 : ix), about which Kelley suggests, "This treatment of magnanimity* and its opposites pride* and pusillanimity derives . . . from Aristotle, *Nicomachean Ethics,* IV, II" (Yale *Prose* 6:737), whereas Lewalski mentions 1. 7, 1098a and 8. 1123–24b (p. 243). Finally, unnamed by Milton, Aristotle (*NE* 4. 1. 2) is credited with making *niggardliness* and *prodigality* the opposites of *liberality* (Yale *Prose* 6 : 779). Buried though they may appear to be among myriad scriptural and other references, these Aristotle-based passages are evidence of the methodical utilization of such details by Milton; eclecticism will bear repeating once more.

Similar emphasis upon Aristotle is found in *Tenure.* In their editions of it both Hughes and Shawcross stress Milton's indebtedness to Aristotle, whatever his many other authorities. For Hughes, "In Aristotle Milton thought that he saw confirmation of his whole case against tyrants as betrayers of a trust from the people" (Yale *Prose* 3:115). As Hughes succinctly states, Milton "took his stand on the fact that 'Aristotle, and the best of political writers have defined a King, him who governs for the good and profit of his people, and not for his own ends' [3 : 202; *NE* 8. 11. 1]. Notwithstanding Milton's Augustinian conception of all human government as a sad consequence of original sin*, his picture of the first king as chosen 'for the eminence of his wisdom

and integrity' [3 : 199] reflects Aristotle's account of the origin of kings in *Politics,* 3. 9" (3 : 111). As Hughes notes, "Milton expected his readers to recognize his authority as Aristotle's discussion of the merits and origin of the various kinds of kingship. . . ." (3 : 199 n42). Hughes stresses the point that "the key principle of *The Tenure*—the distinction between kingship and its perversion, tyranny—is Aristotelian. So is its opening observation that tyrants are fond 'of bad men, as being all naturally servile' [3 : 190]. The same idea stands at the masthead of *Eikonoklastes* . . ." (3 : 111). Moreover, "In the *Rhetoric* [1. 2. 3] of Aristotle the speaker's object in his initial presentation of a subject is recognized as necessarily a vindication of his own character. In the gambit of *The Tenure* Milton gets his 'ethical' effect at the expense of the Presbyterians" (3 : 108). Shawcross, in his "Foreword" to *Tenure* in *The Prose of John Milton* (ed. J. Max Patrick [1967], pp. 337–45), also gives weight to Milton's knowledge of Aristotle: "In *The Tenure* Milton argues that the power of kings and magistrates has been conferred upon them by the people in covenant for common peace and benefit; when their power is abused, it is the people's right and duty to reassume that power or to alter it in whatever way is most conducive to public good. The people's natural rights as God's creatures predicate this conception of the social contract. Its elements as presented by Milton and its abrogation by tyranny should be read against the background of Aristotle's *Ethics,* particularly Book VIII, and *Politics,* particularly Books III, IV, and V, from which it often derives" (p. 341).

In this same edition, Hartmann, whose dissertation upon Milton's early knowledge and use of Aristotle is noted above, observes in the "Foreword" to his translation of *Prol* 7 that, unlike Plato's *Symposium,* Cicero's *Pro Archia Poeta,* and Bacon's *Advancement of Learning,* "Aristotle's influence . . . has been overlooked; perhaps it is merely taken for granted, since much of the curriculum at Cambridge was devoted to the study of his works and commentaries on them. Those unacquainted with that curriculum should be careful to notice that Milton's discussion of happiness in relation to virtue, to friendship, and especially to contemplation, and his emphasis on leisure as a prerequisite for contemplation, correspond to some of the major points in the *Nicomachean Ethics*" [*NE* 10. 7–8; see also *Rhetoric* 1. 2, for the three means of persuasion of which Milton was aware as a type of rhetorical pattern] (*Prose,* ed. Patrick, pp. 8–9). Hartmann makes the specific point that "Milton's speech in praise of learning belongs to the genre which in classical rhetoric is called oratory of display, or, in the opening words of the *First Prolusion,* the 'demonstrative' style of oration. Aristotle [*Rhetoric* 1. 9] specified that the device of amplification in particular should be used in this genre . . ." (p. 12). Such is typical evidence that in both method and matter, from the early *Prol* to *Tenure,* Milton turned to and drew from various works of Aristotle.

Impossible though it may be to exhaust the *loci*—the Ramists preferred "arguments" (Ong, p. 246)—touching Aristotle and Milton, demonstrating Milton's knowledge of Aristotle, it is perhaps less appropriate to speak of influences or indebtedness, of parallels or sources, than of some more elusive relationship, logical or illogical, that describes or defines just what existed and still exists as a common bond between two great and fertile minds. It may be that the question of Milton's substantial familiarity with the corpus of Aristotle is somewhat less complex than that of the extent or degree to which he subscribed to Aristotelian concepts. Obviously, the presence of Aristotelian concepts in Milton, however modified or changed, is far greater than is hinted by identifiable specific references and allusions. Milton may, indeed, have a preference for Plato greater than for Aristotle; but to name "Aristotle, our chief instructor in the universities" (6 : 136), and to speak of "that sublime art which is in Aristotle's *Poetics*" in his treatise *Educ* may be Mil-

tonic reminders that Aristotle still looms large. [PGH]

ARMINIANISM arose in Holland early in the seventeenth century in an attempt to mitigate some of the harsh doctrines of Calvin* and his successors. It takes its name from Jacob Arminius, a professor of Reformed* theology at Leiden from 1603 until his death in 1609; he insisted on his essential orthodoxy and maintained a moderate and conciliatory approach that was in accord with his recurrent pleas for liberty of conscience and mutual toleration* among Protestants. The full wrath of his opponents was vented against his followers at the Synod of Dort (1618–19), called with the express purpose of uprooting the heresies associated with his name.

In 1610 a meeting of Arminius's followers drew up a formal Remonstrance (from which they were frequently entitled *Remonstrants*), which affirmed against Reformed dogma that predestination represents the divine foreknowledge of the faith or disbelief of each individual, who is, however, not coerced by the divine will. The individual, that is, has some freedom of will to choose. This same position appears in chapter 4 of *CD* ("Of Predestination"), and *PL* 3. 98ff. Arminians granted man's depravity but believed that this fact is neutralized by the outpouring of divine grace* to each individual (the "prevenient Grace" of *PL* 11. 1–5) who may respond or not, depending upon his own choice. They believed that Christ's atonement* was for all mankind, depending on the choice of each, and not merely for the Elect (see *PL* 12. 404–10). On the other hand, anyone may successfully resist the outpouring of divine grace upon him; the experience was not, as it was for the Calvinist, irresistible. And finally, even after his conversion the individual may again turn to depravity, an impossibility for the Calvinistic Elect. The Arminian emphasis upon individual freedom is noteworthy; so is its implied tolerance, for in this belief anyone is potentially one of the Elect, in comparison with Calvinism, which recognized only the favored few among a generally depraved humanity.

Despite the hostile treatment meted out to the Remonstrants at Dort (with King James's full sanction) the movement later spread, especially in England under Laud.* As a communicant of the Church of England, Milton certainly felt its influence; his quondam tutor* Chappell* was an Arminian. But with his attacks on the episcopate in the early 1640s, Milton temporarily moved into the camp of the Calvinists proper; accordingly *Apol* (3 : 330) is hostile to the Dutch movement, and *DDD* ranks Arminians with Jesuits (3 : 440). As Milton became disabused of Calvinism he could still mention "the acute and distinct Arminius" as being "perverted" (*Areop* 4 : 313), but thereafter he never attacked the Remonstrants in any way. Rather, it is clear that he turned again to their position, sympathizing with them in *Way* (6 : 366; 1st ed. only) and expressly defending their position as scriptural in *TR* (6 : 168). And as has been noted, *CD* and *PL* are both Arminian.

But Arminius himself had died the year after Milton was born. The "Arminianism" of Milton's maturity traces to contemporary members of the group rather than to its founder. The most famous was Hugo Grotius*, whom Milton sought out in Paris on his trip to Italy; but more influential upon his religious thought would have been the purely theological writer Simon Episcopius (1583–1643) and perhaps Etienne de Courcelles (1586–1659). The former led the movement after the death of Arminius and wrote extensively and systematically upon religious subjects, pieces appearing posthumously in *Works* (Rotterdam, 1650, 1665), especially the *Institutio Theologicarum*. Another important statement of the 1620s was his *Remonstrant Confession*. Besides his systematic arguments upon grace and predestination in the Remonstrant tradition, Episcopius evinces a strong subordinationist position, asserting the inferiority of the Son* of God to the Father* and his beginning in time*. The relationship with Milton's so-called Arianism* is evident, and he may owe something to Episcopius's influence in this respect as well as in his interpretation of grace, free will*, and predestination*. [JD]

ARNE, THOMAS AUGUSTINE (1710–1778), well-known composer of numerous musical plays, oratorios, songs, including music for *Mask* and "Rule, Britannia" from *Alfred*. He also set music for a number of Shakespeare's plays, including *As You Like It*, *The Merchant of Venice*, *Romeo and Juliet*, and *The Tempest*. *Artaxerxes*, his version of Metastasio's *Artasersa*, in February 1762, caused much critical comment because it introduced Italian recitative into English opera. An honorary doctorate of music was conferred on him on July 6, 1759, by Oxford University.

His music for John Dalton's* adaptation of *Mask*, which interpolated material from *L'Al* for the new character Euphrosyne, has been popular since its first performance on March 4, 1738, at the Drury Lane Theatre. *Comus, a Mask: (Now Adapted to the Stage) as alter'd from Milton's Mask* had five editions that year (four in London and one in Dublin) and was often reprinted throughout the rest of the century. Dr. Arne's name was usually cited on the title page. Even in 1773 when George Colman's* revision of Dalton's text appeared, Arne's name continued to be given, despite the differences in text and music. *The Musick in the Masque of Comus. Written by Milton. As it is perform'd at the Theatre-Royal in Drury-Lane. Composed by Mr. Arne. Opera prima* (London : for I. Walsh, [1738]) offered the words and music in score. A number of reprints include one in the 1780s "for the Voice, Harpsichord, and Violin." The most frequent epitome of his work centers on his graceful and flowing melodies. The music has been successfully presented in recent years in the United States and the United Kingdom both in staged and in concert form. It is also available on records.

Arne's oratorio *Abel*, a "sacred drama

for music," was performed at the Theatre Royal in Drury Lane on March 12, 1755, and published in 1775. Its first performance was in Dublin on February 18, 1744, then called "The Death of Abel," indicating its source in Metastasio's "La morte d'Abele." When given at the Haymarket on February 8, 1764, it was named "The Sacrifice." Throughout it shows influence from the language, prosody, and imagery of *PL*. A clear example of debt is heard in the "Hymn of Eve," which was often excerpted for recital. [JTS]

ARNOLD, CHRISTOPHER, a German traveler, who met and became friendly with Milton in 1651. Arnold discussed and described *Areop* in a letter to a friend in Germany, George Richter. The letter is probably dated July 26, 1651, although the notation has also been interpreted as August 7. From this same letter it is known that Hermann Mylius* was residing in London during early 1651, on business for Count Oldenburg*; Milton probably had connections with him at this time. See *Georgii Richteri, J. C., Ejusque Familiarium Epistolae Selectiores* (Nuremburg, 1662), p. 491, for Arnold's letter. The reference to *Areop* is one of the earliest notices extant. On November 19, 1651, Milton himself signed Arnold's autograph album, having had John Phillips first write out a modified quotation in Greek from 2 Cor. 12:9 and an inscription in Latin. The quotation, "I am made perfect in weakness," probably refers to his then near-blindness. [JTS]

ARNOLD, MATTHEW (1822–1888), poet and critic. As poet, he exhibits a minor influence from Milton (see especially J. B. Broadbent, *Essays in Criticism* 6:404–17, for a discussion of *Sohrab and Rustum* and Milton). As critic, Arnold provides extensive and sometimes perceptive commentary on Milton and previous Miltonic critics.

In "Milton" (in *Essays in Criticism,* 2d series, 1888), originally read as an address, Arnold sees the "sure and flawless perfection of his rhythm and diction,"

or "the grand style" as he called it, as Milton's strong point, distinguishing him from the host of followers (Thomson, Cowper*, Wordsworth*) and giving him a place alongside the great poets of antiquity. Arnold sees two further areas of criticism of *PL* that have not yet been properly explored; one is the "management of the inevitable matter of a Puritan epic," or subject as Puritan epic*, and the other is "the architectonics" or structure of the poem. (See also E. M. W. Tillyard's address in *Church Quarterly Review* 148:153–60.)

In "A French Critic on Milton" Arnold examines the criticism of Macaulay (more rhetoric than sound ideas), Addison* ("rests almost entirely upon convention"), Johnson* (while often sound and robust, at many points "not sufficiently disinterested, not sufficiently flexible, nor sufficiently receptive to be a satisfying critic" of Milton), and finally the French critic Edmond Scherer. In Scherer, Arnold finds the most useful and perceptive critic, "well-informed, intelligent, disinterested, open-minded, sympathetic." Scherer, a historical critic (as Arnold points out), discusses the problems the modern reader has with Milton: "*Paradise Lost* is vitiated . . . by a kind of antimony, by the conjoint necessity and impossibility of taking its contents literally." And yet, while the subject may fail the modern reader, there is still Milton's "true distinction as a poet," his "grand style*." Arnold concludes: "Nothing is gained by huddling on 'our great epic poet,' in a promiscuous heap, every sort of praise." We must still confront the question: What do we, as modern readers, get from *PL*? While its fundamental conceptions have become foreign to us, the poem still lives. [WM]

ART OF LOGIC, THE: *see* ARTIS LOGICAE.

ARTHURIAD. Though the word *Arthuriad* does not occur in Milton's works, scholars have found it a convenient term for his projected epic on British legendary

history. The questions of how seriously
Milton considered an Arthurian subject
for his national epic, precisely what form
it would take, whether he actually began
it and whether the language was Latin
or English, when and why he dropped
the project and finally decided against it
have engaged scholars for well over two
hundred years. On all of these points
there are grounds for disagreement, and
it is doubtful that we shall ever be able
to answer them fully and with certainty.
Indeed, the *Arthuriad* may be one of the
persistent myths of Milton criticism.

The evidence that Milton planned and
began an epic on Arthurian materials
rests primarily on two Latin poems:
Mansus, composed during his visit to
Naples, and *EpDam,* written shortly after
his return to England from his continental
journey. *Mansus* devotes only four lines
to the British themes Milton hopes to
sing : native kings (*indigenas . . . reges*)
and Arthur waging wars even under the
earth (*Arturumque etiam sub terris bella
moventem*) or (*aut*) the heroes of the
Round Table and the shattering of Saxon
phalanxes by British arms (*Frangam
Saxonicas Britonum sub Marte pha-
langes* !). *EpDam* in turn gives a slightly
more detailed account of the poet's ambitions. They include virtually the whole
span of British history down to the conception of Arthur : Brutus's voyage to
Britain; Imogene's kingdom; the exploits
of Brennus, Arviragus, and Belinus; the
Armorican settlers under British law; the
magical trick whereby Uther Pendragon,
impersonating Gorlois, Duke of Cornwall,
begat Arthur on the duke's unsuspecting
wife Igraine : "[I shall sing of] The
settlers from Armorica subject at last to
Britons' laws. Next I shall sing of Igraine,
mother-to-be, through fateful trickery, of
Arthur; I shall sing of lying features, of
the taking of arms of Gorlois, guile, all,
of Merlin" (*EpDam* 165ff.).

Though both of these passages specifically name Arthur, they also include
material that is only tangentially related
to him. Moreover, they emphasize different aspects of his career. *EpDam* men-

tions none of his deeds and leaves him
literally *in utero. Mansus* refers explicitly
to only one Arthurian exploit, though it
alludes to two other subjects that would
almost certainly involve Arthur, directly
or indirectly, in the action. The feats of
the heroes of the Round Table might well
begin or end at Arthur's court, even
though the king himself might not take
an active role in the plot. The theme of
British victory over the Saxons would
probably include Arthur's battle at
Mount Badon—though Milton would subsequently express doubts as to Arthur's
role on this occasion. With the exception
of the rather general allusion to native
kings, all of the topics cited in *Mansus*
would appear to center either on Arthur's
own exploits or on those of his court and
comitatus. On the other hand, the subjects
mentioned in *EpDam* bring us merely to
the threshold of the Arthurian era; they
reveal Milton's continued interest in a
British legendary history as material for
poetry, but they do not show conclusively
that he was still planning a poem center-
ing on Arthur. Less than two years after
writing *EpDam* he was still looking not
only for a hero for his patriotic epic but
also for an epic form. In considering
"what King or Knight before the conquest
might be chosen in whom to lay the
pattern of a Christian *Heroe*" (*RCG*), he
makes no mention of Arthur.

The relationship between the subjects
enumerated in *Mansus* and *EpDam* is, in
fact, ambiguous. Do they refer to the
same poem or to different works? Do
they point to a single epic celebrating the
exploits of the Britons from Brutus's
conquests to Arthur's victory at Mount
Badon? Are the obvious differences
between the topics in *Mansus* and *EpDam*
attributable largely to the poet's desire to
avoid repeating in the latter precisely
what he had already said in *Mansus*? Do
the references in *EpDam* indicate a different poetic enterprise; or are they merely
an amplification and extension of Milton's
earlier plans? All of these alternatives are
possibilities, but there is no conclusive
evidence in favor of any one of them.

Except for the fact that both lists are exclusively composed of British topics and that all of the subjects in *EpDam* can be included under the heading *"indigenas . . . reges"* of *Mansus,* the similarities between them are not impressive. The only explicit reference to a possible epic on Arthur occurs in *Mansus; EpDam* offers no solid evidence for either affirming or denying the possibility that Milton may still have been considering a poem centered on Arthur's exploits.

Both lists, moreover, are sufficiently ambiguous to raise doubts as to the precise number of British poems Milton is planning. Are the subjects mentioned in *EpDam* to be treated in one poem or in several? Does the analogous passage in *Mansus* refer to the subject matter of one long epic, two poems, or possibly four? (Milton's use of the conjunction *aut* may be little more than a stylistic mannerism; if taken literally, however, it would appear to indicate a choice between alternative themes.)

The problem is further complicated by the ambiguity of the one line in *Mansus* that does refer explicitly to Arthur: *Arturumque etiam sub terris bella moventem,* which has been variously translated. The majority of scholars have interpreted it as a reference to wars waged "even" underground, but it can also be read as an allusion to an Arthur who himself is "even now" underground stirring up new battles—that is, the future wars that, according to widespread medieval belief, he would subsequently wage on earth on behalf of the Britons. Masson regarded the phrase *etiam sub terris* as a reference to "Arthur's retreat to Faery-land," but this has remained, on the whole, a minority view. Nevertheless scholars who have shared the more widespread opinion—that Milton is referring to subterranean battles —have found it difficult to identify these exploits or to suggest specific literary works in which Milton could have encountered them. Medieval prophecies of the king's future return from fairyland may present a subterranean Arthur, but they do not include subterranean battles.

On the other hand, there is little likelihood that Milton could have known an early analogue recently noted by Alastair Fowler and John Carey, "The Spoils of Annwfn."

Other scholars—Walter MacKellar, Merritt Y. Hughes, Douglas Bush, and others—have detected in Milton's line a reference to the British legend that Arthur was still alive in "the otherworld and would return to rule over the Britons." Allusions to this belief appear in the writings of Wace, Layamon, and Malory, and in a wide variety of less familiar texts. Though this interpretation does not represent Arthur as actually *waging* warfare beneath the earth, it nevertheless portrays him as sojourning underground, awaiting the time for his return to the world of men. But in none of these authors is there any indication that Arthur had ever conducted wars beneath the earth or would ever do so in the future.

The fact that Milton's allusion to a subterranean Arthur occurs in a poem addressed to an Italian nobleman gives additional interest to the Italian traditions that assigned him an underground abode within Mount Etna, in an area closely associated with the Fata Morgana. Gervase of Tilbury recounts a story of how a servant of the Bishop of Catania, seeking a stray colt, ventured into the dark interior of the mountain and encountered Arthur himself, reclining on a royal bed in a palace set in a spacious landscape. The British king informed the youth that he had been brought there after his disastrous battle against Modred and against Childeric (leader of the Saxons) and that he was still recuperating from his wounds. Variations of this tradition occur, as Arturo Graf has noted, in Italian, French, and Germanic poetry. It is quite possible, therefore, that Milton's allusion is merely a variant on the conventional conception of Arthur as *rex futurus,* that it functions as a descriptive epithet rather than as the summary of the argument of a future poem, and that it actually means little more than simply "Arthur, the once and future king." Milton is indeed singling out Arthur for special emphasis among the other "native kings" by mentioning him by name, but this reference does not specify precisely which aspects of Arthur's career the poet intended to celebrate or whether his poem would be exclusively devoted to Arthur.

Though *Mansus* indicates that Milton was at least contemplating the possibility of celebrating an Arthurian theme, it does not suggest that he had committed himself definitely to such a project, that he had actually selected a particular subject, or that he regarded an Arthurian poem as an enterprise for the immediate future. On the contrary, his own expression (*Si quando . . . revocabo . . . Aut dicam*) suggests that he had *not* yet made up his mind and that an Arthurian poem still remained a vaguely defined ambition for the indefinite future. Nevertheless several scholars—David Masson, Hanford, Tillyard, P. F. Jones, Parker—maintain that Milton actually began an epic on Arthur, basing their argument on the passage in *EpDam* relating how "eleven nights and a day ago" the poet's new pipes had fallen asunder under the strain of his lofty song, and had been unable to sustain the *graves . . . sonos* further. Parker interpreted the phrase *undecima . . . nocte* literally, concluding that Milton had actually begun the epic less than a fortnight before writing *EpDam*. This phrase, however, apparently echoes a line in one of Virgil's* eclogues (*Alter ab undecimo tum me iam acceperat annus*); it could be simply a pastoral* convention rather than a literally autobiographical detail. Milton's reference to the pastoral pipe (*EpDam* 156, 169) casts doubt on the assumption that Thyrsis's "grand song" belonged to the epic* genre. The lines on his British themes, and possibly the following lines on his hope to be read throughout Britain (*EpDam* 162–78), are represented as an account of the "grave notes" that Thyrsis had sung earlier and that he had been reserving under the laurel's bark for Damon's ear. Though this passage purports to be a recapitulation of an earlier song, its content is almost entirely

prospective; it is essentially a reiteration of a past statement of Thyrsis's future literary ambitions. (Conceivably the poet may be alluding to the lofty hopes expressed approximately a year earlier in *Mansus*. Though this would obviously require interpreting the phrase *undecima . . . nocte* in a very broad sense indeed —stretching eleven days to almost as many months—it is nevertheless significant that Milton's "grand song" occurs immediately after his account of his sojourn in Tuscany and immediately before his description of the cups that Manso had given him during his visit to Naples. Alternatively, he might be referring to an unfinished Latin poem begun after his return to England, or even to an earlier stage in the composition of *EpDam*.)

It is also possible that the entire incident of the broken pipes was invented in order to permit the poet to introduce the account of his epic ambitions obliquely and less overtly than in *Mansus*. Thyrsis is, after all, fully aware that he may seem boastful or vain (*turgidulus*); and he would surely have appeared even more so, had Milton openly asserted his epic plans instead of introducing them as a recapitulation of a hope already expressed in the past. As the passage stands, Thyrsis's exalted ambitions have been appropriately and decorously fitted into the context of his grief for Damon. As Merritt Y. Hughes has justly observed, in *EpDam* 155–60, Milton is suggesting that "his grief for Diodati . . . prevents him from prosecuting the poetical ambitions which we know from *Mansus* 80–84, that he cherished in Italy." There is no need to interpret the episode of the shattered pipes as authentic autobiography*; this detail may be merely a poetic fiction.

We have no certain grounds, therefore, for concluding that Milton had actually begun his epic on British legend and even less warrant for asserting that the "beginnings of an *Arthuriad*" were among his unfinished and unpublished manuscripts. The greater probability is that the epic plans were long-range projects, that he had no firm intention of implementing them in the immediate future, and that he had not definitely decided on which of several promising British topics to develop. In all likelihood he did not yet feel ready to undertake so arduous a task. Having exercised his powers on the humbler forms of elegy* and pastoral, he would proceed gradually and in due order to the drama, deferring the implementation of his epic schemes until his talents had matured. In the lines immediately following the statement of British themes, the poet declares that he will forsake his pipe or compel it to sing a British song ("aut patriis mutata Camenis / Brittonicum strides!") Most critics take this to mean that Milton will write English in the future, whatever the form.

Though Milton does not indicate the form and method of his poem (or poems) on Arthur—classical epic, romance epic, or episodic chronicle—any of them would have permitted him to include most of the British themes listed in *Mansus* and *EpDam*. For a more-or-less chronological arrangement he had the example of Ovid*, who had declared his intent to sing of the metamorphoses wrought by the gods from the beginning of the world (*ab origine mundi*) to his own times; Tillyard has noted that the vastness of Milton's design could be paralleled in Warner's *Albion's England* and Heywood's *Troia Britannica*. In *RCG* Milton would still be undecided as to whether the rules of Aristotle* or the order of nature* was to be preferred in structuring an epic plot, but he would not consider the possibility of a chronicle-structure for heroic poetry. If Milton attached any authority to contemporary theories of epic and romance when he wrote *EpDam*, he must have conceived his future poetry on British history as a series of separate though related narrative poems or else as a single poem constructed according to the model of classical or romantic epic.

In *Brit* Milton was to question Arthur's historicity: "who *Arthur* was, and whether ever any such reign'd in *Britain,* hath bin doubted heertofore, and may again with good reason. For the Monk of *Malmsbury,* and others . . ., we may well perceave to have known no more of this *Arthur* 500 years past, nor of his doeings, then we now living. . . . But he who can accept of Legends for good story, may quickly swell a volume with trash. . . . As to *Artur,* no less is in doubt who was his Father. . . . And as we doubted of his parentage, so may we also of his puissance; for whether that Victory at *Badon* Hill were his or no, is uncertain; *Gildas* not naming him, as he did *Ambrose* in the former." Arthur is said to have expelled the Saracens, "who were not then known in *Europe,*" to have conquered Friesland "and all the North East Isles as far as *Russia,*" to "have made *Lapland* the Eastern bound of his Empire, and *Norway* the Chamber of *Britain.*" But "when should this be done?" The history of Arthur, as Milton sees it, is fraught with "uncertainties" and "unlikelyhoods"; and even a historian like Buchanan*, who reproaches others "for fabling in the deeds of *Artur,*" relies on "those Fables" and believes things equally "Fabulous." When Milton finally introduced an allusion to Arthur in an epic poem, he indicated his full awareness of the fabulous nature of this material:

> . . . and what resounds
> In Fable or *Romance* of *Uthers* Son
> Begirt with *British* and *Armoric* Knights.
> (*PL* 1. 579–81)

Though the Arthurian legend had never regained the popularity it had enjoyed in late medieval literature, it did continue to attract poets in search of an epic subject. Luigi Alamanni's *L'Avarchide* (published posthumously in 1570) had portrayed Arthur's siege of Bourge. Closely modeled on the *Iliad,* this epic had assigned the British king the role of Agamemnon and converted Lancelot into an idealized Achilles. Spenser*, exploiting the "Tudor myth" of Arthurian descent, had chosen Prince Arthur as the principal hero of his romance-epic and as the exemplar of the universal virtue, Magnificence. In Ben Jonson's* opinion, "there was no such ground" for a heroic poem as "King Arthur's fiction." Dryden* once considered writing an epic "for the honour of my native country" on "King Arthur conquering the Saxons" or alternatively on "Edward the Black Prince . . . subduing Spain . . . ," but the most he could achieve on the former theme was an opera, *King Arthur*. Toward the end of the seventeenth century Richard Blackmore published *two* Arthurian epics. Stillborn, they received an epitaph from Dryden himself : "nothing ill is to be spoken of the dead : and therefore peace to the Manes of his *Arthurs.*"

Milton's *Arthuriad*—abortive, like Dryden's—falls roughly midway between those of Spenser and Blackmore. It is symptomatic perhaps of the decline of the Arthurian tradition that Spenser's epic remained incomplete, that the two major poets of the seventeenth century never wrote their Arthurian epics, and that the *Arthuriads* actually completed were poetic failures. [JMS]

ARTICLES OF PEACE: *see* OBSERVATIONS UPON THE ARTICLES OF PEACE.

ARTIS LOGICAE. Milton's *Artis logicae plenior institutio ad Petri Rami methodum concinnata* is a textbook on logic, done in Latin, as most textbooks still normally were in Milton's day. It consists of the *Dialectic* or *Logic* of the French philosopher and educational reformer Peter Ramus*, virtually intact, fleshed out by a commentary longer than Ramus's text. The commentary was worked up by Milton largely out of other commentators, notably George Downame* or Downham (Dounamus, d. 1634), Bishop of Derry. The title might be rendered in English as *A Fuller Course in the Art of Logic Conformed to the Method of Peter Ramus,* and can be referred to in brief form simply as the *Logic*.

The *Logic* was first published in 1672 and reissued with a new title page the following year, but it was almost certainly a much earlier composition of Milton's, most likely done within the years 1645–1647 (Francine Lusignan, *Artis logicae,* Université de Montréal, 1974), though various other dates from 1629 to 1648 have been proposed. It probably was occasioned by his work in teaching his nephews Edward and John Phillips and a few other boys. Milton may have later revised the manuscript somewhat before he gave it to the printer, although we have no sure indication that he did so. The work has not been published since 1673 except in collections with others of Milton's works. The only English translation published thus far is that by Allan H. Gilbert in *CM*.

Milton's treatment of logic does not deviate in any major way from Ramus's treatment in the latter's final 1572 revision of his *Dialecticae libri duo (Two Books on Dialectic)*. (*See* LOGIC, RHETORIC, AND MILTON.) The body of the work is preceded by Milton's own Preface and followed by a *Praxis logicae analytica,* abridged from Downham, a logical analysis of passages from literature, to which is appended an abridged version of the Latin *Life of Peter Ramus* by the Swiss Ramist scholar Ioannes Thomas Freigius (Freige). [WJO]

ARTS OF DESIGN, Milton and the. Milton's prose and poetry reveal a considerable knowledge and appreciation of the arts of design : painting, sculpture, architecture, and gardens. The poet wrote more specifically of architecture and gardening than of the other arts. His subject matter had something to do with this, but mainly he was better acquainted with these two. The English tradition in building and in gardening was never destroyed as was their tradition in painting and sculpture. The rich deposit of medieval and Renaissance art that formed his background was in a disorderly state. Art museums did not exist, and libraries were not well catalogued. In this era the arts were closely allied with literature in subject matter. In fact there was a very much closer relation between literature and the visual arts in the later sixteenth and earlier seventeenth centuries than has ever existed since. Both were supposed to serve a more than human purpose and to stimulate the moral imagination of man. The Bible narrative, classical mythology*, and medieval allegories* appeared in tapestries, title pages, sculptures, and paintings as well as in literature.

Once the schools and workshops for medieval painting were uprooted by the political and religious upheaval under Henry VIII, it was not easy to establish new ones. Under Elizabeth I, when trade declined with Italy and increased with the Low Countries, artistic ideas came to England through Holland, Germany, and the Netherlands. It is significant that neither Hans Holbein in the sixteenth nor Anthony Van Dyck in the seventeenth century brought into being a native school of painting on English soil. From 1540 to 1650 foreign arts and artists were imported, chiefly from the Low Countries. Though Italy was on everybody's lips, the engravings and architectural decorations that Englishmen knew best were pouring in, uninvited, from the Protestant Low Countries that traded heavily with England.

Painting in Old London was mostly portraits done by foreign artists and found in the homes of royalty, of the landed gentry, and of the well-to-do merchants. A taste for pictures of classical mythologies had not yet been imported from Italy, even though Sir Henry Wotton*, ambassador to Venice; the Earl of Arundel; and Charles I* were bringing to England many such paintings. The Earl of Arundel was a connoisseur of art and had a collection of painting and sculpture at his lovely home on the Strand, part of which was open to the public for a fee. The Royal Collection at Whitehall was also open to the public. Several inventories are extant of these pictures, which list among others Van Dyck's *Cupid and Psyche,* Scarsellino's *Tobias and the Angel,* Tintoretto's *The Muses,* Holbein's *Dance of Death, Adam and Eve* by Mabuse (Jan Gossaert), and

Hieronymus Bosch's *Hell.* The last two are especially relevant to Milton and will be discussed later.

Charles I acquired two famous collections: one of the Gonzaga at Mantua, Italy, full of paintings such as the *Triumph of Julius Caesar;* and from 1627 to 1645 the greater part of Peter Paul Rubens's collection, paintings by Leonardo, Raphael, Titian, Palma Vecchio, Tintoretto, Paolo Veronese, and thirteen by Rubens himself. Rubens was in England from June 5, 1629, to March 6, 1630, as a diplomat to negotiate peace. Milton was at Cambridge and could have seen him when Rubens received an honorary Master of Arts degree there on September 20, 1629. On this occasion Rubens gave Charles I two paintings, *War and Peace* and *St. George,* and was commissioned to paint the ceiling of the new Banqueting House at Whitehall. The canvases were complete in March 1636 and represent allegorically the reigns of James I* and Charles I by such figures as Justice, Peace, Plenty, and Virtues over Vices. In them the boys who load nature's harvest onto carriages measure nine feet. All proportions are colossal, and perhaps Milton thought of this abundance of plenty when he described Satan's banquet feast in *PR* 2. 337ff. Rubens's works must have had a staggering effect when they were seen in London, for by his standard all the other painters working in England probably seemed like pygmies. He influenced Charles I to purchase the twelve noble cartoons of Raphael (each twelve feet high) for use in English manufacturing of tapestry.

Milton lived in the Whitehall area, where the government furnished him and his family with an apartment from November 1649 until December 1651, and J. M. French states that he enjoyed some tapestries from the royal collection, which was being dispersed, "These are to will and require you forthwith upon sight hereof to deliver unto Mr John Milton or to whom hee shall appoint such hangings as shall bee sufficient for the furnishing of his Lodgings in Whitehall." Such biblical, historical, and mythological subject matter as the Samson story, Tobias, the Labors of Hercules, Ceres, Venus and Cupid, Triumphs of Time, Death, Fame, Chastity, and the like were woven into tapestry designs, and Milton could have seen many pieces in the great halls of his day (Whitehall, Middle Temple Hall, Cambridge college halls, Company halls in London, Westminster Hall, Hampton Court Hall) and in private homes.

There are several portraits* of Milton. In his childhood (1618) he sat for Cornelius Johnson (or Janssen) for a portrait showing a lace collar and a burr hair cut. Another was painted in 1629. He had his portrait engraved by William Marshall for a frontispiece to the 1645 edition of his *Poems*. In his 62nd year William Faithorne* drew from life and engraved a portrait for the frontispiece to *Brit*. In addition, the poet's always having a garden where he lived; possessing a family coat of arms in the form of a spread eagle; polishing his education with continental travel; being accomplished in music; and selecting hangings from the King's goods for furnishing his lodgings—all indicate that Milton was half Cavalier in his artistic taste.

Sculpture in Old London was not in a flourishing state. Monumental sculptors and stonemasons trained chiefly in Flanders made the gateways, busts, and monuments. The Earl of Arundel, Charles I, and a few others were bringing in classical sculptures from Italy; Inigo Jones was exhibiting facsimiles of classical statues in his stage scenery for masques. In Milton's lifetime sculptures from Italy began to make their way to London gardens and galleries. During the Renaissance classical sculpture, because of the vicissitudes it had suffered even in Italy, persisted in private collections. In Rome the two important ones were at the Capitol and at the Vatican. In Florence the Medici family had a collection. Medieval sculpture retained its home in the churches, except in Protestant England where the Parliamentarians "purified" many churches and chapels of painting

and sculpture. The demolition crews between 1643 and 1660 were not consistent: Westminster Abbey was left intact, as was King's College Chapel at Cambridge with its beautiful storied windows.

Old London was a walled city with eight gates, each of which had some sculpture as decoration. Around the wall clockwise they were : Ludgate, Newgate, Aldersgate, Cripplegate, Moorgate, Bishopsgate, Aldgate, and Posterngate. The Water Gate at the Duke of Buckingham's York House on the Strand was built after the new fashion in 1623 to 1626 by Nicholas Stone and was ornate and manneristic. At Charing Cross, then an open space at the western end of the Strand but today Trafalgar Square, was erected in 1636 the bronze equestrian statue of Charles I by Hubert le Sueur, a Frenchman who had trained under Giovanni da Bologna in Florence. Milton lived in the Charing Cross area from 1649 to 1651. A bust of Charles I carved in Rome by G. L. Bernini, from a picture painted by Van Dyck, is reported on in a firsthand manner by Nicholas Stone, Junior, son of the mastermason to Charles I, in the diary he kept when he was studying in Rome the very same month Milton was there, October 1638.

Milton took note of monuments and busts. He saw the tomb and bust that Manso had erected to the memory of the poet Marini : "our eyes have seen the poet smiling on us from the bronze so carefully wrought" (*Manso*). Old Manoa takes Samson's body home and foretells : "there will I build him / A Monument, and plant it round with shade / Of Laurel ever green, and branching Palm, / With all his Trophies hung, and Acts enroll'd / In copious Legend, or sweet Lyric Song" (*SA* 1734ff.). It is thought that about 1651 Milton had a bust made of himself, which is now at Christ's College, Cambridge. Certainly Milton was aware of the art of sculpture, but seems to have preferred it for commemorating the constructive and noble deeds of man rather than for an aid to religious devotion. He perhaps had seen the huge collection of sculpture at Arundel

House, estimated by some as better than that at the Louvre, comprised of 37 statues, 128 busts, and 250 inscribed marbles, besides sarcophagi, altars, gems, fragments of antique art.

Public architecture of Milton's London in the main was Gothic. Its buildings were chiefly churches (ninety-odd before 1666), civic halls of Companies, and row houses with part-walls and gabled roofs. Few appreciations of Gothic were written in this age of transition to a preference for classical design; but the young Milton penned one, which could have been based on Old St. Paul's Cathedral next door to St. Paul's School*, which he attended in his boyhood and where he learned

> To walk the studious Cloysters pale,
> And love the high embowed Roof,
> With antick Pillars massy proof,
> And storied Windows richly dight,
> Casting a dim religious light.
> There let the pealing Organ blow
> To the full voic'd Quire below,
> In Service high and Anthems cleer,
> As may with sweetness, through mine ear,
> Dissolve me into extasies,
> And bring all Heav'n before mine eyes.
> (IlP 156ff.)

Sir Henry Wotton and John Evelyn*, together with such designers as Inigo Jones, John Webb, and Sir Roger Pratt, were advocating the classical manner of building as practiced by Andrea Palladio and Vitruvius; but it was not yet popular, and few buildings in this style were actually constructed. Milton chose Vitruvius for an architectural text for his pupils, and even tried his hand at designing an ideal regional academy as a school for future leaders of the country where architecture and gardening were to be part of the curriculum (Educ 4 : 280–83).

In the 1630s Bishop Laud's* return to pre-Reformation ideas in the liturgy produced several Classic-Gothic hybrid church designs : St. Catharine Cree in London and Peterhouse Chapel at Cambridge are examples Milton would have known. Such taste for classical details as decoration on a basically Gothic design is evident in Milton's description of Pandemonium.

There was a great gulf between the taste of the Court and that of the City in the sixteen-thirties and forties. Jones was a Court artist self-trained in Italy, who advocated the new designs, regular (symmetrical) and classical with Corinthian and Ionic pilasters. Although to us he seems to dominate this period, not all his contemporaries would agree. The work of Jones afforded Milton the opportunity of seeing in his home town structural classical buildings taken directly from their Italian source : the Whitehall Banqueting House, the Queen's House at Greenwich, the Portico at Old St. Paul's Covent Garden Piazza and St. Paul's Church, and Somerset House and Chapel. Jones also designed costumes and scenery for masques, some of which Milton certainly saw, for his brother Christopher was a student at the Inns of Court, where masques were a specialty. Jones's most distinguished work is the Banqueting House, which still stands in the Whitehall area. It was unique in that day for its regular design and decoration. This new, exciting building was very like a Greek temple indeed, and on English soil as early as 1622.

Sixteen colleges, mostly Gothic, formed the University of Cambridge. The hall of a college was the most important room. Of the sixteen halls at Cambridge, Trinity College Hall (built 1604–5) was the outstanding one, just as King's College Chapel was the outstanding chapel. The fine roofs of these two halls differ in framing and decoration (one built in 1572 and the other in 1605), but they are both vaulted hammerbeam roofs. A description of Trinity College Hall has survived :

> The whole is roofed with old Oak Beams, very black & dismal, from ye Charcoal wch is burnt in ye middle of ye Hall; & over it in ye middle of ye Roof was an old awkward kind of Cupulo to let out ye Smoak. The Fellows' Table stands on an Eminence at ye upper or S. end of ye Hall, with a Door on ye E. side to go to ye Master's Lodge. The Back of ye Table of ye Fellows had ye Arms of ye College painted pretty high against ye Wall, & below hung a large piece of Tapestry. The

Scholars Tables are on both sides of ye Hall, which is paved with Stone.

See Robert Willis and J. W. Clark, *The Architectural History of the University of Cambridge* (1886). Milton speaks of "the Gates / And Porches wide, but chief the spacious Hall" (*PL* 1. 761–62) with "her stately highth" and her "smooth / And level pavement."

The two major architectural accomplishments at Cambridge while Milton was there were Peterhouse Chapel (1628–1632) and St. John's Library (1624–1628). In design both were a mixture of Gothic and the new classical decorations, as were St. Catharine Cree Church and the Portico on Old St. Paul's in London. All of these are associated with the Laudian Revival. At Oxford Archbishop Laud was sponsoring similar buildings. Milton perhaps associated Classic-Gothic buildings with Laud and his bishops, for architecturally Pandemonium, the glory of Hell, is such a design, as will be shown later. Innovations in the visual arts at Cambridge were in the form of classical decorations on gateways, fountains, and monuments, or Classic-Gothic designs of buildings. A college hall built as late as 1605 was still Gothic in design, based on civic halls in London. Since the young Milton lived here for seven years (1625–1632), the dimly lighted chapels; the stately, spacious halls; and the medieval gardens with their walls, their sparse planting, their walks, dials, arbors, and mounts became a part of his consciousness and later influenced in an undeniable but undeterminable way the poetry of the poet.

Milton loved a garden where he lived and wrote knowingly on gardening (*Animad* 3 : 158–59). Formal gardens, symmetrical with an axial arrangement in the Italian manner, were few in early Stuart England, just as were classical buildings. Not even when Charles II returned from France and tried to do something about the backwardness of England in architecture and gardening did the English people suddenly welcome classical buildings and formal gardens.

The English prefer a natural garden with useful things in it. Henry Wotton, Milton's friend who was considered by Charles I a connoisseur of art, as early as 1624 cast his vote for the natural garden, though he had spent years viewing the continental ones. Milton liked a natural garden. However, the poet also liked the small medieval formal gardens, part of the native tradition of his England. The favorite plan was a square with four paths leading to a little square in the center, where there was a statue or a fountain. The beds were laid out in extravagant and intricate designs. Though such a garden was related to the house, it fell short of participating in a single organic plan for the whole of the terrain as did the axial Italian ones. Statuary was used sparingly; topiary, profusely in these early Stuart gardens. There were alleys, covered walks, arbors, knots, labyrinths, mounts, small fountains, always enclosed within a wall. By contrast, the Italian garden on a grand scale made use of symmetry, terraces, balustrades, grottoes, even waterfalls, great flights of stairs, and an abundance of statuary.

In the early poems Milton is observant of the small English formal gardens with their medieval aspects that he saw in London and Cambridge. "Each lane, and every alley green" (*Mask* 311); "the cedarn alleys" (*Mask* 990); "the smooth enamel'd green / Where no print of step hath been" (*Arc* 84–85); "Hedge-row Elms, on Hillocks green" (*L'Al* 58–59); "arched walks of twilight groves"(*IlP* 133); "the dry smooth-shaven Green" (*IlP* 66); and "trim Gardens" (*IlP* 50) show his alertness to the enclosed English gardens. He is acquainted with the medieval knots, for the flowers in his Paradise are not confined "in Beds and curious Knots" according to "nice Art," but are scattered luxuriantly on "Hill and Dale and Plain" (*PL* 4. 242ff.). Even in his later poems the poet clings to medieval features of English gardens in "Yon flourie Arbors, yonder Allies green / Our walk at noon, with branches overgrown" (*PL* 4. 626–27); "The Woodbine round this Arbour" (*PL* 9. 216); "Among thick-wov'n Arborets"

(*PL* 9. 437); "the shade / High rooft, and walks beneath, and alleys brown" (*PR* 2. 292–93); and "City or Surburban, studious walks and shades" (*PR* 4. 243). The poet in 1637 thought of living at "some Inn of the Lawyers where I can find a pleasant and shady walking-ground" (*Epistol* 12: 29); the Inner Temple, Lincoln's Inn, and Gray's Inn were noted for their charming garden walks and shades.

Milton was sensitive to many charms of the small English garden and also to the variety and contrasts of a natural garden. That he personally preferred one above the other is not recorded, but the poetry leads this writer to believe that he would have liked neither a garden planned too decidedly by "nice Art" nor one too "Wilde above Rule or Art." He writes more lines on nature's beauty (his subject matter lends itself to that), but somehow he always contrives to improve on it. The full-time job of Adam and Eve was trimming and regulating the vegetation of Paradise : "Nature here / Wantond as in her prime, and plaid at will / Her Virgin Fancies, pouring forth more sweet, / Wilde above Rule or Art; enormous bliss" (*PL* 5. 294ff.). However, Milton's garden was not in every way a natural one, but rather a design "cast into a very wilde Regularity," as Henry Wotton proposed as the ideal of English taste in his day. Paradise was enclosed by a circular wall and had one gate out of proportion in size to the rest of the garden, like those shown in medieval paintings of Paradise : "One Gate there only was, and that look'd East" (*PL* 4. 178); "it was a Rock / Of Alabaster, pil'd up to the Clouds, / Conspicuous far" (*PL* 4. 554–46); and "The verdurous wall of Paradise up sprung" (*PL* 4. 143). Milton's "fresh Fountain" that rose up from a large river through veins of porous earth and "with many a rill / Waterd the Garden" (*PL* 4. 229ff.) is certainly made of nature, of various plants and flowers and native rocks.

The poet's Paradise is in a corner of the region of Eden upon the top of a steep hill. The sides of the hill were over-grown with thickets and bushes; above these on the hillside grew the loftiest trees. Higher than the highest of these trees sprung up the "verdurous wall," and within this wall grew a circling row of the finest fruit trees. This idea of a row of trees planted just inside a garden wall was a commonplace in Milton's Cambridge and London. The poet's feeling for symmetry is displayed in his descriptions of first one side of the view in the garden and then the other. On one side were flourishing groves of aromatics and groves of tropical fruit between which stretched "Lawns, or level Downs" where flocks grazed peacefully. On the other side were shady grottoes and caves overgrown with vines heavy with luscious grapes, and a placid lake reflecting the myrtles that fringed its bank. For the touch of symmetry in this scene (*PL* 4. 252ff.), for the tropical fruit, and for the grottoes, Joseph Addison's* remark that "Milton would never have been able . . . to have laid out his Paradise, had he not seen the . . . gardens of Italy" is quite to the point.

Beautiful gardens the poet could have known in the London area are those at the Inns of Court; privately owned gardens on the Strand at Essex House and Arundel House; perhaps the noblest garden in England, Wilton Garden, owned by the Earl of Pembroke; Old Spring Garden, situated at the east end of the Mall between St. James's Park and Charing Cross (Milton's house in 1649 opened on to this garden). Mulberry Garden in the reigns of James I, Charles I, and Charles II is now the site of Buckingham Palace. New Spring Garden across the Thames at Lambeth Palace was later called Vauxhall Gardens. Royal gardens near London were those at Whitehall, at Nonesuch Palace in Surrey, and at Hampton Court, midway between London and Horton.

Milton advised that youths should "see other Countries at three or four and twenty years of age, not to learn Principles but to enlarge Experience and make wise observation" (*Educ* 4 : 290f.). He himself had spent "a year and about three months" in Europe between April 1638 and July 1639. The overall effect on Milton of the abundance and the scale of the arts in Europe as compared to that in his home country must have been considerable even though not precisely measurable. His sensitivity to continental art and his observation of how it permeated the European scene may have had much to do with his deciding on the universal subject of man and woman rather than King Arthur as the subject for his epics. Everywhere he saw the Bible story and Greek mythology woven into colorful, beautiful creations in the visual arts, and no doubt he longed to do the same in literature.

To avoid confusion, this article will mention only three of the cities (Florence, Rome, and Venice) that the young poet visited and only certain items (those which show a close relationship to passages of Milton's writing) among the many, many pieces of the arts available to travelers in that day.

Milton writes specifically of Florence, which is in the valley of the Arno River, where

Through Optic Glass the *Tuscan* Artist views
At Ev'ning from the top of *Fesole,*
Or in *Valdarno,* to descry new Lands,
Rivers or Mountains in her spotty Globe,
(*PL* 1. 288–91)

an area that impressed him with its

Autumnal Leaves that strow the Brooks
In *Vallombrosa,*

about eighteen miles from Florence. Recollection of Italian autumn landscape is evident in his description of

a swarm of flies in vintage time,
About the wine-press where sweet moust is powr'd,
Beat off, returns as oft with humming sound.
(*PR* 4. 15–17)

The churches and religious houses in Florence were mostly Gothic and richly decorated. Within the city were three royal palaces: Palazzo Vecchio with a piazza in front and, to the right, the Loggia di Lanzi with many statues; the Medici Palace on Via Larga; and the Grand Ducal Palace (known today as the Pitti Palace). Beautiful statues dotted these palaces, including Michelangelo's *David,* a Hercules, an Orpheus, Neptune, Ceres, Venus and Cupid, Michael, Adonis, Madonnas, Pan, Jupiter, Vulcan, Judith and Holofernes; and Vasari's vast battle paintings of Florentine wars against Siena and Pisa were in the Great Hall at Palazzo Vecchio.

At Villa Castello, about two miles from Florence, was a great fountain of Hercules and Antaeus, designed by Niccolo Tribolo, and most likely here also were Botticelli's *Primavera, Pallas and Centaur,* and *Birth of Venus,* for these pictures are known to have been in the Florence area in possession of the Medici family at this time. *Primavera* or *Spring* (124" x 80", now in the Uffizi Gallery), is a happy, harmonious picture in which human beings are as natural as the flowers. Venus is conceived as a Madonna; Mercury, as a St. Sebastian. The Graces represent something new in art. Their beauty lies in the linear rhythm of the bodies and the veils undulating continually, yet without action. It is an incarnation of the eternal ideal of the dance. Milton turned to the metaphor of music and dance when he wished to express the highest joy, and in Paradise the "Universal *Pan* / Knit with the *Graces* and the *Hours* in dance / Led on th' Eternal Spring" (*PL* 4. 266–67). The Venus, the Graces, Zephyrus, and Flora of Botticelli's *Spring* may also have been in his mind as he worked out the pictorial scene of Adam's awakening Eve:

he on his side
Leaning half-rais'd, with looks of cordial Love
Hung over her enamour'd, and beheld
Beautie, which whether waking or asleep,
Shot forth peculiar Graces; then with voice
Milde, as when *Zephyrus* on *Flora* breathes,
Her hand soft touching, whisperd thus.
(*PL* 5. 11–17).

In the *Birth of Venus,* Botticelli's conception of Venus is not a Greek one; it is a Renaissance Florentine one. Conscious of her nakedness, she is nearer Milton's Eve than are any of Titian's Venuses. Eve is quite like Botticelli's Venus:

condemned, dragged down in torment. These lines from *PL* are an adequate summary of this colossal painting :

All knees to thee shall bow, of them that bide
In Heaven, or Earth, or under Earth in Hell;
When thou attended gloriously from Heav'n
Shalt in the Sky appeer, and from thee send
The summoning Arch-Angels to proclaime
Thy dread Tribunal: forthwith from all Windes
The living, and forthwith the cited dead
Of all past Ages to the general Doom
Shall hast'n, such a peal shall rouse thir sleep.
Then all thy Saints assembl'd, thou shalt judge
Bad men and Angels, they arraignd shall sink
Beneath thy Sentence.

(3. 321–32)

Milton follows the common opinion of his age by emphasizing the idea that Christ is a powerful, just, stern judge over the idea that Christ is the humble, gentle, merciful Messiah. Both ideas were represented in many *Last Judgments* and in many paintings of the benign Christ.

English travelers were charmed by Raphael's fifty-two Bible pictures in the ceiling of the arcades of one of the three open galleries that Milton would have had to walk through to get to the Vatican Library. That he used Raphael's idea for the creation of the animals in *PL* 7 has been pointed out by S. T. Coleridge, who confused them with the Sistine frescoes. But the animals' coming up from the ground at the creation also appeared in engravings in the 1568 Bishops' Bible that were probably based on Raphael's pictures. Raphael was a great illustrator and a great space-composer, and his painting *The Battle of Constantine against Maxentius* at the Vatican could have helped Milton lay out his battle in heaven. This painting and those at the Ducal Palace in Venice, such as Tintoretto's *Paradise* and the many grandiose battle scenes, must have interested Milton and awakened in the poet as nothing else he had ever seen a longing to try in his own medium, as T. S. Eliot* puts it, images "suggestive of vast size, limitless space, abysmal depth,

and light and darkness," which show up in *PL* and are appropriate "to the genius and the limitations of Milton."

Pinturicchio's ceiling frescoes in the Hall of Saints in the Borgia Apartments at the Vatican glorified the heraldic ox of the Borgia family by representing the myth of Isis and Osiris, the principal deities of Egypt, in a series of episodes. In one scene Isis is depicted in white drapery, finding the scattered members of her husband's body. Lifting in her hands the bloodless head of Osiris, she turns away her face at the horrible sight. His brother Typhon had tragically slaughtered Osiris. M. E. Seaton first pointed out that Milton's comparison of man's attempt at finding Truth with Isis's act of gathering the parts of the body of her husband in *Areop* (4 : 337–38) may have been influenced by the poet's seeing these frescoes. In *Areop* alone, written five years after his return from Italy, Milton gives the symbolism of the Osiris-Isis myth a sympathetic treatment. The whole image persuades the imagination that licensers are violating man's deepest religious instincts by attempting to prevent authors from seeking the torn body of their martyred saint, Truth. The reader's sympathy for the wronged Osiris is attached to Truth and his dislike of the cruel Typhon attached to the licenser. Milton is harsh and unsympathetic with the legend elsewhere. He could have seen the legend related to the figure of Truth on the title page of George Sandys's *Relation of a Journey*, and in many statues.

Walking from the library one could go into the Belvedere or Vatican gardens, where the choice statues of the world were, amid lemon and orange trees. There were exotic trees, curious fountains, shady walks, and a variety of grottoes. One fountain near the gate had water gushing out of the proboscises of bees (bees made up the coat of arms of Pope Urban VIII, 1623–1644).

The recently rejuvenated St. Peter's had been dedicated in 1626 by Urban VIII. When Milton saw it the building was practically complete except for Bernini's colonnade, finished in 1667, and the Sacristy, which was erected by Pius VI in 1780. Rebecca Smith compares Milton's Pandemonium with St. Peter's, his hell with Rome, and his Satan with the pope, but warns against pushing this allegory too far. St. Peter's is not exactly "Built like a Temple" (*PL* 1. 713) with its domed roof and three stories of decorative pilasters. The most convincing arguments she makes are the general effect of vastness and magnificence of the two; Milton's use of "conclave" and "consistory"; and his bee metaphor, comparing the Fallen Angels to bees (a symbol of the Roman Catholic hierarchy) plying in and out of Pandemonium. There were bees on the vines of the four pillars of the newly erected Bernini canopy over the high altar as well as bees on the fountain in Belvedere. Many features of Pandemonium Milton could have seen in several places: gates and porches wide, a façade with pilasters, architrave, cornice, and frieze, a spacious great hall, a high arched roof from which hung many oil lamps, and a smooth and level pavement. No one source will do; the building is a composite of many edifices Milton had seen in London, Cambridge, and Europe. But, in the main, Pandemonium is a product inspired by the visual arts.

Milton warms to the description of it, giving the outside first and then the inside. The exterior façade is evidently only one huge story (like Jones's Banqueting House) and has only Doric pilasters and pillars for decoration (no Ionic or Corinthian ones). The "Golden Architrave" and the roof of "fretted Gold" are more like exteriors in Jones's masque scenery than any exteriors of actual buildings. However, the poet may be transferring what he had seen of the interiors at St. Peter's at the Vatican, or St. Mark's or the Ducal Palace at Venice to the exterior of his "high Capital / Of Satan and his Peers" (1. 756–57). Milton adds to the architrave a cornice and frieze "with bossy Sculptures grav'n" (1. 716), and John Ruskin commented that Milton's "bossy" as applied to Greek bas-relief is a "most comprehensive and expressive" epithet to distinguish this Greek decoration from the flat Gothic kind.

The "ascending pile" had a "stately highth"; "her ample spaces" were covered with an "arched roof," as were the roofs of many great halls Milton could have known. Henry Wotton explained that an arched roof was a vaulted roof in the Gothic manner. Milton gives the "spacious Theatre" in *SA* an arched roof (1605), and the church described in *IlP* has one. Pandemonium's interior lighting, with "Pendant by suttle Magic many a row / Of Starry Lamps and blazing Cressets . . . yeilded light/As from a sky" (*PL* 1. 727ff.), was probably Milton's remembrance of the open hammerbeam Gothic roofs at Whitehall or Hampton Court lighted for masques, or at Trinity College Hall, Cambridge, lighted for plays. The chief room was "the spacious Hall" (1. 762), and after Satan's return from the earth, "that *Plutonian* Hall" with a "high Throne . . . at th' upper end" (10. 444ff.).

The Ludovisi Palace, not far from the Barberini Palace, dates from the seventeenth century; and its park of extraordinary extent was exceedingly beautiful. Along the garden walks were many ancient statues, including the *Dying Gaul*. In the Chorus's description of Samson, "See how he lies at random, carelessly diffus'd,/ With languish't head unpropt,/ As one past hope, abandon'd / And by himself given over" (*SA* 118ff.), Milton may have thought of the *Dying Gaul*. Many copies of it were dispersed through almost all Europe; therefore, Milton may have seen several copies of it as well as the original here at the Ludovisi Palace. The dying Gaul had competed in a public festival to make a Roman holiday, and it cost him his life; Samson was to perform in the public arena of a Philistine festival, and it too would cost him his life.

The Barberini Palace, designed by Bernini and situated on a hillside, had a double portico ascended by two pairs of stairs. The great hall had a frescoed ceiling and the gallery was full of statues and pictures. The theater at the palace was built in 1633. Milton was invited by Cardinal Francesco Barberini* (oldest nephew of Urban VIII and Protector of the English in Rome) to attend a performance at this theater; he gladly went.

On the ceiling in the garden pavilion of the Rospigliosi Palace was Guido Reni's *Aurora Preceding the Chariot of Apollo,* famous over all Rome. Perhaps Milton thought of this painting of the sun's chariot, with the dawn flying before it and seven nymphs—who correspond in number with the Pleiades—trooping alongside when he had the Pleiades dance before the sun at the creation :

First in his East the glorious Lamp was seen,
Regent of Day, and all th' Horizon round
Invested with bright Rayes, jocond to run
His Longitude through Heav'ns high rode:
  the gray
Dawn, and the *Pleiades* before him danc'd
Shedding sweet influence.
                                    (*PL* 7. 370–75).

The creation was in the spring, and in the marginalia of his *Euripides,* Milton noted that it is spring "when the Seven Stars rise in the morning [and] the sun is in Taurus" (*CM* 18 : 313).

Milton admired the government of the Venetian Republic, and most probably took an interest in everything in the Ducal Palace area, including the many statues and paintings. Andrea Rizzo's marble statues of Adam and Eve were on either side of the Giants' Staircase. Adam's mouth is open with a yearning sigh, and perhaps Milton thought of this when he pictured Adam as he learns of Eve's "fatal Trespass" : "[Adam] amaz'd, / Astonied stood and Blank, while horror chill / Ran through his veins, and all his joynts relax'd; / . . . Speechless he stood and pale" (*PL* 9. 889ff.).

On the walls of a small room at the Ducal Palace hung eleven canvases, four by Hieronymus Bosch : *Ascension of Souls to Heaven; Earthly Paradise; Fall of the Rebel Angels;* and *Hell.* Milton would have paid special attention to these panels by a Protestant Fleming whose other painting of *Hell* at Whitehall in London he no doubt knew well. It may have furnished Milton with the idea of a tunnel and bridge from hell to heaven, for in its right foreground was a large tunnel that bridged a chasm and had forms entering it. Bosch's *Ascension of Souls to Heaven* depicts the universe as a concrete cosmic shell with one opening, an idea that Milton also uses, which certainly changes the traditional design of the Ptolemaic spheres. The souls of the blessed are leaving a dark universe and ascending toward a bright area (heaven) through a tunnel of gradations of light, going from dark to the magic realm of pure light. These gradations in the painting are similar to Milton's degrees or steps up to God as indicated by the visible universe suspended from heaven by a golden chain (*PL* 2. 1005), or by steps resembling Jacob's ladder (*PL* 3. 510ff.), a way of getting to heaven.

In the Great Council Hall the wall paintings illustrated pompous episodes in the military triumphs of Venice, such as the Fourth Crusade and conquests of Zara and Constantinople. These large frescoes of battles, together with those at the Vatican and in the Great Hall of Palazzo Vecchio in Florence, may have influenced Milton's idea of battle scenes in heaven (*PL* 5, 6). The painting over the throne in this hall was Tintoretto's *Paradise,* begun in 1587. There are five hundred or more figures arranged in ellipses according to the order of the Litany, Angels, Saints, and the Blessed in increasingly larger circles around the Virgin, who is praying before Christ as the center. The figures are freely hovering and revolving celestial bodies, who perform motions, radiant from an inner light, each one animated and driven by his own spiritual power. Perhaps Milton was impressed by Tintoretto's interpretation of the heavenly regions, for he wrote of the mystical dance of countless angels about the sacred Hill (*PL* 5. 619). Seventeenth-century travelers preferred Michelangelo's *Last Judgment* to Tintoretto's *Paradise,* and Ruskin observed that they did for the same reason people read Dante's *Inferno* and not his *Paradiso.*

The piazza at St. Mark's Church commonly passed as the best in Europe, its buildings mostly Gothic. Marble columns, gold mosaics, and gilded cupolas formed a delightful silhouette against a blue Italian sky. John Evelyn* wrote of the five cupolas on top of St. Mark's Church; they "doe make very goodly faire globes as it were, seene a prety way off, which yeeld a great grace to the church," a prospect similar to Satan's first view of the World : "by break of chearful dawne/ . . . The goodly prospect of some forein land / First-seen, or some renown'd Metropolis / With glistering Spires and Pinnacles adornd, / Which now the Rising Sun guilds with his beams" (*PL* 3. 545ff.). Ruskin wrote in a letter from Venice, "I must quote his [Milton's] description of the temple in my chapter on St. Mark's: 'And higher yet the glorious Temple reared / Her pile, far off appearing, like a mount / Of alabaster, topt with golden spires.' Exactly what St. Mark's is. It was all gilded at top—in old time." It is easy to associate St. Mark's and its pinnacles on top of its towers and cupolas with the church Satan took Christ to in *PR* where he commanded him to stand on a point in mid-air to prove himself the Son of God :

The holy City, lifted high her Towers
And higher yet the glorious Temple rear'd
Her pile, far off appearing like a Mount
Of Alabaster, top't with Golden Spires:
There on the highest Pinacle he set
The Son of God.
                    (*PR* 4. 545–50)

Compared to his inadequate artistic nourishment in Old London, his continental trip must have furnished Milton a liberal education in the arts. The impact of such vast pictures as Michelangelo's *Last Judgment,* the Sistine ceiling frescoes, Raphael's paintings at the Vatican, Vasari's battle scenes in the great hall at Palazzo Vecchio at Florence, those on the walls of the Great Council Hall at the Ducal Palace in Venice, and Tintoretto's *Paradise* above the throne in the same room, on such a well-informed and curious mind as Milton's must have convinced him that the like on such a scale

had not yet been done in literature. In churches, in palaces, in gardens, he saw the Bible narrative and classical mythology depicted in the visual arts by glowing color and flowing lines. It is probable that his understanding of the arts of design considerably determined the subject he chose for his epics and his treatment of that subject on a magnificent and grandiose scale. [ALT]

ARTS OF EMPIRE, THE: *see* CABINET-COUNCIL, THE.

ASCHAM, ANTHONY (1618?–1650), Parliamentarian agent. Ascham, an agent for the Cromwellian government to Hamburg in August 1649, was appointed resident in Madrid in January 1650. The Council of State* made the appointment on January 16 and the Parliament approved on January 31. The appointment, one of several made at this time, aimed at upholding and renewing various diplomatic liaisons. Amendments and corrections to the commission's charges were made on February 2, and letters of credence and a request for safe conduct were prepared for Ascham by Milton two days later (*CM* State Letter 3). A letter to Philip IV of Spain, expressing Cromwell's desire for peace and friendship, is also dated February 4 (*CM* State Letter 4). But the day after his arrival at Madrid, Ascham and his interpreter, John Baptista de Ripa, were murdered (May 27/June 6). The news reached London on June 19, 1650. The assassins were John Guillim, William Spark, and four accomplices. Parliament demanded their apprehension and punishment, and on June 28 the Council ordered a letter sent (*CM* State Letter 13) with such demands as well as the return of Ascham's body and protection for his staff still remaining in Madrid. The six assassins were apprehended, tried, and condemned by the Spanish, but then were given asylum in a Roman Catholic Church (only Spark was Protestant). They escaped later and Spark was recaptured and executed. The remaining five were excepted from an Act of Oblivion in 1652 and provisions were made at this time for

Ascham's dependents. The representative of Charles II* to the Spanish throne during this period was Edward Hyde, Earl of Clarendon*.

Results of the affair continued for some years afterwards. To retaliate, Parliament demanded in July 1650 (and repeated the demand in November) that six persons who had sided with Charles II be seized. Among the six eminent Royalists taken on July 4 was Sir William Davenant*, who had been imprisoned at Cowes Castle on the Isle of Wight. He was sent to the Tower of London, where he remained until October 7, 1652, being freed finally through the intercessions of Milton and others. Correspondence between the Spanish and English exists in 1651–1652 that still alludes to the case. A letter of January 1651 (*CM* State Letter 7) acknowledges letters and a report by the Spanish ambassador, Alphonso de Cardenas, and urges speedy punishment of the murderers rather than absolution because of their religion. Another letter to Cardenas was ordered on January 30, 1652 (*CM* State Letter 8), and a contemporary copy in the archives at Simancos, endorsed in Spanish, was sent to Philip with a letter of February 15, 1652. The various statements urging punishment were translated and published in 1651, and the affair was a main problem in the Spanish treaty of 1655, *Scriptum dom. Protectoris,* allegedly put into Latin by Milton. On July 14, 1660, Ascham was listed along with Milton in *The Picture of the Good Old Cause drawn to the Life in the Effigies of Master Praise-God Barebones, with Several Examples of God's Judgments on Some Eminent Engagers against Kingly Government.*

Milton specifically refers to Ascham twice : once in the second edition of *Eikon* (5 : 286), thus dating that revision after June 19, 1650, and in his letter to John Bradshaw* on February 21, 1653, in which he compared Marvell's* potential favorably with Ascham's. [JTS]

ASCHAM, ROGER (1516–1568), English humanist, friend and pupil of Sir John Cheke*. After studying at St. John's College, Cambridge, Ascham was elected a fellow of his college and appointed reader in Greek and university orator. He subsequently served as tutor in Greek and Latin to Princess Elizabeth, as secretary to Sir Edward Moryson (the English ambassador to Charles V), and as Latin secretary to three Tudor monarchs— Edward VI, Mary, and Elizabeth. His *Toxophilus,* a dialogue on archery or "the schole of shoting," was published in 1545; and his treatise on education, *The Scholemaster,* appeared posthumously in 1570.

Milton's only explicit reference to Ascham occurs in *CB* (18 : 214) under the heading *De Foederatis* (Allies) : "Our league and union with the Scots a thing most profitable, & naturall ever by the Pope sought to be hindered. See Ascams Toxophilus 1. i. p. 38." As Ruth Mohl points out in her notes on *CB* (Yale *Prose* 1 : 502), Milton's page reference fits the 1545 edition of the *Toxophilus.* Mohl (Yale *Prose* 1 : 754) and Hughes (*Complete Poems and Major Prose,* pp. 105, 732) call attention to further parallels between *RCG, Areop, Mask,* and Ascham's *Toxophilus* and *Scholemaster.* [JMS]

ASSER, bishop of Sherborne, friend of King Alfred* the Great, and reputed author of a Latin life of Alfred. Though little is known about Asser's career and though recent scholarship has challenged most of the alleged biographical data concerning him, he is commonly believed to have been born in Wales and to have been a monk of St. David's abbey. Alfred's preface to his translation of Gregory's *Pastoral Care* refers to "Assere minum biscepe." The *Anglo-Saxon Chronicle* records his death under 910, and the *Annales Cambriae* under 908.

Archbishop Matthew Parker's edition of the *Life* was published at London in 1574 under the title *AElfredi Regis Res Gestae* (a title apparently supplied by Parker himself) and in Anglo-Saxon letters. It was based on a manuscript that had been previously owned by the antiquary John Leland, that subsequently passed to the Cottonian collection (Cotton

MS. Otho A xii), and that was eventually destroyed by fire in 1731. Despite protestations of texual fidelity, Parker took considerable liberties with his text, and his edition contained numerous alterations and interpolations. William Camden's* edition, published at Frankfort in 1602–3, was essentially a reprint of Parker's text in Latin letters. It contained, however, an additional interpolation—the notorious passage on Grimbald's quarrel with the king, apparently inserted in order to prove that the University at Oxford was already in existence before Alfred's time.

The *Life* has been described as a "curious mixture of chronicle and biography" (Stevenson, p. lxxx). Beginning with 849, the year of Alfred's birth, it ends abruptly with the year 887, even though it was allegedly written in 893 (Stevenson, p. lxxxii). Though much of the historical material is based on the *Anglo-Saxon Chronicle,* the final twenty chapters "are not derived from any source known to us" (Stevenson, p. lxxx).

In *Brit* (10 : 189–220), Milton cites Asser extensively, both in his text and in his marginalia, as an authority for events between the years 794 and 900. These direct or indirect borrowings from the *Life* have been examined in detail by French Fogle in his edition of *Brit* (Yale *Prose* 5 (pt. 1) : 245–96). In Fogle's opinion, Milton probably used Camden's edition, with its regular type, in preference to the Anglo-Saxon type of the Parker edition. Some of Milton's apparent borrowings from Asser were actually derived from passages interpolated into the *Life* by Parker and retained by Camden, while in other instances Milton combined details derived from later historians with stories derived from Asser (Fogle, p. 290). Thus, in his marginalia, he cites Asser, along with later historiographers, as his source for the story of the wicked Eadburga, wife of Birthric (10 : 191–92)—a theme that he had considered earlier as a possible subject for a British tragedy ("Brightrick . . . poyson'd by his wife Ethelburga . . . "). In Milton's opinion, Asser's authority rested primarily on the fact that he had been "an Eye witness of those times" (10 : 206); and for events not covered by Asser's *Life,* he turned to the *Anglo-Saxon Chronicle* as the most authoritative account (10 : 210) : "Yet these I take (for *Asser* is heer silent) to be the Chief Fountain of our story, the ground and basis upon which the Monks later in time gloss and comment at their pleasure." Among numerous borrowings from the *Life,* we may note Milton's double reference to Asser's opinion that the Danes had come "from the River *Danubius*" rather than from Denmark (10 : 207, 211).

In *CB* (18 : 143) Milton attributes to Asser (through Stow*) the story that King Alfred had "hung chains of gold and bracelets in the crosse high ways to see what theefe durst touch 'em, so severely was justice administerd against them." Nevertheless, as Fogle points out, this episode does not occur in Asser's *Life,* though it does appear in William of Malmesbury* (Fogle, p. 291). [JMS]

ASSOCIATES, PERSONAL. Entries for a number of friends or associates of Milton have been given separately : the Agars, Lieuwe van Aitzema, Arthur Annesley, Christopher Arnold, Samuel Barrow, Richard Barry, John Bradshaw, Valerio Chimentelli, Agostino Coltellini, John Amos Comenius, Abraham Cowley, Carlo Dati, Sir William Davenant, Miss Davis, Henry De Brass, Charles Diodati, Giovanni Diodati, Giovanni Battista Doni, John Dryden, William Dugard, John Dury, the Egertons, Thomas Ellwood, Charles Fleetwood, Antonio Francini, Jacopi Gaddi, Alexander Gill, father and son, Theodore Haak, Samuel Hartlib, Jonathan Hartop, Peter Heimbach, John Hobson, Francis Junius, Edward King, Jean de Labadie, Henry Lawes, Edward Lawrence, Henry Lawrence, Lady Margaret Ley, Antonio Malatesti, Giovanni Battista Manso, Andrew Marvell, Hermann Mylius, Marchamont Needham, Henry Oldenberg, Robert Overton, Nathan Paget, Samuel Parker, Leonard Philaras, Lady Katherine Ranelagh, Lord

Ranelagh (Richard Jones), John Rous, the Rugeleys, Giovanni Salzilli, Andrew Sandelands, Selvaggi, Cyriack Skinner, Ezekiel Spanheim, George Thomason, Katherine Thomason, Moses Wall, Roger Williams, Sir Henry Wotton, Patrick Young, and Thomas Young. A few others may be mentioned here.

Benedetto Fioretti (1579–1642), a grammarian and literary critic, was president of the *Apatisti* when Milton is thought to have visited the academy in Florence. Among the members was Pietro Frescobaldi, to whom Milton sent greetings in 1647 through Carlo Dati*.

John Hall (1627–1656), a precocious poet and essayist, sought out Milton's acquaintance through Samuel Hartlib* in 1646. They seem not to have met in 1647 when Hall settled in London, nor in March 1649 when he became a writer for the Council of State*. Hall was ordered to produce replies to criticisms of the government, including one to William Prynne* (*A Serious Epistle to Mr. Prynne* which attacks *A Legal Vindication of the Liberties of England against Illegal Taxes*), for which Milton may have commended Hall in a lost letter. Whether they ever met in person is uncertain. Hall was the anonymous author of *An Humble Motion to the Parliament of England concerning the Advancement of Learning* (1649) with an allusion to and echoes of *Areop* (pp. 28–29). He was also the anonymous author of *A Letter Written to a Gentleman in the Country, Touching the Dissolution of the Late Parliament* (May 16, 1653), erroneously assigned to Milton by George Thomason*.

The dramatist Sir Robert Howard (1626–1698) was a "particular acquaintance" of Milton, according to John Toland*. Toland quotes remarks that are supposed to have passed between Howard and Milton concerning the republican government and religion. Howard admired Milton, and, according to his widow, Milton liked Howard. It is interesting, therefore, that it is Howard who argues for blank verse* in Dryden's* *Essay of Dramatick Poesy* (1668); Milton added his note on the verse of *PL* in the second issue of 1668 (that is, in the fourth issue of the first edition). Howard's defense of blank verse first appeared in the prefaces to his *Four New Plays* (1665) and *The Great Favourite* (1668).

William Joyner (1622–1706), author of the play *The Roman Empress* (1671) and a Roman Catholic, reported that Milton was not a papist (according to Thomas Hearne) and that they were good friends.

Brian Walton (1600–1661) was curate of All Hallows, Bread Street, during 1624–1628. He later became Bishop of Chester and chaplain to Charles I; he was ejected from all his religious posts during the Interregnum. In 1652 he proposed a polyglot edition of the Bible*, but its expense required government subsidy. Milton tried to acquire support from the Council of State, but they concluded that the project was "more proper for the consideration of the Parliament." *Biblia Sacra Polyglotta* was published in six volumes during 1654–1657. It is conjectured that Milton aided both its content and its publication. Richard Heath*, who seems to have been Milton's student of that name, helped Walton in his work.

A clergyman from Dorchester, a Dr. Wright, visited Milton in 1674, according to Jonathan Richardson*, who repeats a description of the poet and his home. Nothing further is known of this friendship. [JTS]

ASSOCIATES, POLITICAL. Entries for a number of people with whom Milton had some connection because of his Secretaryship have been given separately: Anthony Ascham, John Bradshaw, Oliver Cromwell, Richard Cromwell, Sir Thomas Fairfax, Charles Fleetwood, John Goodwin, Sir Philip Meadows, George Monck, Sir Samuel Morland, John Thurloe, Sir Henry Vane, Georg Rudolph Weckherlin, and Bulstrode Whitelocke. Some political associates became personal associates (e.g., Hermann Mylius). Here are mentioned others of importance to the Interregnum government whom Milton may have known or worked with.

Gualter (Walter) Frost was the general Secretary to the Council of State* in 1649–1652. He died in March 1652 and was replaced by John Thurloe. He must have worked closely and often with Milton in discharging the duties of information disseminator, licenser, and foreign correspondent. Milton undoubtedly often received instructions for state letters from him, and copies of some letters exist in Frost's hand. Perhaps before they were dispatched he reviewed some of Milton's letters and wrote others himself. He was intimately connected, as well, with Hermann Mylius* and the Oldenburg* Safeguard. Entries in the records of the Council of State indicate that he was generally Milton's immediate superior. He was the licenser (that is, editor) of the governmental newspaper *A Briefe Relation of Some Affairs,* which appeared in 1649–1650.

Henry Ireton (1611–1651) was a well-known army leader and regicide, who was buried in Westminster Abbey on February 6, 1651. At the Restoration he was found guilty of high treason, and his body, along with Oliver Cromwell's and John Bradshaw's, was disinterred on January 30, 1661, drawn to Tyburn on a sledge, hanged until sunset, decapitated, and buried beneath the gallows. In addition to possible governmental commerce with Ireton, Milton may have known him through friends. Ireton had married Oliver Cromwell's daughter, Bridget, and she, in 1652, married Charles Fleetwood*.

William Lenthall (1591–1662) was Speaker of the Commons. With the death of Oliver Cromwell he became a spokesman of the government in its transition to Richard Cromwell's control. In 1660 he was one of twenty remaining Interregnum leaders voted to be executed. He signed some of the official state papers prepared by Milton, including the Oldenburg safeguard, and apparently relayed instructions to the Latin Secretary. He was also one of the presiding chancery* officers in the 1654 Milton-Cope lawsuit (chancery proceedings).

Henry Marten (1602–1680) was a member of the Council of State in 1649–1652 and 1660. He probably had frequent communication with Milton, particularly in 1649, over state letters and other duties that Milton discharged for the Council. Copies of two of Milton's letters exist in Marten's hand.

On September 8, 1657, a Mr. Sterry was appointed as a replacement for Sir Philip Meadows in the Foreign Secretary's office. He was one of the secretaries in attendance at Cromwell's funeral. This was probably Nathaniel Sterry (d. 1698). His brother Peter, who has sometimes been suggested as the secretary, was Cromwell's chaplain. He died in 1672. It is interesting to note that he copied out the first seven lines of *SolMus* from the 1645 *Poems*; they are found in a manuscript at Emmanuel College, Cambridge, where he was a student from 1629–1637. This secretary, whether Nathaniel or Peter, would have worked under and with Milton in the last years of the Protectorate. [JTS]

ASSOCIATION COPIES, books thought at one time or another to have been owned by Milton or his immediate family, for example, family Bibles*, and books written by him or others presented to friends. Books that he is known to have owned and books with which he showed a marked familiarity through quotation or allusion are generally included in Milton's library*. Scholars have disproved claims for some alleged association copies; other books have simply disappeared. Eighteenth- and nineteenth-century booksellers' catalogues frequently advertised books with associative value based on family tradition, a smudged signature, the initials "J.M.," autograph notes, and the like. One such example is *Les Delices de la Suisse,* an otherwise unknown volume, for which a Mr. Herber outbid Thomas DeQuincey in 1809; it allegedly had Milton's holograph notes in the margins. More vexing is a copy of Pindar's works with marginal notes, long thought to be in Milton's holograph. The notes were published as authentic in *CM,* but Maurice Kelley and Samuel D. Atkins have shown conclusively that they are not in Milton's hand (see *Studies in Bibliography* [1964]). The volume is owned by the Houghton Library, Harvard University.

Many books allegedly in Milton's private library are now lost. A volume by Theodore Beza*, described as portraits of religious reformers (probably the *Icones,* Geneva, 1580), with Milton's purported autograph, was listed in a catalogue of an autograph collection in Paris in the late nineteenth century, but it has since disappeared. The catalogue also lists as Milton's a book attributed to James V of Scotland; this was *Navigation du roy d'Ecosse,* written by Nicolas de Nicolay, sieur d'Arfeuille et Bel-Air (sometimes Anglicized to Arville). But the DNB also attributes authorship to Alexander Lindsay, the ship's pilot on the occasion of the king's circumnavigation of his realm. The volume, since lost, should contain Milton's autograph and two lines in his own hand, if indeed it is authentic. An item sold by Sotheby's, which has since disappeared, is James I's* *A Remonstrance for the Right of Kings* (Cambridge, 1619); it reportedly included Milton's signature and some notes. Likewise lost are several Bibles said to have belonged to Milton besides the authentic one now in the British Museum, a Geneva Bible (1560), 1581, a Breeches Bible (1588), 1599, 1613 (1614?), a Hebrew Bible (the gift of Thomas Young*), a polyglot Bible (probably Brian Walton's edition), and an edition of the Psalms (1639). Other alleged association copies whose whereabouts are unknown are the *Flores Solitudinis* of Juan Eusebio Nieremberg, translated as *Meditations* (London, 1654) by Henry Vaughan; Joannes Bartholomaeus Marlianus's *Urbis Romae Topographia* (Venice, 1538); Ovid's* *Metamorphoses* (Frankfurt, 1563); Henry Peacham's *Valley of Varietie* (London, 1638); the works of Seneca translated by Thomas Lodge (London, 1620); Florio's translation of Montaigne's *Essays* (London, 1613); and Pascal's *Les Provinciales, or, The Mystery of Jesuitisme* (London, 1658).

A copy of *Apologia per Confessione* (n.p., 1629) was said, in 1883, to have the initials *J. M.* on the title page.

Books with conflicting accounts of authenticity are more tiresome than books merely lost, for there is always the chance that a lost book may come to light and prove to be authentic. A copy of *William Browne's* *Britannia's Pastorals* (London, 1613–1616), in a private collection, contains many marginalia thought by the editors of *CM* to be Miltonic, but recent scholarship dismisses the claim. The New York Public Library has a number of disputed Milton books : a copy of Sir Anthony Fitzherbert's *La Vieux Natura Brevium* (1548) with a signature, inscription and notes, belonged to Milton's father. Thomas Cooper's *Thesaurus Linguae Romanae et Britannicae* (1573), claimed as Milton's by John Payne Collier, is likewise rejected. Ruth Mohl's speculation of holograph marginalia in John Sleidan's* *De Statu Religionis et Reipublicae* (Strasbourg, 1555) has unfortunately been noticed by those who have not looked at the volume itself. Neither are the manuscript notes convincing in the Bodleian copy of Paul Best's *Mysteries Discovered* (London, 1647), nor in Harvard's copy of Thomas Farnaby's *Systema Grammaticum* (1641). The copy of William Ames's* *Conscientia* (Amsterdam, 1635) in the Princeton Library may or may not have been Milton's, but Edward Phillips related that he and his brother studied the text under Milton's tutelage. Other questionable books from Milton's library include Nicodemus Frischlin's *Operum Poeticorum* (Strasbourg, 1595), encased in oak boards from Milton's Barbican house, in the Harvard Library; Olaus Magnus's *Epitome de Gentibus Septemtrionalibus* (Antwerp, 1558) at the Milton Cottage at Chalfont; Richard Smith's *The Middle State of Souls,* translated by Thomas White (1659), now in the University of Illinois Library; and *Negotiation de la paix* (1576) in the Library of Congress.

Students interested in the problems of Milton's library may profitably consult the commentary and notes in Parker's *Milton,* and Jackson C. Boswell's *John Milton's Library.* [JCB]

ASTRONOMY: *see* COSMOLOGY; SCIENCE, MILTON AND

AT A SOLEMN MUSICK. This 28-line poem appeared in both the 1645 and 1673 editions of Milton's poems. Three and a half drafts of it appear in *TM,* the indications being that Milton composed it there shortly after commencing the manuscript itself. Its date of composition therefore depends upon when Milton began the manuscript, a date traditionally assigned to the early 1630s but more recently to 1637 by John T. Shawcross (*Modern Language Notes* 75 : 11–17).

The three-and-a-half drafts tell us much about Milton's habits of composition. The first contains the essential outlines of the last, suggesting that Milton had the poem blocked out in his mind before ever setting it down on paper. Having blocked out the poem, he then subjected it to intense line-by-line criticism. The best study of that process is P. L. Heyworth's (*Bulletin of the New York Public Library* 70 : 450–58). Professor Heyworth demonstrates that Milton's revisions show him keenly aware of euphony and of decorum, trying to make each phrase sound right while tailoring it to enhance the effect of dignity that he wanted the entire poem to achieve. Euphony, for example, dictated his changing the phrase, "sacred Psalmes / singing," which appears in the first and second drafts, to "holie Psalmes singing" in the second and succeeding drafts in order to avoid excessive alliteration, while decorum led him to omit the description in the first draft of "youthf[ul cher]ubim as "sweet-winged squires" from subsequent ones, "squires" seeming perhaps too earthbound for heavenly creatures. Having subjected each line to careful scrutiny, Milton once again considered the poem as a whole, excising a number of lines and significantly expanding the last part (lines 19–25 in the final draft) in order

to strengthen the firm and subtle structure of the poem's final version.

In its final version, the poem divides into three parts. In lines 1–16, the poet hears solemn music, a blending of voice and verse. It is worth noting that "solemn" in the seventeenth century possessed none of the somber overtones it now has. Rather, it suggested festivity, albeit of a stately and formal nature, so that it is entirely appropriate that this music present to the poet's "high-rais'd phantasie" the heavenly music made when the angelic spirits join in song with the souls of the faithful "before the saphire-colour'd throne." In lines 17–24, the poet hopes that we may join in that music as we were able to do before sin destroyed the universal harmony of which we were once a part. In lines 25–28, he concludes with a brief supplication that it be not long until we renew that song, God uniting us to his celestial consort "To live with him, and sing in endles morn of light."

Metrically, *SolMus* is a rather free imitation of the Italian madrigal form. Most of its lines are pentameter, although there are three seven-syllable lines and a concluding Alexandrine. The first four lines rhyme *a b a b.* Thereafter, the poem disposes itself into couplets with the exception of lines 9 and 15, which rhyme with each other. It divides into only two sentences; and these are by no means of equal length, the first two parts combining into a sentence of 24 lines and the second into one of only 4 lines. The ingenuity with which the syntax is handled in the first sentence is remarkable, an early example of "the sense variously drawn out from one Verse into another" that was to be the metrical strategy employed by Milton to such marvelous effect in *PL.*

Long and complex traditions lie behind the ideas in the poem. That music could induce ecstasy, that it had beneficent effects upon its auditors, that the world itself was constructed on musical lines —these ideas, which are as old as the Pythagoreans* and Plato*, had been enriched by many centuries of repetition and commentary when they reached Milton. Because of his musical bent, they were especially appealing to him, and it is interesting to note their appearance in his other poems, although as always, Milton is selective in utilizing tradition. Significantly, for example, the "solemn music" is not music alone, but a blending of music and poetry. The emphasis on the closeness of the arts is traditional, but it is also characteristically Miltonic. He referred to them in *AdP* as "arts of one blood and kindred studies" and especially praised his friend Henry Lawes* for teaching English music how to fit itself to the sense and rhythm of the lyrics for which he wrote.

In keeping with the practices of his age, Milton adorned his poem with materials drawn from classical and pagan literature. The sirens whose powers he invokes in the opening lines, for example, derive from figures who appear in the *Odyssey* and in the *Argonautica* of Apollonius of Rhodes. Their ability to pierce "dead things with inbreath'd sense" suggests other classical legends—that of Orpheus*, whose beautiful music attracted trees and rocks to him, and that of Amphion, whose music caused stones to move and build themselves into the walls of Thebes. Such materials, however, have been Christianized and coexist easily with the details of the heavenly music drawn from the Book of Ezekiel and from the Book of Revelation. [ERG]

AT A VACATION EXERCISE IN THE COLLEGE. First published in the 1673 *Poems* with a note indicating composition at age nineteen, *Vac* should be read in conjunction with Milton's *Prol* 6, of which it was a part. The prolusion was written to be delivered at the Vacation Exercise of July 2, 1628, which opened the long summer holiday. Most of our knowledge of the Exercise derives from Milton's performance. From it we learn that the Exercise was given "according to custom, with almost all of the young men of the institution assembled" and that it was "the almost annual observance of a very old custom." The master of ceremonies,

in this case Milton, was known as "Father," while the other participants in the program were introduced as his "sons."

The portions of Milton's performance that have survived divide into three sections : (1) a Latin oration on the subject "That sometimes sportive exercises are not prejudicial to philosophic studies"; (2) a more informal address, still in Latin, filled with bawdy, topical humor; (3) a set of English verses. At the conclusion of the verses, a note observes that *"The rest was Prose";* but whatever this may have been —perhaps Milton's introduction of his other "sons," perhaps some concluding remarks—it has been lost. Milton's switch from Latin prose to English poetry must have been surprising to his audience, for it was against university statutes. His rhetorical excuse, Parker notes, "would be a preamble to introducing his 'sons' " (*Milton,* p. 45). More basic may have been a well-founded desire to show what he could do in English verse as opposed to Latin prose.

Written in couplets, the verse reveals a variety of influences—Jonson*, Spenser*, and Drayton; but it is not merely derivative. In the lines where Milton lists possible epic subjects, he speaks—perhaps for the first time—with his own unique accent. His list of epic subjects rounds out a number of interesting comments on poetry and language. Having stated that he has "packt the worst" into the Latin portions of his address, he admonishes the English language to bring from its wardrobe its "chiefest treasure" :

Not those new fangled toys, and triming slight
Which takes our late fantasticks with delight
. . . .

The identity of these "late fantasticks" is debatable. W. J. Harvey has suggested that the fad indicated is the "cult of 'strong lines' " associated with the Metaphysicals (*Notes and Queries* 202 : 524). Perhaps, however, we should not look so far afield for an identification. Having noted that "the midsummer frolic for which these verses were written consisted of numerous skits and recitals," John T. Shawcross tentatively suggests that "Milton's fellow performers were the 'late fantasticks'" (*The Complete English Poetry of John Milton* [1963], p. 33). Milton, at any rate, wished to give his audience more. For his "fair Assembly's ears," he wished to clothe his "naked thoughts" in the "richest Robes" that English could offer, but he frankly admitted that he would rather use English for "some graver subject." He then listed some topics that he regarded as appropriate for serious English poetry. The list is of great interest for Milton's future poetic ambitions, although one need not assume that Milton at this point was dedicating himself to epic poetry. At nineteen, he had a disposition toward the serious that the years were to confirm, but for the present he was content merely to glance at suitably epic subjects, then to proceed to the introduction of his "sons."

For the occasion, Milton had assumed the role of *Ens*, the Aristotelian* principle of Absolute Being. His eldest son was Substance; his other sons, the accidents of Substance: Quantity, Quality, Relation, Place, Time, Posture, Possession, Action, and Passion. Milton's humor is topical throughout, its topicality being divisible into two kinds: (1) that devoted to the scholastic logic so familiar to his audience; (2) that devoted to the persons taking part in the celebration. An example of the first kind is his professing fear that Substance, according to a prophecy, "Shall subject be to many an Accident." This is amusing because in scholastic logic, Substance could only be known through its "accidents." An example of the second is his using the name of the boy who played Relation, Rivers, as the excuse for his working in a Spenserian catalogue of English rivers. Perhaps another example of this kind of humor is his telling Substance that "O'er all his Brethren he shall Reign as King," for it may be that Edward King*, whom Milton later commemorated in *Lyc,* took the part of Substance. [ERG]

ATONEMENT, THE. The Atonement has never been defined by the Church in the sense that the triune Godhead and the dual nature of the Christ have been dogmatically affirmed. It remains a mystery whose capital aim is to uphold the "at-one-ment" of God and man through the Christ Jesus.

Of the four major theories of the Atonement normally distinguished by historians of dogma, the earliest revolved about the Pauline statement that "as by one man's disobedience many were made sinners, so by the obedience of one shall many be made righteous" (Rom. 5:19). This view of Jesus as the second Adam was early enforced by such apologists as Justin Martyr, who introduced the concept of Mary as the second Eve (*Dial. cum Tryph.* 3), and Irenaeus, who stressed the parallel between the tree of knowledge in Eden and the tree of Calvary that was used to build the Cross (*Adv. haer.* 5. xvii, 3). From this premise it was argued that the Christ "recapitulated" in his Person the entire human race and that he achieved man's redemption as the representative of mankind (cf. Eph. 1:10).

A second interpretation—the "ransom" theory—maintained that the Son* gave his life as a ransom for many and was incarnated so "that through death he might destroy him that had the power of death, that is, the devil" (Mark 10:45, Matt. 20:28, Heb. 2:14). While several Fathers accepted the view that the ransom for man's acquittal was paid to Satan, a number of extreme views led in time to a violent reaction. "Since a ransom belongs only to him who holds in bondage," wrote Gregory of Nazianzus, "I ask to whom was this offered, and for what cause? If to the Evil One, fie upon the outrage!" (*Orationes* 45. 22).

The most popular theory of the Atonement proved to be St. Anselm's interpretation in *Cur Deus homo*? Man's first disobedience was now seen as a violation of the honor of God; and before normal relations with the Deity could be reestablished, "satisfaction," in the sense of reparation for the dishonor caused, had to be rendered. In Anselm's terms, since no one could satisfy God except God himself, and since no one ought to do so save man, the task had to be assigned to "one who is God-man" (2. 6).

The interpretation advanced by the Reformers retained elements from the previous theories but emphasized in juridical terms that the Atonement was a legal transaction, a "contract" (to use Donne's favorite word), whereby the debt paid to the Supreme Judge was considered to be both the satisfaction demanded by divine justice and the just punishment required for our sins. Protestants, led by Luther's* statements in his commentary on Romans (3 : 3; 4 : 19, etc.) and by Calvin's* in his *Institutes* (2. xii. 3, etc.), inadvertently distinguished between the Father* as the guardian of divine justice and the Son as the exclusive manifestation of divine love —precisely the emphasis upheld by the earlier tradition of the contending "four daughters of God" (cf. Ps. 85 : 10), whom Giles Fletcher* in *Christ's Victory and Triumph* (1610) reduced to two, Justice and Mercy.

The same distinction, and the same "severe contention," appear in *PL* 3. Elements of the previous theories were retained by Milton as by the Reformers: the Anselmic stress on satisfaction, drastically qualified, is present at every turn; the ransom theory is also stated explicitly, with the Father as the recipient of that ransom (3. 221; 10. 61; 12. 424); and the recapitulation theory is likewise expounded, with the Christ regarded as the second Adam (3. 285ff.; 11. 383), but also with Mary viewed as the second Eve (3. 387; 10. 183). At the same time Milton re-created the very atmosphere of the criminal law court already present in Protestant theology. Man, we are told again, disobeyed the divine behest and brought death upon himself and posterity; the divine decree that created him immortal could not be revoked, being, like all heavenly laws once enacted, "Unchangeable, Eternal" (3. 127); to rescind

it was to go against the prescribed standards of divine justice : "Die hee or Justice must" (3. 210); someone had to substitute for man and thereby pay the "rigid satisfaction, death for death" (3. 212). Milton's contemporaries likewise state that the satisfaction exacted by the Father was marked by its "rigour and severity." But as Lancelot Andrewes* observed, "GOD [cannot] *forgive* offences to Him made. . . . His *Justice* and *truth* are to Him as *essentiall*, as *intrinsecally essentiall*, as His *Mercy* : of equal regard every way as deare to Him. *Justice* otherwise remains unsatisfied : and satisfied it must be, either on Him, or on us" (*XCVI Sermons* [1641], p. 101). [CAP]

ATTRIBUTIONS. Over the years various tracts, poems, and other items have been attributed to Milton, sometimes because of the subject matter, sometimes because of initials attached, sometimes as hoaxes. Following is a list alphabetized by title or by identifying terms of such tracts or poems which are known to have no connection with Milton or which are not given serious consideration as Milton's today. However, at times a title may still be found in library catalogues under Milton's name. *See also* ADAPTATIONS, LITERARY; CANON; and PAPERS, STATE. Given here is the date of first publication only, which is not necessarily the date of attribution :

"Ad Christinam Reginam" (1681), also attributed to Marvell*; first line : "Bellipotens virgo, septem Regina Trionum."
Alarum to the Officers and Souldiers of the Armies, An (1660).
Argument or Debate in Law: of the Great Questions concerning the Militia, A (1642), by J[ohn] M[arch?].
"Breif Description of Genoa, A," essay in Columbia MS, pp. 4–5.
Breviary of the History of the Parliament, A (1650), English translation of *Historiæ Parliamenti Angliæ Brevarium . . . autore T. M.* (1650), by Thomas May*.
Canterburies Dreame (1641).
Copy of a Letter from an Officer of the Army in Ireland, A [1656], by R[ichard] G[oodgroom?].

"Directions to a Painter," four poems all with the same title in *Poems on Affairs of State* (1697), also attributed to Sir John Denham; first lines: "Nay Painter, if thou dar'st design that Fight," "Sand—ch in *Spain* now, and the Duke in love," "Draw *England* ruin'd by what was giv'n before," "Painter, where was't thy former work did cease."

Discourse Shewing in What State the Three Kingdoms Are in, A (1641).

Distich on Alexander More* (1652), "Ad Bontiam Salmasiae Domesticam"; first line: "Galli è Concubitu Gravidam Te, Pontia, Mori."

Epigram on Pope Urban VIII (1692), also attributed to Thomas Brown; first line: "Estne Papa Christianus?"

Epigrams on Prince Charles (1636), one in Latin, one in English, also attributed to John Meredith; first lines: "Vivat io Vivat Principes Carolinus, et Orbi," "Flourish braue Prince, out shine thy Glorious Name."

Epistola ad Pollionem, Miltonis (1st ed. in Latin, 1738; in English, 1740), by William King.

Epitaph on a Rose Tree, manuscript, in copy of the 1645 *Poems*, by J. [?] M., dated October 1647; first line: "He whom Heaven did call away."

Epitaph on Cardinal Mazarin (1692), sixty-eight lines, also attributed to Thomas Brown; first line: "Hic jacet Julius Mazirinus."

"Epitaph on Madam Elizabeth Swettenham, An" (after 1673); manuscript; first line: "If cheerfull, chaste as the snows."

"Epitaph on Moll Cutpurse," verse epitaph on Mrs. Mary Frith (1662); first line: "Here lies under this same Marble."

Epitaph on Thomas Young*, on tombstone, dated 1655; first line: "Here is committed to earth's trust."

Epitaph on William Staples, on monument, dated 1650; first line: "Quod cum coelicolis habitus, pars altera nostri."

"Extempore upon a Faggot, An" (1705), also attributed to Earl of Rochester, and also called "A Description of a Maidenhead"; first line: "Have you not in a Chimney seen."

"Fragment of Milton. From the Italian, A" (1773); first line: "When in your language, I unskill'd address."

Grand Case of Conscience, The (1650).

Great Brittans Ruine Plotted (1641); version of *The Plot Discovered and Counterplotted*.

"I am old and blind!" (1848), by Elizabeth Lloyd Howells; appears also under the title, "Milton's Prayer of Patience."

Inscription in Latin, replacing Charles I's picture in the Old Exchange, dated August 10, 1650.

Jus Populi (1644), by [Henry Parker].

Kings Cabinet Opened, The (1645).

"Lavinia Walking in a Frosty Morning" (1640), by Mr. I. M. (according to Henry Lawes's* *Second Book of Ayres* [1655]); first line: "In the non-age of a winters day."

Legal Index, in Columbia MS, pp. 144–52.

Letter to George Wither, in Wither's *Se Defendendo* (1643), p. 3, by J. M.

Letter Written to a Gentleman in the Country, touching the Dissolution of the Late Parliament (1653), by [John Hall].

Life and Reigne of King Charls, Or the Pseudo-Martyr discovered, The (1652).

Lines in a Bible, manuscript, beside 1 Macc. 14; first line: "When that day of Death shall come."

Lord Bishop None of the Lords Bishops (1640), by [William Prynne?*].

Man Wholly Mortal (1655), second edition of *Mans Mortalitie,* in which Milton allegedly caused a passage from Peter du Moulin's* *The Anatomy of Arminianisme* (1620), pp. 66–67, to be inserted on pp. 26–27.

Mans Mortalitie (1644), also attributed to Richard Overton.

Mercurius Politicus, alleged editor from September 1650 through March 1652, as well as frequent contributor; Milton licensed the periodical from March 17, 1651, through January 22, 1652, but the only sentence that he may have written is in No. 91, February 26–March 4, 1652, p. 1443.

Morland*, Sir Samuel, address to the Duke of Savoy on the Piedmont Massacre, 1655 (published 1658).

Newes from Hell, Rome, and the Inns of Court (1642), by J. M.

Novae Solymae libri sex (1648), by [Samuel Gott*].

Observations upon His Majesties Late Answers (1642), by [Henry Parker?].

"Of Statues & Antiquities," essay in Columbia MS, pp. 3–4.

"On Day Break" (1786); first line: "Welcome, bright chorister to our hemisphere."

"On Mel Heliconium," by J. M., manuscript poem in Alexander Ross's* *Mel Heliconium* (1642); first line: "These shapes, of old transfigur'd by the charmes."

"On the Librarie at Cambridge" (1851), by J. M., dated 1627; first line: "In that great maze of books I sighed and said."

"On Worthy Master Shakespeare* and His Poems" (1632), by I. M. S. [allegedly, John Milton, Student]; first line: "A Mind reflecting ages past, whose cleere."

"Our lives are albums, written through" (1876), by John Greenleaf Whittier.

Panegyrii Cromwello Scripti (1654), two panegyrics, attributed to Joao Rodriguez de Sá e Meneses and to a Jesuit.

Parliamenti Angliae Declaratio: in qua res numperum gestae (1648), translation of *Declaration for the Satisfaction of the Kingdom touching the late Proceedings of the Parliament*, largely by Bulstrode Whitelocke*.

Pious Annotations upon the Holy Bible, by John Diodati* (1643), alleged translator or supervisor of English translation.

*Plain English to his Excellencie the Lord General Monck** (1660).

Plot Discovered and Counterplotted, The [1641]; version of *Great Brittans Ruine Plotted*.

Prefatory tribute to Edward King* in *Justa Edovardo King naufrago* (1638).

Reasons why the Supream authority of the three nations is not vested in the Parliament (1653).

Reply to the Answer . . . to . . . Observations upon Some of His Majesties Late Answers (1642), by J. M.

Right of the People over Tyrants, The (1644), nonexistent; confusion over *Pro Populo Adversus Tyrannos*, for which *see* ADAPTATIONS, LITERARY.

Sabandiensis in Reformatam Religionem Persecutionis Brevis Narratio (1655), by B. M.

Satyr against Hypocrites, A (1655), by John Phillips.

School-Lawes, or Qui Mihi in English Verse (1650), by J. M.

Short View of the Praelatical Church of England, A (1641), by [Richard Bernard?].

Sonnet "Found in a Glass Window in the Village of Chalfont, Bucks" (1738), by Alexander Pope* and Lord Chesterfield; given in a letter from Pope to Jonathan Richardson, July 18, 1737; first line: "Fair Mirrour of foul Times! whose fragile sheene."

Soveraigne Salve to Cure the Blind (1643), by J. M.

Stanzas on Engraved Scenes illustrating Ovid's* *Metamorphoses*, manuscript, in edition of 1563; first stanza and line: "Of Chaos. 1. the world created. A Chaos of all confus'd on heapes doth ly."

State of Church Affairs, The (1687), also attributed to Sir Christopher Milton.

Treatise of Magistracy, A (1647), by [Mary Pope].

Treatise of Monarchie, A (1643), by [Philip Hunton].

True Character of an Untrue Bishop, The (1641).

True Description or Rather a Parallel between Cardinall Wolsey, . . . and William Laud, A* (1641).

True Portraiture of the Kings, The (1650), by [Henry Parker].

Tyrannicall-Government Anatomized (1642), translation of George Buchanan's* *Baptistes*

(1578), given in revised form by Francis Peck*, *New Memoirs of Mr. John Milton* (1740), pp. 265–428.

"Upon a Fly that Flew into a Lady's Eye" (1687), also attributed to John Cleveland; first line: "Poor envious soul! What couldst thou see."

Special attention must be given to two other attributions, which normally would be considered under the state papers: *Scriptum Parlamenti Reipublicae Angliae De iis quae ab hac Repub. cum Potestatibus Foederatarum Belgii Provinciarum Generalibus, & quibus progressibus acta sunt*, and *Scriptum Dom. Protectoris Reipublicae Angliae, Scotiae, Hiberniae, &c. Ex consenu atque sententia Concilii Sui Editum; In quo hujus Republicae Causa contra Hispanos justa esse demonstratur*. The first is a Latin translation of *A Declaration of the Parliament of the Commonwealth of England, Relating to the Affairs and Proceedings between this Commonwealth and the States General of the United Provinces of the Low Countreys*, printed July 9, 1652, by John Field; it appeared on July 29, 1652, from Dugard's press. There is another edition of the English version in 1652 (and in 1732) and various translations into Danish, Dutch, German, Italian, and French, all of which are supposed to be drawn from the English version. An order to turn *A Declaration* into Latin, French, and Dutch was given by the Council of State* on July 13, 1652 (perhaps to Milton), and another order for the printer William Dugard* to talk to Milton about printing the manifesto in such translations, dated July 20. Whether Milton was the translator of any of these versions, particularly that in Latin, is uncertain, but the facts are suggestive.

The second item is a translation of *A Declaration of the Lord Protector of the Commonwealth of England, Scotland, Ireland, etc., published by the advice and with the consent of his Council; in which the cause of the Commonwealth against the Spaniards is shown to be just*, printed around October 26, 1655, by Henry Hills and John Fields; another issue with a different title page came out around the same time, and a few days later there was a reprint in Edinburgh by Christopher Higgins. The Latin version was also printed by Henry Hills and John Fields, perhaps around November 23. These printers also produced for the Council an official version in Spanish. There were two Dutch translations and one Germon. In 1738 Thomas Birch* attributed the Latin version to Milton in his collection of the prose (1 : xxxiv), in which he published both the Latin and the English. In the same year appeared *A Manifesto of the Lord Protector of the Commonwealth of England, Scotland, Ireland, &c. Published by Consent and Advice of his Council. Wherein is shewn the Reasonableness of the Cause of this Republic against the Depredations of the Spaniards. Written in Latin by John Milton, and First Printed in 1655, now translated into English,* published by the bookseller Andrew Millar. Another edition was put out for T. Cooper in 1741, under the title, *A true Copy of Oliver Cromwell's Manifesto Against Spain, Dated October 26, 1655;* there is a reference to Milton in the preface, p. [v]. This edition was alleged to have been taken from the original manuscript in English. Whether Milton was the translator of the Latin version is most uncertain. [JTS]

AUBREY, JOHN (1626–1697), an antiquarian who compiled important topographical materials and biographical notes. He collected firsthand information about Milton the man, his family, and his works from Milton's relatives and friends. This work, "Minutes of Lives" of various eminent people, was undertaken around 1681–1682 for Anthony Wood*, who employed the notes on Milton for the life of the poet in *Athenae Oxoniensis* (1690). The manuscript (one of the two original volumes now being lost) was given to the Ashmolean Library by Aubrey, and is in the Bodleian Library, cat. MS Aubrey 8. Ff. 63–68b are devoted to Milton. It contains additions and corrections in Edward Phillips's hand. Aubrey's main sources of information, besides Phillips, were Milton's widow and his brother Christopher, in addition to Theodore Haak*, a Mr. Packard (perhaps an error for Jeremy Picard, one of Milton's amanuenses*), Abraham Hill (treasurer of the Royal Society), and others. His work has often been adversely criticized, for example, by Wood himself, for its disorder, for Aubrey's lack of literary discernment, for its lack of evaluation of material; but it is nonetheless an important source of anecdotal information and personal descriptions, not otherwise recorded. Aubrey obviously was not learned in Milton's works, although he was familiar with them before he undertook the "Minutes," and he did not usually even seek out copies of the volumes he was citing. For the scholar as well as the biographer, however, Aubrey's notes on Milton are a necessary beginning. "Biographical Notices of John Milton" was first published in *European Magazine* 28 (1795) : 184–86; a fuller version appeared in *Letters Written by Eminent Persons in the Seventeenth and Eighteenth Centuries* (1813) by William Godwin*. Subsequent editions (such as Helen Darbishire's popular one in *Early Lives of Milton*) have not been entirely accurate.

Further references to Milton will be found in a letter to Wood, dated May 18, 1675 (Bodleian, MS Wood F.39, ff. 296–97), containing biographical notes; another letter to Wood, dated May 25, 1684 (Bodleian, MS Wood F.39, f. 372), on *Sonn* 15 and 16, indicating Aubrey's perusal of *TM*; in *The Natural History of Wiltshire,* ed. John Britton (London, 1847), a comment on p. 50, written ca. 1670; and in *Wiltshire. The Topographical Collections of John Aubrey,* ed. John E. Jackson (Devizes, 1862), containing quotations from *Brit* and some allusion, pp. 66, 74, 258 (the preface being dated April 28, 1670). [JTS]

AUDEN, W. H.: *see* INFLUENCE ON TWENTIETH-CENTURY ENGLISH LITERATURE, MILTON'S.

AUGUSTINE, ST. Milton's theology of the Fall of Man* is substantially that of St. Augustine, which is that of the Christian tradition as a whole. Milton considered Augustine "The Most judicious of all the Fathers" and found the theology of that Father a stimulus to his own thinking, as is clear from over forty-five references to Augustine in the prose works. Augustine's definition of original sin*, which inaugurates the poet's discussion of this most important dogma in *CD* becomes the theological basis for *PL*.

For Augustine, God created all things good; and because they are good, no positive reality is evil* : evil denotes the privation of good (*Civ.Dei* 11. 21. 22). Hence, Milton's God says of Adam, "I made him just and right," and adds, "Such I created all th' Ethereal Powers" (*PL* 3. 98–100). Evil is really an absence or a perversion of good; and this perversion arises when a creature, through pride, becomes more interested in itself than in God. Satan, the proud angel, was the first who turned from God to himself by refusing to be a subject and by making himself a tyrant over his own subjects (*Civ.Dei* xiv. 11). In Milton, Satan "thought himself impaird" (*PL* 5. 665); he is "self-begot, self-rais'd / By our own quick'ning power" (5. 860); he is "Emperour with pomp Supream" (2. 510), "great Sultan" (1. 348), "Tyrant" (4. 395), and "Monarch" (2. 467). Although all things are created good, they are not equally so. Some are more excellent than others; and yet all, from the highest to the lowest order, are good. All is a scale* or hierarchy of natures (*Ench. ad Laurentium* x). In Milton, God created the angels the most excellent creatures with Satan the greatest "in Power, / In favour and praeeminence" (5. 660–61), superior even to Adam and Eve, who were "Favour'd of Heav'n so highly" (1. 30) yet created "less / In power and excellence" (2. 349–50). And it is Satan's rebellion against this hierarchy that accounts for his own misery. In an angelic world, the higher that one ascends, the clearer becomes the image of God; and Satan as Lucifer has

the clearest image. The being most like God, though most obviously dependent upon him, will have, paradoxically, the highest degree of causality and, in that sense, of independence. The danger of the fall will be greatest where it will be least justified; where there is the greatest joy, there will be, with rejection, the greatest pain. This accounts for Satan's cry, "O had his powerful Destiny ordaind / Me some inferiour Angel, I had stood / Then happie" (*PL* 4. 58–60). Adam and Eve, with all their prerogatives, had a lesser degree of causality because they were lower in the scheme of creation*. As unjustifiable as was the Fall of man, still more unjustifiable was the fall of the angels : theirs was the higher creation and the clearer image of God. This accounts for Milton's God's pronouncing in Book 3 that there will be no redemptive grace for the fallen angel as there will be for fallen man (128–34). The irony of Satan's situation stems from the Augustinian paradox that the corruption of the best becomes the worst and that from the worst God brings forth the best —a tenet that functions significantly for the central irony of the epic.

Milton's treatment of preternatural Adam and Eve relies heavily upon Augustinian teaching. According to Augustine, Adam and Eve were created totally free; in the epic we read that God "formd them free, and free they must remain" (3. 124). They were endowed with preternatural and supernatural gifts in the most perfect way; in the epic Raphael says, "Abundantly his gifts hath also pour'd / Inward and outward both, his image faire" (8. 220–21). Yet their freedom had one restriction : in the epic Adam and Eve are told "Amid the Garden by the Tree of Life, / Remember what I warne thee, shun to taste" (8. 327–28). Concerning Adam and Eve's preternatural gifts, Augustine taught that they were created immortal, which meant simply that it was not necessary that their bodies should die (*posse non mori*), not that it was impossible that they die (*non posse mori*) (*Civ.Dei* 13. 9). The privilege of immortality of the body was conditional upon the divine prohibition; and when they transgressed, this gift was lost : "that Forbidden Tree, whose mortal tast / Brought Death into the World" (*PL* 1. 2–3). They were given the gift of impassibility, which freed them from all pain and suffering; but Augustine is careful to aver that this prerogative did not make them dehumanized or immune from natural bodily discomforts. He says that they would have known hunger and thirst because their bodies, which were animal, not spiritual, required meat and drink to satisfy hunger and thirst (*Civ. Dei* 13. 23). Significantly, Milton places a dinner scene in Book V, wherein Adam and Eve entertain Raphael. They were endowed with the gift of superior knowledge infused by God and not acquired by the use of human faculties. This is most manifest in the epic when Adam calls out the names of the birds of the air and the beasts of the land soon after the Creation. And Augustine teaches that this superior knowledge did not imply that the progenitors could not increase in knowledge and learning : hence Adam's quest for knowledge from Raphael and the incidents of curiosity in the epic. Finally, they were gifted with integrity or freedom from any movement of the lower faculties (sense and imagination), which were not under the control of the higher faculties (reason and will) (*Civ. Dei* 14. 15ff.). Since the Fall consisted in man's disobedience to his superior, it was fittingly punished by man's loss of authority over his inferiors, that is, over his passions and his physical organs (*Civ. Dei* 14. 15). Milton's handling of the two love* scenes, one before the Fall and one after the Fall, is a poetic statement of this teaching. Before the Fall, the love act, voluptuous though it is, is performed with the utmost tenderness and under the direct control of the will. After the Fall, the sensual appetites usurp the reason and will, and unbridled passions dominate the act.

The Fall consisted plainly and simply in disobedience, in Adam and Eve's doing precisely what they were told not to do, and it resulted from pride. The scenes wherein Adam requests knowledge, Eve has a nightmare, and Eve gives in to vanity at the pool, which take place before the actual transgression, should not perplex readers as they have the critics, who misconstrued these incidents as sins and the progenitors as already fallen. Augustine maintains that it is one thing not to have sin and another not to abide in that goodness in which there is no sin (*De Corruptione et Gratia* 10. 26). The incidents prior to Book 9 indicate that Adam and Eve are falling from perseverance, are failing to abide in that goodness in which there is no sin, but such incidents are not tantamount to the Fall. The actual Fall took place with the eating of the apple; and for Augustine, the iniquity of violating the prohibition was all the greater in proportion to the ease with which it might have been kept (*Civ. Dei* 14. 12).

Augustine's paradox of good-from-evil is a familiar feature in Milton's epic. The motif is used twice in the seventh book. It is included in the hymn sung before the Son journeys out into Chaos, and it is part of the celebrations that take place on his triumphant return. Milton maintains that "God eventually converts every evil deed into an instrument of good, contrary to the expectation of the sinner, and overcomes evil with good" (*CD* 8). In the epic, all Satan's "malice serv'd but to bring forth / Infinite goodness, grace and mercy" (1. 217–18); his "spite . . . still serves His glory to augment" (2. 384–86). The angels point out : "his evil / Thou usest, and from thence creat'st more good" (7. 615–16). Adam's astonishment in finding himself an instrument in Satan's rebellion and an instrument in God's providence is a poetic statement of the Augustinian formula "O felix culpa." "O goodness infinite, goodness immense ! / That all this good of evil shall produce, / And evil turn to good" (12. 469–71). [PAF]

AUSTIN FRIARS, DUTCH REFORMED CHURCH OF, the oldest of

Dutch Protestant churches and located on Broad Street, London. This congregation had its beginnings in the reign of Henry VIII, when persecution in the homelands swelled the colonies of Flemish and other foreigners that had been dwelling in England during the Middle Ages. With the accession of Edward VI in 1547, the Reformation not only took permanent root in England, but came to bear an increasingly Calvinist stamp, as foreign laymen and divines were encouraged to immigrate to further reformation and the economy. In 1550 the famous Polish reformer John à Lasco was recognized as spiritual leader of the foreigners in the realm, and on July 24 a royal charter was granted for a Dutch (Germani) congregation, which received as its place of worship the Church of Austin Friars, the largest friars' church in England before the suppression of the monasteries. Like the French, Italian, and Spanish exile churches, which initially shared the same premises, the church government of Austin Friars was presbyterian*, with ministers, elders, and deacons designated by the members themselves on democratic principles. In this the foreign churches were remarkable exceptions by law to the episcopal system of the native church, the one Anglican feature being the office of superintendent, originally assigned to à Lasco, which subjected the consistory to state authority. As its members were technically aliens, the church's responsibilities included a broad range of political, social, judicial, educational, and ecclesiastical functions, and after the Netherlands provinces renounced allegiance to Philip of Spain, Dutch ambassadors used the community as their official place of worship. During the reign of Queen Mary the papacy was restored, but under Elizabeth the foreigners were allowed to reconstitute themselves with the presbyterian format of their churches intact. The queen was careful to prevent an independent Calvinistic church polity, however, and kept central power in the hands of Anglican prelates by transferring the superintendency to the Bishop of

London. Among the various communities of Reformed "strangers" in Britain, Austin Friars was the leader, being the largest and most influential. Abroad, the London community meant more to the home churches than they to it, for initially the Reformation was spread in Flanders and Holland by Dutch merchants who for the most part attended Austin Friars in their intercourse between British and Netherlands ports. Prior to 1571, when much of the northern Netherlands was still in Spanish hands, the Dutch and Flemish churches were still in the process of forming, whereas the London congregation was already organized, having pioneered the use of the Dutch language in doctrinal teaching and liturgy, including books of instruction, a translation of the Bible, and its own rhymed version of the psalms. Not until the continental churches had developed their own confessions and external manifestations were the London forms replaced, and only late in Elizabeth's reign did the London church come to follow the Netherlandish church, not vice versa. Although the court had favored the strangers in London against the dislike of the local populace, the chronic impecuniousness of King James* and rivalry provoked by the astonishing rise of the United Provinces occasioned many difficulties. Prosperous foreigners were always suspect of economic crimes, and members of the community were again and again singled out by the courts for special taxation, exorbitant fines, and inhibition of commercial activities. But as a body thoroughly orthodox in doctrine and properly obedient to the State Church, Austin Friars exemplified James's concern for the Reformed* churches during his efforts against Arminianism* at home and in the United Provinces before the Synod of Dort of 1618–19. In fact, the King himself took a personal hand in resuscitating the moribund Italian congregation associated with the Dutch at Austin Friars, and the ministers of these churches were on the best of terms with the Archbishop, George Abbot, the Bishop of London, and the royal chaplains. Hence, Milton's friendship with people like Charles Diodati brought him into contact with Reformed emigrés such as Caesar Calandrini*, Predicant to the Italian church and soon to be minister at Austin Friars itself. With the accession of Charles I* and the rise of William Laud*, the church entered on hard times. As Bishop of London and Archbishop of Canterbury, Laud was determined to force aliens to conform to Anglican practices, and he used the powers of superintendency to suppress the Dutch community. Despite resistance and delaying tactics, he nearly succeeded, but when the English Puritans rebelled, Laud's measures recoiled. As Austin Friars was irrefutable proof that in doctrine and spirit the Church of England had from the beginning conceived of itself as one with the Reformed churches, ever honoring Calvinistic ministry as legally valid, so, among the indictments brought against him, Laud was charged with attacking the traditional rights and liberties granted to the Reformed churches of the Dutch and French in England. The Puritan regimes, of course, extended full liberty to the congregation in the exercise of its religion and discipline. Under the Protectorate Austin Friars was called on, as it had been so very frequently in the past, to come to the aid of victims of the Counter-Reformation, this time the Waldenses*, and the congregation worked closely with the government in rendering assistance. As the State Papers and his famous sonnet on the Piedmontese show, Milton was personally involved in these matters, and at this very time he used the Consistory of Austin Friars also to secure information from Geneva about Salmasius* and More* in Holland. Though the Restoration of 1660 brought the reestablishment of the Episcopal Church, hostile measures were not taken against Austin Friars, and with the Act of Toleration of 1689, the difficulties of the past vanished. [PRS]

AUTOBIOGRAPHY, MILTON'S. Although he wrote no formal autobiography, Milton left sufficient information that John Diekhoff could collect from his writing a good-sized book, *Milton on Himself* (1939). The reasons for such statements are both personal and religious. Thus he identified himself personally with every cause in which he participated. In turn he was frequently attacked by his opponents and subjected to personal vilification; to this he responded with explanations and information from which a remarkably full autobiography may be reconstructed. Almost every prose piece contains some reference to his ideas and activities.

In a somewhat different way he writes about himself in his poetry, focusing, for instance, upon his literary aspirations in *Lyc,* recording particular events in most of his sonnets, entering his own epic in its invocations and angelic songs, and being somehow involved in the characterization of Samson and of Jesus in *PR.* Autobiographical concerns probably account for the fact that he dated almost all of the poetry he wrote before the age of twenty-one and then printed in 1645 and 1673, for the most part in chronological order within the various forms that he practiced. The Latin poems are printed together in the order of their composition, as are the sonnets. But at the beginning of each printing *Nat* appears out of its proper place, probably to interest a prospective reader more than would his earliest printed work, the translation of Psalm 114. Slight inconsistencies in strict chronology or in Milton's assigned dates, detected by modern scholarship, suggest that his memory was sometimes at fault and that he did not keep a diary.

Furthermore, it seems that Milton tried to print everything that he had written so that the student of his life would have a complete record. Thus in 1645 he included the *Passion,* which he acknowledges to be unsatisfactory; by 1673 he had come across a copy of his very early *FInf,* which the author of *PL* must have recognized as lacking any intrinsic literary value: it could be interesting only as part of a full autobiographical statement of his poetic growth. For the same reason he published his college essays, the *Prols,* and he is the first Englishman to collect and print his own familiar letters. Milton evidently assumed that his readers would be interested in such autobiographical materials.

A major reason for this self-concern lay in the seventeenth-century religious milieu. Men believed that God's Providence* exerted itself in everyone; biography and autobiography accordingly became a record of how such divine Providence guided the individual, affording some insight into God's activity and some judgment as to a man's ultimate destination as one of the saved or damned. For the pure Calvinist the result had been irrevocably predestined; the individual could only record in his diary or autobiography his wonder and admiration as this divine plan worked out for him in time. It always centered in a single great illumination like that of St. Paul, in which he realized that he was saved, passive though he was in the process. Such an account constitutes John Bunyan's *Grace Abounding to the Chief of Sinners.*

But Milton's autobiographical statements dwell upon his own activities more than upon God's Providence for him. Furthermore, he never mentions having undergone the experience of conversion. These characteristics may reflect his Arminianism*, with its stress upon the individual's own choice, which results in good works insofar as he voluntarily follows divine guidance. Milton believed himself to be led by Providence, like Adam and Eve at the conclusion of *PL;* but the responsibility to follow that directive lay within his own control, with concomitant spiritual dangers. Thus Samson sinned by following his own inclinations that led him to the woman of Timna. Milton's extensive autobiographical statements are thus his own testimony to the righteousness of God working in him and his own response to such divine Providence, although to unsympathetic readers they have seemed little more than self-righteous exculpation. [WBH]

AUTOGRAPHS. Aside from manuscripts* of works, marginalia* in various volumes, and entries in presentation* copies of the works, holograph items such as signatures and notes occur in a variety of places. The following list cites known examples chronologically; omitted are reported but unproved occurrences and the work of amanuenses* :

1623, November 7, witness signature on marriage settlement for Anne Milton and Edward Phillips; in Morgan Library.

1629, February 10 (?), supplicat for degree of A.B.; University Subscription Books, Christ's College*, Cambridge.

1629, March 26, signature on articles for degree of A.B.; University Subscription Books, Christ's College, Cambridge.

1632, July 3, signature on articles for degree of A.M.; University Subscription Books, Christ's College, Cambridge.

1638, June 10 (May 31 O.S.), inscription (11. 1022–23 of *Mask* and Horace*, *Epistles,* I, xi, 27) and signature in autograph album of Count Camillo Cerdogni; in Harvard University Library.

1639, March 29, letter to Lukas Holste* (*Epistol* 9); in Vatican Library, Barb. Lat. 2181, ff. 57–58.

1639(?), nine corrections in *Mask,* 1637, including one change of word; in Carl H. Pforzheimer Library.

1639(?), corrections in *Lyc* in *Justa Edovardo King naufrago** in copies owned by Cambridge University Library and British Museum.

1645, April 11, witness signature on will of William Blackborow; in Somerset House, Prerogative Court of Canterbury, 82 Twisse (copy).

1645(?)–1652(?), entries in family Bible* through and including "My daughter" in references to Deborah; British Museum, Additional MS 32310.

1646, January (?), inscription and list of works in volume of eleven tracts sent to John Rous* at the Bodleian, with eleven corrections in *Ref* (nine certainly by Milton); Bodleian Library, 4° F.56.Th, now Arch.G.e.44.

1646, December 13, witness signature on will of Richard Powell; in Somerset House, Prerogative Court of Canterbury, 52 Fines.

1647, January (?), corrections in second volume of 1645 *Poems* sent to John Rous at the Bodleian, pp. 22, 28, 39, and 36 (second pagination); Bodleian Library, Arch, F.f.9.

1647, January 23, one-word correction in "Ad Ioannem Rousium" in John Phillips's hand; Bodleian Library, Arch. F.f.9.

1647, April 20, letter to Carlo Dati* (*Epistol* 10); in New York Public Library.

1649, April 2, corrections in state letter to Hamburg in Henry Marten's hand; in Brotherton Collection (Leeds University), Marten-Loder MSS, 3S, XI, f. 1.

1649, April 2, corrections in another state letter to Hamburg in Henry Marten's hand; in Brotherton Collection (Leeds University), Marten-Loder MSS, 3S, XI, f. 2.

1649, April–May (?), corrections in translation of letter from Princess Sophie to Prince Maurice in John Phillips's hand; in Public Record Office, SP Dom. 18/1, No. 55, f. 142.

1650, February 16, signature on receipt of payment from Rodolph Warcupp*; owned by Historical Society of Philadelphia.

1650, April 30, entry in Order Book of the Council of State*; Public Record Office, SP Dom. 25/6, unpaged.

1651, February 25, note and two signatures on petition concerning lands owned by the Powell family; Public Record Office, SP Dom. 23/101, p. 928.

1651, February 25(?), signature on schedule for income from lands owned by the Powell family; Public Record Office, SP Dom. 23/101, p. 929.

1651, February 28, signature on affidavit concerning Richard Powell's debt; Public Record Office, SP Dom. 23/101, p. 931.

1651, November 19, signature on inscription and quotation from 2 Cor. 12:9 in John Phillips's hand in autograph album of Christopher Arnold*; British Museum, Egerton MS 1324, f. 85v.

1656, September 26, signature on quotation from 2 Cor. 20:9 in amanuensis's hand in autograph album of John Zollikofer; in Stadtbibliothek St. Gallen (Switzerland), Bibliothek der Vadiana MS 92a.

1659, November 29, signature on discharge of Richard Powell's bond; Public Record Office, C 152/61.

1663, February 11, signature on allegation to marry Elizabeth Minshull; Faculty Office of the Archbishop of Canterbury, Ecclesiastical Court for the Issue of Marriage Licenses.

Four other items from the Order Book of the Council of State should be mentioned, although certainty of Milton's autograph is lacking: 1) February 18, 1650, in SP Dom. 25/64, p. 3; 2) February 23, 1650, in SP Dom. 25/64, p. 30; 3) June 14, 1650, in SP Dom. 25/64, p. 447; 4) June 25, 1650, in SP Dom. 25/64, p. 478. Generally the hand is only similar to Milton's; the spelling seldom reflects his practices. There were also four entries and a Latin note in Mary Powell Milton's

Bible, supposedly in Milton's hand, but the Bible has now disappeared. Thomas Birch* transcribed these notes (now in British Museum, Additional MS 4244, ff. 52–53), but he included a full note concerning Deborah's birth, which seems unlikely to have been Milton's. [JTS]

AVARICE, or covetousness, one of the traditional deadly sins*, denotes the excessive desire for wealth or material goods. In his entry on covetousness (*avaritia*) in *CD* (17:229–31), Milton confines himself to citing a number of biblical condemnations, including such familiar ones as St. Paul's equation of covetousness with idolatry (Eph. 5:5) and his assertion that "love of money is the root of all evil" (1 Tim. 6:10). More detailed analyses of other forms of avarice occur in the section on social ethics that occupies chapters 11–17 of Book 2.

The Mammon of *PL* embodies various aspects of avarice. Even before the rebellion, he is described as admiring more the riches of heaven's pavement than "aught divine or holy else enjoy'd / In vision beatific" (1.683–84). Later, when the fallen angels begin to recover from their defeat, it is Mammon who leads the forces who mine and refine the ore for the building of Pandemonium (1.678–709). And in the infernal council it is Mammon who rejects the idea of returning to heaven either as a conqueror or as a suppliant; rather, he argues, let us raise up objects of magnificence, "and what can Heav'n shew more?" (2.270–73). Avarice as exemplified in Mammon thus passes through three stages: the contemplation of wealth for its own sake, the creation of new wealth by the application of skill and labor, and the lavish expenditure of this new wealth on objects of beauty. For the concept of these stages and for much of the imagery, Milton drew extensively from the Cave of Mammon episode in Spenser's* *Faerie Queene* 2.7; behind the depictions of both poets lies Aristotle's* analysis of miserliness and prodigality as the vices opposed to the virtue* of liberality.

Avarice is depicted on the human level

in the third vision that Michael presents to Adam toward the conclusion of *PL*. The workers on the plain are skillful artificers who create the "Arts that polish Life," yet they are "unmindful of thir Maker" and fail to acknowledge his gifts (11. 556–627). Resemblances have been noted between this scene and the description of Mammon and his followers in Book 1. These workers fit the description of the men who, at the suggestion of Mammon, "ransack'd the Center, and with impious hands / Rifl'd the bowels of thir mother Earth / For Treasures better hid" (1. 684–88).

Elsewhere in the poetic works the power of wealth is depicted. Samson states that the spousal embraces of Dalila were "vitiated with Gold" (*SA* 389) and later accuses her of betraying him out of weakness for "Philistian gold" (line 831). But the Christ of *PR* sets man an example by successfully resisting a temptation to wealth even under the guise of using it for a noble purpose (2. 406–86). [RF]

AYLMER, BRABAZON (fl. 1671–1707), bookseller of St. Michael's, Cornhill. Aylmer had been apprenticed to Luke Fawne on January 21, 1660, and made free of the Company of Stationers on February 11, 1667, but his known work dates a few years later. He had various connections with Milton and his works during the last quarter of the seventeenth century, possibly through the bookseller Edward Millington (fl. 1669–1698), or Edward Phillips, or Daniel Skinner*. Aylmer had tried to publish Milton's letters, both the state papers* and the personal letters, but he was denied permission to put out the former. Perhaps this occurred in 1673–1674, for in 1674, through negotiations with a mutual friend (perhaps Millington), he obtained additional material from Milton to publish with the personal letters. This material was the seven college prolusions, which he added to *Epistolarum Familiarium Liber Unus*, licensed on May 26, 1674, and entered in the Stationers' Register on July 1. In the meantime the state papers were published in Holland. Aylmer's preface to the familiar letters,

"Typographus Lectori," supplies much of the information above. Probably the arrangement of the prolusions is not chronological but rather by length, and probably the designation *Liber Unus* was simply a hopeful addition on his part rather than an indication that Milton had a manuscript of further letters. Edward Phillips's *Letters of State* (1694) lists no printer or publisher; possibly Aylmer finally did produce further letters, the state papers.

Milton's translation of the document concerned with John Sobieski's election to the kingship of Poland, *A Declaration, or Letters Patents* (July? 1674) was also published for Aylmer, and perhaps was undertaken because Aylmer realized its significance politically at that time. On October 27, 1680, Samuel Simmons* sold his rights to *PL* to Aylmer, who registered the poem in his name on July 24, 1683. He sold half his rights to Jacob Tonson* on August 17, 1683, and the remainder on March 24, 1691. No edition came out, however, with Aylmer's name listed. The important fourth edition was published in three issues in 1688, during the time that Aylmer held rights to the poem. In 1682 he published *Mosc*, which he says in a preface, "Advertisement," "was writ by the author's own hand, before he lost his sight." When he obtained the manuscript is not known, but perhaps it was given to him along with the prolusions to fill up the slim volume of letters and then held as an inappropriate addition. The reason for publication delay is not known. Whether Aylmer had anything to do with other works of Milton's is not in evidence.

It has been suggested that he was the bookseller who was a pallbearer at Milton's funeral (see John Ward's* notes in BM, Additional MS 4320, f. 232v), but identification is most uncertain. [JTS]

BACON, FRANCIS. In the years following his death, an increasing luster grew about the name and works of Sir Francis Bacon, Baron Verulam, Viscount St. Albans (1561–1626). Like many other seventeenth-century Englishmen, John Milton apparently read some of Bacon's works with care and regarded him as an English classic. Much has been said of a speculative nature about Milton's supposed Baconianism at Cambridge; more concrete evidence of his use of Bacon's works exists in his controversial writings. However, Milton's relationship to Bacon has seemed a paradox. Both men vigorously criticized the reigning scholastic system of education; both urged that men should devote their energies to practical measures for their own improvement. But Bacon's emphasis fell on scientific and technological progress, a direction of thought that was revolutionary in his time, while his views on church and state were reform-minded, but essentially conservative. Milton, on the other hand, ardently supported the most radical theories and acts in the political and religious affairs of his times, even while his largest concepts of human betterment ran in ethical and idealistic channels that flow back through the earlier humanists to St. Augustine* and Plato*. In evaluating Bacon's influence on Milton (or anyone else) it is most important to determine which of Bacon's many works seem to have had the most impact on the person influenced. Although Bacon's very name may have raised hackles in the bastions of scholasticism, certain of his works, such as the *Advancement of Learning* and even the *Essays*, which we may see as fraught with changing ideas of conduct and mores, could be comfortably embraced by any moderate intellectual or courtier or citizen.

Bacon's influence in the universities, particularly Cambridge, his *alma mater,* during the second and third decades of the seventeenth century is often assumed by scholars, although in fact little documentary evidence crops up before the century's fourth decade. Bacon sent personal letters with copies of his works to Oxford and Cambridge, and was fulsomely thanked by the former in a letter reprinted in *Baconiana* (1679), pp. 204–6. His scheme to found a lectureship in natural philosophy at both universities, however, came to nothing when his estate was found at his death to fall far short of his bequests. A history professorship established at Cambridge by Fulke Greville may represent the embodiment of some Baconian ideas (see J. Bass Mullinger, *The University of Cambridge from the Election to the Chancellorship in 1626 to the Decline of the Platonist Movement* [Cambridge : Cambridge University Press, 1911](p. 81); but the lectures were canceled and the professorship allowed to lapse after the first incumbent, the Dutchman Isaac Dorislaus, was thought to have reflected unfavorably on the royal prerogative in his first course of lectures, delivered December 7 and 12, 1627, on Tacitus (see Mullinger, pp. 83–89). Milton, having been admitted to Christ's College* in the spring term, 1625, was in residence at Cambridge during these abortive attempts to broaden the curriculum in a Baconian way. It has become a commonplace of criticism to refer to Milton's attachment to "the Baconian faction" while at Cambridge; Tillyard even speculates that the clash with his first tutor*, Chappell*, an extremely prominent and subtle disputant and supporter of scholastic Aristotelianism*, came about because of the pupil's outspoken adherence to the Baconian party of educational reformers (*Milton: Private Correspondence and Academic Exercises* [1932], p. xxii). No one has provided names and evidence for the existence of a Baconian faction at Cambridge as early at the late 20s and early 30s. Published references to Bacon and his works and lists of books in private libraries of Cambridge personalities of the period suggest that Bacon's less scientific works, such as the *Essays* and the *Advancement of Learning,* had the greatest currency. Indeed, of the three great processes into which Bacon once divided his Instauration, the *Pars destruens* ("unbuilding part") and to some degree the optimistic rhetoric of the *Pars praeparans* ("preparative part") are all that took hold of many minds at first; the *Formula ipsa interpretationis* ("true formula of interpretation"), as Bacon foresaw, being deeper and far more technical, appealed to fewer and was embraced in its details by almost none. The *Pars destruens* particularly, in its hostility to the fruitless multiplication of controversies and the empty, unproductive verbalism of scholasticism, fell on many willing ears; Bacon's criticisms often parallel the attacks on the established educational system put forth by earlier humanists such as Erasmus*, Colet, and Cheke*, and by the Ramists*. Milton's enunciation of similar anti-scholastic ideas can only be called Baconian in the loosest sense.

Milton's prolusions provide ample evidence of their student-author's active and vigorous dislike of the reigning curriculum at Cambridge; they offer also, in content and occasionally in diction, some evidence that his criticism was tinctured by Baconian colors. Milton twice alludes to the hostility and distaste he encountered from the Cantabrigian academic community "on account of disagreements over our studies" (12 : 207; cf. 12 : 121). Those "differences" probably centered on his scorn for the scholastic system, voiced at length in the third prolusion, and his advocacy of what amounts to an alternative curriculum stressing poetry and rhetoric*, natural philosophy, and history and sociology (see *Prol* 3, 4, 5, and 7). In *Prol* 3 Milton uses language of praise and reprobation that seems to echo Bacon's. But the actual standard of judgment he applies is Horatian*, rather than Baconian : these studies are neither *delightful* nor *useful*. He contrasts their lack of "power to stir up the passions of the soul" (12 : 165) with the charms of poetry, rhetoric, and history. Such moral, ethical, and aesthetic concerns are the very grain of Milton's thought, and represent a widely differing emphasis from Bacon's pragmatic and "technical" bent. The Verulamian-sounding language that criticizes scholastic disputation as a "logomachy" that does not eventuate in *public welfare* or yield honor or *utility* (12 : 169) and the proposed alternative, a curriculum including geography, history, poetry, sociology, politics, and natural philosophy, simply overlies and embellishes an ethical or rather a spiritual end

expressed in Platonic phraseology : "finally, what is after all the most important matter, let [the mind] learn thoroughly to know itself and at the same time those holy minds and intelligences, with whom hereafter it will enter into everlasting companionship" (12 : 171). Milton may seem to be asking seventeenth-century "how" questions (see Kathryn A. McEuen, Yale *Prose* 1 : 247 n17), but the traditions in which his thought moves are one in spirit with those of Erasmus, Ficino, Cicero*, or Plato. Even in the finest of the prolusions, the seventh, with which Bacon's name is usually associated, Milton's moving paean to natural history* is only the conventional argument for admiration tending to the glory of God. Bacon's originality had introduced the principle of active control of nature, built on understanding and enlisted in the service of man under the aegis of the second table of the law and the Gospel command of charity. These distinctive and characteristically Verulamian ideas leave no traces on Milton's thought and expression (*see* SCIENCE, MILTON AND).

Historiography* also occupies a prominent position in Bacon's interests and exhortations. Milton praises history by precept in *Prol* 3, and by example in *Prol* 5. Further explanation of what besides delight can be expected of history comes in *Prol* 7. McEuen has listed some of the parallels between this prolusion and the *Advancement*, which Milton apparently read attentively (Yale *Prose* 1 : 287). Milton's main argument turns on the superior suitability of knowledge to happiness, in this life as well as in the next. Once again he argues that it is a great thing for our *delight* "to have comprehended every law of the heavens and of the stars," and of meteorology, mineralogy, zoology, and anatomy as well. There is no mention of power over nature or repairing the ruins of our first parents by remedying the natural shocks that flesh is heir to since the Fall. Similarly, when Milton adds history to the mind-expanding categories of learning, though he recommends its study for "practical judgment and morals," he has no specific directives for its practical application to either our personal or state affairs such as Bacon supplies in the doctrine of the *faber fortunae* (architect of fortune). Milton's survey of the "vicissitudes of kingdoms, nations, cities, peoples" that one views through history as if able "to reside in every age as if alive, to be born a contemporary of time itself" goes back in its term of encomium at least to Diodorus* Siculus, rather than to Bacon's favorite "modern" Florentine political historians.

If one is inclined to associate Bacon with some "Faustian urge of Renaissance man," then Milton's entire praise of knowledge in *Prol* 7 may be seen as loosely Baconian in its exultation and sense of human power and potential. But it is not specifically Baconian in any identifiable details as, for example, John Webster's *Academiarum Examen* (1654) is. *Prol* 7 resembles most Book 1 of the *Advancement*, one of the least technical of Bacon's writings on his own testimony. McEuen asserts that it is conjectural whether Milton had read the *Novum Organum* when he wrote the prolusions, but guesses that he probably had on the grounds that the work was published in 1620 and "Milton was an adherent of the Baconian faction at Cambridge" (Yale *Prose* 1 : 247 n17). She admits, however, that he never refers to the work in any of his writings, early or late. In fact, the only reference to Bacon's logic* in Milton's writings comes in an insignificant analogy in *Logic,* and it does not refer to the book that chiefly embodies the model of Verulamian induction at work (11 : 23–25). If Milton did read the *Novum Organum,* his silence on it throughout his life, as well as on other available scientific works such as the *Sylva Sylvarum* and the various histories published in 1638 at London, in Latin, as *The Natural and Experimental History for the Foundation of Philosophy,* seems finally much more significant than the possibility that he turned their leaves. In the actual constructive portions of the *Great Instauration,* however confusedly put forth, Milton found nothing he could

use, nothing that seemed immediately relevant to his chief concerns, which were social and ethical* in more traditional ways. Like that of many of his contemporaries, Milton's "Baconianism" was the product of a spirit of the age, a busy practical and utilitarian concern for the active life and human progress that went hand in hand with a hostility to scholastic verbalism and haggling and to all apparent relics of medievalism and monkishness on the one hand, and an intoxicating anticipation and exaltation at the possibilities for man on the other. This set of attitudes found its most prestigious and eloquent, though not by any means its sole spokesman, in the great Verulam. Milton's association with a supposed Baconian faction at Cambridge can scarcely be regarded as an incontrovertibly demonstrated fact in the absence of further evidence of the membership of the faction and in the face of the negative evidence that Milton never mentions such an alignment himself.

More than a decade after his university days, Milton had occasion to refer to Francis Bacon's opinions and prestige again, but in very different contexts. Bacon wrote two major statements on church affairs, *An Advertisement Touching the Controversies of the Church of England,* first published in 1641 as *A Wise and Moderate Discourse concerning Church Affaires,* and *Certaine Considerations, Touching the better Pacification and Edification of the Church of England,* first published, anonymously, in 1604 and reissued anonymously in 1640. Milton knew both tracts, as George Whiting has demonstrated (*Milton's Literary Milieu* [1939], pp. 267–69), although he makes much more use of the former, which, written in 1589 during the Marprelate pamphletwar, provides many apt comments on the violent controversies of 1641. He seems to have read them hot off the presses; an entry in *CB* (18 : 180), an oblique reference to a "learned English writer" in *Ref* (3 : 18; cf. Whiting, p. 268), and a reference in *Animad* (3 : 111–12) show that he knew them before they were called to his attention by their use in the *Modest Confutation* by his anonymous antagonist. Whiting has made the appropriate comparisons and generalizations afforded by an examination of Bacon's views on church reform and Milton's. It is sufficient to say here that Bacon's discourses are indeed "wise and moderate" in contrast to the zealous and fiercely partisan Milton, and that both Milton and the prelatical Modest Confutant with equal unfairness mine the sentences of the irenicist solely for the gems that show well in the light of their own polemic position. The Confutant may have somewhat the better conscience in the matter (though Whiting thinks it "not improbable that Milton derived from Bacon's tracts more support, moral if not factual" than his survey of the actual positions of the two men can indicate [p. 281]), since Bacon, unlike Milton, obviously had no interest in hewing down episcopacy root and branch—an operation that he, like Charles's bishops, regarded as dangerously subversive to the state itself—and indeed did not favor extreme positions of any sort. Milton also finds support for his opposition to licensing in Bacon's tracts on church affairs (*Areop* 4 : 326, 332f.), although Bacon (who, as Don M. Wolfe points out, "profoundly distrusted the free trade of ideas Milton was to picture in *Areopagitica*" and "had no confidence in the political or intellectual future of the humble man" [Yale *Prose* 1 : 27]) could scarcely have endorsed the position his observations were pressed to serve.

An interesting opportunity to assess the impact of rhetorical exigencies on Milton's structuring of an argument presents itself in his seemingly contradictory estimates of the value of utopias in *Apol* (3 : 294–95) and *Areop* (4 : 316–18). The same ethical idealism and practical didacticism would seem to sustain both positions, in fact : it is the sublime wit in "teaching this our world better and exacter things, then were yet known, or us'd," that evokes his praise of Plato, More, and Bacon in the first instance (in contrast to Bishop Hall's* supposed lack of

such redeeming high seriousness in *Mundus Alter atque Idem*), and the danger that Plato's authority in favor of censorship will make against his own efforts to show us how "to ordain wisely as in this world of evill" that leads him to deprecate utopias in general in the second (and in any case, *"Atlantick"* there may as well refer to Plato's Atlantis in the *Critias* as to Bacon's unfinished ideal society). On the whole, nothing that Milton says, even in the toils of polemic strife, ever implies that he has anything but the highest respect for Bacon.

As summary statements, those offered by Whiting and E. L. Marilla ("Milton and Bacon : A Paradox," *English Studies* 36 [1955] : 106–11) are difficult to fault in their large emphases. Whiting sees Milton as "the fervent idealist" whose zealous partisanship blinds him to the virtues of his opponents and the vices of his own party—a view that might be modified by noting simply that Milton's massive sense of unity, harmony, and decorum, while embracing much, simply cannot embrace the cool, dispassionate observation and compromise that make Bacon "the practical statesman" and an artist of the possible (see Whiting, p. 278). In addition Whiting's overstatement ignores Milton's rhetorical stance. Marilla notes as his central "paradox" the "fundamental difference in their philosophy of life," linked only by deep concern for the imperfections of this world and scorn for the "speculation" of the universities, and by a positive belief that it is "the obligation of every capable person, in the interests of humanity, to commit himself to the purpose of improving the conditions of that world" (p. 106). Marilla observes that Milton shares with Bacon chiefly in the negative portions of Bacon's attempts to clear the mind of man from idle and useless concepts, and at least in his earlier years, in the general spirit of optimism that characterizes the Baconian venture. Milton admires Verulam as a great Englishman and a great mind, and uses him as a weighty witness even in his maturity when it suits his purposes; but he cannot have found in the real central concerns of the *Great Instauration* and the Baconian analysis of the arts of life much to command his continued attention or assent. On the whole, they labored in different vineyards. [MLD]

BAILLIE, ROBERT: *see* ANTAGONISTS.

BANQUET OF JESTS, A. One of the most popular miscellanies of witty pieces of prose and poetry, *A Banquet of Jests* went through a number of editions, but some editions were totally different from others and some duplicated parts of the previous contents. The editions of 1640 (the sixth) and 1657 included "Another on the same" and "Hobson's Epitaph" (attributed). The compiler has sometimes been identified with Archie Armstrong, a well-known Court jester who lent his name to other miscellanies and whose jests at first were apparently their main contents. But his connection with *A Banquet of Jests,* or at least the 1640 and 1657 editions, is not evidential. [JTS]

BAPTISTES: *see* ATTRIBUTIONS.

BAPTISTS: *see* ANABAPTISTS AND BAPTISTS.

BARBERINI, FRANCESCO, CARDINAL (1597–1678). The Cardinal was prime minister of Rome and chief counselor to his uncle, Pope Urban VIII (Maffeo Barberini, 1568–1644). The Casa Barberini was a social and diplomatic center of Rome, and during his second visit to Rome in February 1639, Milton attended a public musical entertainment there through Lukas Holste*, secretary and librarian to the Cardinal. The entertainment may have been Giulio Rospiglioni's comic opera *Chi soffre speri,* with music by Virgilio Mazzocchi and Marco Marazzuoli and the stage design by Bernini. It was presented on February 17, 1639. The greeter for the occasion was the Cardinal's brother, Antonio, and in the large audience was Cardinal Mazarin of France. Milton would not have heard Leonora Baroni* at the Casa Barberini, as formerly alleged, because women were not admitted. The day after the entertainment, we learn from a letter to Holste, dated March 19, 1639, and written when Milton had proceeded to Florence, Milton was granted an audience with the Cardinal, who was a patron of the arts and the founder of the Barberini Library, which Milton undoubtedly visited. Oddly, Milton does not mention the Cardinal in the section of *2Def* dealing with his Italian trip. [JTS]

BARETTI, GIUSEPPI: *see* ANDREINI, GIOVANNI.

BARLOW, JOEL: *see* INFLUENCE IN AMERICA, MILTON'S.

BARON, RICHARD (d. 1766), editor of Milton's prose. A staunch republican, he published Algernon Sidney's *Discourse Concerning Government* (1751), the revision of Thomas Birch's* edition of Milton's *Prose Works* (1753), the first separate edition of *Eikon* since 1650 (1756, 1770), and Marchamont Needham's* *The Excellency of a Free-State* (1757). Baron reprinted the second edition of *Eikon;* all other editions since 1650 had used the first. The introduction was on "The Transcendent Excellence of Milton's Prose Works." Baron's revision of Birch includes the first printing of Moses Wall's* letter to Milton. [JTS]

BARON, ROBERT: *see* INFLUENCE ON LITERATURE, MILTON'S.

BARONI, LEONORA. Three Latin epigrams supply the information that Milton heard the famous Leonora Baroni (1611–1670) sing during his trip to Italy in early 1639. The poems were almost expected reactions to praise the occasion, which was in Rome. There is nothing unusual in Milton's having written them. It has often been assumed that Milton heard the celebrated diva at the Casa Barberini*, but recent argument has denied that even she, as a woman, would have been allowed to sing there. The musical entertainment that Milton heard may have been Giulio Rospiglioni's comic opera *Chi soffre speri,* on February 27, 1639; Leonora was a friend and protégé of the composer, and perhaps his mistress. Milton's praise of Leonora seems hyperbolic, but it is standard and not excessive when compared with others'. There is nothing suggestive of love poetry, despite Jonathan Richardson's* attitude and attempt to link the Italian sonnets with her. Leonora was from Naples and the daughter of the well-known musician Adriana Baroni, both of which facts are alluded to in the epigrams. [JTS]

BAROQUE, MILTON AND. The origin of the term *baroque* is still controversial. René Wellek has recently suggested "a confluence of . . . two words of different etymologies." In his opinion, the Italian word *barocco* derives (as B. Croce suggested) from the mnemonic term *baroco,* the "fourth mode of the second figure" of the syllogism. On the other hand, the French adjective *baroque* apparently derives from the Portuguese word *barroco,* "a jewelers' term for the irregular, odd-shaped pearl . . . " (see "The Concept of Baroque in Literary Scholarship" and "Postscript 1962" in *Concepts of Criticism,* ed. Stephen G. Nichols, Jr. [1963], pp. 69–127). In the sixteenth and seventeenth centuries, Continental authors sometimes ridiculed sophistic or pedantic hair-splitting as "arguments in *baroco.*" During the eighteenth century the term *baroque* usually meant "extravagant" or "bizarre" and was applied pejoratively to architectural and musical styles* that violated neoclassical canons of classical form and good taste. Burckhardt applied this term to what he regarded as the "decadent" phase of Renaissance architectural style, and Heinrich Wölfflin subsequently analyzed it in more favorable terms, tracing its development from the "classical" style of the High Renaissance in painting and sculpture as well as in architecture and suggesting analogies in literary history.

In *Renaissance and Baroque* (1888)

Wölfflin compared the poetry of Tasso* to baroque art, contrasting it with the "Renaissance" style of Ariosto*. Subsequently, in *Principles of Art History* (1915), he analyzed the evolution of the baroque style in the visual arts in terms of a five-part schema of antithetical pairs: linear and painterly, plane and recession, closed and open form, multiplicity and unity, absolute and relative clarity. (For the subsequent diffusion of the term and the application of Wölfflin's categories to literature, see Wellek, "Definitions"; also Wolfgang Stechow, *Journal of Aesthetics and Art Criticism* 5 : 109–15. In *JAAC* 12 : 421–37, John H. Mueller reexamined the "historical shifts in meaning" of this word and the problem of its validity as a musicological concept.) Eighteenth-century critics condemned the music of Rameau as "bizarre, baroque, et dépourvu de mélodie" and that of Durante as "baroque, coarse, and uncouth." Recent criticism of baroque music often describes the period as having a "heterogeneous and often unrelated group of traits. . . ." Many of these are "mutually contradictory" or "so general and abstract that they are quite as applicable to almost every other period in history." In Mueller's opinion, it is "illogical to assume" that men of the Renaissance were "languishing in emotionless frustration awaiting the 'richer vocabulary' of the baroque and romantic ages which would permit them to release their profoundest sentiments," and such an analysis "points up the fallacy of exclusive subjectivity which permeates so much of the discussion on the nature of baroque. . . ."

Many of the scholars who have adopted this term as a literary category—Praz, Warren, Croll, Warnke, Nelson, Daniells, Sypher, and others—or have attempted to exploit Wölfflin's schema are aware of the difficulties involved and the need for critical restraint. The Wölfflinian categories concern technical problems peculiar to the visual arts, and their relevance to literature depends partly on the hypothesis of a basic psychological or spiritual unity underlying the culture of an entire age. Skeptical of the assumptions of *Geistesgeschichte* and of literary or visual styles as projections of individual or collective tensions, historians frequently differ in their interpretation of historical trends and their relevance to literature and art. Against the overemphasis on the Counter-Reformation element in the baroque, Wellek stressed the significance of "unmistakable Protestant baroque" in several countries. He was critical not only of efforts to "define baroque in purely stylistic terms," but of most "ideological or socio-psychological" explanations and of endeavors (potentially more successful) to define it in terms of "a philosophy or a world-view or even a merely emotional attitude toward the world." The student of baroque as a period-style, in literature or in art, must also take into account the problem of differentiating it from mannerism* (which Wölfflin's schema ignored), national and individual variations, and alternative conceptions of the baroque as a particular phase of late Renaissance or post-Renaissance style and culture and (more broadly) as a recurrent phase not only in ancient and medieval Europe but also in other cultures.

Like Tasso*, Shakespeare*, Vondel* —and, indeed, Dryden*, Molière, and Racine—Milton has been classified as a baroque writer. Though Schirmer excluded him from this category, Wellek and Rosemund Tuve cited a wide variety of authors—Meissner, Reynold, Cerny, Hatzfeld, Lebègue, Buffum, Raymond, Rousset—who regarded Milton as a baroque artist. Hatzfeld went so far as to describe him as "the most hispanized poet of the age, who to the foreigner appears the most baroque" (Wellek, "Definitions"). In *Die geistesgeschichtlichen Grundlagen des englischen Literaturbarocks* (Munich, 1934), Paul Meissner perceived in the literature of the seventeenth century a reflection of the dualistic tendencies and split ("zweispältig") character of the age —an "antithetic" and divided "feeling for life" (*Lebensgefühl*) that stood in striking contrast to the harmonious tendencies of humanism*. Examining the tensions of the

period in terms of six antitheses (expansion and contraction, macrocosm and microcosm, sin and redemption, faith and reason, absolutism and democracy, and atectonic and tectonic style), Meissner found these polarities present in the works of Milton as well as in those of his contemporaries (cf. pp. 43, 165, 210, 217, 260, 262).

In "The Baroque Element in Milton" (*English Miscellany* 1 : 31–42), Margaret Bottrall denied that Donne* and the *concettisti* are "baroque poets" and preferred the term *mannerist*; it was "precisely their mannerisms which so worried Dr. Johnson." Though Crashaw may properly be called baroque, Donne and Quarles, Herbert and Benlowes are essentially "mannerist" poets. Milton, on the other hand, is "the one major poet whose work exemplifies the full grandeur of the baroque style." Censuring E. I. Watkin for excluding Milton from this category on the grounds that he "was too classical and too Hebraic to be called baroque," Bottrall found Milton "characteristically baroque in his audacity of enterprise," the "amplitude and richness" of his poetic descriptions, his "fondness for figures hurtling through space," his attitude to his material, and his synthesis of impressions related to different senses. Satan's cherubic disguise recalls a Bernini angel, and his palace of Pandemonium "suggests the gorgeousness of a baroque church. . . ."

In *Poetry and Humanism* (1950; rept. 1970), M. M. Mahood likewise saw Milton as essentially a "baroque artist." In mood and tone and in subject matter his *Nat* belongs to the baroque tradition. It possesses "a Baroque amplitude of conception," and like the finest contemporary works of art in the grand style, "it is saved from turgidity by the vigour of its movement." In *PL* Milton's comparison between the field of Enna and the garden of Eden achieves a "typical Baroque fusion," and his infusion of "intellectual humility into the humanist faith in scientific method" in the dialogue on astronomy is a "striking example of the strenuous Baroque attempt at reintegration." No work is "more characteristic" than *SA* "of the Baroque age, when the perennial conflict between a true and false humanism was intensified by the moral, political and economic individualism of the Renaissance." Similarly, it is "in keeping with the Baroque spirit" that his reconciliation between the medieval *contemptus mundi* and "the Renaissance thirst after glory . . . should be effected through transcendence rather than through compromise. . . ."

In Milton's representation of the third temptation in *PR*, Hanford perceived "one of the high moments of Milton's art, an English masterpiece of the baroque, analogous to great Italian painting" (*John Milton, Englishman* [1950], p. 244). Hanford also suggested that *PL*, with its "fusion of Christian and pagan imagery, its visualizations of Biblical legend and of classical mythology, its rich perspectives and its profusion of detail," may be "best illustrated" by the paintings that had confronted Milton in Italy (p. 118).

Wylie Sypher's *Four Stages of Renaissance Style* (1955) examined the analogies between the verbal and visual arts during the three centuries from 1400 to 1700, distinguishing between "Renaissance," "Mannerist," "Baroque," and "Late-Baroque" phases and applying Wölfflin's categories to Milton and other writers. Sypher saw *Lyc* as "perhaps the greatest mannerist poem, and one where the planes of reality are so interchanging and complex" that we shall never be able to "read" it fully. *PL* and *SA* represent "the fruition of a Counter-Reformation style in literature." The images of Satan in Hell and the infernal council are "composed in baroque space . . . ," and the scene at Hell-gate reveals the poet's "baroque vision." The action in *SA* possesses "the public dimensions of high-baroque art. . . ." *PR* portrays "a late-baroque encounter of opposing spiritual forces"; like Racine, Milton refuses to be "seduced by any magnificent high-baroque spectacles. . . ." Just as Racine "destroyed the heroic idols of the baroque theater,"

so the Milton of *PR* destroys "his baroque idols also, and the violence of his Protestant austerity speaks . . . against the Counter-Reformation rites. . . ."

In Sypher's opinion, the differences between Milton's two epics reflect the differences between baroque and late-baroque. The Council of Trent* had inaugurated a "phase of reintegration in the arts," resolving the "unresolved tensions" of mannerism in a style that "returns to the idealism of the renaissance grand style for some of its formal laws, but exercises these laws with an exultant . . . spirit and a satisfaction in the textures of the material world." The baroque style formally resolves the mannerist tensions in dense masses of material, redundant statement, kinetic energy, . . . a monumental academic balance, and flashing color and light." It depends not "upon mannerist contingencies, but upon assurances and certainties," and wins assent "through its power over the sensorium alone." The "supreme baroque literature" appears not in Tasso, but in *PL* and *SA*.

The late-baroque style is characterized by "exaggerated contrast or counterpoise," and its differences from the preceding baroque phase may be illustrated by comparing Dryden's "Song for Saint Cecilia's Day" with the verse paragraphs of *PL*. The "heroic style of late-baroque" is subsequently "purified under academic jurisdiction" and finally "achieves intense moral and psychological force in the controlled, naked style of Racine and Milton's *PR*, a style marked by dramatic conflict and a spiritual testing of baroque energies."

In *Milton, Mannerism and Baroque* (1963) and in several essays—such as *University of Toronto Quarterly* 14: 393–408 and *Journal of Aesthetics and Art Criticism* 5:115–21—Daniells considered Milton as primarily a "baroque craftsman." Emphasizing the element of paradox and ambiguity in *PL* and the contrast between the poetic methods of Milton and Spenser*, he interpreted *PL* as "a piece of Baroque structure," emphasized the baroque elements in *PR* and

SA, and analyzed the mannerist elements in *Lyc* and *Mask.* In utilizing Wölfflin's categories of Renaissance and baroque style and in applying the concepts of art history to literature, he recognized their limited validity in literary criticism and was usually cautious in applying them.

In *Comparative Literature Studies 3:* 95–108, Joseph Frank reexamined Milton's major poetry, taking "as a point of departure one persistent trait that seems to distinguish . . . Baroque architecture, painting, and sculpture." It is the "overcoming of self-imposed obstacles, combined with a strong sense of tradition" that makes Milton "a Baroque artist," deliberately distorting "traditional materials in order to make his creative acts more difficult, his productions more sensational, his talents more conspicuous." Milton's "poetry generally becomes more Baroque as his theology becomes less assured. . . ." *Mask* is more baroque than *L'Al* and *IlP,* and its "uncertainties and irresolutions" may be "deliberate and audacious." Though *Lyc* seems "a medley of irresolutions, conventions, fragments" when taken line by line, the ensemble seems "resolved, unique, unified." *PL* is "the great example of a Baroque epic," *PR* is "fully as Baroque" as its predecessor, and *SA* is "essentially Baroque in its stretching of a traditional form."

In *Baroque Lyric Poetry* (1961), Lowry Nelson, Jr., emphasized the structural role of time and drama in the poetry of Milton and his near-contemporaries. He called attention to Milton's use of space in *PL,* to "the panoramic, almost hallucinatory shifts in space" in *L'Al* and *IlP,* and to "the juxtaposition of distant places" in *Lyc* and later poems. The "contemporaneous" presentation of two time planes in *Nat* resembles the "confusion of tenses" in Góngora's *Polifemo.* In *Lyc* he observes "the gradual process of reconciling the movement of tenses from the remote past with the main time plane . . . ," as well as an instance of the trend "in Baroque poetry toward greater dramaticality. . . ." In both respects it "stands as one of the most nearly complete fulfillments of

peculiarly Baroque tendencies in style."

W. R. Parker* called attention to "the crowded, almost baroque panels" that predominate in *Nat (Milton,* p. 63). Douglas Bush observed that in "conception, ordered development, and ordered exuberance of rhythm" this poem "had no English predecessor or successor" and suggested that "those for whom the word has a meaning may call the poem baroque" (*John Milton* [1964], p. 36). Balachandra Rajan commented that if *Nat* is baroque, "it is so in a manner decidedly Miltonic," and its "controlled exuberance . . . finds echoes in unexpected places such as the eulogy of discipline" in *RCG (The Lofty Rhyme* [1970], p. 13).

Mario Praz suggested that England "offers the almost paradoxical case, on the one hand, of a literature to which the definition Baroque seems to fit to a nicety . . . and, on the other hand, of an art in which Baroque characteristics appear only late and briefly. . . ." While recognizing the pitfalls involved in fitting art-historical categories to literature, he nevertheless recognized "a kinship of taste between creative *concetti* . . . and certain devices and surprising effects of Baroque architects and painters," and he noted that certain characteristics of English litterature of the late sixteenth and early seventeenth centuries were first interpreted as baroque but have since been recognized as mannerist. Though Praz regarded the label *baroque* as a misnomer when applied to Donne, he argued that in the case of Milton and Crashaw "one may speak of an English literary Baroque with much more foundation than for Shakespeare . . ." (*Modern Philology* 61 : 169–79).

Observing that the term *baroque* became "a stylistic as well as a periodic description," Frank Kermode extended this category to Milton's poetry as well as to Bach's music, Leibniz's philosophy, and "some Hellenistic sculpture." He found Góngora's Latinism more like Milton's than like Donne's and suggested that, as in Milton, this produces "an untranslatable *asprezza,* a harshness made of meaning, but not Donne's kind of harshness." On "a cursory glance there are more differences than resemblances in the poetry of the three great 'baroque' poets." Though continental theorists are "usually ready to call Milton a baroque poet," nobody "ever seriously called him a metaphysical*" (*The Metaphysical Poets* [1969], pp. 14–16). In *The Age of the Baroque* [1952], pp. 45–48), Carl J. Friedrich detected this sense of power in Milton "as he faced the cosmic struggle of good and evil, of God and Satan. . . . There was in Milton, more perhaps than in any other poet of his time, a deep sense of the dynamic spiritual potential of language. . . . A sense of power calls in the artist for the capacity to portray, to dramatize tension; that is the quintessence of baroque." Friedrich regarded Milton's Satan as perhaps "as striking a portrayal of baroque man as the age created" and called attention to the "baroque word-painting" —ornate and artificial—in Milton's description of the "procession of evil spirits leagued with Satan."

Rosemond Tuve's essay (in *Milton Studies in Honor of Harris Francis Fletcher* [1961], pp. 209–25), criticized the tendency to treat *baroque* and *mannerist* as dogmatic categories, and questioned the validity of the "familiar differentiating traits" and criteria usually employed in order to define and delimit these categories. Though critics still tend to adduce two sorts of criteria—"touching stylistic elements or touching attitudes of mind"— the majority of attempts to demonstrate Milton's baroque qualities neglect the former criteria and overstress the latter. Such criteria as far-fetched metaphors, "superabundance of images," the desire "to surprise and startle," and artistry "for its own sake" are essentially subjective. But these difficulties in "criteria touching stylistic matters" seem slight in comparison with criteria "erected directly upon our conceptions of the author's state of mind." The criteria of not being "at home in the world" and "disturbed balance" as indexes of mannerism or baroque reveal the "fatal shortcoming of all criteria based on attitude and state of mind"—the fact that in literature the criteria "must immediately count on perfected decisions concerning the most problematic and the last thing we know about any work, the full nature and import of the entire poetic subject." Stressing "the intimate relation in literature between poetic subject and the decorum of the piece," Tuve doubted the value of *baroque* and *mannerist* as "categories through which we will group poems more reliably and understand them more fully."

In spite of its "difficulties and the increasing welter of its meanings," the term *baroque* remains (as Wellek observed) "the one term for the style between the Renaissance and classicism which is sufficiently general to override the local terms of schools," and its discussion has "contributed enormously to our understanding of a time and art which was for a long time ignored, disparaged, or misinterpreted." In his judgment, this is "sufficient justification for its continued use," and we would be wise to accept this verdict. [JMS]

BARROW, SAMUEL (1625–1682), physician whom Milton may have known during the 1650s when, according to Masson, Barrow was secretary to General Monck* and chief physician to his army, but almost nothing is known of their subsequent relationship. Masson cites no source for his statements, and inferences that Milton and Barrow were good friends really have no foundation. The forty-two commendatory lines *In Paradisum Amissam Summi Poetæ Johannis Miltoni* prefixed to the second edition of *PL* were initialed S. B., M.D., whom John Toland* identified as Barrow. The poem emphasizes the universal range of Milton's epic and deprecates Homer* and Virgil* in comparison. "Whoever reads these lines will think that Homer sang only of frogs, Virgil only of fleas." S. B. also notes that Satan "walks hardly less great than Michael himself." [WM]

BARRY, RICHARD, 2nd Earl of Barrymore (1630–1694), son of Alice (Boyle) and David Barry (1604–1642), Viscount Buttevant. He may have spent as long as two years (1645–1647?) as Milton's student while the poet resided in his Barbican house. To escape the terrors of the siege at Youghal, Barry (descended from a distinguished Irish family) and his mother journeyed to London in July 1645; there Lady Alice and her son shared the house occupied by Alice's sister, Katherine, Lady Ranelagh*. Perhaps she had been introduced to Milton by Samuel Hartlib*, or perhaps also having read Milton's essay *Educ,* Lady Ranelagh may have suggested the poet as a likely tutor for the fifteen-year-old earl. Barry's grandfather, the first Earl of Cork, had included a liberal sum (£200 per year) in his will for the boy's education. What Barry gained from Milton's instruction we may never know, and what we do know of his later career may be stated in a few facts.

In Paris in 1649 he married Susan Killigrew, a maid of honor in the court of Henrietta Maria. He was later to marry —in London in 1656—Martha Lawrence, daughter of Amy (Peyton) and Henry Lawrence*, who was then President of Cromwell's Council of State*. At the Restoration, Barry retired to Ireland; in 1666 records reveal his marriage to Dorothy Ferrer. Although he managed extensive lands and was in a position to exert considerable political influence, his political career in Ireland was a particularly undistinguished one. [JGT]

BASIL THE GREAT, one of the Fathers of the Greek Church. He was born about 330 and died in 379 at Caesarea, where for the last nine years he had served as Bishop, succeeding Eusebius*, the most learned man of his day and a great favorite of Constantine*. Basil himself had been trained in Constantinople and Athens in philosophy and rhetoric, gaining fame as a champion of the orthodox faith against Arianism*. Now he is chiefly remembered for reforming the liturgy, founding monasticism, and

writing a series of sermons on the opening of Genesis, the six days of creation, entitled *Homiliae in Hexameron.* From Basil's *Homiliae in Psalmos* Milton draws in *CB* such seminal notions as : "Basil tells us that poetry was taught by God to kindle in the minds of men a zeal for virtue" (18 : 139). He also quotes Basil in *Ref,* and the hexameral* material in *PL 7* undoubtedly derives in some degree from Basil's work. [PMZ]

BATE, GEORGE: *see* ANTAGONISTS.

BEDE, THE VENERABLE, was born around 673 near the monastery at Jarrow, at Monkton in County Durham. He died in 735 at the same monastery, at which he had spent most of his life. At the age of seven, Bede began his education at Jarrow, where he was ordained deacon twelve years later. In 702 or 703 he was ordained a priest, and he devoted the remainder of his life to study and writing. His early works, including a tract on versification, *De Arte Metrica,* are of little importance beside his mature studies such as the *History of the Abbots of Wearmouth and Jarrow* and a *Life of Cuthbert* (in verse and in prose). But his major work was the *Ecclesiastical History of the English Nation,* for which he drew materials "either from ancient documents, or from the tradition of the elders, or from [his] own knowledge." For this attempt to distinguish between fact and fiction in recording historical events of the early English church, he earned the title "Father of English History." The *Ecclesiastical History* remains a major source of information about the early church, and its tales of Caedmon and Edwin of Northumbria are classic.

Its earliest printing appeared at Strasbourg, possibly in 1475. The first modern English translation was published in 1565, at Antwerp. However, the 1643 parallel text edition of Abraham Wheeloc* served as Milton's most immediate source. Wheeloc's edition, published at Cambridge, offered the first printing in England of the Latin text and the first printing of

Alfred's Old English translation. Milton's interest apparently lay with the Latin version, since there is small likelihood that he could read Anglo-Saxon*.

In 1639 Milton had undertaken "a systematic examination of British history" (French Fogle, *Milton as Historian. Two Papers* [1965], p. 3). Although in this period he mentions Bede twice in *CB* —once using the story of Caedmon to illustrate "De Poeticâ" ("A marvelous and very pleasing anecdote is told in Bede's History about an Englishman who suddenly by act of God became a poet" [18 : 139]) and again indicating Bede as a source used by Holinshed* (18 : 169)—the *Ecclesiastical History* was clearly not yet one of his major sources for early historical materials. Dissatisfied with sixteenth- and seventeenth-century historiography*, Milton saw in the Wheeloc edition an opportunity to learn English history from its primary sources. The Latin version of Bede, which "he was to depend on constantly for the Saxon period of his *History of Britain*" (Fogle, Yale *Prose* 5 : xxxvii), along with the *Anglo-Saxon Chronicle* (also published by Wheeloc), Lambarde's* *Archaionomia*, Spelman's* *Concilia*, and Ussher's* *De Primordiis*, supplied him with hitherto unavailable and generally accurate data on early English history and may have inspired him to undertake his own full-scale history of England.

Much of the moralistic tone of Milton's *Brit* may be traceable to that of Bede. "In Bede, the English reformers found memories of a native, undefiled Christianity contending with Roman corruption" (Kliger, *Goths in England* [1952], p. 80). But in *Brit*, Milton holds both Britons and Saxons in contempt, seeing "old English immorality not as ordinary sinfulness but specifically as the folly of a people who have an exceptional genius for liberty but who lack the requisite wisdom to reap its fruit in a democratic government" (Kliger, p. 152). Like Gildas*, one of Bede's major sources, Milton saw history, the great teacher, primarily in terms of "divine reward and punishment" (Fogle, *Milton*

as Historian, p. 15). He could hardly help seeing a parallel between the Englishmen of Bede's time and those of his own.

Milton's other specific references and indebtedness to Bede are less significant. In *PrelE*, he uses Bede along with Sulpicius Severus* as authority for praise of clerical poverty ("As for those *Brittaine* Bishops which you cite, take heed what you doe, for our *Brittaine* Bishops lesse ancient then these, were remarkable for nothing more then their poverty, as *Sulp. Severus,* and *Beda* can remember you of examples good store" [3 : i, 98]). Again in *Hire*, Bede is cited as authority, this time for Milton's condemnation of tithing (6: 65). He is also referred to in *1Def* (7 : 437), as well as briefly noted in the "Outlines for Tragedies" (18 : 242) and "Marginalia" (18 : 329, 330). Possibly the idea in *PL* 4. 20 that Satan creates his own hell* is derived in part from Bede. [AA]

BEELZEBUB. Originally the chief god of the Syrians, the idol of the Ekronites (2 Kings 1 : 2), Beelzebub is a corrupted term more properly written Baalzebub or Beelzebul. Nothing being more common than for the deities of one nation to be converted into the demons of another, Beelzebub was designated by the Hebrews and also by Jesus as the supreme evil spirit. The popular appellation, "lord of flies," derives from the legend that Beelzebub appeared as a fly and from the belief that his temple was infested with flies, which some authorities believe he had the power of driving away. According to Alexander Ross* (*Pansebeia* [London, 1653]), Beelzebub was variously taken for Jupiter, Priapus, Sumanus, and Pluto; and according to biblical commentators (Renaissance and modern) his name, as used in the New Testament, denotes the "Evil One" (i.e., Satan, Belial).

If Beelzebub's and Satan's names are used interchangeably in the New Testament, where Beelzebub is called the prince or chief of devils (Matt. 12 : 24, Mark 3 : 22, Luke 11 : 15), Beelzebub is distinguished from Satan in the Apocryphal* Gospel of Nicodemus, which records a dispute between Satan, "the prince and captain of death," and Beelzebub, "the prince of hell" (15 and 18 : 14). Beelzebub upbraids Satan for persecuting Christ; and Christ, in return for being able to rescue Adam and his sons from hell, gives Beelzebub dominion over Satan, who is described by his new superior as "prince of destruction, author of . . . defeat and banishment . . . prince of all evil, author of death and source of all pride" (18 : 1, 12).

There are, then, two traditions : one that identifies Beelzebub and Satan, another that differentiates between them. During the Middle Ages the first tradition gained predominance because of the authority assigned to Scripture and because of the pressure such authority exerted on literary tradition. Beelzebub, for instance, is the name by which Dante* refers to Satan (*Inferno* 34. 127); and this same tradition extends into the Renaissance, which accounts for the fact that where Tasso* writes "Belzebú" in *Gerusalemme Liberata,* Fairfax can translate the name "Satan" (7. 99). In the mystery plays, these two traditions converge. The names of Lucifer, Satan, Beelzebub, and Belial appear in the various cycles, and when they do, Satan and Lucifer always refer to the same person, whereas the names Beelzebub and Belial are sometimes used synonymously with the name of Satan and at other times they are used to mark a distinction between the three devils (see · L. W. Cushman, *The Devil and the Vice* [1900], esp. pp. 18–20). However incidental this latter tendency may be in exegetical and literary tradition, it is of central importance to occult literature, where Beelzebub and Satan are regularly distinguished from each other.

Once they differentiate Beelzebub and the other demons from Satan, the occultists proceed to rank them in a hierarchal order that parallels the divine order from which they have fallen. This practice, authorized by the Apocryphal Book of Enoch and encouraged by Thomas Aquinas*, was popularized by Johannes Faustus in *Miraculous Art and Book of Marvels* (1469), Robert Burton* in *Anatomy of Melancholy* (1621), and Thomas Heywood in *The Hierarchie of the Blessed Angells* (1635). The system, presented embryonically by Faustus, is modified and amplified by Burton and Heywood.

Related to the occult tradition of the demonic hierarchy is the iconographic tradition of representing the devil with three faces—a tradition that derives from the Gospel of Nicodemus and the Good Friday Sermon of Eusebius of Alexandria. The references to the devil as "three-headed Beelzebub" find analogues in other trinitarian conceptions of evil—the three-headed Hecuba, for example, and also the three-headed Cerberus. In Christian art the diabolic trinity develops as a parallel to and parody of the heavenly Trinity*. The tradition of a three-headed devil, found in paintings, works of sculpture, and manuscript ornaments, culminates in Dante's portrayal of the three-headed Lucifer (*Inferno* 34). Most important, however, is that in this tradition the previous ones converge. Not only is the devil given three faces in the typical representations of him, but additional faces are fixed to his shoulders, knees, and lower parts, each with its distinctive physiognomy recalling the infernal hierarchy. Whereas the different faces point to the tendency of distinguishing between the different devils, their close identification with Satan suggests that the artist admits as a possibility the interpretation that sees the devils as extensions of Satan, revealing in caricature the many facets of his evil nature.

The uncertainty about the relationship that exists between the devils and Satan as manifested in Christian drama and iconography* and articulated by Aquinas persists into the Renaissance and is doubtless behind Milton's decision to allow both traditions to exist side by side but not with equal authority. Milton seems to have believed with Dr. Johnson* that "what philosophy suggests to us on this topic is probable : what scripture tells us is certain" and with John Rainolds that while "gross ignorance will interpret allegory literally . . . truly learned men, comprehending subtlety, will discern its deeper meaning." In Milton's prose works the names of Beelzebub and Satan are used interchangeably, but in *PL* the two traditions—one of them differentiating the various demons*, the other consolidating them in the figure of Satan—converge and are brilliantly reconciled.

In his initial reference to Beelzebub (Belzebub in *RCG* 3 : 216, and *DDD* 3 : 437; Beëlzebub in *3Def* 9 : 279; Baalzebub in *SA* 1231), Milton suggests that while "the common people had a reverent esteeme" for Christ, "the gowned *Rabbies* . . . were of opinion that he was a friend of Beelzebub" (*Animad* 3 : 131). This reflection is reiterated in *RCG*, where Milton recalls that Christ was identified with Beelzebub by the "predecessors" of the prelates, and in *CD*, where Milton recalls that the Pharisees, accusing Christ falsely "of acting in concert with Beelzebub," sinned "unpardonably" against "the Father himself," since He was the spirit working within the Son and thus the one whom the Pharisees identified with "the prince of the devils, or an unclean spirit" (14 : 397). These reflections point back to Matthew 10 : 25; 12 : 24, 26–28; Mark 3 : 22; and Luke 11 : 15, 18–19. In *CD* Milton also asserts his belief that Satan "has obtained many names corresponding to his actions" and thus associates him with Beelzebub, Abaddon, Apollyon (15 : 111). In other prose references, adopting from political rhetoric* the device of identifying his opponent with the devil, Milton says that not even Beelzebub would commit "such a peece of folly" as "to divide against himself and pervert his own ends" (*DDD* 3 : 437); and later, having attributed to Beelzebub ferocity and confidence, Milton says of Alexander More* that one "would almost think him another Beëlzebub, but that he merely cast out flies" (*3Def* 9 : 279). These references to Beelzebub in Milton's prose reveal his familiarity with traditions—scriptural, patristic, literary, and occult—involving the infernal deities.

Grant McColley (*Paradise Lost: An Account of Its Growth and Major Sources* [1940]) explains that in *PL* Milton observes the traditional hierarchy of devils at the same time that he omits many of its minute particulars; but like other recent commentators, McColley ignores the fact that in observing this tradition Milton appears to embrace an incidental rather than central tradition of Christianity. Given Milton's insistence in *CD* that the devils "retain . . . their respective ranks" in hell (1 : 9), his differentiation of the various devils is less than curious; but given Milton's practice of not contradicting Scripture, together with his insistence in the same work that Beelzebub is just another name for Satan, his differentiation of Beelzebub (and also Belial, Mammon, and Moloch) seems a violation of the tradition Milton holds in greatest esteem. This realization caused Coleridge* to object to Milton's "addition of Fiction": "Readers have learnt from Milton alone, that Satan & Beelzebub were different Persons (in Scriptures they are different names of the same Evil Being)." Milton's "Fiction," Coleridge continues, "produces an effect too light, too much savoring of capricious Invention, for the exceeding solemnity of the subject" (*Romantics on Milton*, ed. Joseph Wittreich [1970], p. 211). The same point was made a century before by Defoe who, attempting to correct Milton's mistaken understanding of "the History of the *Devil*," argues that the names of Beelzebub, Belial, Mammon, and Moloch—"all names proper and peculiar to *Satan* himself"—are derived from and adapted to "the several shapes he has appeared in to do his mischief in the world" (*History of the Devil* [1727], pp. 39, 43).

Coleridge's and Defoe's objections recall an understanding articulated by Milton himself—an understanding as prevalent in their time as it was in Milton's. Lucas Debes insisted that the various devils are "spectres" of Satan, the same spirit in different manifestations. Similarly, John Deacon and John Walker argued that the various princes of the different infernal orders are "all joyntly *combined* together in *Satan* himselfe" (*A Summarie Answere* [1601], p. 149). Whatever qualities the princes of hell exhibit, whatever powers they execute, are "onely in *Satan* himselfe, and not peculiar to any of the rest" (ibid.). This is the view Milton adopts in *PL,* along with another, also formulated by Deacon and Walker, of how evil should be portrayed : any attempt to depict the devil or to conceptualize evil should be done through allegory* and metaphor where more is meant than is literally expressed. The various devils (Beelzebub, Belial, Mammon, and Moloch), then, may be understood at different interpretative levels of *PL.* At the literal level of Milton's epic the devils may be distinguished, but at the symbolic level of the poem these devils are manifestations of Satan—the fragments of a fallen deity—exposing his evil.

Like his contemporaries, Milton acknowledges an infernal hierarchy; but his own hierarchical conception of the fallen deities consolidates and confuses the order codified by Burton and Heywood. Milton makes Beelzebub Satan's subordinate instead of the reverse. He also allows Moloch to represent the first rank of devils, the false gods, rather than Beelzebub, and associates him with the third rank, the vessels of anger and fury, rather than Belial. The effect of these confusions and consolidations is important. By seeming to confuse the various orders and the devils associated with them, Milton creates the impression that at different times the infernal deities engage in all these activities; and by consolidating the usual nine orders within the figures of Belial, Mammon, and Moloch, Milton suggests that the archfiend and his subordinate epitomize the various aspects of evil that these figures shadow forth. Thus the first two books of *PL* dramatize Milton's belief that Satan has "obtained many names corresponding to his actions." Beelzebub, Belial, Mammon, and Moloch are first associated with Satan's evil and then with Satan himself; distinct from Satan in Book 1, the various devils (but especially Beelze-

bub) in Book 2 are represented as fragments of Satan's personality. Satan's words to Beelzebub are pertinent : "Both waking we were one," he acknowledges (5. 678).

The "characterizations" in Book 1 not only "prepare the Reader's Mind for [the devils'] respective Speeches and Behaviour in the second and sixth Book"; but just as important, the "Firmly Exprest" characterizations in Book 1 establish the allegorical connections exploited by Milton in Book 2 (see *Milton: The Critical Heritage,* ed. John T. Shawcross, p. 171). The council scene is less a genuine debate than an imaginative rendering of what Calvin* describes as the "subtle methods Satan employs, presenting all the while an appearance of discord, in order to entrap the minds of men" (*Commentary on a Harmony of the Evangelists,* trans. William Pringle [1845], 2 : 68). At the symbolic level this is the point of view that Milton adopts; at the literal level, however, he pursues the Augustinian* notion that God subsumes all the pagan deities and heavenly spirits : all are contained in His person and are essential to His unity. Part of Milton's effort to underscore parallels between the demonic and heavenly trinities and to make appropriate distinctions, the council scene dramatizes the notion that not God but the devils are divided into parties and engage in strife. It also implies that, just as God imparts his image to those who follow him, so Satan's image is imparted to his followers.

Milton's conception of Beelzebub in *PL* derives from the traditions previously described; from the Mummers' plays, where Beelzebub is represented as Satan's subordinate; and probably from "an allegorization invented by St. Jerome* and cited by Valeriano in his discussion of the fly as a symbol of pertinacity" (*Poems of John Milton,* ed. John Carey and Alastair Fowler [1968], pp. 466–67n). Milton's conception of Beelzebub may also owe something to Vondel's* *Lucifer,* where Beelzebub is depicted as Satan's subordinate, and to John Selden's* description of him in *De D[i]is Syris* (1617).

In *PL* Beelzebub is quickly discerned by Satan (1. 78–81). Second only to Satan, he is described as Satan's "bold Compeer" (1. 127), as his "neerest mate" (1. 192); and he is addressed by Satan as "Fall'n Cherube" (1. 157) after Satan has explained that he and Beelzebub are "joynd/ In equal ruin" (1. 90–91). Beelzebub, apparently, is the first to be tempted and the first to succumb. As he is awakening, Satan "in secret" issues a directive (5. 671–93); and Beelzebub, following it and falling, "together calls . . . the Regent Powers." In the infernal council scene, except for Satan, "none higher sat" (2. 300) than Beelzebub, who, rising to speak, seems "A Pillar of State . . . Majestic though in ruin" (2. 301–9). Just as Beelzebub reflects Satan's consciousness—"still crude in its range of awareness"—in Book 1, so he represents the finer consciousness of the archfiend in Book 2 (Arnold Stein, *Answerable Style* [1953], p. 50). The "spokesman for Satan's more considered view" (Stein, p. 40), Beelzebub presents the plan earlier "devis'd" by Satan—an "easier enterprise" than invading heaven (Moloch's proposal) and one more plausible than achieving peace (the proposal of both Belial and Mammon). To this plan (2. 365–72) the devils give "full assent." Beelzebub's oratorical victory is in reality a victory for Satan, who insinuated the plan adopted by the council and who, in turn, offers to execute it.

Since Voltaire*, critics have recognized the necessity of the infernal council, but they have tended to stress its importance as a vehicle for action rather than for ideas and character. John Peter and Merritt Y. Hughes, usually at odds, are the exception. As characterization, Hughes finds the council scene "indispensable." The portraits of Belial, Mammon, and Moloch, in their monolithic simplicity, suggest the tendency of the morality play to decompose human nature into its constituent parts; but these fragments of a personality are gathered together in Beelzebub, who most closely resembles Satan. In the council scene, Beelzebub's character is fully formed; and his speeches here (2. 310–78, 390–416) reveal an eloquence, an awareness, a firmness of conviction, lacking in his earlier ones (1. 128–55, 272–82). Beelzebub is one of four participants in the consult which, for John Peter, is less "an actual discussion" than a "train of thought." If "on one level [the literal] the debate can be accepted as a debate, on another level [the symbolic] it can also be accepted as a dramatized account of Satan's inner motives" (*A Critique of Paradise Lost,* [1960], p. 42). Here Beelzebub is to Satan what in Book 3 the Son is to the Father—a "Similitude/ In whose conspicuous count'nance, without cloud, / [Satan is] Made visible" (3. 384–86). The various proposals advanced during the consult are not so much different alternatives as they are "the processes through which [Satan's] own mind has been moving" (Peter, p. 42)—a point that Milton himself emphasizes in the argument appended to Book 2, saying not "the devils debate" but "Satan *debates*." The participating devils, then, are an index to Satan's own thought processes; they are "psychological fragments" of him (a point Peter chooses not to press).

The artistic method employed in the intensely emblematic council scene is allegory—what Blake* would call "sublime allegory"—the sort that converts upward into myth* rather than downward into history. Milton seems not to exploit political connections between historical figures and the devils, as Masson, Raleigh, and Verity would have us believe. Instead, he uses the consult to recall the processes of mythic decomposition, mythic doubling, and mythic condensation as they operate within the complex tradition that has gathered around the figure of Satan (see Edward Langton, *Satan: A Portrait* [1945], with Rwkah Schärf Kluger, *Satan in the Old Testament,* trans. Hildegard Nagel [1967]). The pagan gods were originally associated with Satan, but not without preserving their distinction from him, as part of an effort to fragment and thereby elucidate a complicated archetype. In Milton's epic scheme, Satan's intricate character is dissolved into its component parts (Belial, Mammon, and Moloch). Complementing the technique of decomposition is the technique of doubling with Beelzebub, a less colorful Satan, representing in bold outline Satan's chief faults; he is the most complete manifestation of the evil Satan embodies because he is also a consolidation of the perspectives on evil presented in the characterizations of Belial, Mammon, and Moloch. In the figure of Beelzebub, the satanic archetype is reconstituted for Milton's fit audience. The various devils remain, of course, but as psychological projections rather than as separate entities. These are the mythic processes involved in Milton's allegory, but there are minute particulars as well.

Invoking the tradition of the three-headed Beelzebub, Milton represents satanic evil through the respective vices associated with Belial, Mammon, and Moloch in Book 1 and satanic method through the proposals they advance in Book 2. At this point in his epic Milton seems less concerned with the tradition of the seven deadly sins* (but see Robert C. Fox, *Texas Studies in Language and Literature* 2 : 261–80) than he is with the tradition of the three master categories of sin—a tradition that Belial, Mammon, and Moloch together suggest. The sins of youth, manhood, and old age—lust, avarice, and pride—are associated with Belial, Mammon, and Moloch respectively and with the temptations* of the flesh, the world, and the devil presented by necessity in the first instance, fraud and persuasion in the second, fear and violence in the last. The proposals advanced by the three devils in the council scene establish this latter connection between them and the triple-temptation sequence : Moloch appeals to fear and violence, Mammon to necessity, and Belial to fraud and persuasion, which provokes the authorial intrusion at the end of his speech.

Allegory, says William Butler Yeats, requires "a right knowledge for its understanding." These traditions of identifying and distinguishing between the infernal deities, ranking them hierarchically, and portraying their prince iconographically with three faces greatly illuminate the art and meaning of the infernal consult in Milton's epic. But one further tradition, assumed throughout this discussion, requires notice. The epic council scene, from its very inception, was allegorical and possessed a local significance, the pressure of which was felt throughout the entire epic. The tradition is continued, not broken, by Milton. The immediate effect of the infernal council is to expose Satan in all his evil to those who can read and comprehend, but this scene also adumbrates what is to come. It parodies the heavenly Trinity and is a reverse image of the parallel episode in Book 3, and by alluding to both the three master categories of sin and the methods of temptation associated with them it points to Milton's more extended portrayal of Satan's evil in the subsequent books. Having here invoked the master categories of sin*, Milton uses this conception to foreshadow the more elaborate tradition of the seven deadly sins that manifests itself most completely in the seven animal disguises assumed by Satan in Books 4–9. Finally, though the specific proposals of Belial, Mammon, and Moloch are not adopted by Satan's council, the methods of temptation suggested by them are employed by Satan, first when he inspires Eve's dream and then when the formal temptation occurs in Book 9. No other episode in *PL* more fully reveals the syncretic mind of a poet who by consolidating traditions triumphs imaginatively over them. [JAW]

BELIAL. Discord is Belial's first name, says Prudentius*, and heresy* his second. Rendered as a proper noun but not used as a proper name in the Old Testament, Belial means "worthlessness," "wickedness," "lawlessness," "destruction." In phrases like "children of Belial" (Deut. 13 : 13, Judg. 20 : 13, 1 Sam. 10 : 27, 1 Kings 21 : 13, 2 Chron. 13 : 17), "sons [or daughters] of Belial" (Judg. 19 : 22; 1 Sam. 1 : 16, 2 : 12, 25 : 17; 2 Sam.

23 : 6; 1 Kings 21 : 10), "man [or men] of Belial" (1 Sam. 25 : 25, 30 : 22; 2 Sam. 16 : 7, 20 : 1; 1 Kings 21 : 13), Belial's name —used as a designation for certain classes of people—means *"the man of sin, or the Lawlesse one"* (George Sandys, *Sacrae Heptades* [1625], p. 91). Appellations like these, says John Diodati*, refer to those who have given themselves over to lewdness and licentiousness, to those who are notoriously evil and desperately wicked— those who are like Satan himself. On other occasions in the Old Testament, Belial's name designates one who gives false testimony (Prov. 19 : 28) or one who plots evil (Nah. 1 : 11), and in Nahum 1 : 15 and Hebrews 2 : 1 the word is used to designate a malevolent power or demon*. In the Apocrypha*, on the other hand, Belial (often written Beliar or Berial) is used as a proper name for Satan, a practice brought into focus by words ascribed to Belial in the Gospel of Bartholomew:

> At first I was called Satanel, which is interpreted a messenger of God, but when I rejected the image of God my name was called Satanas, that is, an angel that keepeth Hell . . . I was formed the first angel.

This tradition persists in other Apocryphal writings. Associated with lust, fornication, covetousness, rebellion, and destruction, Belial is the Antichrist (depicted as an emissary from Rome), the angel of lawlessness, and the leader of the false prophets; he is chief of the seven spirits of deceit, and he combines the twofold mischief of wrath and lying (see Fragments of a Zadokite Work 6 : 9–10, 7 : 19, 9 : 11, 15 : 5; Book of Jubilees 1 : 20, 15 : 33; Sibyline Books 3. 63, 73; Martyrdom of Isaiah 1 : 8–9; 2 : 4; Testaments of the Patriarchs—Reuben 2 : 4, 4 : 11, 6 : 3; Simeon 5 : 3; Levi 3 : 3, 18 : 12, 19 : 1; Judah 25 : 3; Issachar 6 : 1, 7 : 7; Zebulun 9 : 8; Dan. 17, 47, 5 : 1, 10–11; Nephtali 2 : 6, 3 : 1; Asher 1 : 7–8, 3 : 2, 6 : 4; Joseph 7 : 4, 20 : 2; Benjamin 3: 3–4, 8, 6 : 1, 7 : 1–2). Here Belial is identical with the Belial represented by St. Paul in the New Testament : "And what concord hath Christ with Belial? or what part hath he that believeth with an in-

fidel?" (2 Cor. 6 : 15). In the words of John Calvin*, "Paul has employed the word [Belial] here to mean devil, the head of all wicked persons [Satan]" (*Commentary on the Epistles,* trans. John Pringle [1849], 2 : 259).

Milton not only quotes St. Paul's words to the Corinthians in *DDD* (3: 407–8) but, commenting on the "antagony between Christ and Belial," insists, like St. Jerome*, that there can be "no communion" between them (3 : 410–11). The sons of Belial (*Apol* 3 : 307), from Milton's point of view, are "the draffe of men," exhibiting "unbridl'd and vagabond lust," for whom "no liberty is pleasing" (*DDD* 3 : 370); they are men whom Milton comes to identify with "seisure" of liberty and with violence (*Hire* 6 : 68). "The dissolutest Spirit . . . The sensuallest . . . The fleshliest Incubus," who elsewhere in Milton's poetry advises Satan to "Set women in [Christ's] eye and in his walk" (*PR* 2. 150–53; see also 2. 172–226), Belial as portrayed in the epic catalogue of *PL* comes "last" : ". . . a Spirit more lewd / Fell not from Heaven, or more gross to love / Vice for it self" (1. 490–92). The position assigned to Belial is significant. He comes "last" not only "because he had no local cult" and is, in the poem, timorous and slothful (*Poems of John Milton,* ed. John Carey and Alastair Fowler [1968], pp. 490–91n) but because, as Charles Dunster earlier observed, "The *last place* in a processional catalogue, is . . . a *post of honour;* and Belial's rank among the fallen Spirits, the preeminence in wickedness and talents ascribed to him . . . peculiarly entitles him to fill it" (*Poetical Works,* ed. Henry John Todd [1809], 2 : 338; see also David Masson, *Poetical Works* [1874], 3 : 125).

Gathering together the various traditional conceptions of Belial, Milton associates him with lust and with violence. Both aspects of Belial's character emerge in the Old Testament and in the Apocrypha, but in the occult literature Belial is associated primarily with the latter quality : he reigns as prince of the third order of devils—the "vessels of death . . . vessels of fury . . . vessels of wrath" (Henry Cornelius Agrippa, *Three Books of Occult Philosophy*, trans. J. F. [1651], p. 398; but see also Robert Burton*, *Anatomy of Melancholy* [1621], 1 : 2, i. 2). Having already identified Moloch with the first rank of devils (the false gods), Milton now associates Belial with the second rank (the spirits of lies), but not without preserving the usual connection between Belial and the forces of violence. Milton's sketch in Book 1 of *PL* introduces the character who emerges in the subsequent books. The association of Belial with lust and with violence blurs the division that seems to separate Moloch and Belial in the second book; and by pointing to Belial's haughtiness, arrogance, and pride, it anticipates Belial's scoffing speech to Satan (6. 620–27).

Delivered "with perswasive accent" (2. 118), Belial's council speech (2. 119–25) begins by disposing of Moloch's proposal, which Belial says is grounded "on despair / And utter dissolution" (2. 126–27). "In act more graceful and humane" than Moloch, but in actuality base, timorous, and slothful, Belial answers Moloch's proposal point by point, stressing the impossiblity of penetrating heaven by deception or by might. "They who counsel Warr*," says Belial, destine us "to eternal woe" (2. 160–61). Observing that the affliction and pain the devils previously experienced have subsided, Belial concludes that in time God may remit his anger, in time "This horror will grow milde, this darkness light" (2. 220). The speech, its counsel of "waiting," provokes an authorial intrusion : "Thus Belial with words cloath'd in reasons garb / Counsel'd ignoble ease, and peaceful sloath, / Not peace . . ." (2. 226–28).

The best drawn of Milton's devils except for Satan himself, Belial "is too well-bred to rage, too disillusioned to aspire, too consummate an artist to press his points" (E. E. Stoll, *Modern Language Notes* 48 : 419). But however plausible, however realistic Belial's speech may seem, Milton wrote into it, line after line, the professions of a sophist. Those professions

elicited his disdain. Belial's speech is founded upon the same error as Claudius's speech in *Hamlet* (3. iii. 36–72); both of them create expectations of forgiveness without offering repentance. This is the false premise that Milton's intrusion nudges the reader into perceiving. Milton's adoption of the demonic perspective in these initial books also causes him to express disdain for Belial who, when considered "in terms of those attributes concerned with leadership, political power, and secular heroism," is "at the base of the pyramid," even if from an earthly perspective "the pyramid is oddly reversed." In comparison with Moloch, "Belial is an evil which hardly threatens at all"—or hardly seems to threaten until we learn in Book 8 that Satan wears the mask of Belial in tempting Adam and Eve and, so doing, precipitates the fall from Eden (see Joseph H. Summers, *The Muse's Method*, p. 92).

This realization invites us to consider Belial as a manifestation of Satan—an epitome of the fraud and deception that cause the fall of everyman. Like Moloch, Belial, traditionally identified with Satan, is one of his three faces. In character, Belial suggests lust and sloth (the first master category of sin); in action, he points to the temptations of the world that are shrouded in deception. If the distinction between Moloch and Belial is blurred by their mutual association with violence, the division between Belial and Mammon is bridged by their mutual association with the temptations of the world. (*See also* BEELZEBUB.) [JAW]

BENLOWES, EDWARD: *see* IMITATIONS.

BENTLEY, RICHARD (1662–1742), major scholar and critic of classical texts in the late seventeenth and eighteenth centuries. He attempted to apply his reconstructions of texts such as of Horace* (1711) and of Terence (1726) to *PL*. His work on the spuriousness of the *Epistles to Philaris* in 1697 (expanded in 1699 with an allusion to Milton on p. ci) undoubtedly also emboldened him in his attack on the text of the epic. Besides, he had been in controversy through most of his scholarly life and the specter of antagonism would hardly deter him. Although his edition of *PL* appeared in 1732, it had been announced and denounced before that time. As early as March 5, 1730, a letter to *The Grub-street Journal*, no. 9, discussed needed emendations for the epic. Adverse editorial opinion, letters to the editors, and poems attacked Bentley, who frequently responded, always signing himself Zoilus (a Greek grammarian and textual critic), during 1730–31. An unpublished letter from his nephew Thomas to Bentley's later critic Zachary Pearce, dated April 20, 1731, told of trying to dissuade him from his enterprise. (The letter is in the Alexander Turnbull Library, Wellington, New Zealand.) What finally emerged in January 1732 as a new edition proposed a number of new readings in footnotes, with reasons for those readings. From his first work on the project in 1730 the emendations seem to grow in quantity and nature in an attempt to prove himself and to belittle his critics rather than as a result of careful and scholarly examination of text.

Bentley had found what he considered inaccurate quantities in the verse, erroneous, meaningless, or inconsistent language or metaphor, and passages that did not have the Miltonic touch or that appeared to be extraneous. To justify his wholesale revision Bentley hypothesized an ignorant editor intervening between Milton's manuscript (itself produced by an incompetent scribe) and its printed form. Revisions of words or lines and insertions of passages were supposed to have occurred through whim or ignorance. The fact of Milton's blindness* seems to have given rise to this theory, for obviously the case of *PL* was totally different from what Bentley had encountered in the text of, say, Manlius (1739). His introduction, which discusses editions*, publishers*, and the epic's relationship with *PR*, is built on misinformation or mis-interpretation and a lack of scholarly investigation. Reactions to the edition, pointing out some of its errors but primarily contradicting Bentley's poetic judgment, were numerous; some few, however, approved.

The main rebuttal agannst this edition was *A Friendly Letter to Dr. Bentley. Occasion'd by His New Edition of Paradise Lost. By A Gentleman of Christ-Church College, Oxon.* [that is, Zachary Pearce], published also in January 1732. It was greatly expanded into three separately printed parts with continuous pagination, *A Review of the Text of Milton's Paradise Lost: In Which the Chief of Dr. Bentley's Emendations Are Consider'd, and Several other Emendations and Observations Are Offer'd to the Public* (1732–1733). Like others, Pearce pointed out errors in reading and understanding, the lack of knowledge of certain words and concepts, and Bentley's illogical suppositions and conclusions. Yet he too shows no clear understanding of the poem by today's standards. The controversy continued in little ways through the next twenty or so years, with "slashing" Bentley, as Alexander Pope* ridiculed him in the *Dunciad*, reflecting the most generalized opinion.

One of Bentley's emendations is universally accepted ("Soul" for "Fowle," 1667; "Foul," 1674, in 7.451) and another sometimes is cited ("swelling" for "smelling" in 7.321). The effect of Bentley's work for Milton studies, however, was ultimately positive. It sent readers back to the text, both to recognize (though still today less pervasively than it should be) that the received texts may contain errors and to examine more carefully the meaning, prosody, structure, and inter-relationships of the text. Such study led in the eighteenth century to important investigations of Milton's style, language, and verse. Bentley's efforts well exemplify the eighteenth-century doctrines of correctness and "neoclassicism," while also pointing to the denigration of celebrated writers who had become too powerful forces on the culture of the times for some to accept. [JTS]

BERGE, ERNST GOTTLIEB VON: *see* TRANSLATIONS OF MILTON'S WORKS

BERNI, FRANCESCO (ca. 1497–1535), an Italian writer of satiric and burlesque poetry, best known for his recasting (*rifacimento*) of Matteo Boiardo's* *Orlando Innamorato*. Four quotations from his work were included in Milton's *CB* and several allusions to the poem occur in both *PL* and *PR*. In *CB* Milton identified Berni as the author of a stanza quoted in the category on lying. His illustration of slander carried Boiardo's name, though the stanza can be found in Berni's *rifacimento* (1545). Milton correctly quoted Berni in the third citation but did not include the book number (1); in the fourth illustration, he included both poets' names, but again seems to have taken the stanza from Berni's work. Berni wrote in various verse forms, especially *capitolini;* his name has even been given to one particular style, called *bernesco.* Berni hesitated to publish his recasting of *Orlando Innamorato*; after his death, Pietro Aretino had a hand in seeing it through the press. Symonds asserted, however, that Aretino edited the poem, suppressing stanzas that showed Berni's Lutheran sympathies (*Italian Literature,* 2 : 315–16, 475–79). The popularity of Berni's *rifacimento,* proved by numerous editions in the sixteenth century, had waned by Milton's day. [RMa]

BEZA, THEODORUS (1519–1605), a minor Burgundian nobleman, trained in classics, law, and theology. Converted to Protestantism in 1548, he moved to Geneva to become Calvin's* disciple and assistant; he succeeded Calvin as the religious and political leader of Geneva and as champion of the Protestant cause in Europe. Of his many writings (poems, plays, satires, editions, translations, textbooks, sermons, political and religious tracts) nearly thirty titles were translated into English during his lifetime, including Arthur Golding's version (1575) of the biblical tragedy *Abraham sacrifiant.* Beza befriended several persons directly or indirectly known to Milton, among them Andrew Melville, teacher of Milton's tutor Thomas Young*; Sir Henry Wotton*, the admirer of *Mask*; Jean Diodati*, uncle of Milton's friend Charles Diodati*.

Milton numbers Beza among the great reformers (*Tetra*), quotes from Beza's *Icones* or *Portraits of Great Men* (1580) in support of Bucer (*Bucer*), and explicitly differs with Beza's *Treatise on Repudiation and Divorce* (1587) five times in *Tetra*. Beza's *Major Annotations to the New Testament* (1594) is referred to eight times in the course of *CD* and is the focus of Milton's counter-arguments in *DDD*. It is impossible to measure the debt arising from Milton's known use of Beza's famous scholarly translations of the New Testament into Latin. Of the several editions, Milton may have preferred that of 1589, which gives the Vulgate version along with Beza's Greek and Latin texts (H. F. Fletcher, *The Intellectual Development of John Milton* [1956] 2 : 108). [JRM]

BIBLE, MILTON AND THE. The important place held by the Bible in his erstwhile Roman Catholic father's Anglican household must have deeply impressed the young Milton. At St. Paul's School* Milton studied it in the original languages, also joining in the devotional reading of a chapter of the Bible in English every morning at seven o'clock, followed by prayers in Latin. The young man so progressed in his biblical studies that at some time prior to March 1625, when Milton wrote to thank him for it, Milton's favorite tutor, Thomas Young*, sent the young poet a Hebrew Bible from Hamburg. Milton's comment that "the meanest Christians," a category he would not have been likely to include himself in, had the common experience of hearing verses of Scripture read daily (*Apol* 3: 346) implies that his own youthful study was far deeper and broader. And it must have been considerably reinforced and encouraged by the rector of the family's congregation, All Hallows Church, Bread Street; a blunt, plain-spoken man, Richard Stock urged his parishioners to read their Bibles continuously, and he often supported biblical statements by reason and by quotations from the Church Fathers (Parker, *Milton,* 1 : 9–10), a method followed by Milton throughout his life, though with decreasing emphasis on the Church Fathers.

Judging by Milton's remarks in *Educ* and elsewhere, Cambridge University made a mostly negative contribution to his notions of proper Bible study, in somewhat the same way, perhaps, as Ovid's* eroticism had determined him toward chastity. His observation on the effect of substituting "ragged Notions and Babblements" for the clear light of the Scriptures being either "an ambitious and mercenary, or ignorantly zealous Divinity" (*Educ* 4 : 279) may have inspired his portrayal of the young men in his projected school closing each day's studies by bringing all under the "determinate sentence of *David* or *Salomon*" (*Educ* 4 : 284), and progressing toward the ideal of reading the Bible in the original languages (cf. *Hire* 6 : 96).

Although *TM* includes about a hundred possible literary subjects from the Bible and from British history, the biblical subjects predominate and are elaborated more fully than the historical; thus as early as 1640–1642 those subjects which were to become the basis for his greatest works—the Fall of Adam, the Judgeship of Samson—were already being contemplated. Milton himself may have thought that the most effective culmination of all his study of the Bible would be his *CD,* a "wholesom bodie of divinitie . . . without schoole terms and metaphysical notions" (*Hire* 6 : 78), a work he declared to be his "best and richest possession" (*CD* 14 : 9), though few modern readers would agree. But his poetry is such that one cannot long avoid grappling with the Bible, especially as seen through Milton's eyes. And his mature view, quite sophisticated for his day, yet utterly devout, is best expressed in chapter 30 of Book 1 of *CD.* It is summed up succinctly in *PL,* when Michael refers to

> the truth . . . .
> Left onely in those written Records pure,
> Though not but by the Spirit understood.
> (12. 511, 513–14)

For Milton the canon of Scripture is the Jewish and Protestant canon of the Old Testament and the Protestant canon of the New Testament; the Apocrypha* and Pseudepigrapha "are by no means of equal authority with the canonical, neither can they be adduced as evidence in matters of faith" (*CD* 16 : 251). The apocryphal books are rejected for three reasons : they are not extant in the Hebrew language, they are never quoted by the New Testament writers, and they contain much that contradicts canonical Scripture. Yet Virginia Mollenkott has demonstrated that Milton used the Apocrypha to a surprising extent throughout his works, though always following the principle that it is not a proper basis for doctrine. The canonical Scriptures themselves, Milton believed, are to be promiscuously read by all, even the most unlearned, since God has made them "partly by reason of their own simplicity, and partly through the divine illumination, . . . plain and perspicuous in all things necessary to salvation" (p. 259).

He believed that one who engaged in public interpretation of the Scripture should be trained in the original languages of Hebrew and Greek, exercise contextual considerations, have the ability to distinguish between literal and figurative expressions, take care to collate and compare texts, give regard to the analogy of faith, develop his competence in dealing with problems of grammar and syntax, and firmly reject inferences from the text that do not "follow necessarily and plainly from the words themselves" (p. 265). As far as private interpretation is concerned, "Every believer has a right to interpret the Scriptures for himself, inasmuch as he has the Spirit for his guide, and the mind of Christ is in him; nay, the expositions of the public interpreter can be of no use to him, except so far as they are confirmed by his own conscience" (p. 265). Milton recognizes a twofold Scripture: one external, the written word, and the other internal, the Holy Spirit written in the hearts of believers and assisting them in understanding the holy writings. Since the church is based on the Bible, "the church cannot be the rule or arbiter of that on which it is itself founded" (p. 269). Furthermore, since the text of the written word is in many places corrupted through transmission, the internal guide of the Holy Spirit is superior to the external guide of the Bible. "It is difficult to conjecture the purpose of Providence* in committing the writings of the New Testament to such uncertain and variable guardianship, unless it were to teach us by this very circumstance that the Spirit which is given to us is a more certain guide than Scripture, whom therefore it is our duty to follow" (pp. 277–79). His reasoning here is admittedly circular : "we set out with a general belief in their [the Scriptures'] authenticity, founded on the testimony either of the visible church, or of the existing manuscripts; afterwards, by an inverse process, the authority of the church itself, and of the different books as contained in the manuscripts, is confirmed by the internal evidence implied in the uniform tenor of Scripture, considered as a whole; and, lastly, the truth of the entire volume is established by the inward persuasion of the Spirit working in the hearts of individual believers" (p. 279).

In the last analysis, then, truth is to be discovered within, though the initiation of the process leading to its discovery is attributable to the written word without. It follows, then, that to yoke the conscience* of the individual believer is to yoke the Holy Spirit himself, a manifest sacrilege if not an unpardonable blasphemy. Michael's rhetorical question, "for on Earth / Who against Faith and Conscience can be heard / Infallible?" (*PL* 12. 528–30) needs no answer; yet he prophesies that forcers of conscience will continue to presume and to wield great power against humble believers until Truth herself returns to earth with the person of her divine Master, Jesus Christ. Since he held such convictions it should not be surprising that Milton uses every persuasive means, open or subtle, to appeal to the biblical knowledge of his reader, for only by inner acceptance can the truth of the outer testimony be corroborated.

The influence of the Bible in Milton's writings is so pervasive and so powerful that an accurate and complete assessment hardly seems to be possible. At any rate such a full assessment has yet to be made, though several valuable book-length studies and many helpful articles and notes have appeared during the twentieth century. Before 1929 information on Milton's use of the Bible was available through the annotations of his various editors* and commentators, but only in a random and unsystematic way. But with the publication of Fletcher's *The Use of the Bible in Milton's Prose* (1929), a fresh interest was awakened in a more methodical exploration of the ways of Milton with the Bible. Although much remains to be done, the work of scholars of Fletcher's generation and thereafter now enables us to see Milton with a new clarity as a master of artistically integrated biblical quotation, echo, and allusion.

Fletcher's study is valuable, indeed irreplaceable, for students of Milton, but it focuses narrowly on explicit references or quotations and leaves untouched Milton's subtlety in achieving indirect, even subliminal, effects. Contrary to Fletcher's assumption that "The collation of [chapter and verse citations in *CD*] with a Biblical text constitutes a basis for the investigation of Milton's knowledge of Scripture and employment of it which leaves nothing to be desired" (p. 13), Milton's use of the Bible in his prose, like much of his use in his poetry, is often aimed at the reader's subconscious awareness of biblical similitude rather than at his conscious recognition of particular texts.

A much-needed corrective to the over-emphasis of Saurat (1925) on esoteric sources for some of Milton's unorthodox ideas is provided in Conklin's *Biblical Criticism and Heresy in Milton* (1949), where the primary aim is to show that many of Milton's "heresies"* are the direct result of his knowledge of the original languages and of his careful methods of exegesis and interpretation. Kurth's *Milton and Christian Heroism* (1959) sets *PL* and *PR* within the tradition of a search for forms worthy of the epic themes of the Bible in seventeenth-century England; it demonstrates that the superiority of Milton's achievement in his major and minor epics consists, at least partially, in his combination of hexameral*, Old Testament, and New Testament subject matter within the larger vision of the cosmic drama and the course of universal history as viewed by all branches of Christendom, a combination that could be at once the culmination of an English tradition of sacred heroic poetry and of the more general Renaissance aspirations to produce the ideal Christian epic*. Three years after Kurth's book, H. R. MacCallum published a significant essay on "Milton and Figurative Interpretation of the Bible." The issues MacCallum raises have not been adequately dealt with in subsequent scholarship, particularly his contentions that "Imagery and metaphor play a subordinate role in Milton's conception of biblical interpretation and in the theology which he elaborates from his study of the Bible" and that Milton "upholds the Protestant rejection of multiple meanings, rejects allegory as an instrument of exegesis, permits a compound sense but prefers types clearly established by the New Testament, denies all authority to types in matters of doctrine and discipline, and stresses the spirituality of the antitype" (*University of Toronto Quarterly* 31 : 409). Yet it must be pointed out that MacCallum's contentions need qualification in the light of Milton's insistence on the sovereign right of the Spirit within the believer in matters of interpretation, whether literal or figurative; and it is the influence, after all, of the "Celestial Patroness" that controls all that Milton writes, particularly his poetry.

In the first extensive study of its kind, the present author's *The Bible in Milton's Epics* (1962) attempts to categorize and analyze the effect on the reader of Milton's manifold uses of Scripture in *PL* and *PR*. A basis for this work was furnished by the more than 1,300 citations to specific texts recorded by Milton's editors from Hume (1695) to Hughes (1957), yet over 800 additional references to the Bible in particular lines of the two epics have been added. Milton depends heavily on biblical echoes to impress the reader with the superhistorical truth, the ultimate reality, of his fable; to remind him of the original Hebrew and Greek Scriptures lying behind the English translations; to develop associations between well-known figures in the Bible and the characters of the epics, associations that would both affect the reader's emotional response to the characters and provide a deeper dimension to the dramatic characterization; and to combine with classical epic conventions so as to transform the genre from a glorification of human virtues into a celebration of the loving providence of God in overruling man's sinfulness for his own ultimate good.

In a University of Illinois dissertation, "The Relations Between Classical and Biblical Allusions in Milton's Later Poems" (1967), Anne Bowers Long goes far beyond the suggestion that Milton amalgamates pagan mythology* and the Bible in order to make of the epic a divine poem; she argues persuasively that Milton, and such Puritan contemporaries as Golding and Prynne*, see classical myths as closer to the Gospel dispensation than the Mosaic law because they "represent human efforts to understand the spirit of the law by the law of nature in the heart without the guidance and imposition of external law" (p. 34). Thus Milton intends by his conjunction of classical myths and biblical allusions to stress "the renovation of the natural faculties of man before, and along with, spiritual enlightenment" (p. 35). This important study challenges both sides in the critical controversy over Milton's use of mythology in his later poems; one side is inclined to assign an arbitrary negative denotation to myth, the other side, an arbitrary positive denotation. But Long maintains that Milton is consistent in his connections between mythology and upright and fallen characters, and that the reader who learns to perceive the spirit and disregard the letter of the myths as well as of the Bible will grasp Milton's faith that the remnant of the divine image in the hearts of men not only robs them of excuse for unbelief but allows them to grow to belief as well: "if a pagan proceeds in the process of regeneration through response to the imperfect law of nature, he may be able to use his reason, memories, and imagination to prophesy in mythology the significance of the covenant of grace" (p. 32). Long concludes with regard to *PL* in particular: "Milton uses the tradition of parable-making to drive his readers from the letter to the spirit, to encourage them to grow in understanding. This process of growth is the meaning of the ways of God and is the subject of the poem" (p. 177).

Another dissertation equally deserving of publication and a wide audience among students of Milton is Virginia Mollenkott's "Milton and the Apocrypha" (New York University, 1964). Milton's references to the Apocrypha throughout his works are catalogued and its influence on the structure and imagery of his major poems is demonstrated. Though she sometimes strains to make connections, as when some of Milton's nonbiblical Platonic ideas are traced to the Apocrypha instead of to Plato* (p. 72) or when the angel Raphael's intuitive intelligence is connected with Daniel's inspired exoneration of Susanna in the Apocrypha (pp. 79–80), Mollenkott has produced a valuable study. Among the more impressive of her discoveries is the relationship between Second Esdras and the cycle of sins that Adam sees in the visions of *PL* 11. The five visions recapitulate the sins of Satan, Eve, and Adam in a pattern perhaps suggested by 2 Esdras 3:5–10. "Like Dante's descriptions of sin in the *Inferno,* the visions of Book 11 strip away any semblance of glamor in the sins of Satan, Eve, and Adam. Satan's so-called glorious revolt against God becomes Cain's beating his

brother to death with a rock and finally becomes the bloody massacre on the Plain; Eve's [inabstinent] eating of the forbidden fruit becomes the hideous Lazar-house and finally the rioting which ends in the desperation of drowning; and Adam's fondness for the creature rather than the Creator becomes the thoughtless reveling of the Tents of Wickedness, in which are spawned the brutal giants" (p. 211). Altogether Mollenkott identifies eighteen clear references to the Apocrypha in Milton's prose (correcting Fletcher, who had mentioned only two) and some three hundred and forty in the poetry. His most frequent allusions are to the Wisdom of Solomon and to Ecclesiasticus, with 2 Esdras and Tobit running close behind. His allusions to the Apocrypha in the prose are often in a disparaging vein, yet his "interpretation of a canonical passage sometimes seems to be wrenched in the direction of an Apocryphal doctrine" (p. 239). In his poetry, Milton apparently follows two main principles: the Apocrypha is to be used only when the canonical details can be made fuller and more vivid by apocryphal material; and the Apocrypha is never to be used where it in any way contradicts the Protestant canon.

Although J. M. Evans, in *Paradise Lost and the Genesis Tradition* (1968), has shown the influence of *Apocalypsis Mosis* and *Vita Adae et Evae* on the tradition with which Milton's *PL* is aligned, no study has been made of Milton's use of the Pseudepigrapha. The rather surprising influence of the Apocrypha established by Mollenkott should encourage efforts to discover evidence of Milton's knowledge of specific details from the Pseudepigrapha, and from the New Testament Apocrypha as well.

Until recently knowledge of Milton's use of extrabiblical Semitic sources was limited to the studies published by Fletcher. There are now, however, encouraging signs of the entry into Milton studies of those with a firsthand knowledge of Hebrew* and of rabbinical writings. Harold Fisch's *Jerusalem and Albion: The*

Hebraic Factor in Seventeenth-Century Literature (1964), including three important chapters on Milton, has been followed by other essays by Fisch and studies by Samuel Stollman, Kitty Cohen, and others. Efforts have even been made by Fletcher and Kermode to trace some features of Milton's prosody back to Hebrew poetry, though Hunter sees its features as attributable to Sylvester's translation of du Bartas* and to the metrical psalters. Perusal of *Dissertation Abstracts* shows that interest in Milton's Hebraic sources has been lively over the past few years, and what has already appeared in print augurs well for Milton studies in this important area.

Milton's knowledge of New Testament Greek and its influence in his poetry has yet to be fully explored. Sellin's important essay "Milton's Epithet Agonistes" (*Studies in English Literature* 4:137–62) is a move in the right direction, but research by scholars in other fields has not been fully utilized in the study of Milton. For instance, V. C. Pfitzner's *Paul and the Agon Motif* (1967) and J. P. Sampley's *"And the Two Shall Become One Flesh"* (1971) investigate the traditions associated with New Testament words and concepts that are central in understanding Milton's Samson and Adam and Eve.

Milton's first poetical effort extant is "A Paraphrase on *Psalm* 114," composed according to his own notation at the age of fifteen. Surveying the whole panoramic sweep of Milton's work with the clearer vision retrospect provides, one can see this as significant, even prophetic. The child who, grown old, was to produce in English in the major genres of poetry biblical paraphrases and extrapolations that aftertimes would not willingly let die —for two hundred years largely because of their biblical texture and for much of the next hundred in spite of it—this child in his Englishing of a psalm shows himself the father of the man. Much is here in seminal form : the expansive periphrasis "blest seed of *Terah's* faithful Son" for the Authorized Version's "the house of Jacob"; the oblique suggestion at once of

the long continuous sweep and the tortured schisms of Hebrew history in the phrase *blest seed* (the spondaic emphasis reminding us of such comparatively *un*blessed descendants as Lot, Ishmael, Esau —and of the Pauline stress on the culmination of the continuity of Abrahamic faith in Gentile Christians); the strenuous reach for such learnedly allusive place names as *"Pharian* fields," connecting Egypt with Pharaoh and the isle of Pharos in the mouth of the Nile; the evocation of the creature's breathless awe in the face of evidence of the Creator's infinity and eternity : "Shake earth, and at the presence be agast / Of him that ever was, and ay shall last." Even the enjambment of "hide his froth becurled head / Low in the earth" heralds Milton's use of prosody to obscure end-rhyme and, ultimately, presages his mature preference for the blank verse* period.

One must admit, of course, that this early psalm is unremarkable for its own sake, though it does compare quite favorably with the Countess of Pembroke's versified psalms and even with the mature Sidney's*; but as a harbinger of characteristics of the mature Milton's biblical poetry it is quite remarkable. Later Milton would develop strikingly new techniques of transforming biblical material into poetry, as in *Lyc,* where the fusion of ancient Greek myth, Hebrew Old Testament, and Christian New Testament is so effectively achieved as to become ever after one of the hallmarks of Milton's poetic style. When Lycidas's apotheosis makes him at once an Apollo, a translated Elijah, a member of the Bride of Christ, and a guardian Genius (*Lyc* 168–85), we have in miniature a style of allusion that will fill vast canvases in *PL,* as when Satan, beholding God's golden scales in the heavens, becomes simultaneously an Achilles, a Hector, a Turnus, a Belshazzar, and a Pontius Pilate (*PL* 4.990–1015). Obviously, it is in his major poems that he transforms scriptural and classical allusions into poetry of the highest, noblest art, but such an achievement was built upon experimentation with such materials in his early poetry and prose; it is ultimately an achievement that supports his profoundest convictions about the nature of man, the nature of God, and the physical and spiritual circumstances within which God and man can commune. For Milton's use of the Bible is not for mere adornment, nor is his use of the classics. His method reveals his theme, almost is his theme, by the time *PL* is published. Meanwhile the road to, and from, Paradise is strewn with abundant evidence of his ever-developing artistry in the affective use of the Bible.

A foreshadowing of his ability, unmistakably revealed in *Lyc,* to fuse classical and biblical allusion may be seen in Milton's early *FInf,* though it is a pale example indeed. Speculating on the origin of the beautiful infant, the poet considers as one alternative that she was a goddess who fled Olympus when the Titans besieged Heaven (*FInf* vii; cf. Ovid *Met.* 1. 151–62). Implied here as well is a reversal of the biblical story of the giant sons of God taking wives of the daughters of men (Gen. 6 : 4–5). But the association, like the poem generally, is rather awkwardly strained; the contrasting reminiscence, whether intentional or not, further fragments a poem whose struggle for coherence is already virtually lost.

In *Sonn* 7 (1632?) biblical ideas control the movement from discouragement over time's stealing away opportunities for achievement to a calm acceptance of time's slow guidance within the will of God. Behind the poem lies the well-known passage beginning "To every thing there is a season, and a time to every purpose under the heaven" (Eccles. 3 : 1–8); the image shifts from Time* as a thief to Time as a divine guide, and the turning point comes with the mention of "some more timely-happy spirits," as though in the very complaint that Time blesses some more appropriately than others lies the implicit recognition that God controls Time from the vantage point of Eternity ("All is . . . as ever in [God's] eye"), and that, therefore, whatever Time does is a part of God's plan. He is the "task-

Master" whose eye sees "All" as "is"— past, present, and future as now. Therefore, as Christ is figured by the "thief in the night" (1 Thess. 5 : 2) in His second coming, Time is figured as a "subtle thief," because in both instances the result of their "theft" is to release the Christian from "merely mortal dross" into a higher level of spirituality—if one has "grace to use it so." Similarly, God is called "task-Master," the epithet used in the Authorized Version for the Egyptian slave drivers (Exod. 1 : 11, 3 : 7, 5 : 6), because what appears to be a situation in which God forces one of his servants to make "bricks without straw," that is, to show a bud or blossom without inward ripeness, is actually a temporary and only apparent hardship that may ultimately result in a far greater future than would be realized without it. The ultimate result for Israel is Jehovah's sending Moses as a deliverer in response to their prayers and their establishment as an independent nation in the Land of Promise (Exod. 3 : 7–8); in the light of these biblical overtones, the poet sees his unknown future as a fixed goal in the mind of God, a goal that he cannot miss since the will of Heaven works together with time and God's grace to guide him to "that same lot."

Although none have the extraordinary depths of suggestion that his mature allusions show, Milton's other sonnets of the 1645 edition contain effective kinds of biblical echo and reference. For example, the young lady of *Sonn* 9 had followed Jesus' advice to enter "the strait [i.e. narrow] gate; for wide is the gate, and broad is the way, that leadeth to destruction, and many there be which go in thereat" (Matt. 7 : 13). She is seen among the "few there be that find" the narrow way as she labors up the hill of truth. But his most significant praise associates her with Mary of Bethany, with Ruth the Moabitess, and with the wise virgins of Matthew 25. Both biblical women are emblems of Faith*; and Ruth is, in addition, representative of Charity*, her name itself meaning "kindness," and her conduct throughout showing love*. The wise virgins symbolize Chastity, but also Good Works through their shining lamps (Matt. 5 : 15–16) and Hope* through the provision of oil in their lamps (Matt. 25 : 4).

Lyc is in many ways a microcosm representative of Milton's major work: a pagan pastoral* genre, framed for lament and earthly consolation, is infused with Christian ideas of virtue, salvation, and moral responsibility, and strikes in its conclusion a note of positive Christian triumph; the diverse motifs are brought together in a final crescendo to support a brief apocalyptic* vision and then smoothly muted for the quiet pastoral close. In short, a classical form is altered so thoroughly that the form has never since been quite what it was before Milton used it. And it is hardly an exaggeration to say that the poet's chief agent in such an application of classicism is the Bible. On the first several readings it appears that the biblical element enters with "The Pilot of the *Galilean* lake" (*Lyc* 109) and is confined to the condemnation of the corrupt clergy (through 131). But the biblical echoes start much earlier, with the first line in fact : "Yet once more" applies specifically to the poet's launching against his inclinations into a funeral elegy; but in the light of the apotheosis of Lycidas, when it is remembered that this is a biblical phrase (Heb. 12 : 26–27; Hag. 2 : 6–7) connected with God's purpose to judge and renew in righteousness the whole earth, the reader may see "Yet once more" as forecasting, within the poem, both the judging of the clergy and the beatitude of the translated Lycidas. Thus the "melodious tear" expresses genuine sorrow, but it is not the sorrow of "others who have no hope" (1 Thess. 4 : 13); "once more" points as surely toward God's victory for His people as the later "smite once, and smite no more" (*Lyc* 131) assures the hireling shepherds of final judgment at the close of the second movement.

The first movement ends with the promise of God's omniscience and justice in rewarding the faithful : "As he pronounces lastly on each deed, / Of so much fame in Heav'n expect thy meed" (*Lyc* 83–84). God must have the last word on the deeds of men, for only in his "pure eyes" and "perfect witness" can true fame be determined from an eternal point of view (Rev. 14 : 13; 1 Cor. 3 : 13–15). The third climax is signalled more openly by the near-quotation, "And wipe the tears for ever from his eyes" (*Lyc,* 181; Rev. 7 : 17, 21 : 4), itself preceded by eight lines (173–80) containing at least one biblical allusion each (John 6 : 19–20; Rev. 22 : 1–2; Rev. 7 : 14; Rev. 14 : 3–5; Rev. 1 : 5–6; Rev. 5 : 8–10; Rev. 11 : 15–17). The tremendous increase in biblical reminiscences in this final climax, especially when there are earlier stretches of fifty lines and more without them, foreshadows Milton's practice in *PL,* where Books 11 and 12 increase the density of biblical echoes per line until very little nonbiblical diction finds its way into long passages, but then the epic closes with a marked slacking off of such language. In *Lyc* the shift is more abrupt; the beautifully simple *ottava rima* that closes the poem contains not a single allusion to the Bible.

In sum, then, Milton in *Lyc* reinforces the architectonic structure at strategic turning points with concentrations of biblical echoes, making it possible at the same time to emphasize by contrast passages that are free of biblical reference, such as the Orpheus* section and the inquest into the cause of death. Thus it almost appears that the poem is falling apart into two fragments, one pagan and one Christian. Then the alternating mythological and biblical passages are welded into one with the equation of Lycidas with the morning sun, the saints in Heaven, the resurrected Christ, and the guardian Genius of the shore at the apocalyptic climax, a unifying climax prepared for by the biblical allusions in the preceding high point of each movement. With such "large recompense" accomplished for Lycidas, the poet shifts point of view to show the swain, calmed by his elegiac song, in a completely neutral pastoral scene, neither distinctively Christian nor pagan, of no time and place and yet of all times and all places.

By contrast with *Lyc, Mask* makes relatively little use of the Bible. Of the seven identifiable allusions, the most important is the reference of the Attendant Spirit to the spiritual weapons necessary to combat the forces of evil* (*Mask* 610–14; Eph. 6 : 10–17), which is relevant to the Elder Brother's confidence that his sister is safe because her chastity clothes her in "compleat steel" (420). But with regard to the use of the Bible, *Mask* fits more logically within its period than does *Lyc;* that is, *Lyc* gives far more evidence of poetic maturity in this respect than do any of the other poems of the 1645 edition.

From his earliest entry into the anti-episcopal controversy with *Ref* (1641) Milton uses the Bible quite obviously and straightforwardly to bolster his views and to raise doubt about the views of the supporters of the bishops. But what often goes unnoticed in these tracts, as well as in the tracts on divorce* and other subjects, is his subtle weaving of scriptural phraseology, imagery, and syntax into the fabric of his argument in such a way as to result in a persuasive effect subliminally rather than consciously. Thus his opening address, "Written to a friend," in *Ref* leans heavily on Paul's opposition of flesh and spirit, though Milton quotes neither Paul nor Jesus' own saying, "The spirit indeed is willing but the flesh is weak" (Matt. 26 : 41). His powerful picture of a religion fashioned by tradition "to bring the inward acts of the *Spirit* to the outward, and customary ey-Service of the body, as if they could make *God* earthly, and fleshly, because they could not make themselves *heavenly,* and Spirituall" with the result that "all the inward acts of *worship,* issuing from the native strength of the SOULE, run out lavishly to the upper skin, and there harden into a crust of Formallitie" (*Ref* 3. i. 2–3) depends for its full effect on the reader's remembering both the flesh-spirit contrast of the New Testament and such Old Testament comparisons between hypocritical formality in

religion and a diseased body covered with "putrifying sores" (Isa. 1 : 6). The only salvation from complete atheism for such a ceremoniously idolatrous church, argues Milton, has been "custom and the worm of conscience," perhaps reminiscent of the worm especially prepared by God to rob Jonah of his protective gourd-vine and make him aware of his essentially blasphemous attitude toward the love and mercy that God exhibits to non-Jews (Jon. 4 : 7–11).

Again when he favorably compares "the sober, plain, and unaffected stile" of the Bible with the Fathers' ornate style, especially their "fantastick, and declamatory flashes; the crosse-jingling periods which cannot but disturb, and come thwart a setl'd devotion worse than the din of bells, and rattles" (*Ref* 3. i : 34), there is a glance at Roman Catholic bells in religious ceremonies but there is also an implication that such language grates harshly on the ears of settled devotion because it lacks charity for independent and dissenting sects : "Though I speak with the tongues of men and of angels, and have not charity, I am become as sounding brass, or a tinkling cymbal" (1 Cor. 13 : 1).

When he criticizes the bishops for striving through their preaching "to set at nought and trample under foot all the most sacred and life blood Lawes, Statutes, and Acts of *Parliament*" (3. i. 57), the underlying suggestion is that they damage not only the civil rights of free Christians but also that they have a scorn for the true Gospel, like those who have "trodden under foot the Son of God, and hath counted the blood of the covenant . . . an unholy thing, and hath done despite unto the Spirit of grace" (Heb. 10 : 29). Even veiled threats of the revolution and the consequent desolation of the country lurk in the obscured allusion to Christ's sad response to Jerusalem's rejection of Him in the exhortation : "But let us not for fear of a scarre-crow, or else through hatred to be reform'd, stand hankering and politizing, when God with spread hands testifies to us, and points us out the way to our peace" (*Ref* 3. i. 73). Milton surely has in mind the occasion when Jesus "beheld the city, and wept over it, saying, if thou hadst known, even thou, at least in this thy day, the things which belong unto thy peace!" (Luke 19 : 41f.); "How often would I have gathered thy children together, even as a hen gathereth her chickens under her wings, and ye would not! Behold, your house is left unto you desolate" (Matt. 23 : 37–38). For his peroration, Milton prays for victory for the right and for God's vengeance on enemies of the true biblical faith with a psalmlike repetitiveness : "let them all take Counsell together, and let it come to nought; let them Decree, and doe thou Cancell it; let them gather themselves, and bee scatter'd, let them embattell themselves, and bee broken, let them imbattell, and be broken, for thou art with us" (3. i. 78). His concluding curse on those who wish their own high dignity and rule at the expense of the servitude of their country—"[Let them] be thrown down eternally into the *darkest* and *deepest* Gulfe of HELL" (*Ref* 3. i. 79)—has the ring of an imprecatory psalm : "Let death seize upon them and let them go down quick into hell" (Ps. 55 : 15).

Milton continues his subtle interweaving of biblical phraseology and imagery throughout his obvious appeals to texts of Scripture in *RCG* (1641–42), and he makes clear as well that an argument from the implications of Scripture, even from the silence of Scripture, is as valid for him as an argument from what is "formally, and profestly set downe" (*RCG* 3. i. 184). After prefacing the first book with a defense of his youthfulness for such a controversy (a defense alluding to Paul's exhortation to Timothy, "Let no man despise thy youth; but be thou an example of the believers. . . . Neglect not the gift that is in thee, which was given thee by prophecy" [1 Tim. 4 : 12, 14]), he proceeds to defend the presbyterial* system and to attack the episcopal system with very little direct quotation but with much paraphrase, allusion, and imaginatively extended imagery. For example, Paul's

statement to the Corinthian church, "I have espoused you to one husband, that I may present you as a chaste virgin to Christ" (2 Cor. 11 : 2), is connected with the story of the extensive period of preparation undergone by Esther and the other candidates for Queen of Persia (Esther 2 : 12–17) to establish the common-sense principle that "of any age or sex, most unfitly may a virgin be left to an uncertaine and arbitrary education" (*RCG* 3. i. 188); *ergo,* the church's government is not left to man's discretion but is plainly "platformed in the Bible," since it would be both unsound and untrue to assume that God would be more careless of the preparatory discipline of the bride for his son than Ahasuerus was of his wives and concubines. Again, in arguing against the Old Testament Law as a pattern for church government under the Gospel, without directly quoting Paul's Galatian epistle (a declaration of Christian independence from the Mosaic Law), Milton alludes to the Pauline image of the Law as a schoolmaster, a pedagogue, with no further authority over mature free-born sons (Gal. 3 : 24–26) and asks : "How then the ripe age of the Gospell should be put to schoole againe, and learn to governe her selfe from the infancy of the Law, the stronger to imitate the weaker, the freeman to follow the captive, the learned to be lesson'd by the rude, will be a hard undertaking to evince from any of those principles which either art or inspiration hath written" (*RCG* 3. i. 196–97).

In *RCG* Milton first reveals his remarkable ability to create vivid "cartoon scenes" from scriptural hints without quoting texts. Yet by this method he is able to provoke at once in the mind of the sympathetic reader amusement at the caricature of the episcopal targets of his scorn and implicit agreement with the underlying principle because of its roots in biblical authority. *RCG* exhibits two outstanding examples of this technique. After alluding several times from the very beginning of Book 1 to the angel of Revelation who measures God's temple with the rod of discipline (Rev. 11 : 1–2), Milton uses the foursquare image of the New Jerusalem, measured by an angel as a fifteen-hundred mile cube (Rev. 21: 15–17), without mentioning the source of his image. A presbyterial assembly is made up of councils like that called in Acts 15, where "no faithfull Christian was debarr'd" (*RCG* 3. i. 217), each council being a "right homogeneous and constituting part being in it selfe as it were a little Synod, and towards a generall assembly moving upon her own basis in an even and firme progression, as those smaller squares in battell unite in one great cube, the main phalanx, an embleme of truth and stedfastnesse" (3. i. 217). Contrary to this presbyterial cube with its biblical basis in the New Jerusalem stands "Prelaty ascending by a graduall monarchy from Bishop to Arch-bishop, from thence to Primat, and from thence, for there can be reason yeilded neither in nature, nor in religion, wherefore, if it have lawfully mounted thus high, it should not be a Lordly ascendent in the horoscope of the Church, from Primate to Patriarch, and so to Pope. I say Prelaty thus ascending in a continuall pyramid, . . . her pyramid aspires and sharpens to ambition . . ." (3. i. 217–18). Soon the "most dividing, and schismaticall forme that Geometricians know of . . . as it happens in such pointed bodies meeting, fall to gore one another with their sharpe spires for upper place, and precedence" (3. i. 218). The animated figures collapse together as Milton imagines the proud bishops scorning the idea that the "high rear'd government of the Church should so on a sudden, as it seem'd to them, squat into a Presbytery" (3. i. 219). The images sum up the whole argument of Book 1 : a truly New Testament form of church government is represented by the cube, not the pyramid; but error canonized by custom has so fueled human pride that the bishops think it the worst of indignities to assume the lowly form of brethren among brethren represented by the four-square shape of the New Jerusalem itself.

Similarly, in Book 2, Milton does not refer directly to the entry of Christ into Jerusalem on the back of an ass, but he uses that image to contrast with a ludicrous caricature of the pomp and power of the bishops being worshiped by the people of England as an "ass bestriding a lion."

> But it is observable that so long as the Church in true imitation of Christ can be content to ride upon an Asse carrying her selfe and her government along in a mean and simple guise, she may be as he is a Lion of the tribe of *Juda*, and in her humility all men with loud Hosanna's will confesse her greatnes. But when despising the mighty operation of the spirit by the weak things of this world she thinks to make herself bigger and more considerable by using the way of civil force and jurisdiction, as she sits upon this Lion she changes into an Asse, and instead of Hosanna's every man pelts her with stones and dirt. (3. i. 252)

Such "cartoon scenes" stick in the mind and may well have gone much further in persuading Milton's readers toward his point of view than his more outraged and indignant (and much more obvious) appeals to biblical analogies, such as those in his peroration comparing the King to Samson with his head in the harlot lap of the prelates and comparing prelaty to Sodom and Gomorrah as the Parliament, like God of old, prepares to destroy the episcopal government of the church, bringing "such a dead Sea of subversion upon her, that she may never in this Land rise more to afflict the holy reformed Church, and the elect people of God" (3. i. 279).

In *Areop* the title itself may conceal an allusion to the Bible. The connection on the surface, as Milton himself points out, is with Isocrates, who wrote to the parliament of Athens from his private house; but there are perhaps intentional parallels with the Apostle Paul's sermon on the Areopagus in Acts 17. Both orators praise their audiences for their sincere wish to serve truth but point out where they are wrong in their assumptions. There is wisdom among the Athenians in seeking to know a God higher than any they currently worship, but their error is in trying to represent such a God by icons or to house him in temples (Acts 17: 24–25). The Parliament of England has passed an act governing the printing of books and some provisions of it are beneficent; the error they must now be made aware of lies in the deleterious effects that will grow from the licensing of books. That is, as the Athenians sincerely seek to know God but are prevented from so doing by their lack of divine revelation, the English sincerely seek to forward the cause of truth but are actually hindering it by their neglect of the revelation they already have. Paul appeals to the national pride of the Athenians by quoting one of their own poets to support his theology of the "unknown god" (17 : 28), and Milton appeals to the pride of the English in having initiated the principles of reformation and recovery of truth, pointing to Wycliffe as the pioneer without whose work Luther* and Calvin* might never have been known. Milton refers to Paul's example in quoting pagan authors, including the occasion in Acts 17, to support his ideal of "promiscuous reading," but he provides no explicit hint of an intentional parallel between his oration and Paul's. It can hardly be doubted, however, that the members of Parliament or contemporary readers of Milton's tractate would have thought of Paul's sermon to the Areopagus upon reading *Areop,* though perhaps few of them would have bothered to pursue the thought.

In *Tenure* (1649) and *CivP* (1659) Milton argues for consistency in interpreting Scripture and in the practical applications that should logically follow from one's interpretation. Among many such abuses of biblical texts there was the contention of the royalists, lately joined by the Presbyterians, that the king was above the law because King David had prayed in Psalm 51 "Against thee only have I sinned." Milton comments, revealing his opposition to literalistic interpretation of texts in a vacuum, "Whatever his meaning were, any wise man will see, that the

pathetical words of a Psalme can be no certaine decision to a poynt that hath abundantly more certain rules to goe by" (5 : 13). Another abuse that particularly provokes Milton in *Tenure* is the royalist dependence on the letter of Paul's words to the Romans, "Let every soul be subject to the higher powers. For there is no power but of God : the powers that be are ordained of God. Whosoever resisteth therefore the power, resisteth the ordinance of God; and they that resist shall receive to themselves damnation. For rulers are not a terror to good works, but to the evil. Wilt thou then not be afraid of the power? do that which is good, and thou shalt have praise of the same : For he is a minister of God to thee for good. But if thou do that which is evil, be afraid; for he beareth not the sword in vain : for he is the minister of God, a revenger to execute wrath upon him that doeth evil" (Rom. 13 : 1–4). In *CivP*, Milton takes up this passage phrase by phrase, pointing out that he had "through Gods assistance" explained this "most wrested and vexed place of scripture" more than once : "heretofore against *Salmasius*, and regal tyranie over the state; now against *Erastus*, and state-tyranie over the church" (6 : 17).

The contradictory position of Protestant persecuters of Protestants becomes again in 1673 one of the main emphases of Milton's *TR* : "What Protestant then who himself maintains the same Principles, and disavows all implicit Faith, would persecute, and not rather charitably tolerate such men as these, unless he mean to abjure the Principles of his own Religion?" (*TR* 6 : 170). In such passages may be sensed the indignant fervor of Michael as he reveals the distant future to Adam.

> Truth shall retire
> Bestruck with slandrous darts, and works of
> Faith
> Rarely be found : so shall the World goe on,
> To good malignant, to bad men benigne..
> (*PL* 12. 535–38)

The combined intellectual and devotional energy that Milton poured into his study of the Bible flows through all his works to the reader, and when one kind of energy seems to predominate, the impression may well result from the modern reader's preference for one over the other. For example, *CD*, like other of Milton's prose works, often seems to the modern reader to be dissolving into the very scholastic rationalization that Milton repudiates in the preface to his "best and richest possession" (*CD* 14:9), sometimes in those very passages which must have seemed to Milton to be most charged with worshipful devotion. For example, when he concludes his arguments against the Calvinistic doctrine of reprobation, he sounds cooly rational, even sophistical, to a modern ear, but to a seventeenth-century ear accustomed to hearing casuistical justifications of God's having arbitrarily damned millions to hell from all eternity, Milton's prose may well have throbbed with a warm appreciation for God's compassion toward man.

> Inasmuch, therefore, as there is no condemnation except on account of unbelief or of sin, . . . the texts themselves which are produced in confirmation of the decree of reprobation will prove that no one is excluded by any decree of God from the pale of repentance and eternal salvation, unless it be after the contempt and rejection of grace, and that at a very late hour.
> (*CD* 14:155–57)

On the other hand, a passage in *PL* that appears to express pure, spontaneous praise is rather an intensely concentrated verbalization of a long theological tradition of the strife of mercy and justice within the divine mind. Addressing the Father, the angels sing of the Son, immediately following his offer to redeem man,

> He to appease thy wrauth, and end the strife
> Of Mercy and Justice in thy face discern'd,
> Regardless of the Bliss wherein hee sat
> Second to thee, offerd himself to die
> For mans offence. O unexampl'd love,
> Love no where to be found less than Divine!
> Hail Son of God, Saviour of Men[!]
> (*PL* 3. 406–12)

Patrides has shown this apparently ex-temporaneous outburst of praise to be actually a poetic culmination of a long Christian tradition based on Psalm 85:10—"Mercy and truth are met together: righteousness and peace have kissed each other" (*Milton and the Christian Tradition* [1966], pp. 122ff., 131ff., 155ff.). The point is that for Milton, as for most of his contemporaries and predecessors, intellectual ratiocination and spiritual devotion were inseparable, two sides of the same coin, and though poetry is "more simple, sensuous, and passionate" than logic* and rhetoric*, Milton's comparative adverb is relative, not superlative. Therefore, though Milton's major poetry seems to be the epitome and finest flowering of his mastery of the art of transmuting the Bible into literature, one should recognize the anachronistic tendency involved in such a view of Milton's art. Although he himself says in the preface to the second book of *RCG* that writing prose is the labor of his left hand, he clearly had a regard "to Gods glory by the honour and instruction" (3. i. 236) of his country, and wished to be "an interpreter & relater of the best and sagest things" among the citizens of his native island (3. i. 236).

> For me I have determin'd to lay up as the best treasure, and solace of a good old age, if God voutsafe it me, the honest liberty of free speech from my youth, where I shall think it available in so dear a concernment as the Churches good. (3. i. 232)

Eliot's comment that Milton's prose is "the prose of a poet," though intended as dispraise, can be seen as praise by those who, like Kester Svendsen, have marveled at Milton's Latin and English prose and have speculated that he might never have developed his superior and unique epic style without the discipline of writing the many works that at the time must have seemed frustrating distractions from his main mission in life (Yale *Prose* 4. ii. 687, 693).

Milton's multifaceted uses of the Bible in his epics are amazingly effective when they are fully recognized, and through the aid of diligent editors and commentators modern readers can overcome the handicap of biblical illiteracy and appreciate what these allusions do for the poems and what they show us about Milton the artist. Precisely because he took the Bible seriously as God's revelation to men and because he believed that "it is only to the individual faith of each that the Deity has opened the way of eternal salvation" (*CD* 14 : 5), Milton feels free to extrapolate imaginatively from the letter of Scripture so long as he stays within the spirit of its teaching and trusts the assistance of "that eternall Spirit who can enrich with all utterance and knowledge" (*RCG* 3. i. 241). Yet he recognizes the important role of "industrious and select reading, steddy observation, insight into all seemly and generous arts and affaires" (3. i. 241) and thus, more often than not, keeps his imagination in line with established Christian tradition, as Patrides, Evans, Lewalski, and others have demonstrated.

In his epics Milton may be seen as a Christian poet, believing in the biblical basis of his subject and communicating the conviction of superhistorical reality, of truth, even in the invented parts of his fable. He is revealed as a Renaissance man who has taken all learning for his province, particularly linguistic and literary learning, by his allusions to the Scriptures in their Hebrew, Greek, and Latin forms, allusions for which he found "fit audience . . . though few" in the seventeenth century and finds even fewer today. That his are the most dramatic of epics is especially impressed upon the reader familiar with the techniques of biblical allusion employed by Marlowe and Shakespeare* on the Elizabethan stage, techniques present in embryonic form even in the earlier English mystery plays. And since his major poems are both epics, though one is the full-blown classical epic of great action played out on a broad multileveled stage and the other is the briefer Jobean epic of intense debate in a private setting, he successfully confirms as tools for the Christian warfare such epic devices as the epic simile, reiteration of formulaic phrases, catalogues, eloquent speeches, and scenes of single combat. Finally, the two epics are unified in theme and revealed as complementary parts of a greater whole by the many cross-referencing strands thrown out by each to the other, strands that are anchored at each end by biblical reference and allusion.

In both epics, Milton creates such density of biblical reference and allusion that even the reader who knows the Bible well, or perhaps one should say especially the reader who knows the Bible well, has difficulty determining where Milton adheres to the letter of Scripture and where he departs from it. As one gives himself more and more to the suspension of disbelief, the impression of authoritative reality becomes so strong that one no longer makes the effort to distinguish biblical fact from Miltonic imaginative interpretation. For example, in the description of Eve's temptation by the serpent in *PL* and in that of Satan's temptation of Jesus in the wilderness in *PR,* Milton communicates scriptural reality through his imaginative presentation: he follows the Bible so closely in certain crucial passages that the events have the air of having really happened as he portrays them, though a later cold-eyed comparison readily shows that Milton freely expands, extrapolates, and rearranges incidents and dialogue.

The Genesis statement of the serpent's superior subtlety becomes the basis in *PL* for Milton's substitution of a gradually progressive temptation for the abrupt approach of the serpent in Genesis 3 : 1. Eve's initial surprise at the serpent's ability to speak, the serpent's claim to have already eaten of the forbidden fruit, his flattering seduction that leads Eve to the very foot of the tree—these are all Miltonic additions (some of which are shown by Evans to correspond to rabbinic and/or medieval Christian tradition) that seem so "right" that the reader of *PL* is recapitulating (with less excuse) Eve's experience of being deceived even as he reads of her deception. By the time the dialogue becomes basically biblical, Milton can transpose speeches and otherwise shift emphases without objection from the reader. In Genesis the serpent first questions Eve concerning God's command, deliberately enlarging it to all the fruit of the Garden and thus impugning the goodness of God: "Yea, hath God said, Ye shall not eat of every tree of the garden?" To which Eve replies, "We may eat of the fruit of the trees of the garden: But of the fruit of the tree which is in the midst of the garden, God hath said, Ye shall not eat of it, neither shall ye touch it, lest ye die." (Gen. 3 : 1b–3) His sly suggestiveness has led her to exaggerate God's command ("neither shall ye touch it") and to mitigate its force simultaneously ("lest ye die," instead of "in the day that thou eatest thereof, thou shalt surely die" [Gen. 2 : 17b]). Yet in Milton's account, the serpent has developed such eager anticipation in Eve as he leads her to the hitherto nameless tree of such great virtue, that she speaks first, already hinting her disaffection with God in her tone:

Serpent, we might have spar'd our coming hither
Fruitless to mee, though Fruit be here *to excess,*
The credit of whose vertue rest with thee,
Wondrous indeed, if cause of such effects.
But of this Tree *we* may not taste *nor touch;*
God so commanded.
(*PL* 9. 647–52, italics added)

Her "indeed" is picked up by the serpent, sensitive to the tone of her words. Though he cannot have missed her emphasis on "this Tree," he questions whether God has prohibited all the fruit of the garden.

Indeed? hath God then said that of the Fruit
Of all these Garden Trees ye shall not eate,
Yet Lords declar'd of all in Earth or Aire?
(9. 656–58)

Showing that before the Fall the principle of the Sermon on the Mount that an inner motive toward a sin is tantamount to the sin (Matt. 5 : 27–28) is not applicable, the epic voice carefully designates Eve "yet sinless" (9. 659) even though her almost petulant words show all too clearly her incipient rebellious attitude. "Of the Fruit / Of each Tree in the Garden we may eate,/ [any *other* old trees; but who needs them?]. But of the Fruit of this fair Tree amidst / The Garden [this very special one in its especially prominent place] God hath said, Ye shall not eate / Thereof, nor shall ye touch it, least ye die" (9. 659–63). Such a scene fulfills the requirements of most modern readers through portraying quite accurately and realistically a psychological crisis leading to a decision. Much of Milton's perennial durability as a poet lies in his amazing power to supply the demands of succeeding generations of readers, to provide aesthetic satisfaction or intellectual stimulation or both in times as widely different as his own day and ours—and as different from either as all those periods between his and ours.

The order given to Satan's temptations of Jesus in *PR* is Luke's rather than Matthew's, but Milton manages to harmonize the synoptic accounts in such a way as to convince the reader familiar with all New Testament references to the temptation of Christ by Satan that his account has the authoritative reality of the Bible behind it. Aside from the greater artistic and dramatic advantages to be gained by closing the brief epic with the striking scene on the pinnacle of the Temple, Milton can create a greater aura of biblical reality by using Luke's order and weaving in allusions to the other Gospels as he details the temptations. For one thing Luke explicitly claims that "having had perfect understanding of all things from the very first" he is writing down the events of the life of Jesus "in order" (1 : 3), while Matthew makes no corresponding claim. For another, Luke closes the temptation story with the statement that the devil had "ended *all* the temptation" (4 : 13), implying that the pinnacle test was the final one. Again, Matthew makes no such statement following the mountaintop scene, but merely records that "the devil leaveth him" (4 : 11).

In his effort to harmonize these accounts, Milton's description of Satan's "Feigning to disappear" (4. 397) after the mountaintop temptations is apparently an allusion to Matthew's version, and this is doubtless one reason for Milton's inclusion of the storm scene between the temptation to accept the kingdoms of the world, including worldly knowledge, and the temptation to cast himself down from the Temple. For the complementary balance of the two epics, a more important structural reason is to show Satan falling as a result of his desperate use of force at the end of *PR*; therefore, we have come full circle since we first saw him falling through the failure of his force at the opening of *PL.* Arranging the temptations as he does enables Milton to follow through on the distinction God the Father makes in looking ahead toward the temptations: Christ is to prove himself able to "resist / All his sollicitations, and at length / All his vast force, and drive" Satan back to Hell (1. 151–53), so that he who gave up force in favor of fraud in *PL* has now in desperation given up fraud to resort once again to force since all his wiles have failed. After the storm scene he comes to Jesus,

Yet with no new device, they all were spent,
Rather by this his last affront resolv'd,
Desperate of better course, to vent his rage,
And mad despight to be so oft repell'd.
            (*PR* 4. 443–46)

Thus when Satan says, "Another method I must now begin" (4. 540), he describes his own circle, for the way of force against the Son of God was his initial method. The statement of a few lines earlier that Satan has found Jesus "Proof against *all* temptation as a rock / Of Adamant" (4. 533–34), may indicate that the temptations as solicitations to sin have now ended and that what follows is primarily a test or trial by ordeal. Again, as in *PL,* the Son wins by an apocalyptic parousia, much less spectacular but no less effective, a corroboration of Raphael's account of the first fall of Satan (*PL* 6) and a repudiation of Satan's (*PL* 1 and 2). Poetically, the stroke is brilliant, while at the same time,

the reader's conviction of biblical authority is established.

One aspect of Milton's use of the Bible in his epics, and to some extent in all his writings, one that in the twentieth century restricts his fit audience to fewer comparatively than it would have done in the seventeenth, is his frequent appeal to a reader's knowledge of the original Hebrew and Greek texts and of the Latin versions, particularly the Vulgate of Jerome. At times he transliterates Hebrew or Greek words into English and includes within the immediate context an English translation, thus alerting the reader to the etymological sense of a familiar word or to the connotations in English of an unfamiliar word from the original biblical text; at other times he provides variant translations for texts familiar from the Authorized Version, translations that he prefers to those widely received. And there are a few times when he echoes the words or phrasing of the Latin Bible, depending on his reader to respond to the allusion, yet not so heavily as to rob the passage of meaning for the reader with no Latin. For instance, when in *PL* Beelzebub asks

who shall tempt with wandring feet
The dark unbottom'd infinite Abyss
And through the palpable obscure find out
His uncouth way,

            (2. 404–7)

"Abyss" is transliterated from a Greek word meaning "unbottom'd," therefore of infinite depth (the "bottomless pit" of Rev. 20:1, KJV), and the "palpable obscure" alludes to the "tenebrae . . . tam densae, ut palpari queant" of the Vulgate (Exod. 10:21; "Palpable darkness" occurs again in *PL*, 12. 188). Again, in both *PL* and *PR* Milton provides a literal translation of a Greek word as a name for Satan, though in the King James version the word is used as an abstract rather than as a proper noun. The request in the Lord's Prayer, "deliver us from evil" (Matt. 6:13a), could be more literally translated "deliver us from the Evil One." Milton so translates the word, using "the Evil one" as a name for Satan in crucial scenes of both epics (*PL* 9. 463 and *PR* 4. 194). To these few examples could be added dozens more, all of which convince the informed reader that here is a poet whose linguistic versatility in biblical exegesis and interpretation wins for his opinions on such important theological subjects a respectful and considerate hearing.

PL is the most dramatic of epics; indeed, Milton at first contemplated writing the story of the Fall of Man* in dramatic form, and when the form changed to epic in his imagination, many characteristics of drama remained. Not the least of these is his use of biblical allusion for dramatic effect, a use that is clearly in the tradition of medieval and Elizabethan drama, most notably of Marlowe and Shakespeare. Biblical references, quotations, and allusions establish setting, including psychological mood or atmosphere as well as physical setting; contribute to the illumination of or foreshadow the direction of movement in the action, or plot; intensify irony and other special effects gained by how a character, or the epic voice, uses language; and more fully rounds out the epic characters, giving them a depth and complexity that would have been difficult to achieve by any other means. Satan's fall through Chaos, his and his followers' being chained on the lake of fire, the brimstone, fierce flames, and "darkness visible" of Hell's landscape—all are based on biblical images from the Old and New Testaments. Heaven, too, is a scriptural Heaven primarily, though both Hell and Heaven have some features drawn from nonbiblical classical and Renaissance literary conceptions.

But it is on the Garden of Eden that Milton lavishes most profusely his echoes of the Bible—the Genesis garden, Solomon's garden for his Shulamite bride, Susanna's apocryphal garden, the pastoral beauty of David's psalms and the prophets' visions of restored Israel, the celestial flora of the New Jerusalem, all and more are appealed to as enriching associations along with the gardens of Alcinous in Homer*, the Elysian fields in Virgil*, and the beautiful places of Ariosto*, Tasso*, Spenser*, Camoëns*. The *topos* of the *locus amoenus,* as described by Curtius and traced through the Christian epic by Giamatti, had never before Milton been so thoroughly baptized in the waters of Scripture. A passage that epitomizes Milton's technique of amalgamating the conventional elements of a literary *topos* with biblical images and phrases is that in which Eve is discovered alone by Satan on the day of the Fall (*PL* 9. 425ff.). The conventional features are also from the first three chapters of Genesis : the grove, the fountain and rivulet, the mixed forest, the flowers, the soft breeze, the sound of birds are all concentrated around Eve, but "in *her* look summs all Delight" (9. 454; italics added). Since Eden means pleasant or delightful and the Garden is the most pleasant plot, Eve becomes an island of pleasure amidst pleasure, a fulfillment of the biblical words, "A garden inclosed is my sister, my spouse" (Song of Sol. 4 : 12). It is as though the pains Milton has taken to make his garden both beautiful and biblical are means toward the end of personifying Eden in Eve, are a way of making setting serve character and both serve theme, since "loss of Eden" for Adam is loss of Eve (9. 910; 8. 470–80).

Similarly in *PR* one of the most effective uses of biblical allusion for establishing setting that will at once delineate character, emphasize the importance of preceding action, and highlight theme occurs when Satan's temptations have all been overcome and a "fiery Globe" of angels lifts Christ from the pinnacle of the temple and

> in a flowry valley set him down
> On a green bank, and set before him spred
> A table of Celestial Food, Divine
> Ambrosial, Fruits fetcht from the tree of life,
> And from the fount of life Ambrosial drink,
> That soon refresh'd him.
>
> (4. 586–91)

By contrast with the threatening wilderness of most of the poem, this is a peacefully pastoral scene reminiscent of Eden and representative of Christ's having now regained Eden by having qualified himself as example and redeemer of mankind. But biblical words and phrases add considerably to the dramatic effect of the setting: having passed through the "valley of the shadow of death," Jesus now is resting in "green pastures" and God has sent angels to prepare "a table before [him] in the presence of [his] enemies" (Ps. 23:2, 4–5). The whole scene becomes prophetic of his future success in the glorious work as "Queller of Satan" (4. 634), just as the psalmist sees his Shepherd's present blessings as assuring that "goodness and mercy shall follow me all the days of my life: and I will dwell in the house of the Lord for ever" (Ps. 23:6). At the end of the poem Jesus "unobserv'd / Home to his Mothers house private return'd" (PR 4. 638f.), but the triumphal scene with the angels foreshadows the time when he will reign in triumph from his Father's throne.

As the example just cited indicates, biblical references in both epics often serve to foreshadow forthcoming action within the poems themselves and, sometimes simultaneously, to place the present action in the context of eternity and of God's inevitable victory over Satan and evil. For example, when Adam and Eve leave the Garden of Eden at the close of PL, biblical allusion to the story of Lot and his family's deliverance from Sodom show the real significance of the action to be merciful rather than vengeful and it also points forward to the good that God will bring out of man's sin. Michael is called the "hastning Angel," when he takes "In either hand" Adam and Eve, our "lingring Parents," from Eden (12. 637–38), and these allusive modifiers remind the reader of when the "Angels hastened Lot . . . and while he lingered, . . . laid hold upon his hand, and upon the hand of his wife" (Gen. 19:15f.). Sad as their leaving Paradise has to be, compared with the death from which they are reprieved and the dreadful faces and fiery arms at the gate behind them, given the opportunity to choose a place of rest with God's providential guidance and reconciled to each other and to Him, what our first Parents have to look forward to is almost beatific.

Addison* (Spectator no. 297 of 1712) felt that PL was flawed because it did not have a happy ending and that Milton, "sensible of this imperfection in his fable, . . . endeavoured to cure it" by the humiliation of Satan in Book 10 and the visions of the future in Book 12, and many readers have agreed with his judgment. Yet Addison missed Milton's most effective means of mitigating the sad ending; certainly the end of PL is not made happy by biblical allusion, but the poignant sense of loss is carefully blunted by the long-range expectation of God's victory through the seed of the woman.

Words and phrases from the Bible are used by Milton to achieve ironic contrast or other dramatic effects as a result of the reader's memory of their original context. In the Son's* expulsion of the rebel angels in PL 6, he is associated with Moses' leading the people of Israel out of Egypt and across the Red Sea, while Satan and his forces are seen as types of Pharaoh and his armies. The Son commands the good angels to "Stand still" and watch as God's power drives out the rebels through a breach in Heaven's wall (PL 6. 800ff.) just as Moses commanded the Israelites to "stand still, and see the salvation of the LORD" (Exod. 14:13) as the Egyptians rode into the open Red Sea, only to be overwhelmed by the waters within a few minutes. Thus the biblical words are used in a situation similar to the biblical one; but one of Milton's more effective devices, borrowed and developed from similar uses of the Bible in Marlowe and Shakespeare, is the complete reversal of the context and purpose of the biblical language being echoed. By such means Satan reveals himself as a perfect anti-Christ, since it is often in his speeches that reversals of Christ's words in the Gospels occur. Arguing that the fallen angels must plan a new strategy against God, Satan says,

> our better part remains
> To work in close design, by fraud or guile
> What force effected not;
> (1. 645–47)

he is turning upside down the admonishing words of Christ to Martha that "the good part" of contemplative devotion that Mary had chosen would bring forth more lasting results than the busy household activity of Martha (Luke 10:41–42). In a similar way, to justify his bringing sin and death into the innocent world of Eden, Satan sarcastically twists "Freely ye have received, freely give" (Matt. 10:8), words spoken by Jesus in giving the gift of the Spirit to his disciples to empower them to bless suffering humanity. Though unheard by them, he addresses Adam and Eve:

> my dwelling haply may not please
> Like this fair Paradise, your sense, yet such
> Accept your Makers work; he gave it me,
> Which I as freely give.
> (4. 378–81)

Milton uses the Bible very effectively in characterization, primarily through associating his epic characters with well-known persons of the Bible. As seen through biblical allusion, Satan has the proud vanity of Nebuchadnezzar (1. 570–73; Dan. 5:20), the malice disguised as piety of Herod (3. 667–72; Matt. 2:8–12), the unrepentant materialism of Esau (4. 79–85; Heb. 12:16–17), the cowardliness of Belshazzar (4. 1010–12; Dan. 5:6, 27), the self-righteousness of the Pharisees (5:788–92; John 8:33–36). The Son of God, Adam, Eve, Abdiel, and others are similarly characterized by biblical associations, and in PR both the protagonist and the antagonist are rounded out as characters by biblical allusion, though in the brief epic Satan is more often associated with direct biblical statements about him than with villainous characters and Jesus becomes the one seen in the light of biblical heroes: Daniel, Elijah, and most notably, Job.

The interconnections between PL and PR that indicate Milton's intention to complement each epic with the other are primarily biblical. The opening lines of the two poems reflect the unity of theme that is maintained throughout: "For as by one man's disobedience many were made sinners, so by the obedience of one, shall many be made righteous" (Rom. 5:19). What is lost through the dis-

obedience of Adam in PL is restored through the greater man of PR. And different as PL and PR are stylistically and structurally, thematically they are opposite sides of the same coin, each asserting in its own way eternal providence and justifying the ways of God to men; this thematic unity is highlighted particularly by the epic convention of reiteration, a convention Milton successfully transforms into an integral part of the wholeness of vision achieved by reading the two epics together and being alert to the cross-referencing of biblical words and phrases. Examples are the words *serpent, air,* and *seed.* The Genesis account does not identify the serpent as Satan, but Milton depends on the reader's awareness of the New Testament identification (2 Cor. 11:3, Rev. 12:9, 20:2) to give the word an ominous sound wherever it occurs. Both his first reference to Satan in PL and his penultimate reference in PR are to the "Infernal Serpent" (1. 34; 4. 618), and all the occurrences of the word in between (some 40 or more) carry ominous overtones to some degree. After the Fall neither the angels (10. 1–5, 19–21) nor man (9. 1067–69) nor woman (9. 1149–50) can have a simple admiration for the serpent as a living creature, for he is associated too closely with the Adversary of God and man. Yet after Book 10 (and including 10. 1032–34), the references to the serpent in PL and in PR are connected with the promise of his future bruising by the seed of the woman, thus shifting in its connotations from dread to hope as Christ gives evidence in PR of his ability to inflict upon the serpent his "last and deadliest wound" (4. 622). The biblical promise that the woman's seed would bruise the serpent's head (Gen. 3:15) becomes a motif of both poems, and the conventional reiteration of words and phrases in the epic form is grasped by Milton as an opportunity for emphasizing the theme of both epics. Furthermore, by alluding often, from the opening books of PL to the end of PR, to Satan's destiny as "prince of the power of the air" (Eph. 2:2), Milton makes of the culminating scene on the pinnacle of the temple in *PR* a fitting climax to both epics at once; unlike Antaeus, defeated by Hercules in the air because he was out of touch with his native element, the earth, Satan is defeated by Christ in the very domain Satan prides himself on having become ruler over.

Milton's primary sources for *SA* were Judges 13–16, Hebrews 11, and the body of traditional commentary and interpretation that had accreted to these biblical references to Samson, much of which is surveyed in F. M. Krouse, *Milton's Samson and the Christian Tradition* (1949). Less clear to modern readers but probably clearer to those of the seventeenth century are Milton's many allusions to other passages, particularly those in the New Testament which, when recognized, help shape reader response to the characters and to the central development within Samson. Most of Milton's changes in and additions to the Judges account seem to be controlled by a wish to substantiate Hebrews 11 : 32–34 by revealing Samson as the Old Testament hero who best fits the category of those who "through faith . . . out of weakness were made strong" and by a concomitant desire to associate Samson with Paul as the foremost of merely human New Testament heroes, one who found that by God's grace his greatest strength came in his time of greatest weakness (2 Cor. 12 : 9). Samson, too, demonstrates the Pauline discovery that through faith in God, "when I am weak, then am I strong" (2 Cor. 12 : 10b). As Kirkconnell has shown, Milton departed from the practice of his predecessors in treating the Samson story by making the drama psychological and spiritual rather than external and physical. Milton demonstrates the paradox of God's spiritual strength gradually becoming perfect in Samson's weakness through his use of the choric sounding-board and his careful orchestration of choral songs and visitors. Such Miltonic additions to Judges as the reappearance of Dalila, the invention of Harapha, the prolongation of Manoa's life beyond his

son's, and the introduction of a group of Danites before Samson's death all contribute to the development within Samson of the faith and the inner illumination necessary to his final victory in death; by the end of the fifth episode Samson's movement from human weakness to divine strength is completed and there remains only the working out in physical action of what has already happened within. Milton's delineation of this psychological and spiritual progress depends on the skillful and decorous meshing together of many small details of characterization and language. Subtle biblical echoes, especially from the New Testament, achieve in the reader's mind an association with the Apostle Paul as a biblical hero whose victories are clearly those of the spirit over the physical world.

Paul is an example from the New Testament of one who "out of weakness [was] made strong" (Heb. 11 : 34) and it is he to whom God said, "My strength is made perfect in weakness" (2 Cor. 12 : 9). *Samson* is transliterated from a Hebrew word meaning "strong," and *Dalila* combines *dallah,* "weak," with *lah,* "nothing" rather than the transliteration of the Authorized Version, *Delilah,* meaning "languishing, pining." Thus when Dalila pleads her weakness as an excuse and points out to Samson "To what I did thou shewdst me first the way" (*SA* 781), he cannot deny it, and her name intensifies both his repeated charge of effeminacy against himself (410, 562) and her claim that she and he are, after all, two of a kind : "Let weakness then with weakness come to parl / So near related, or the same of kind" (785–86). Samson's real triumph in resisting Dalila, then, is in overcoming the Dalila within himself to the extent that he refuses to excuse himself or to blame God for his erstwhile weakness; as he puts it, "All wickedness is weakness" (834). The Dalila episode provides the most striking instance in the drama of like purging like : "sowr against sowr, salt to remove salt humours" ("Of That Sort of Dramatic Poem Which Is Called Tragedy," prefacing the drama.)

Samson's opening soliloquy reveals his conscious misunderstanding of his plight and at the same time suggests to the reader the process by which he will come to understand and to grow to spiritual strength. When he concludes, "Suffices that to me strength is my bane, / And proves the sourse of all my miseries" (63–64), he is both right and wrong. Weakness really has been his downfall, as his outcry "O weakness!" some 160 lines later shows, and as he himself comes to see in the mirror of himself, Dalila, weakness personified. His physical strength will prove his killer but will also bring the Israelites their deliverance from Philistine rule, the purpose for which he was born. His "Suffices" is an ironic echo of God's answer to Paul when the apostle begged for the removal of his "thorn in the flesh" (the Chorus calls a bad wife, like Dalila, "a thorn / Intestin" [1037–38]) : "My grace is sufficient for thee" (2 Cor. 12 : 9). Like Paul, his thorn of weakness not removed but transcended through faith, Samson demonstrates at last a "vertue which breaks through all opposition, / And all temptation can remove," a renewal of strength in the midst of weakness that "Most shines and most is acceptable above" (1050–52).

Other parallels between Samson and Paul can be seen. As Paul always considered himself a prisoner, not of Rome, but of Christ—that is, his imprisonment was for a divine purpose unknown to him—so Samson is a prisoner, not of the Philistines or of his own body, but of God (SA 7, 1170; Philem. 9, Eph. 3 : 1). As Paul was convinced that God's plan for him antedated his conversion or even his separation from his "mother's womb" (Gal. 1 : 15), Samson knows himself "a person separate to God" (31), "destin'd from the womb" (634) to great exploits as Israel's deliverer. Paul recognized his responsibility to submit willingly to "the dispensation of God" (1 Cor. 9 : 17, Col. 1 : 25); Samson knows he "must not quarrel with the will / Of highest dispensation" (60–61). Paul feared letting his body subjugate his spirit lest he "should be a cast-away" (1 Cor. 9 : 27); Samson fears that God has "cast [him] off as never known" (641; Matt. 7 : 23). Paul cried out in despair at being bound in his nature to the dead body of the old Adam : "O wretched man that I am! Who shall deliver me from the body of this death?" (Rom. 7 : 24). Samson bemoans his "life half dead, a living death, / And buried; but O yet more miserable! / My self, my Sepulcher, a moving Grave" (100–102). And when Samson, feeling "rousing motions" within, says in calm resolution to the Philistine officer, "I am content to go" (1403), he has learned Paul's great lesson : "For I have learned, in whatsoever state I am, *therewith* to be content" (Phil. 4 : 11). A partial explanation of the power of Milton's story of Samson's phoenixlike rise from hopelessness to victory lies, then, in such subtle appeals to the biblical knowledge of his reader to underscore the poem's regenerative theme and imagery.

Probably no other single work can compete with the Bible for the distinction of most influential source of Milton's ideas and modes of expressing those ideas. The explicit references are too frequent and too obvious to the reader who is himself familiar with the Bible for such a conclusion to be questioned; almost as clear are the multitudinous hints and suggestions of biblical parallels that are only implied. Yet the body of Milton's work, particularly the poetry, is not, as Raleigh* thought, a "monument to dead ideas," interesting merely as a museum showcase example of an outworn theology; the volume and vitality of modern criticism and scholarship on Milton testify to his continuing relevance, to the responsiveness of contemporary readers to his vision of man and of man's relationships with man, with the world around him, and with transcendent reality. E. N. S. Thompson once suggested why Milton's work continues to appeal so strongly to readers who no longer share his faith in the dependability of the biblical revelation upon which all of his work is based : "It is the work of a man who has read the Bible with a poet's heart" (*Essays on Milton* [1914]). [JHS]

BIBLES. It can be assumed that Milton owned and used various versions of the Bible, in various translations, and that he may have inherited his father's Protestant Bible and his mother's. But despite a number of alleged autographed copies that have appeared, we know of only a few certain volumes. His "family" Bible, in which he recorded vital statistics, was a 1612 edition of the Authorized Version; it is extant in the British Museum, where it is catalogued Additional MS 32310. Because "its diction, its imagery, its rhythms, early became a part of him" (Parker, *Milton*, p. 10), romantic speculation envisions the Bible as a gift from his parents on his fourth birthday, but when he acquired it is unknown, for the handwriting postdates 1639. He owned a Geneva Bible at some time, but this has disappeared as far as we know. A copy of the 1560 Geneva edition was said to exist with his autograph as late as 1911; this may now have emerged as Elizabeth Minshull's Bible. A gift of a Hebrew Bible was sent to him by Thomas Young*, perhaps early in 1627 from Hamburg where Young was pastor to the English Merchant colony. It has disappeared. Milton's first and third wives also each had Bibles. Mary Powell's Bible, probably a copy of the Authorized Version, passed to her daughter Deborah and then to Deborah's daughter Elizabeth Foster, who allowed John Ward* to examine its family notations in February 1738 and who on January 6, 1750, showed it to Thomas Birch*. Its whereabouts thereafter are unknown. A Bible was listed in the inventory made of Elizabeth Minshull's effects, but whether this was a Geneva version is uncertain (it is, however, listed as large). A volume with a spurious signature of the poet is now in the University of Texas Library, and this has been said to have been Milton's widow's. He certainly owned a Latin Bible, the translation of Tre-

millius* and Junius*, but a copy has never been identified. One final item should be noted. Brian Walton's *Biblia Sacra Polyglotta,* in six volumes, published in 1654–1657, was championed by Milton in proceedings for aid from the Council of State* in 1652, and it was almost certainly Milton's former student Richard Heath who assisted Walton in his work. Its use in *CD* assures Milton's ownership. [JTS]

BIBLIOGRAPHY. For all practical purposes, bibliographical interest in Milton began in the nineteenth century when Henry J. Todd* included a great deal of bibliographical matter in his notes to the second edition of *Some Account of the Life and Writings of John Milton* (1809). Many other scholars published lists of studies during this century, among them a thirty-nine page bibliography compiled by J. P. Anderson, included in Richard Garnett's *Life of John Milton* (1890). However, E. N. S. Thompson's *John Milton: A Topical Bibliography* (1916) was the first extensive bibliography published. Thompson's work contains 104 pages, and it was intended to be selective. Under each topic, the arrangement of titles is chronological. Thompson included editions, books, and articles that he considered to be most significant. His volume was frankly exploratory.

David H. Stevens followed Thompson, with his *Reference Guide to Milton from 1800 to the Present Day* (1930, repr. 1967). Stevens's work contains items published through 1928. He obviously was influenced by Thompson, for his entries are arranged chronologically. Stevens's first section is devoted to bibliographical and reference works. Then ten sections are devoted to editions of Milton's works. Other sections list translations, biography, general criticism, tributes and ascribed works, editors of Milton, epic, metrics, and Milton's influence.

Stevens's volume contains 302 pages, with 2,850 entries. It is incomplete, as almost every bibliography is, but it includes most of the significant editions of scholarship and some trivial items. It is generally accurate, though the index, which is chiefly an author index, is faulty. Stevens wrote brief annotations for many of the entries and longer ones for a few.

Another useful volume is Harris F. Fletcher's *Contributions to a Milton Bibliography, 1800–1930, Being a List of Addenda to Stevens' Reference Guide* (1931, repr. 1967). This volume contains 138 pages of entries and an index of 28 pages. The arrangement is chronological, not topical, and items are indexed by subject as well as by author. Fletcher had access to the vast holdings in the library of the University of Illinois, and he added considerably to Stevens's first systematic attempt to compile a complete bibliography for Milton. For example, for the year 1900 he listed articles describing the 1638 *Lyc,* discussing Milton's "simple, sensuous, and passionate" definition of poetry, depicting Milton's Satan and his conception of evil, and so on. He listed an unnoticed edition of Macaulay's *Essay on Milton* and another edition of *PL.* Although many of Fletcher's entries are minutiae, his volume is of value to the graduate student as well as to the Milton specialist.

Calvin Huckabay's *John Milton: A Bibliographical Supplement, 1929–1957* (1960, repr. 1967) was intended as a supplement to Stevens's and Fletcher's bibliographies. He enlarged and updated this work, which was subsequently published as *John Milton: An Annotated Bibliography, 1929–1968* (1969). The latter volume contains 392 pages, with 3,932 entries. Huckabay was influenced by Stevens in his method of classification of items. Editions and translations are listed chronologically, but other entries are listed alphabetically. Some items are cross-listed. The index is mostly an author-editor index, and probably the chief fault of the volume is the lack of a subject index, which, it is hoped, will become a separate undertaking. Annotations often consist of direct quotations from the works themselves. Much of the compilation of

the revised bibliography was done at the Bodleian Library and the British Museum. It attempts to bring together all significant scholarship on Milton, both American and foreign. Because the book went to the press in October of 1968, listings for that year are incomplete.

One of the most useful bibliographical tools available is the second volume of W. R. Parker's *Milton* (1968). In his commentary, notes, index, and finding list, Parker notes and often comments on much of the scholarship of the past. He deals with almost every facet of Milton criticism. For example, he lists (p. 680) three items on the perverse theory that Milton was an albino and then cites from Stevens specific pages that list other articles on the subject. He cites essays on Milton's cottage at Chalfont St. Giles (p. 1106). He lists a score of recent books on *PL* (pp. 113–14) and library holdings of first and subsequent editions of Milton's works. The volume is a virtual mine of information concerning Milton scholarship. Of special interest is the suggestion here and there of subjects that need further research and exploration.

Many selective bibliographies are useful to the student of Milton. Among others are several published by Merritt Y. Hughes in his various editions of Milton, such as his *Complete Poems and Major Prose* (1957) and his *Paradise Lost* (1962). Also, the bibliographies in John T. Shawcross's edition of *The Complete Poetry* (1963, rev. 1971) and J. Max Patrick's edition of *Prose* (1967) are helpful. James H. Hanford's Goldentree bibliography of Milton (1966) is extremely useful for undergraduate and graduate students, as is the bibliography in the latest edition of his *A Milton Handbook* (1970), which he revised with James G. Taaffe. One of the best annotated reading lists for *PL* and *PR* appears in C. A. Patrides's edition of *Milton's Epic Poetry: Essays on* Paradise Lost *and* Paradise Regained (1967). The section on Milton in the *Cambridge Bibliography of English Literature* (1941) was compiled by D. H. Stevens; its supplement (1957) is by W. Arthur Turner,

Alberta T. Turner, and W. Edson Richmond. It has been revised by C. A. Patrides (1973).

Many specialized bibliographies on Milton have been published. These include W. R. Parker's "Contributions to a Milton Bibliography" (*The Library*, 4th ser. 16 : 425–38), which deals with Milton and his early printers, and F. F. Madan's bibliographical studies of Salmasius's* *Defensio Regia* and Milton's *Pro Populo* (*The Library*, NS 4 : 119–45; and 5th ser. 9 : 101–21). These, however, are listed in the larger bibliographies.

In the area of Milton bibliography the greatest need at present is for a volume that deals with material published prior to 1800. Shawcross is currently compiling a *Milton Bibliography: 1624–1800*. In the meantime, his editions of *Milton: The Critical Heritage* (1970, 1972) contain much helpful information, such as personal statements and contemporary evaluations (1628–1674) and eighteenth-century comment (1700–1731 and 1732–1809). Bibliographical data accompany each entry in these volumes.

Two journals are of special interest in connection with current scholarship on Milton. These are *Seventeenth-Century News*, edited by J. Max Patrick and Harrison T. Meserole, and the *Milton Quarterly*, edited by Roy C. Flannagan. Both contain articles, reviews, and abstracts of recent studies on Milton. Of value also is the list of works in progress, which is printed in the annual dinner booklet of the Milton Society of America*. Finally, the PMLA Annual Bibliography attempts a complete listing of scholarship, including Milton, in the seventeenth-century English literature section. [CH]

BIGOT, EMERIC (1626–1689), French scholar who visited Milton. Early in 1657 he wrote to Milton asking his help in checking some passages in his study of parliamentary procedures. Milton answered (*Epistol* 21) on March 24 and supplied Bigot with needed references; Milton also accepted Bigot's offer to obtain books for him and requested several published in Paris. [WM]

BIOGRAPHERS, MILTON'S. Early biographers of Milton's life depend on autobiographical* accounts, primarily that in *2Def,* and on personal knowledge of Milton, his close relatives, or associates. The notes collected by John Aubrey* for Anthony Wood* are dated ca. 1681 and were derived from interviews. Despite the inexactness of some of his informants' memories, Aubrey's notes supply many details concerning the private man as well as remarks about the works, Milton's writing habits, and the more usual biographical materials. The so-called Anonymous Life, now credited to Milton's pupil, amanuensis, and friend Cyriack Skinner*, is the source for some unique statements. It is dated around 1687. Skinner's knowledge is, of course, most detailed and reliable for those periods when he was in close association with Milton—the early and middle 1640s, the mid-1650s, and the earlier 1660s. The life of Milton appearing in Wood's *Athenae Oxonienses* ("Fasti") in 1691–92 is based on Aubrey's notes and certain letters from Aubrey. Wood often extrapolates information with invalid inferences or emphases; he offers no new, reliable information. Setting a pattern for other biographers and particularly for biographical dictionaries, Edward Phillips is the major source of our knowledge of his uncle's life—for example, residences, the nature of Milton's tutoring, certain family matters. Unfortunately Phillips is sometimes unreliable (particularly with dates and chronology) and his employment of the autobiographical section of *2Def* created misreadings that have tended to assume factual status. His "Life of Mr. Milton" appeared in 1694 as an introduction to his translation of the *Letters of State;* a catalogue of Milton's works is appended. The first separately printed biography was John Toland's*, first written for *A Complete Collection of the Historical, Political, and Miscellaneous Works* (1698) and reprinted by itself the next year. Toland pulls together previous scholarship, relying heavily on Phillips and expanding (not always accurately) on him. Toland had read the prose (including two previously inedited works) and presented analyses or interpretations of them in their historical contexts. The arguments aroused by the life were concerned with Toland's religious precepts, which he set forth within his discussions of Milton's ideas. Likewise he draws information and inferences from Milton's familiar letters. While Toland's sources seem not to be first-hand, his review of existing information, some of which had not previously been used and some of which was ancillary, is important in developing a full biography.

Eighteenth-century biography depends on the aforementioned lives by Wood, Phillips, and Toland. For a new edition of *PL* in 1725 Elijah Fenton* wrote a life that contains analyses of some of the poems and tries to align them chronologically with the biography. His inferences are not always correct. The life prefacing *Explanatory Notes on Paradise Lost* (1734) by Jonathan Richardson* reports stories about Milton heard contemporaneously by the author or told to him by those who purportedly knew Milton. The biographical comments introducing Thomas Birch's* edition of the prose in 1738, in addition to using the recently discovered *TM*, have the advantage of being able to cite interviews with Milton's daughter Deborah Clarke and his granddaughter Elizabeth Foster by Joseph Addison*, John Ward*, or Birch himself. (Some notes made by Ward exist in manuscript.) Further interviews with Mrs. Foster supply some information for Thomas Newton's* famous "Life" in the 1749 variorum edition of *PL*. During the first half of the century various documents were also discovered and digested into Newton's work. Fenton's briefer life (one often abbreviated even further) and Newton's much longer one examine the works, particularly the more popular poetry, and thus supply literary criticism that became influential in creating attitudes toward Milton. Both lives were repeatedly repub-

lished (or abbreviated) in editions of the poetry throughout the century in England, the Colonies, and on the Continent. The first biography written outside England, other than such dictionary notices as Pierre Bayle's (1690ff.) and Johann Christian Gottsched's* (1760), was Louis Racine's* in 1754, a major contribution in Milton's developing reputation.

The last quarter of the eighteenth century saw a most important biography emerge—that by Samuel Johnson* in 1779. Produced as part of the series called "Lives of the Poets" to accompany new editions of the British poets, Johnson's "Life of Milton" is both biography and literary critical survey of the poems. Evaluations of the poetry often depend upon Johnson's view of Milton the man —that is, the alleged regicide and liberal thinker—and of certain genres (like the sonnet*) or modes (like the pastoral*). But though all these are negative, Johnson is also positive in his view of the companion poems, *Mask*, and *PL*. Johnson supplies no new biographical information; yet his connection with the benefit for the impoverished Mrs. Foster in 1750 and the controversy over the allegations of William Lauder* in 1749–1751, among other matters, yield significant remarks.

To offset the effect of Johnson, William Hayley* produced a life of Milton (1794) that is highly commendatory and that was most significant in fashioning the Romantic attitude toward Milton. Its reconsideration of *PL* and the usually neglected *PR* was to be a factor in the emergence of the renewal of interest in epic, particularly the brief epic. At the end of the century also researches by Thomas Warton* and Henry John Todd* turned up new documents (e.g., the records concerning the nuncupative will*, the Bridgewater MS, letters), an often-successful kind of investigation that continues today. Contributing such research have been Joseph Hunter (1850), W. D. Hamilton (1859), Hyde Clark (1859), Joseph L. Chester (1868), James Holly Hanford (1921, 1925), David H. Stevens (1927), B. A. Wright (1931), and J. Milton

French (1939). A number of nineteenth- and twentieth-century biographies supplied accounts for an expanding reading public; for example, Todd's (1801), Charles Symmons's (1806, 1810), John Mitford's (1832, 1851), Joseph Ivimey's (1853), Thomas Keightley's (1855), Mark Pattison's (1879, etc.), Richard Garnett's (1890), William P. Trent's (1899), Sir Walter Raleigh's (1900), Rose Macauley's (1934), Hilaire Belloc's (1935), Paul Phelps Morand's (1939), F. E. Hutchinson's (1946), Hanford's (1949), Emile Saillens's (1959, trans. 1964), and Douglas Bush's (1964). Special kinds of biographies or approaches or periods are Denis Saurat's *Milton Man and Thinker* (1925, 1944), E. M. W. Tillyard's *Milton* (1930, 1949), Dora Neill Raymond's *Oliver's Secretary* (1932), Don M. Wolfe's *Milton in the Puritan Revolution* (1941), Arthur Barker's *Milton and the Puritan Dilemma* (1942, 1956), Donald L. Clark's *John Milton at St. Paul's School* (1948), J. Milton French's *The Life Records of John Milton* (1949–1958; five vols.), and Harris F. Fletcher's *The Intellectual Development of John Milton* (1956–   ; two vols. to date). Three important subsidiary biographies should also be mentioned : Ernest Brennecke's *John Milton the Elder and His Music* (1938), Willa McClung Evans's *Henry Lawes* (1941), and Donald C. Dorian's *The English Diodatis* (1950). But the three towering biographies are those by David Masson* (1859–80; six vols. plus an index in 1894; vol. 1, revised 1881; vol. 2, revised 1894), Alfred Stern* (1877–79; two vols.), and William Riley Parker* (1968; two vols.).

Masson's *Life* covers not only Milton's biography but the history of Milton's age. It compiles all information known around the end of the nineteenth century, places Milton into his literary and political contexts, and offers evaluations of all the works. At times, however, it engages in speculation and cites conjectures as if they were facts. But the biography is indispensable despite more recent findings and competitors; no other single work on Milton is the source of so much information

related to him and his writings. Stern's biography, often overlooked because it has not been translated from the German, reexamines the author's work and adds important material from Stern's researches into the German relations with Cromwell's England and German reactions to Milton the controversialist and the poet. Parker's biography purposely eschews contextual and literary considerations, concentrating instead on directly important biographical material. An extensive index makes readily available information about scholarship, allusions, bibliographic matters, and the like, in addition to references to biographical subjects both large and small.

Throughout the second volume of his biography Parker indicates the remaining gaps in knowledge about Milton's life, works, relatives, and associates*. Research may fill in such gaps, but the investigation will have to lead through genealogical, political, manuscript, municipal, and other public records not only in England and not only for the immediate Milton family. For the state of Milton biography is such today that it can confidently be said that more detail is known about him than any other comparable author of his era. [JTS]

BIOGRAPHY, MILTON'S. Milton was born on Friday, December 9, 1608, in his father's home on Bread Street, London, at 6 :30 in the morning, and was baptized at All Hallows, Bread Street, on December 12. His father, John Milton, was a scrivener, whose family came from Stanton St. John, Oxon. The Miltons were Roman Catholics, but John, Sr., in the early 1580s, espoused Protestantism, and the poet was thus brought up in a Calvinistic* household. His mother, Sara Jeffrey, of St. Swithin's parish, London, came from a family apparently related to Bradshaws, Castons, and Haughtons, names formerly assigned to her. John, Sr., came to London around 1583, and married Sara some time between 1590 and 1600. One older sister and one younger brother survived infancy; *see* Anne (Milton) Phillips (Agar) and Sir Christopher Milton. Because of his father's various business ventures, in some of which Milton himself became involved, Milton did not have to pursue gainful employment during his life, although he did receive a salary as a secretary to the Council of State*.

Through the year 1632 Milton was being educated ostensibly to become a minister. In his early years he was tutored privately, but the name of only one teacher is known, Thomas Young*. Young, a minister originally from Scotland, may have served as tutor* around 1618–1620. He was an important influence on Milton in religious matters and may have been the major link in Milton's entry into pamphleteering during the episcopal controversy. During this period of study at home, Milton seems to have read a great deal, and late-night study may have contributed to the weakening of his eyes. Around 1620 Milton began attending Alexander Gill's St. Paul's School*, located only a few blocks from his home. Perhaps the decision to attend a formal school was prompted as much by Young's removal to Hamburg because of difficulties with the Church authorities as it was by Milton's level of learning. Milton remained at St. Paul's until early 1625. Here his friends included Charles Diodati* and Alexander Gill, Jr.*, one of the instructors, though not Milton's.

Next Milton attended Christ's College*, Cambridge, where he was admitted on February 12, 1625, and from which he matriculated on April 9. Why he chose Christ's College over others is not known, but its reputation was high and its faculty well known. Milton received the Bachelor of Arts degree on March 26, 1629, and the Master of Arts degree on July 3, 1632. He was constantly in Cambridge from 1625 through 1632, except for vacations spent, apparently, at his family's home or homes, and except for two other periods. During these years the family still lived on Bread Street, until 1631 when they moved to Hammersmith*, then a suburb to the west of Westminster. It is possible that Milton sojourned at some country place during a vacation or two, with or without his family, but there is no evidence. It may

be that *L'Al* and *IlP* reflect a country vacation, and the Seventh Prolusion alludes to such a vacation, but this may be a reference to being in Hammersmith in the summer of 1631. The two further periods when Milton was not in Cambridge were the Lent Term of 1626 (until April 19) and the period when the university was closed due to the plague, from April 17, 1630, to around January 1631. In the first instance Milton was rusticated* because of a disagreement with his tutor William Chappell*. Upon his return he was placed under Nathaniel Tovey*, who remained his tutor through his remaining years at Christ's. This arrangement proved successful and Milton, upon graduation as Bachelor of Arts, was fourth on the University honors list and first from his College.

During his years at Christ's Milton produced various academic exercises, seven of which survive, and various poems, some of which are "academic" (i.e., the result of some occurrence in the college community such as the death of an official). Whether Milton rejected a clerical career for himself while still at Christ's (specifically around the end of 1629, when he was beginning his graduate studies and when he produced *El6* and *Nat,* or later) is debated. At least his continued study through 1632 aimed at a clerical career and the period thereafter until around the summer of 1637 seems to make no firm commitment one way or another. It has been argued that disillusionment with the ministry had grown during these years after graduation, but that a decision against a clerical career had not really been made (or admitted) until around the summer of 1637. Any decision in favor of a poetical career (rather than simply a continuance of poetic writing) is dependent upon the foregoing, and thus has been dated around 1629, around 1632, or around summer 1637.

Despite the honors as an undergraduate and a successful graduate career, Milton did not receive a fellowship in 1632. Perhaps he did not seek one, and perhaps his removal to his father's house from 1632 through 1638 was necessitated by the age and increasing infirmity of his parents rather than reaction to a lack of academic preferment. The reasons for Milton's actions from 1632 through 1638 have been debated by scholars through the years, with arguments ranging from disappointment at not receiving a fellowship to rejection of a clerical career, from familial duties to pursuit of a poetical career. Normally a graduate of Milton's social status would have proceeded to further study at a college (often the same one), sometimes leading to a divinity degree, or at one of the Inns of Court, sometimes leading to a law degree, or to a sojourn abroad, roughly for about a year. Milton's actions in 1632 to 1638 encompass all these courses in a way, since he retired to his father's home for study, considered removal to one of the Inns of Court in November 1637, and traveled on the Continent from around April 1638 through August 1639.

From July 1632 through around the middle of 1635 Milton lived with his parents at their home in Hammersmith. At this time he wrote *Sonn* 7, *Arc,* and *Mask,* and perhaps other poems. The last two works indicate Milton's acquaintance with the Bridgewater (or Egerton*) family, probably through their music teacher, Henry Lawes*, who wrote the music for both works and took part in them. In 1635 the Miltons moved to Horton*, Bucks, and here Milton resided until he left for the Continent. He worked through his studies chronologically and geographically so that by November 1637 he had reached the thirteenth century and had begun an investigation of independent Italian city-states. The Horton period, which was once thought to date from 1632 through 1638, saw the death of Milton's mother on April 3, 1637, a culmination in the soul-searching *Lyc* in November 1637, and finally a move to independency by traveling to the Continent. What other poems were written during the Hammersmith–Horton studious

retirement and their exact order are debated. *TM,* Milton's poetic workbook, was begun during the period (although a suggestion that it may have been begun before Milton's graduation is still sometimes heard), but specifically when is uncertain. Usually proposed has been 1632 or 1633, on the basis of the dating of *Arc,* which begins the notebook, and on the omission of *L'Al* and *IlP,* generally accepted as 1631. The dating of a letter to an unknown friend*, which includes a copy of *Sonn* 7, is likewise pertinent. The recent redating of *Arc* in May 1634 nullifies some of the arguments for an early date. On the other hand, one suggestion dates the manuscript from around autumn 1637 and accordingly raises questions concerning the dates of the letter and such poems as the three English odes*. Milton's rejection of a clerical life and acceptance of a poetical career is significant for which dating is preferred. A question that all of this raises is, Does *TM* reflect work contemporary with the original composition of the poems it records or does it reflect later recording for revision and for a single repository of poems of a given period? (Of the poems entered earliest, only *SolMus* is not a transcription from some earlier copy.)

During this studious retirement* (1632–1638) Milton also began his extant *CB,* which records ideas and points of view from his reading and which seems to aim at preservation of such ideas for future use in his own writing. The date at which Milton began to keep this miscellany is likewise uncertain: the usual date has been around 1635 with suggestions before that time and even during his university days and after that time in autumn 1637 on the basis of career decision. A few entries have been dated on the basis of position on the page and handwriting as 1635–1637? and many others as 1637?–1638? or, of course, later, even after Milton became totally blind. The date of *AdP* has likewise been placed anywhere from 1631 through March 1638 on the basis of the answers to the preceding question about Milton's biography. By March

1638 Milton's publications were only *Shak* in the Shakespeare* Second Folio (1632) and *Mask* in 1637 or early 1638, with *Lyc* following sometime in 1638 (and whatever was meant in a letter to Alexander Gill, Jr., concerning "printed" ghost-written material).

Sometime by the beginning of April Milton had decided to travel to the Continent and spoke of his trip with Sir Henry Wotton*. The Italian journey*, as it is called, concentrated on stays in Florence, Rome, Naples, and Venice, although other Italian areas were visited as were France (particularly Paris) and Switzerland (particularly Geneva). (*See also* ARTS OF DESIGN.) The period was to be one of the most important in Milton's biography because of the encouragement it yielded for a poetic career, because of the friends met and discussions held, and because of his immediate contact with the culture of Italy. Several Latin poems were also composed during this trip. Milton seems to have returned to England in August 1639. During his travels his good friend Charles Diodati had died and perhaps his sister Anne (Phillips) Agar. Instead of returning to his father's home, where his brother Christopher and his family had been residing from around the end of 1637, he took lodgings in London, where he began schoolteaching with his sister Anne's sons, Edward and John Phillips, as his first pupils. (*See* RESIDENCES, MILTON'S, for the various moves made as his own family group and employment altered.) John Phillips came to live with him in 1639 and Edward sometime later. Edward, the older, remained until around 1647 and visited periodically thereafter, remaining relatively close to his uncle. John remained until his majority in 1652, but thereafter appears to have had little contact with his uncle. Both served as amanuenses* to Milton. Other pupils were added as day students through around 1647, although there were brief periods of tutoring of a few boys after that date as well. (*See* STUDENTS, MILTON'S.) The nature of Milton's "private academy" can be inferred from *Educ* and Edward Phillips's *Life* of his uncle.

In 1642, perhaps in May, Milton married Mary Powell of Forest Hill, Oxon; much uncertainty surrounds the date and circumstances of the marriage (for which *see* MARY POWELL), but at least it is evident that she was much younger than he (sixteen and thirty-three respectively) and that she was expected to serve as a kind of step-mother to the Phillips boys, aged twelve and eleven. Within a few months, Mary had returned to her parents' home and was not to return until the middle of 1645, the Civil War perhaps contributing to the delay. In the meantime Milton's father had moved in with him in April 1643 and his eyesight began to fail noticeably around autumn 1644. Mary and John's first child, Anne, who was retarded (?) or spastic (?), was born on July 29, 1646, and their second child, Mary, on October 25, 1648. Milton's in-laws moved in with him in 1645 and stayed through autumn 1647, and his father died probably on March 13, 1647. Domestically, therefore, Milton's life in the 1640s involved a series of changes and adjustments, difficulties and resolutions, and a not entirely stable household.

From autumn 1639 through the end of 1648 Milton continued his personal studies, making the majority of entries in *CB*, for example, and engaging in various prose and poetic writings. His private studies, though interrupted by public controversy, seem to have aimed at the production of a significant tragedy on one of several themes, the most detailed treatment and greatest amount of work being given to what became *PL*. (*See* DRAMATIC PLANS.) Some minor poems were composed in these years, including his tribute to Diodati, *EpDam* (1639), *Sonn* 8–15, and *Rous*. The first edition of the minor poems in 1645 may owe something to Milton's annoyance with public reaction to his prose tracts and may represent a different kind of activity in poetry rather than prose, which was more firmly resumed from 1645 through 1648. The contention that the two major poems published in 1671 may have been begun during this period is accepted by some scholars but rejected by most.

Into Milton's private life, studies, and poetic writings were thrust two groups of controversial tracts as well as his two most popular prose pieces. The first group —those five tracts dealing with the question of an episcopal system within the English Church, as fostered by Archbishop William Laud* and championed by Bishop Joseph Hall*—emerged in early 1641 and continued to engage Milton through April 1642. Possibly Milton was brought into the pamphlet war by Thomas Young and possibly his debut was "A Postscript" added to Smectymnuus's* *An Answer to a Booke entituled, An Humble Remonstrance* (March 1641). It is conjectured also that the friend to whom Milton's first acknowledged effort in the controversy, *Ref* (May 1641), was addressed was Young. *PrelE* (June–July?) and *Animad* (July) followed swiftly, and then *RCG* (January ? 1642) and *Apol* (April 1642). Milton's arguments for the abolition of episcopacy, and in effect the establishment of presbytery*, are historical, logical, and confutational of episcopacy's adherents. He is both vituperative against his opponents and somewhat confessional of his own life and hopes. The second group of controversial tracts, four (in a sense, five) dealing with advocacy of divorce*, appeared from August 1643 through March 1645. Like the antiprelatical tracts, these argue their thesis through historical awareness as well as biblical interpretation, through logic*, confutation, and in one case, vituperation. The divorce tracts are *DDD* (the second edition of 1644 so greatly expanding the first as to constitute a second tract), *Bucer, Tetra,* and *Colas.* Neither group of writings seems to have had more than ephemeral impact and reaction, and the latter group placed a notorious reputation upon Milton as a "divorcer" or "fornicator." The two prose works of this period lying outside either group are *Educ* (June 1644) and

Areop (November 1644). Neither seems to have created much stir in its own time, but both became significant by the end of the century, a significance that continues to the present day despite educational reforms and permissive attitudes toward censorship. Though published later, a few other prose works were written or begun during the 1640s: see *Accedence Commenc't Grammar* (1669), *Brit* (1670), *Logic* (1672), *CharLP* (1681), *Mosc* (1682), and perhaps *CD* (1825).

In January 1649, during the trial of Charles I*, Milton wrote his first anti-monarchical tract, one of his most philosophically important, *Tenure.* It aided in bringing him to the attention of the new government then being formed, and on March 15, 1649, he became Secretary for Foreign Tongues to the Council of State*. He continued in a secretarial position until at least October 22, 1659, when a salary payment is recorded. Six months later the Restoration was to take place and Milton found himself in a precarious situation because of his work for the Cromwellian government. In 1650 he had lost much of the sight in his left eye and was totally blind* by February 1652. His illness and reduced proficiency brought him assistance in his office and during the later years of his tenure he was really a "Latin Secretary," the popular though not entirely accurate title by which many referred to him throughout his years of service. As Latin Secretary he was reduced to the rather perfunctory duty of translation of documents into or out of Latin, without leeway for originality and without other responsibilities or commissions he had enjoyed in the earlier years of the republic. Among such commissions were the charge to make clear the late king's and the Earl of Ormond's* duplicity in the *Articles of Peace* (see *Observations,* May 1649) and to refute the popular sentiment for the late king as martyr, raised by *Eikon Basilike*. Eikon* (October ? 1649) became one of the two works detrimental to Milton's reputation in later years as a regicide and revolutionary.

Another commission was to answer Salmasius's* *Defensio regia pro Carolo I* (which appeared in England in November ? 1649), and of all Milton's works, prose or poetic, it was *1Def* (February 1651), which was best known in his day, most reprinted and read, and most notorious. *Eikon* and *1Def* were publicly banned and burned in France and, after the Restoration, in England, and they called forth the most numerous counter-arguments of all the tracts. *1Def* was additionally the subject of three German dissertations within a few years' time. The controversy that developed out of Milton's work brought forth *Responsio Ad Apologiam Anonymi* (1651) from his nephew John Phillips, with his assistance in answer to John Rowland's *Pro Rege et Populo Anglicano Apologia*; Milton's *2Def* (May 1654) against Pierre du Moulin's* *Regii Sanguinis Clamor ad Coelum;* and his *3Def* (August 1655), which opposed Alexander More's* statements in *Fides Publica* and *Supplementum*. All of these works, in Latin to reach a continental audience, defend the Commonwealth or attempt to refute monarchic stands, and, like other of Milton's tracts, they often become vituperative and biographically personal.

Concluding Milton's attention to public controversy and life are a series of arguments against the Restoration or attempting to alter the monarchic settlement that was inevitably upon England in 1659–60. See *CivP* (*February* 1659), *Hire* (August), *A Letter to a Friend, Concerning the Ruptures of the Commonwealth* (October 20; published in 1698), "Proposalls of certaine expedients for the preventing of a civill war now feard, & the settling of a firme government" (autumn; published 1938), *Way* (March 1660 and April 1660), *PresM* (March ?; published 1698), and *BN* (April). In spite of some full rebuttals, these tracts had no effect in deflecting the Restoration or influencing its form and settlement. The confusion of 1660 with its change of governments, punishment of parliamentarian leaders, and acts to propagandize the people saw Milton at first sought for

punishment and in hiding, passed over by the Act of Oblivion (August 29), finally apprehended, perhaps on out-of-date orders, and imprisoned from around October through December 15. Milton's release would seem to have been effected by various friends, including Sir William Davenant* and Andrew Marvell*, upon payment of a fine. There is little to wonder at Milton's retirement from public life from 1661 until his death.

During the 1650s Milton's personal life was beset by illness and death, and his personal studies and writing had but spasmodic attention. Milton's eyesight continued to fail during 1649–February 1652, when he became totally blind. Accompanying the troubles with his eyes was frequent general illness. His only son, John, was born on March 16, 1651, but was dead by June 16, 1652. His wife Mary gave birth to their fourth child, Deborah, on May 5, and died a few days later. On November 12, 1656, he married as his second wife Katherine Woodcock. She gave birth to a daughter Katherine on October 19, 1657, but both were soon dead—Milton's wife on February 3, 1658, his daughter on March 17, 1658. Understandably, the period of 1652–53 saw Milton recuperating from his losses and his ill health, and during this time, perhaps somewhat also through 1654 and 1655, he may have returned to personal studies and writing, though not exclusively. If so, there is no certainty as to what he was working on; suggestions have included a second edition of the minor poems, *PL, SA, PR,* and *CD*. From 1655 through 1658 he more certainly was working on such projects, and *PL* and *CD* must have received most attention, if not all. The remaining minor poems were composed between 1652 and 1658 (?)—*Sonn* 16–23 and *Ps* 1–8.

The last fourteen years of Milton's life were undoubtedly devoted to his writing, whether completion or revision of previously started works, or new composition, or publication (some of which publication has already been noted). *PL* was completed by 1665 (published 1667) and revised around 1674, when the second edition appeared. *PR* and *SA* were composed, or completed, or revised for publication in 1671 (various theories have been proposed for the dates of composition). *Brit* was completed or readied for publication in 1670. *TR* (May ? 1673) became Milton's last original work published in his lifetime, for *A Declaration, or Letters Patents* (July ? 1674) is a translation. Moves were made to publish a second edition of the minor poems and *Educ* in November ? 1673; the State Papers, which did not appear, however, until 1676 in Amsterdam; and *Epistol,* which were published in May 1674 with seven college prolusions. Publication of *CD*, composed apparently around 1655–1660 and showing some revision thereafter, may have been contemplated, although it was not printed until 1825.

While Milton had employed scribes as early as 1637 and his nephews may have served in that capacity from 1642 onward, it was during his governmental employment and after his reduced eyesight that Milton worked through various amanuenses*. Sometimes scribes were specially hired, sometimes they were friends. His scribes or servants, and his daughters Mary and Deborah, read to him; his daughters may also have written down notes and the like for him, but they did not handle full-scale scribal jobs. He taught a bit, for example, Thomas Ellwood*, and such students might do a scribal chore now and then. He seems to have established a routine of work, Bible reading, general reading, and dictation in his later years. At times in the 1650s and less often in the 1660s and 70s he was visitd by foreign dignitaries or by such well-known people as Marvell and John Dryden*, and by close friends like Dr. Nathan Paget*. The one interruption from these years in London came during the visitation of the plague and subsequent fire in 1665–1666. Milton and his family escaped London from around June 1665 to around February 1666 through the help of Ellwood, who found a small house for him at Chalfont St. Giles,

Bucks, the only Milton "residence" still standing.

Milton's household in 1661 consisted of his three daughters and whatever servants* he was able to afford, but at least a housekeeper-governess was required. On February 24, 1663, he married Elizabeth Minshull, whom he met through her kinsman Dr. Paget. Stories of the relationship between the step-daughters and step-mother conflict, and the daughters' attitudes toward their father are variously reported. It would seem, however, that the girls were not happy under their much-older father's strictness and demands, and they may simply have wished to assert themselves as individuals and as independent. Such attitudes, plus the not-uncommon frictions between step-relatives, may have caused upsets in the household during the 1660s. All three daughters seem to have left on their own before 1669 and not to have visited thereafter (at least not often). Most of the reports of family difficulties are given in the depositions concerned with Milton's nuncupative will*. Deborah, though, in interviews during the eighteenth century, seems to have spoken well of her father; and her daughter, Elizabeth Foster, gives no indication of serious friction between father and daughter. We have no real evidence of other relatives' attitudes toward Milton or their frequency of visits, relatives like Thomas Agar*, his brother-in-law, or Richard Powell*, another brother-in-law, or his brother Christopher's children. Christopher did visit at times, and despite their political differences, they seem to have been on good terms.

In his last years Milton had recurrent attacks of gout*, and in 1674, when his brother Christopher was visiting him, he expressed his wishes for the disposal of his possessions in case of his death. This so-called nuncupative will was examined in the Prerogative Court of Canterbury a month after Milton's death, but it was not probated. A settlement was reached leaving £100 to each of the daughters (plus some items of furniture and the like to

Deborah) and the remainder of the estate to Elizabeth.

Milton died on Sunday, November 8, 1674, of the gout, and was buried on Thursday, November 12 in St. Giles, Cripplegate. Death was probably caused by heart failure due to illness, such as the gout, rather than by gout directly. The death date is an inference from 1) the record of burial and 2) the statement of his servant Elizabeth Fisher*, made on December 15, that he had died on a Sunday about a month before. He apparently expired in his sleep sometime between retiring on Sunday and being found dead the next morning. (*See also* DISINTERMENT, MILTON'S.) [JTS]

BION, born in Smyrna, wrote in the second half of the second century B.C. Of his poetry only some fragments, an epithalamion for Achilles sung by "Lycidas" (possibly by a follower rather than by Bion himself), and the *Lament for Adonis* survive. The *Lament for Bion* (see MOSCHUS) honors Bion as a pastoral* poet, a "neatherd" who sang for the nymph Galatea and drank the water of the Sicilian river Arethusa. Although Bion's *Lament for Adonis* is not itself pastoral, the poem influenced the development of the pastoral elegy. It offers a lush account of the death of Adonis and the extravagant grief of Aphrodite. Hanford* suggests that the poem was too decadent for Milton's taste. *Lyc* and *EpDam* show no signs of having been influenced by it. [JRK]

BIRCH, THOMAS (1705–1766), historian and biographer*. Birch was ordained a deacon of the Church of England on January 17, 1730, and a priest on December 21, 1731. A supporter of Whig* doctrine in the church, he was granted the degree of Doctor of Divinity in 1753, despite his lack of a university education. He was elected a Fellow of the Royal Society and a Fellow of the Society of Antiquaries in 1735; he was secretary to the Royal Society from 1752 to 1765.

Birch wrote the first scholarly account of Milton's life, which appeared in his edition of the prose works : *A Complete Collection of the Historical, Political, and Miscellaneous Works of John Milton* (1738). He began the biography around August 25, 1737, and delivered part of it to the printer on January 13, 1738. The printer's work was complete by February 25, and the two volumes were advertised as published on March 24. In the midst of the printing, on February 11, Birch interviewed Elizabeth Foster*, Milton's granddaughter, who had seen John Ward* the day before. As the biography was being set Birch also added material that the unreliable Ward had gathered from his talk with Mrs. Foster and, earlier, his interview with her mother, Deborah Clarke. (Birch's *Account of the Life of John Ward LL.D., Professor of Rhetoric in Gresham College* appeared posthumously in 1766.) Included in Birch's life of Milton are remarks on the then newly discovered *TM*, with some corrections of the printed texts of the poems recorded there. Later Birch saw Mrs. Foster again on January 6 and November 13, 1750; the further information gathered was employed in the second edition of the prose works in 1753. This edition was supervised by Richard Baron* and altered a number of earlier statements; for example, Milton's alleged forgery of Sidney's prayer from *Arcadia* into *Eikon Basilike** was now rejected. Pertinent notes by Birch on Milton also appear in British Museum Additional MSS 4244, ff. 52–53; 4472, f. 3; 4478c, f. 248b; and 35,397, f. 321b. Birch aided in the benefit for Mrs. Foster and officiated at her funeral on May 14, 1754.

Birch's edition of the prose includes John Phillips's *Responsio, Scriptum dom. Protectoris,* allegedly turned into Latin by Milton, and its English version called *A Manifesto of the Lord Protector,* Edward Phillips's translation of the *Letters of State* as well as *Literae,* and Joseph Washington's translation of *1Def* as well as the original Latin, and it inserted *CharLP* into *Brit.* The second edition, entitled *The Works of John Milton,*

Historical, Political, and Miscellaneous, printed two letters to Milton from Andrew Marvell* and Moses Wall*, which had not previously been known.

An editor of *A General Dictionary, Historical and Critical: In which a New and Accurate Translation of that of the Celebrated Mr. Bayle, with the Corrections and Observations Printed in the Late Edition at Paris, Is Included,* ten vols. (1734–1741), along with John Peter Bernard and John Lockman, Birch was responsible for the additions concerning Milton, which are quite numerous. Citations appear under Adam, Addison*, Andrewes* (vol. 1), Ariosto* (vol. 2), Offspring Blackall, Charles Blount (vol. 3), Chaucer*, Edward Coke*, Cromwell*, Davenant*, Dryden*, Laurence Echard (vol. 4), Tanequi le Fevre (vol. 5), Hobbes* (vol. 6), Marvell*, Milton, Alexander Morus* (vol. 7), Henry Oldenburg*, Samuel Parker*, John Phillips, Matthew Prior, Sir Walter Ralegh* [Rawlegh], Roscommon (vol. 8), Spenser*, Toland* (vol. 9), Thomas Wagstaffe, and "Critical Remarks on the New Edition of Moreri's Historical Dictionary, Published in 1704" (vol. 10). The scholarly and thorough treatment of Milton's relationships with the above people and the frequent quotations from his works amplified or corrected numerous earlier accounts and indicated Milton's influence on such people as Blount, Echard, and Prior. The entry on Milton (7 [1738]: 567–88) includes the first printing of the two drafts of a letter to an unknown friend* and plans and subjects for literary work given in *TM.* The remarks on Louis Moreri's Dictionary (10 [1741]: 513–15) correct errors and counter Moreri's adverse criticism of Milton as person, thinker, and poet. In his edition of *A Collection of the State Papers of John Thurloe, Esq;* seven vols. (1742), various state papers connected with Milton are given, as well as allusions in letters and the like from or to Thurloe*. The original documents are in the Bodleian Library. Of importance to Milton studies, also, are two other works of Birch's, the remarks and characters written to accompany *Heads of Illustrious Persons of Great Britain,* two vols. (1743–1752; rptd., 1756, 1813), which includes George Vertue's engraving from the Onslow portrait*, and *The Court and Times of Charles the First,* two vols. (1849). [JTS]

BLACKALL, OFFSPRING: *see* Toland, John.

BLACKBOROUGH FAMILY: *see* Relatives.

BLACKBURNE, FRANCIS: *see* Criticism.

BLACKMORE, SIR RICHARD: *see* Imitations.

BLAKE, WILLIAM (1757–1827). No English poet felt the burden of the past more acutely than John Milton, and no English poet made a bolder attempt to cast off that burden. For this reason, Blake's admiration for Milton deepened into the kind of veneration he had for no other poet; and for the same reason, Blake was willing—despite his militant iconoclasm—to take "dictation" from his predecessor. "I dare not pretend to be any other than the Secretary," writes Blake; "the Authors are in Eternity." And later he says, "I have the happiness of seeing the Divine countenance in . . . Milton more distinctly than in any prince or hero."

From the beginning to the end of his artistic career, Blake worked with and within the Milton tradition. Not only did he make engravings of Satan after designs by Stothard and Fuseli*; but, beginning in 1788, he made a series of original designs for Milton's poetry (most of them for *PL*) that eventually led him to do his first complete set of designs for a poem by Milton. This set of designs for *Mask,* completed in 1801, was followed by another set for the same poem, two sets for *PL,* two for the *Nat,* and later a set for *L'Al* and *IlP* and one for *PR.* A third set for *PL* was begun for John Linnell in 1822 but never completed. Each time Blake reillustrated a poem by Milton, he brought it into closer alignment with Milton's text, revealing with greater precision the spiritual essence of the poems those designs accompany. At the same time that Blake is commenting on Milton's work through his illustrations*, he is allowing allusions to Milton's poetry to multiply in his own poems and with such calculation that they create their major context.

S. Foster Damon has observed that Blake's *Songs* are his *L'Al* and *IlP, Thel* is his *Mask;* behind Blake's *Visions of the Daughters of Albion* are Milton's divorce tracts, behind *America* are the political pamphlets, behind *The Marriage of Heaven and Hell* is the kind of thinking found in *CD. PL*, finally, provides the context for *The Four Zoas* and *Milton,* while *Brit* offers one for *Jerusalem (The Divine Vision,* ed. V. DeSola Pinto [1957], pp. 92–95). The point is an important one, but it is also too simple in many of its particulars, and in others it is simply mistaken. Blake could not have known *CD* (it was not discovered until 1823 and was published in 1825). More pertinently, *Ref,* in its themes, and *RCG* and *Areop,* in both their themes and structure, resemble *The Marriage,* just as in both these respects *PR* resembles *Milton* and *Jerusalem,* and resembles them so closely that Milton's epic should be regarded as the prototype for Blake's. Believing, as Blake did, that "Imitation is Criticism," he wrote poems that are doubly significant: primarily they are the vehicle for Blake's own imagination; secondarily they are interpretations of their predecessor's vision. As interpretations, Blake's poems combine with his illustrations to provide a sustained symbolic commentary on Milton's canon.

That Blake felt Milton's influence from *Poetical Sketches* to *Jerusalem* has often been observed, but that Blake's opinion of Milton was continually being altered is a point too often ignored. The kind of criticism offered against Milton in *The Marriage* becomes more equivocal as Blake becomes more convinced that not Milton but Milton's commentators offer the greatest obstacle to penetrating the poet's vision.

The assertion that "Milton wrote in fetters when he wrote of Angels & God, and at liberty when he wrote of Devils & Hell . . . because he was a true Poet and of the Devil's party without knowing it" has occasioned considerable misunderstanding. The aside, usually attributed to Blake, is made by the Devil, whose perspective is as partial as that of the angels whom he is assailing. Like Milton, Blake warned against confusing the voice of the persona with the voice of the poet. In an annotation to Swedenborg's *Heaven and Hell,* Blake writes, "Thus fools quote Shakespeare; the above is Theseus' opinion Not Shakespeare's. You might as well quote Satan's blasphemies from Milton & give them as Milton's Opinions."

In *The Marriage,* Blake's Devil distinguishes between Milton's conscious and unconscious meanings at the same time that he calls Milton "a true Poet." Therein lies one of his errors, for from Blake's point of view a true poet, who is also a prophet, knows and understands what he utters; to think otherwise involves "a most Pernicious Falshood." There is, nevertheless, an element of truth in what the Devil says; and even if the Devil himself does not perceive that truth, Blake does. When the Devil identifies Milton with "the Devil's party" he employs a commonplace of political rhetoric. After the Restoration, as Christopher Hill has shown in *Antichrist in Seventeenth-Century England* (1971), it became increasingly dangerous to pursue the course of associating the powers either of state or of religious institutions with the devil; but it was common enough for conservative forces, both during the Restoration and throughout the eighteenth century, to employ this rhetorical weapon in dealing with political radicals and religious dissenters. Indeed, Blake's Devil is not the first eighteenth-century "critic" to apply this label to Milton (see Francis Blackburne's *Memoirs of Thomas Hollis* [1780], pp. 621, 625).

Blake is a supreme ironist engaged, in *The Marriage,* in the same kind of ironic play that Milton engaged in with Satan. When Satan says in *PL* that "The mind is its own place, and in itself / Can make a Heav'n of Hell, a Hell of Heav'n" (1. 254–55), he articulates sentiments with which Milton himself can in a sense agree. The irony lies in the fact that what is true from the human perspective is not true from the demonic one. Similarly, the irony in the remark made by Blake's Devil lies in the fact that Blake, in possession of a larger consciousness and thus aware of subtleties that his devil does not perceive, has him use a term of abuse and apply that term approvingly to Milton. In this sense, the Devil is to Blake what Milton's Beelzebub is to Satan, and what Satan sometimes is to Milton—a witless spokesman who never exhibits the same largeness of perspective as the figure with whom he is identified. When, echoing the vocabulary of Milton's Beelzebub (cf. *PL* 2. 240), the Devil says that Milton was of "the Devil's party," he points to precisely those qualities (sublimity, majesty, and energy) which both Milton and Blake could admire if they were invested in a "moral" character. In *PL* they are not; and thus Satan, whom Blake will later represent as Milton's spectre, his selfhood, must be repudiated. At the same time, Blake's Devil, without knowing it, makes a statement with which Blake can agree. To associate Milton with "the Devil's party" is to acknowledge, from Blake's point of view, precisely that which the Devil seems to deny : that Milton was radical in his politics and revolutionary in his theology, a view that makes a great deal of sense when we return the Devil's quip to the larger context of *The Marriage* and read it in terms of the rhetorical strategy that Blake here employs.

The Marriage is a satire cast in the form of prophecy. It is about the formation of the prophetic character and is structured around the opposition between the true and the false prophet—an opposition exploited by Milton himself in his most abusive political pamphlets. It also takes its argument of contraries, its themes of spiritual perception and apocalypse, and its purpose of transforming an entire civilization into a nation of visionaries from Milton's early prose works. To perceive the Miltonic context that Blake gives to *The Marriage* is the first step toward understanding his rhetorical strategy. For Blake, Milton's vision may have failed him in *PL,* but not so completely and not in quite the sense that the Devil suggests; in any event Milton's vision was recovered when he wrote *PR,* which explains Blake's repeated allusions to Christ's temptation in the wilderness in the later plates of *The Marriage* and also his remark to Henry Crabb Robinson : "Milton . . . in his old age . . . returned back to God whom he had had in his childhood." The pattern of Milton's life provided Blake with a neat contrast to the pattern of Swedenborg's: whereas Swedenborg established a sect, subverting the revolutionary character of his early thought and embracing the Calvinistic* notion of predestination* that Blake so deplored, Milton moved steadily away from institutionalized religion, casting off Calvin's doctrine in *PL* and formulating a radically new version of Christianity in *PR.* When this pattern of opposition is discerned, we see Milton emerging from *The Marriage* not as a target of ridicule but as a type of the true prophet. It is this figure whom Blake celebrates as the "Awakener" in the epic poem for which Milton provides the title.

In 1803, Blake expressed his wish "to speak to future generations by a Sublime Allegory, which is now perfectly completed into a Grand Poem." Presumably the poem to which Blake refers is *Milton* —a poem written "without Premeditation" "on One Grand Theme, Similar to Milton's Paradise Lost." Blake's comments are doubly significant, pointing as they do to the poem of which *Milton* is a direct criticism and pointing, too, to the critical tradition that Blake's own epic materializes. When Blake wrote *The Marriage* his interest centered in the intellectual substance of Milton's poetry. In *Milton* that interest persists; but now, under the patronage of William Hayley, Blake has developed an interest in Milton's art. Yet, whatever Blake's interest and however great his admiration for his predecessor, Milton is not beyond criticism. *Milton* is written as a celebration of Milton, more precisely as a celebration óf that moment when Milton perceives his intellectual error and casts it off. Milton's error is threefold, having affected his art and his vision, and having extended beyond both to affect his personal relationship with his wives and his daughters; it is consolidated in Satan, who is Milton's spectre and who must be cast off before the poet can assume the posture of the redeemed man and before he can take on the task of redeeming Blake's society.

Blake's ambivalence toward Milton is deftly presented in the Preface to his poem. Having taken his epigraph from *PL,* having alluded to Milton's distinction between the Daughters of Memory and the Daughters of Inspiration, and having placed Milton within the line of visionaries who oppose the artifice of the Classics with the sublime art of the Bible, Blake equivocates: Milton was a true poet, *but* Milton was also "curb'd by the general malady & infection from the silly Greek and Latin slaves of the Sword." Blake argues that Milton is circumscribed by the very traditions from which Blake would liberate poetry. However, the lyric that follows mitigates this criticism. That lyric (and this point is seldom noticed) is a song of *the* bard, a song that derives its motifs and themes from Milton's prose works and that culminates in the characteristically Miltonic image of the poet-orator as a mental warrior who will cast the morning beam of reformation.

By 1808 a first version of Blake's *Milton* was probably completed, and by 1810 two copies were made. During this same period, Blake completed two sets of designs for *PL,* and the differences between these sets are of real import. The first set is composed of twelve designs, the second, as it survives, of only nine—the illustrations of Satan calling up his legions

and of Satan, Sin, and Death are missing; so is the illustration of the judgment of Adam and Eve. For all these absent illustrations there are separate designs that could conceivably be part of a complete second set of designs that later was broken up. It may be argued, however, that Blake deliberately omitted the three designs from the second set, in which case he reveals a significantly altered understanding of Milton's vision. Blake's second set of designs appears to be less an effort to correct Milton's vision than an effort to reveal the Christocentric character of Milton's theology. Such a conclusion is consonant with the omission of the Preface in the last two copies of *Milton,* which were made around 1816, and with the new character of the illustrations to *L'Al* and *IlP* and to *PR,* which were also underway about this same time. At the outset, Blake had used his verbal and visual commentaries, like *Thel* and the *Mask* designs, to correct the mistaken vision of his predecessor. With his newly acquired appreciation of both Milton's vision and his artistry, he is now concerned with revealing the Miltonic vision rather than with altering it. Milton's poetry, from Blake's point of view, is clouded in misunderstanding, and Milton is partly at fault—he has allowed the large outlines of religious orthodoxy to obtrude upon his poem, and he has allowed his narrative to obscure his vision. Milton's purpose was to criticize the very theology he postulated; and thus the poet's commentators, who read with their doors of perception closed, are likewise responsible for the cloud of misunderstanding that envelops Milton's poetry.

When Blake omitted the Preface from the last two copies of *Milton* he, in effect, deleted the bold attack on Milton the artist. By shifting the accent from the oppression of Milton by tradition to a celebration of the poet's freedom from it, Blake shows Milton to be a poet who, in the words of Angus Fletcher, "treats literary tradition like an entrepreneur, tinually making 'mergers'" (*The Transcen-*

dental *Masque* [1971], p. 193). In the investing one work with another, conprocess, Blake also shows Milton to be the prototype of the revolutionary artist: Milton radically alters traditional forms in order to display his own genius and in order to achieve a perfect coincidence between those forms and the radically new vision with which those forms are invested; the emblem for the new order that the poet seeks to create is not the individual poem but the one grand poem to which all the individual poems contribute. Nowhere is this more evident than in Milton's epic endeavors.

Like many of his contemporaries, Blake located the truly revolutionary moment in the history of epic poetry within Milton's achievement; but that moment, Blake would argue, occurs in the writing of *PR* rather than of *PL*. Milton's diffuse epic—in an important sense an anti-epic—leaves the classical epic* in ruins, but out of those ruins Milton creates a new kind of epic, intensely dramatic (though the drama is introspective and psychological) and rich in potential. *PR* represents the emergence of a new tradition that Milton's successors may use as freely and as innovatively as Milton used the traditions that he inherited. By purging the epic of its atrophied conventions, by fracturing the customary relationship between the poet and his audience, by creating a new scheme of values rather than codifying those that pertain, by forging an alliance between epic and prophecy, Milton created a tradition in which Blake could comfortably ensconce himself and a tradition of which Blake was the first, and is still the most brilliant, exponent. It has been suggested by Harold Bloom that Milton was "a colossal Covering Cherub, who prevented the Romantics from certain achievements" (*Studies in Romanticism* 9 : 231). The contrary is true. From Milton, Blake and his contemporaries learned not to contain tradition but to circumvent it. Thus Milton, who initially seemed a burden to the poet, became his liberator—the liberator

not of Blake only but of all the poets who are generally subsumed under the rubric of "the Romantics." [JAW]

BLANK VERSE. In *Ref* (1641) Milton "rendered" some lines from Canto 19 of Dante's* *Inferno* in "English blank Verse" thus :

Ah *Constantine,* of how much ill was cause
Not thy Conversion, but those rich demaines
That the first wealthy *Pope* receiv'd of thee.
(3 : 26)

In his 1668 note on "The Verse" of *PL*, however, he identified "the Measure" of the epic as "*English* Heroic Verse without Rime, as that of *Homer* in *Greek,* and of *Virgil* in *Latin* . . ." (2 : 6). The phrase implies that "*English* Heroic Verse" may be written with or without rhyme, and Spenser's* earlier remark to Lodowick Bryskett (quoted in Bryskett's *A Discourse of Civill Life;* see H. S. V. Jones, *A Spenser Handbook* [1947], pp. 31, 127) that he had "undertaken a work . . . in *heroical verse* under the title of a *Faerie Queene*" would seem to confirm this. George Puttenham provides more explicit evidence, saying of Chaucer*, "His meetre Heroicall of *Troilus* and *Cresseid* is very grave and stately, keeping the staffe of seven and the verse of ten" (G. Gregory Smith, ed., *Elizabethan Critical Essays,* 2 vols. [1904], 2 : 64). It is the "verse of ten," the English decasyllable (or "iambic pentameter" line; *see* VERSIFICATION) which is, then, the "Heroic Verse" of Milton and his great predecessors.

The "blank Verse" quoted above (and a few other examples are to be found here and there interpolated in Milton's prose) is also decasyllabic verse, without rhyme, like that of *PL*. We might suppose that the adjective *blank,* used of verse, could mean only "unrhymed," and thus that those portions of the choruses of *SA* which are without rhyme might also be called blank verse, as might the pentameters and trimeters of Milton's "The Fifth Ode of *Horace*. Lib. I. . . . Rendred almost word for word without Rhyme" though regularly arranged in quasi-stanzaic form. In general, however, the term seems from the beginning of its use to have been applied all but exclusively to unrhymed pentameters, divided, if at all, irregularly, into verse paragraphs, not (as they might be) regularly, into something like stanzas.

English blank verse is generally held to have been written first by Henry Howard, Earl of Surrey (1517–1547), on the pattern of the Italian *versi sciolti* (*endecasillabi sciolti*); it is worth remarking that even in its origins, thus, the blank verse line differs metrically from its correspondent line only in the absence of end rhyme—and so, essentially, not at all, end rhyme being a structure the existence of which cannot be detected in the line looked at by itself. Surrey translated Books II and IV of the *Aeneid* into competent but rather stiff unrhymed pentameters. The first original English poem in blank verse is Gascoigne's didactic satire *The Steel Glas* (1576); prosodically its extraordinary feature is that it shows a *metrical* caesura (as distinguished from a simple pause, a sense break) for possibly the first and probably the last time in the history of English accentual-syllabic verse. The caesura falls all but invariably after the fourth syllable of the ten-syllable line, whether or not the sense admits of a pause at that point: "My sistr' and I, into this world were sent" (line 59; see *The Complete Works of George Gascoigne*, ed. John W. Cunliffe, 2 vols. [1907], 2: 144). In "Certayne Notes of Instruction" (1575) Gascoigne suggested that there are "pauses or restes in a verse, whiche may be called *Ceasures*," and which "have bene first devised (as should seeme) by the Musicians . . ."; he voices the opinion that "in a verse of tenne [syllables]" the "Ceasure" "will best be placed at the ende of the first foure sillables . . ." (Smith, 1 : 54). Gascoigne had some knowledge of French and Italian verse, in which there is a caesura—usually identified with a sense break—after the fourth or the sixth syllable of the decasyllable/hendecasyllable. Gascoigne's dramatic blank verse in *Jocasta* (Acts 2, 3 and 5) does not show the invariable "Ceasure" after the fourth syllable; though many or even most of the lines are doubtless susceptible of it, verses such as the following, which could have appeared in *The Steel Glas* only exceptionally, are not uncommon :

Polinices. Out of my kingdome am I driven by force
(2. 1. 556)
Eteocles. As though thy divelishe deedes were hid from him.
(2. 1. 565)

Dramatic blank verse, in the event, was to be developed fully in the next fifty years, a period during which—so great was the ascendency of rhyme in other than dramatic poetry—the writing of nondramatic blank verse was scarcely further attempted. Verse that is seriously intended to relate to speech, in ways however complex and (sometimes) indirect, must, it would seem, show less obvious artifice than other verse, and sixteenth- and seventeenth-century dramatic blank verse does indeed show a relative naturalness of sound patterning, a syntactic simplicity, and a progressive tendency toward metrical variation—especially toward the orchestration of the rhythms of speech fragments as line fragments against a carefully controlled base—that provide us ultimately with examples of the art that conceals art as astonishing as any to be found in the history of English poetry. Since many of the playwrights of the period in question wrote important nondramatic verse as well, it is inevitable that some of the ease and flexibility developed in the writing of the dramatic line should have carried over into the writing even of rhymed verse; but the more extreme freedoms of dramatic verse introduced a disorder, or an apparent disorder, that would have destroyed stricter verse forms. A full analysis of those freedoms cannot be attempted here; we must concern ourselves only with the background of the dramatic blank verse of *Mask* and of *SA*.

Even the dramatic line began, as all critics are agreed, simply enough, its ten syllables fairly regularly iambic in accentuation, and characteristically end-stopped. One of the clearest functions of rhyme in accentual-syllabic meter being identification of the line end, and thus the outlining, as it were, of the form of the verse, one can see why early practitioners of blank verse felt that if it was to be used without rhyme, the decasyllable could not also be enjambed. Gradually, of course, such self-conscious rigidities were relaxed. Use of the "feminine ending," a final unstressed syllable sometimes called "redundant" or "extrametrical," which makes a hendecasyllable of the English decasyllable, was never wholly restricted to dramatic verse, but provided from the beginning a safe kind of relaxation, a mild variety of movement, appropriate to it. Much later Samuel Johnson* was to object (in *Rambler* essay #88) to Milton's use of such endings in *PL*. He quotes 9.1178 and 1183, then says, "Verses of this kind occur almost in every page; but though they are not unpleasing or dissonant, they ought not to be admitted into heroic poetry, since the narrow limits of our language allow us no other distinction of epic and tragic measures, than is afforded by the liberty of changing at will the terminations of the dramatic lines, and bringing them by that relaxation of metrical rigour nearer to prose" (*The Works of Samuel Johnson* [1958–], 4 : 104).

There is more variety possible to the use of the feminine ending than might at first be imagined. In Italian verse there is found rarely a line with a double feminine ending, an *endecasillabo sdrucciolo;* Sir John Harington, Thomas Heywood, and Joshua Sylvester, among other poets, tried to naturalize this line in English, but with no permanent effect —possibly because in verse divided into feet the line cannot be differentiated except through its context from a hexameter with a final pyrrhic :

And that his noble force and magnanim(itie,
Had still preserv'd the flowre of her
    virgin(ity
    (Harington, *Orlando Furioso* 1.55.7–8)

In whose dead face he red great magnanim-
  |i-ty.
        (Spenser, *F.Q.* 2.8.23.9)

Such a hexameter as *F.Q.* 1.10.46.9,

Of God and goodnesse was his medita|ti-on,

would without question be read out of context, or in another context, as a hendecasyllable; the feminine ending that is itself a contraction of two unstressed syllables occurs not infrequently in dramatic blank verse, and at times even in nondramatic blank verse :

Against the canon laws of our founda(tion
    (*Mask* 807; cf. *F.Q.* 1.10.46.9 above)
Soon as the Potion works, their human count'-
  (nance
    (*Mask* 68; with this line contrast Shake-
      speare, *Antony and Cleopatra* 4.14.85,
Turn from me then that noble coun|te-nance.])
As if she would her children should be
  rio(tous
             (*Mask* 762)
In his redemption, and that his obe(dience
          (*PL* 12.408)
Irresolute, unhardy, unadven(trous
        (*PR* 3.243)
To accept of ransom for my son their pris'(ner
  (*SA* 1460; contrast *Coriolanus* 1.9.83,
He cried to me; I saw him pris|on-er

Contrast also, for example, *King Lear* 2.4.145 with *Richard III* 4.4.480, *Mask* 155 with *Mask* 364. The reader will observe that, just as the longest of these lines could in the proper context be read as hexameters, so the shortest could —again in the proper context—be read as tetrameters with feminine endings. Such often-quoted lines as *PL* 8.216, "Imbu'd, bring to thir sweetness no satie(tie" (see also *PL* 9.249 and *PR* 1.302), correspond to, for example, *Mask* 762, et cetera; as the reader finds it easier or more difficult to contract their endings, those endings will seem to him to have in lesser or greater degree the *sdrucciolo* effect.

A second variation of the feminine ending is that the eleventh syllable may be an unaccented monosyllable :

Where may she wander now, whether betake
  (her
            (*Mask* 350)

Against a foe by doom express assign'd (us
(*PL* 10.926)
Of what I suffer here; if Nature need (not
(*PR* 2.249)
Who this high gift of strength committed to
(me,
In what part lodg'd, how easily bereft (me,
Under the Seal of silence could not keep,
But weakly to a woman must reveal (it
(*SA* 47–50)

Obviously, both the frequency of occurrence and the nature of the feminine endings used will qualify the effect they have upon the reader.

A final variation may be mentioned. If the so-called redundant syllable may be an independent monosyllabic word, that word, though initially admissible as a feminine ending only if it is relatively unstressed, may in the practice of one or another poet be allowed to bear more than the conventional degree of accent —to the danger, of course, of the reader's sense that it is "extrametrical." In the dramatic verse of John Fletcher we find, for example,

Norfolk: That blind priest, like the eldest
son of For(tune,
Turns what he list. The King will know
him one (day.
Suffolk: Pray God he do! He'll never know
himself (else.
(*Henry VIII* 2.2.21–23)

Unless "iron" is contracted to a monosyllable in *Mask* 490 as it is in *PL* 3.594, Suffolk's line is paralleled in

Com not too neer, you fall on iron stakes else;

in any case Milton is held to have been following the dramatic verse of Fletcher, or equally difficult models, in writing such lines as

Bore a bright golden flowre, but not in this
(soyl
(*Mask* 632)
If in my flower of youth and strength, when
all (men
Lov'd, honour'd, fear'd me, thou alone could
hate (me
Thy Husband, slight me, sell me, and forgo
(me;
How wouldst thou use me now . . .?
(*SA* 938–41)

In *SA* 939 the final "me" seems at first to be relatively unstressed; when we understand that the structure is appositive, the full phrase "me/Thy Husband," we must reread to increase the stress on "me." The effect is very strange, even —as Milton must have recognized and accepted—awkward.

Variation of the prosody of the dramatic line by the admission of extrametrical syllables *within* it, rather than at its end, presents difficult problems; there must always be problems when the reader cannot differentiate between what is metrical and what is extrametrical. For dramatists of the late 1500s and early 1600s, inheritors and fashioners of a line composed of five duple measures, within which apparently supernumerary syllables might occur only if they could in effect be eliminated through one or another familiar kind of metrical compression, any but a final extrametrical syllable must ordinarily seem simply to change some iamb into an anapest, in exact contradiction to the nature of the meter. Only if the extra syllable could be set apart in some way, clearly marked or identified for what it was, would this not be so. Marlowe occasionally treated one or more of the unstressed syllables at the end of a polysyllabic proper name as extrametrical, at line end or within the line:

How now my Lords of *Egypt* & *Zenoc(ra[te]*?
(*Tamburlaine,* Part I, 309)
Both we (*Therida[mas]*) will intrench our men
(*Tamburlaine,* Part II, 3397)
Amongst which kings is *Alexan[der]* the great
(*Dr. Faustus,* 1035)
Oh trusty *Ith[imore]*; no servant, but my
friend
(*The Jew of Malta,* 1344)

(The line numbering is as given in C. F. Tucker Brooke, ed., *The Works of Christopher Marlowe* [1910].)

An interjection, or a word repeated, may in dramatic verse be identified as extrametrical:

Melt and lament for her.
[O,] God's will! much better
(*Henry VIII* 2.3.12)

One syllable against him?
        Yes, [yes,] Sir Thomas.
        (*Henry VIII* 5.1.39)

But in each of these examples the line is divided between two speakers; in a divided line an extra syllable may be identified if it occurs at the point of division, and so in, for example, *Henry VIII* 5.1.39, the "him" may be accounted the extra syllable. Compare *Mask* 614,

And crumble all thy sin[ews].
        Why prethee Shepherd,

in which either the bracketed syllable or "Why" (as an interjection) may be taken as extrametrical.

    But if the last syllable of a speech ending within the line may be treated as extrametrical, then the syllable preceding any strong midline sense break within a speech may be treated in the same way :

T'oppose your cun[ning]. Y'are meek and
    humble-mouth'd
        (*Henry VIII* 2.4. 107)
Alone, and help[less]! is this the confidence
        (*Mask* 582)
Some touch of your late bus[iness]. Affairs
    that walk
        (*Henry VIII* 5. 1. 13)
And earths base built on stub[ble]. But com
    let's on
        (*Mask* 598)
And wisdom of my Coun[cil]; but I find none
        (*Henry VIII* 5. 3. 136)
Cramms, and blasphemes his feed[er]. Shall
    I go on?
        (*Mask* 778)
Out of a foreign wis[dom],—renouncing clean
        (*Henry VIII* 1. 3. 29)
Made Goddess of the Riv[er]; still she retains
        (*Mask* 841)
They are (as all my other com[forts]) far hence
        (*Henry VIII* 3. 1. 90)

And, once one learns to watch breaks in syntax as points at which the meter of the line may be loosened by the admission of an extra syllable, lighter and lighter breaks will serve :

I was then pres[ent], saw them salute on
    horseback
        (*Henry VIII* 1. 1. 8)
To quench the drouth of *Phoe[bus]*, which
    as they taste
        (*Mask* 66)

But for that damn'd Magi[cian], let him be
    girt
        (*Mask* 601)

Mask shows the midverse extrametrical syllable between speeches (406, 614, 661), at strong midline pauses (301, 582, 598, 778, 841), and at lighter pauses (485, 604, 801, in addition to the lines quoted just above). In 598 and 801 a somewhat redundant connective may seem to be extrametrical; 485 may be reduced to ten syllables by metrical compression. One line in *Mask* is unusually difficult :

If you let slip time, like a neglected rose.
        (742)

Here "time," though stressed, may (altogether exceptionally) be extrametrical; the comparison would be with *Mask* 632. The alternative is to read "If you let" as the only genuine trisyllabic foot in Milton, or to read " 'F you let" as of two syllables. "If I" seem to coalesce into a single syllable in *Henry VIII* 1.4.26 and 5.4.23.

    The dramatic blank verse of *Mask* differs from that of *SA,* as the non-dramatic verse of *PL* and *PR* differs. That *SA* "never was intended" by its author "to the Stage" may account for a part of the contrast between *Mask* and *SA*. What role time plays in that contrast is not certain, since (among other things) the date of *SA* is not certain; some critics feel that it was written shortly before its publication, others place it as early as the latter 1640s. It may have been written early, at least in considerable part, laid aside, and revised more or less extensively before it was allowed to reach print.

    The verse of *Mask* is, in any event, so much earlier than the rest of Milton's blank verse that it has still in some ways a Jacobean, even an Elizabethan flavor. Shakespeare and John Fletcher, as has been suggested, were among those who provided models for its versification; and there is something of Spenser in all of Milton's early verse. There are three examples of recession of accent (a phenomenon much more common early than late) in the first forty lines of *Mask*: "sérene" (line 4), "énthron'd" (11), and (probably) "pérplex't" (37). Prosodically a signal feature of Elizabethan verse was its use of extended, as well as of contracted, forms. The *-ed* ending is pronounced seventeen times in *Mask* in words in which it might have been contracted: see, for example, "unadornèd" in line 23, "mis-usèd" in line 47, and "charmèd" in line 51. Even more notable are "Con-sci-ence" in *Mask* 211, "de-lu-si-on" in line 364, "Con-tem-pla-ti-on" in line 376, "sus-pi-ci-on" in line 412, "vi-si-on" in line 456, "con-ta-gi-on" in line 466, "le-gi-ons" in line 602, "ap-pa-ri-ti-on" in line 640, "con-di-ti-on" in line 684, and "com-plex-i-ons" in line 748; these could all be paralleled in Spenser, his contemporaries, and his followers. *PL* and *PR* contain no lengthened forms of the type of "Con-sci-ence"; the occurrence of a few comparable forms in SA (in, for example, lines 104, 668, 669, 705, 1660, and 1663) is possible but doubtful.

Certain of the contractions and other metrical compressions of Elizabethan and early Jacobean verse are also characteristic of their time; thus monosyllabic "i'th',", "o'th',", "by th'" and "to th',", which are common especially in the early drama, all but disappear from English verse as the seventeenth century wears on. In *Mask* "i'th'" occurs four times (in lines 281, 300, 381, and 530; it occurs three times also in the late psalm translations), "o'th'" appears in line 445 of the masque, "by th'" probably occurs in 514 (the structure is ambiguous), and "to th'" is to be found in 621, as well as in *Vac* 38, *Shak* 9, and *Lyc* 80. "I'th'" occurs in *PL* 1.224 and 11.432; neither this nor the related short forms occur in *PR* or *SA*. Apart from the familiar apocopation of "the" before a noun or adjective beginning with a vowel, *Mask* shows few examples of metrical compression involving more than one word; the most difficult of these, "th' all giver would be' unthank't would be unprais'd" (line 722, as the MS has it, in Milton's hand), has also many parallels in late sixteenth- and early seventeenth-century verse, especially dramatic verse. Metrical compression in *PL*, *PR*, and *SA* is more common; much of it

is more complex still, and more sophisticated. See VERSIFICATION.

Both *Mask* and *SA* contain passages that are not in pentameter verse. In *Mask*, as in other masques, there are songs; there are also extended passages of tetrameter verse, parts of which resemble closely the verse of *L'Al*, reveal an occasional intermixing of pentameters with tetrameters in a style very like that of certain passages in William Browne* of Tavistock's *Britannia's Pastorals*.

The odes and choruses of *SA* are much more complex. The poem opens with a monody one area of which (lines 80–97) somewhat resembles *Lyc*, and the irregular *canzoni* that underlie that poem, in mingling trimeters with the pentameters of which it is principally composed. But the *Prologos* of *SA* is generally unrhymed (see, however, later observations in this essay on rhyme in Milton's blank verse), and before it closes, it has introduced at least two tetrameters, and one line (104) which could be either a pentameter or a tetrameter with a feminine ending. The unexpected shifts in form, the uncertainty, forewarn us of an even more unorthodox verse management to come.

The choral odes are in an irregular verse the effect of which is incomparably strange, all but unparalleled in English poetry. The lines appear to be basically accentual-syllabic (though some critics have suggested that their formal affinities are rather with classical quantitative verse), but they are of differing and oddly disproportioned lengths; sequences occur that one could scarcely find in stanzaic verse. In particular the choruses contain many hexameters that occur in the midst of sentences, and are not, therefore, used to sum up and conclude, as they are in post-Spenserian verse generally; the choral verse also combines headless lines (especially headless tetrameters) with markedly longer or shorter full-syllabled lines in such a way that uneven leaps result. Further, Milton's refusal to provide a norm, a key to line length, means that some lines will have differing lengths depending on whether or not we read certain possible metrical compressions:

Made Arms | ridic|ulous, | useless | the for|ge-ry
                                                    (131)
                        | useless | the forge(ry (?)
(x) Har|dy and | indus|trious to | support
                                                    (1274)
Hardy and| (?)

Since unquestioned examples of hexameters, pentameters with feminine endings, headless pentameters, and tetrameters can all be found in the choruses, there is nothing to tell us certainly how to read the lines above and others like them; simply, we must make whatever choice seems to us best, and read in accordance with the principles underlying that choice. We may hope, but we can do no more than hope, that Milton's choice, and the principles underlying it, would have been the same.

What were Milton's models for this strange verse? If, as has been argued elsewhere ("The 'Dry' and 'Rugged' Verse," *The Lyric and Dramatic Milton*, ed. Joseph H. Summers [1965], pp. 115–52), the form of the choruses of *SA* is an unorthodox development from the rhymed irregular verse of Cowley's* *Pindarique Odes*, then those choruses must have been written, or largely rewritten, after 1656. But the whole history of English irregular verse, and a technical originality and formal skills of the most astonishing kind, lie behind the verse of the choruses of *SA*; if they seem light years distant from anything in *Mask,* so are they light years distant from *PL* and *PR,* and the point is rather to respond appropriately to their strangeness than to attempt to "place" it, or reduce it through comparisons.

There is no certain example of the midverse extrametrical syllable in *SA*; it would be comfortable to read lines like

Out, out *Hyae*[*na*]; these are thy wonted arts
                                                    (748)
Tongue-doubtie Gi[ant], how dost thou prove
    me these?
                                                    (1181)

as showing the extrametrical syllable, but "Hyaena" may instead be dissyllabic (cf. tetrasyllabic "humiliation" in, for example, *PL* 10. 1092 and 1104), and "Giant" may be monosyllabic (cf., for example, mono-

syllabic "quiet" in *SA* 1724, monosyllabic "riot" in *PL* 1. 499). Most of the lines in *Mask* which appear to show the midverse extrametrical syllable have no other formal explanation, or none that does not involve even greater difficulties and unlikelihoods. Since only one line in all of *PL* and *PR,*

Both Good and E[vil], Good lost, and Evil got,
                                                    (*PL* 9. 1072)

suggests at all strongly that we read it as showing the midverse extrametrical syllable, and since that usage is in any event associated rather with the verse drama than with other forms, editors have been reluctant to read *PL* 9. 1072 as it is represented (for illustrative purposes only) above. Robert Bridges* (in *Milton's Prosody* [1921], p. 33) suggests that "Good and Evil" in the line is "an error of the scribe or the printer" for "Evil and Good," which, he says, "gives a better verse." Milton does not seem elsewhere in his poems to have treated "evil" as a monosyllable (as against treating, for example, "evil and" as dissyllabic); but earlier poets had often employed it thus. In Sidney*, for example, we find monosyllabic "ev'll(s)" often; and see, for example, *Astrophil and Stella* 78. 14,

Is it not evill that such a Devill wants hornes?

What Milton intended in *PL* 9. 1072 we do not know; but it remains likely, on the whole, that in his poetry use of the midverse extrametrical syllable is restricted to *Mask*.

There is one long passage of stichomythia in *Mask* (276–89); one-line speeches cluster occasionally and briefly in *SA,* as in 1308–9, 1345–47, and 1569–70, but the device is never sustained for long enough to give the formal and artificial effect that Milton clearly sought (for whatever reason) in *Mask* 276ff. On the other hand, fewer lines in *SA* than in *Mask* are divided between two or more speakers; the breaking of the line in dialogue, or the blurring of line boundaries, is, of course, a gesture in the direction of naturalism in verse drama. Nonetheless, the formal management of

SA is in general such that the dialogue in it seems much more natural than does that in *Mask*. Both works consist largely of long speeches—what Saintsbury calls "tirades" (*A History of English Prosody*, 3 vols. [1908–1910], 2 : 233). But the rhythm of the set pieces of *Mask* (some of them very great set pieces) is expansive and leisurely almost throughout; it is the rhythm at times of exposition, at times of declamation. In *SA,* on the other hand, the central encounter between Samson and Dalila (remarkably dramatic in itself, though it is made up almost wholly of long speeches) tips some kind of balance, and the following episodes, involving Harapha and the Messenger, move more and more rapidly, the pulse of thought, speech, and action quickening with a responsiveness that *Mask* cannot—and doubtless does not seek to—rival.

Even within "tirades," as has been suggested, the diction and rhythms of *SA* seem less poetic, closer to speech, than do those of *Mask*. There is a slightly higher rate of enjambment in the later poem than in the earlier one; at the same time there are relatively more midline pauses in *SA* than in the masque, and there is more variety in their placement. Altogether, the syntactical unit conforms less to the metrical unit (the line) and its proportioned subdivisions and multiples in *SA* than in *Mask*; the result is that *SA* seems less artificial. Finally, the incidence of feminine endings is twice as high among the 1,329 pentameters that fall outside the passages of irregular verse in *SA* as it is among the 791 unrhymed pentameters of *Mask;* and four in fifteen of the feminine endings in *SA* (as against only three in fifteen of those in *Mask*) are monosyllables or contractions. All this affects both the rhythms and the tones of the two poems. *SA,* with more than one line in six a hendecasyllable and feminine endings often grouped together (see 47–50 and 938–41, already quoted, 215–18, 233–36, etc.), has a flexibility and an informality, at times a kind of rough simplicity and urgency, that is scarcely to be found elsewhere in Milton's work.

The Milton who wrote *PL, PR,* and *SA,* in whatever order he wrote them, was older and in every way more experienced than the Milton who wrote *Mask;* if it is reasonable to compare *Mask* and *SA* as forms of the drama, it is as reasonable to compare the three longer poems as composed in varying degrees of late and mature work. And indeed we need not differentiate too sharply between dramatic blank verse and the blank verse of Milton's epics; long sequences of *PL,* and most of *PR,* consist largely of soliloquy and dialogue, and even the narration of the epics is in a voice so personal and "involved" as to seem, again and again, dramatic. Dialogue and soliloquy in *SA* are on the whole more naturalistic than they are in parts of the epics; but the quarrels between Adam and Eve, and some interchanges between Jesus and Satan, are as lively as those between Samson and Dalila, Samson and Harapha. In general, decorum rules here as everywhere in Milton's verse : supernatural characters do not speak quite as human characters do; Adam and Eve fallen are human in a sense in which they were not, quite, before their fall. The feminine ending, that familiar resource of dramatic verse, occurs more frequently in the blank verse of *SA* (in which all the characters are human) than in any other of the late blank verse; but it occurs more frequently in *PR*—in which Jesus is represented as intensely human, though not frail—than in *PL,* and it occurs very much more frequently after the fall in *PL* than before it. There are in fact more feminine endings in *PL* 9 and 10 than in all the other books of the poem put together (about 72 : 70); there are as many in *PL* 10 alone (52) as in *PL* 1 through 8. The first feminine ending in the poem that consists of a separate monosyllable occurs in *PL* 10. 781, in Adam's long and moving soliloquy; there are in the 125 lines of that soliloquy more feminine endings (13) than there are in any other single *book* of the poem except Book 9. The statistics here coincide with the impressions the reader receives; *PL* 9 and 10 differ from the remainder of the poem in ways that require no explanation here.

It remains, perhaps, to discuss the ways in which *PL* (and *PR*) differ from *SA* and *Mask*, and the ways in which the verse of *PL* attains the character that has set it apart from all other blank verse in English. Unlike *Mask* and *SA*, *PL* and *PR* are, of course, written throughout in pentameters. Milton's 1668 statement on "The Verse" of *PL*, explaining his rejection of rhyme for that poem "as a thing of it self, to all judicious ears, triveal and of no true musical delight; which consists onely in apt Numbers, fit quantity of Syllables, and the sense variously drawn out from one Verse into another, not in the jingling sound of like endings" (2 : 6) gives us information about his formal intentions in the writing of the sustained blank verse of the long epic that cannot help being of use to us, though it must be interpreted with great care.

It may be remarked to begin with that neither "apt Numbers" nor "fit quantity of Syllables" refers to the number of syllables in the line; Milton would scarcely have thought that a matter requiring explanation or comment, and if explanation had been needed, the phrase *"English Heroic Verse"* would have been sufficient. "Apt Numbers" means "suitable rhythms," or more exactly, "a versification sensitively adjusted to the nature of what is being said at any given time." "Quantity of Syllables" refers, as in classical verse, to duration, and "fit quantity" means "appropriate brevity or length." This does not mean that the verse of *PL* is quantitative, composed in accordance with a metrical schema of conventionalized shorts and longs; it means that Milton was concerned as he wrote to avoid unusual tenuity or weight in syllables, unusual lightness or heaviness of movement, where his intellect and his ear, working together, told him they were inappropriate. Study of the syllables that precede pause in *PL* —either end-of-line pause or internal pause—would show that these are, very much more often than not, quantitatively long; and some editors and critics feel

that Milton came to use spelling (as far as, in his blindness, he was able to do so) to make quantitative discriminations. Thus the alternative spellings of "woe" in *PL* 9. 132–34,

> all this will soon
> Follow, as to him linkt in weal or woe,
> In wo then. . .

may be intended to direct us to hold the vowel in "woe," and to produce that in "wo" more briefly. Similarly, the –ee spellings of the personal pronouns may in their intention have more to do with vowel quantity and quality ("mee," for example, insuring the pronunciation [mi:], as against [mɪ]) than with unusual stress or emphasis—though the more lightly "me" is stressed, of course, the more likely it is to be pronounced [mɪ]. We must remind ourselves that quantity and stress, though they are indeed related, are not the same; and we must take seriously Milton's own values as he expressed them. Few would suggest, on the other hand, that it is easy to translate those values into a fully articulated system or systems—or even that it would be appropriate to try to do so.

The rebellious and deceitful angels who worked, through the first night of the war in heaven, against their kind, "With silent circumspection unespi'd" (*PL* 6. 523), are those who, themselves deceived, much later, in their final triumph,

> fondly thinking to allay
> Thir appetite with gust, instead of Fruit
> Chewd bitter Ashes, which th' offended taste
> With spattering noise rejected . . .;
> (*PL* 10. 564–67)

who then "With hatefullest disrelish writh'd thir jaws" (10. 569). And the poet who wrote both 6. 523 and 10. 569 knew as much about the physical nature of English—about tenuities and heavinesses of sound, freedoms and interferences, "apt Numbers, fit quantity of Syllables"—as would seem possible. We may go on to note that in *PL* 10. 563 (not quoted) there are pauses after the fifth and eighth syllables; that in 10. 564 the pause comes after the second syllable ("Deceav'd; they

. . ."); that in 565, the pause comes after the sixth syllable; in 566, after the fifth; in 567, after the seventh; and that in 569, there is no punctuated pause—so that we have as well an example of "the sense variously drawn out from one verse into another." As every analyst of Milton's prosody has observed, pause is used in *PL* with seemingly endless variety. Let the reader compare, for example, the pauses in 4. 641–56 with those in 5. 28–52, those in 2. 815–16 with those in 9. 510–12; let him compare the jagged starts and stops of 6. 834–9 with the remorseless flow of 840–43. But we must not be concerned solely with the line and its proportioning; for the combination of midline pause with enjambment produces, of course, syntactical sequences which, if the place of the pause is varied, are of varied lengths. Thus 10. 564–65 ("they fondly thinking . . . gust") is of 8 plus 6 or 14 syllables; 565–66 is of 4 plus 5 or 9 syllables; 565–67 is of 5 plus 7 or 12 syllables. The effect of a 5 plus 7 combination is rhythmically different, it goes without saying, from that of a 6 plus 6 combination; cf. *PL* 4. 646–47. Milton gives us divided phrases as brief as "the gray / Dawn" in *PL* 7. 373–74; he gives us extended passages virtually without pause:

> Up he rode
> Followd with acclamation and the sound
> Symphonious of ten thousand Harpes that
>   tun'd
> Angelic harmonies. . . .
>   (*PL* 7. 557–60)

Both the three syllables of 7. 373–74 and the 29 syllables of 7. 557–60 we hear in counterpoint to the ten syllables of the blank-verse line; as the sense is "variously drawn out" in other lines we hear falling rhythms against rising rhythms, odds against evens. From time to time, however, Milton will give us a series of clear, simple pentameters, or will resolve a complex movement in a line that we hear very much as a line, so that we may not lose our sense of the basic meter:

> Now to th' ascent of that steep savage Hill
> Satan had journied on, pensive and slow;
> But further way found none, so thick entwin'd,
> As one continu'd brake, the undergrowth
> Of shrubs and tangling bushes had perplext
> All *path* of M*a*n or Bea*st* that *past* that way.
>   (*PL* 4. 172–77)

In the first two of these lines syntax is conformed to meter, though not clumsily or monotonously; in the last line, after the tangling of the intervening phrasing, syntax and sound patterning work together to return us to our sense of the whole, the fundamental, and the unitary.

But the structures of which we become conscious as we read and reread *PL* are many. At times Milton makes us aware of the definition of phrases briefer than the line by rhyming rhythms:

> they but now who seemd
> In bigness to surpass Earths Giant Sons
> Now less than smallest Dwarfs, IN NARROW
>   ROOM
> THRONG NUMBERLESS, like that Pigmean
>   Race
> Beyond the *Indian* Mount, OR FAERIE ELVES,
> Whose midnight Revels, by a Forrest side
> Or Fountain some belated Peasant sees,
> OR DREAMS HE SEES, while over-head the
>   Moon
> SITS ARBITRESS, and neerer to the Earth
> Wheels her pale course. . . .
>   (*PL* 1. 777–86)

It may be oversubtle to suggest that "EARTHS GIANT SONS" is expanded in "NOW LESS THAN smallest DWARFS" (less is more!), and that its rhythm is mirrored at last (that is, reversed) in "WHEELS HER PALE COURSE"; but it is Milton himself who trains us to hear such patterns. Doubtless they exist in all his poems; but in *PL* they occur frequently, taking their place among the extraordinary devices which substitute their versions of order for the order represented by conventional rhyme, and our awareness of their presence is therefore of more than passing importance.

Clearly, the rhyming and related patterning of rhythms may help to support the structure of the line, or it may give us the sense that there is an unusual harmony in a cluster of lines,—or even in a sequence of some length. Our subject begins, in short, to be the verse paragraph. Critics have had the somewhat undefined sense that *Mask* (and perhaps *SA*) does not display the formal control of multi-linear structures that *PL* and *PR* display; but it seems clear that in drama, the speech plays the part of the verse paragraph naturally, and that it was only when he addressed himself to the writing of the more complex narrative verse of epic that Milton found himself faced with the necessity of devising an equivalent. In lyric the stanza mediates between the basic line and the form of the whole; in rhymed epic it mediates between line and canto, as the canto mediates between stanza and book. In drama, verse or prose, occur the more or less natural divisions of line or sentence, speech, scene, act. Modular division seems as necessary to the construction of epic as to that of any other form. It is only another evidence of Milton's greatness that he was able to devise a formal unit not regularly rhymed, not necessarily brief, sufficiently coherent but sufficiently flexible, intermediate between the line and the book. The speech in drama provides a model, and its properties might at times, with little reinforcement, serve epic also. But something additional, parallel, was required—and found.

The basic structure of the verse paragraph is of course syntactical; we need not detail here the inversions, qualifications, and suspensions, some of them patterned on grammatical structures in other languages—Italian, Latin, Hebrew—that enabled Milton to lengthen and sustain the rhythms of his narrative, giving many lines together a connectedness and an even density of thought. It is our task rather to try to understand how Milton uses structures of sound to help mold the paragraph—now to give firmness, texture, and harmony to some part of it, now to provide a larger form, less immediate perhaps to our senses, but finally in some way receivable, appreciable. Just as the reader needs some organization of thought to help him move between line (or sentence) and episode, canto or book, so he needs

some formal order or orders to mediate between line and paragraph. He needs to be aware now of the line itself, now of parts of adjacent lines together, now of the coherence of clusters of lines; the poet is continually at work expanding the dimensions of the orders the reader can perceive.

The rhyming of rhythms is one such order, and it can accomplish much more, more variously, than can here be illustrated. James Whaler, in *Counterpoint and Symbol* (*Anglistica* 6 [1966]; see especially chaps. 1 and 2, pp. 13–50), has pointed out other orders, what he calls "cross-rhythmic constructions," within the verse paragraph—constructions based on the line but crossing its boundaries, at once retaining and expanding the figure it makes:

> Soon had his crew
> Op'nd into the Hill a spacious wound
> And dig'd out ribs of Gold. . . .
> (*PL* 1. 688–90; Whaler p. 29)

> For us alone
> Was death invented? or to us deni'd
> This intellectual food. . . ?
> (*PL* 9. 766–68; Whaler p. 30)

It is possible to point to even larger emergent structures (still within the verse paragraph), structures that bear momentary resemblance to stanzas. Thus we are aware of something like a quatrain effect in *PL* 8. 1–4 and in 12. 606–9. And not infrequently a midline stop will end a series of lines with the kind of authority that often attends the conclusion of a stanza with a short line:

> Well have ye judg'd, well ended long deb*ate*,
> Synod of Gods, and like to what ye *are*,
> Gr*eat* things resolv'd; which from the lowest d*eep*
> Will once more lift us up, in spight of F*ate*,
> N*eere*r our *anc*ient S*eat*. . . .
> (*PL* 2. 390–94)

A variation of this effect occurs in the lines that lead up to *PL* 7. 557–60, already quoted:

Yet not till the Creator from his *work*
Desisting, though unwearied, up re*turn*d
Up to the Heav'n of Heav'ns his high ab*ode,*
Thence to behold this new created *World*
Th' addition of his Empire, how it shew'*d*
In prospect from his Throne, how good, how
    faire,
Answering his great Idea. Up he *rode*. . . .
                                        (7. 551–57)

In all of the passages just cited or quoted, of course, alliteration, assonance, slant rhyme, rhyme itself define the proportions that give us the momentary sense of stanza. Much that is sensitive and illuminating has been written about the use of rhyme in all its forms in the "blank" verse of *PL*; it is nonetheless safe to say that the subject has scarcely begun to be treated adequately. Here it must concern us principally to note the relationship of sound patterning to the construction of the verse paragraph. We have seen how Milton uses such patterning at times to define the metrical unit, the line itself, in (for example) *PL* 4. 177; and 11. 642, though the specific pattern it displays is quite different, may be quoted to similar effect:

Giants of mi*ghtie Bone,* and *bou*ld empr*ise.*

But the poet interested in building toward the verse paragraph finds ways, of course, with these means also of subordinating the line to larger structures, of knitting lines together:

            mean while murmuring waters fall
Down the slope hills, disperst, or in a Lake,
That to the fringèd Bank with *Myrtle c*rownd,
Her *chryst*al mi*rr*or holds, unite thir streams.
                                        (*PL* 4. 260–63)

The "mirroring" of sounds in the last two of these lines provides a breathtaking image of the sense. A pattern rather more general in effect unites, for example, *PL* 4. 605–6:

                        *Hesp*erus that led
The *st*arrie *Host,* rode brighte*st.* . . .

Note how in these lines the sounds that contribute to the pattern come together, then dissolve, permitting the reader to continue with scarcely a pause—avoiding, that is, the effect of finality that full end rhyme so often gives.

There could be no end to appropriate quotation here, but for illustrating the use of emergent patterns of sound to bind together clusters of lines within the verse paragraph, a final passage must suffice:

                    though in *H*eav'n the Trees
Of *li*fe ambrosial frutage b*ear,* and *vines*
Yield Nectar, though from off the *boughs* each
    Morn
We *b*rush mellifluous D*ewes,* and *find* the
    ground
Cover'd with pearly *g*rain: yet God hath *here*
*V*aried his *bounty* so with new de*li*ghts,
As may comp*are* with *H*eaven. . . .
                                        (*PL* 5. 426–32)

Obviously not all patterns present have been indicated; further, elements of the patterns shown connect with other sounds, to make other patterns in the lines preceding and following. In some passages in *PL* sounds drop before us like the bits of colored glass in a turning kaleidoscope, constantly evolving new patterns, creating a stability of change. But we do not neglect meaning while we attend to the patterning of sound, for the two are, again and again, fully comprehensible only in terms of each other. There are in any event kinds and kinds of meaning; the sound patterning in *PL* is exactly supportive of the kinds of meaning that Milton wishes us, in the reading of that poem, to entertain.

As we have known since John S. Diekhoff published his "Rhyme in *Paradise Lost*" (*Publications of the Modern Language Association* 49 : 539–43), there is a considerable amount of full end rhyme in *PL* (and *PR*); but analysts seem scarcely to have begun to show us how much there is and what its uses are. To begin with, we must note that at line ends as well as within lines Milton gives us, where his formal purposes suggest its appropriateness, a continual modulation of sound patterning that has something of the formal usefulness of rhyme without its obtrusiveness and finality. To choose a passage almost at random,

          As when Heavens *Fire*
Hath scath'd the *Forrest* Oaks, or *M*ountain
    Pines,
With singèd top thir stately growth though
    *b*are
Stands on the *b*lasted *Heath. He* now
    pre*par'd*
To sp*eak*; whereat thir doubl'd *R*anks they
    bend
From wing to wing, and half enclose him
    round
With all his *Peers.* . . .
                 (*PL* 1. 612–18)

Less than two lines later, "Peers" is rhymed, unexpectedly, by the first word in 1. 620, "Tears"; three-and-a-half lines later the paragraph ends. When one notices that the first seven lines of the following paragraph end with the words "Powers," "strife," "dire," ("change,") "mind," ("Depth,") and "fear'd," it will be seen how continuation of the patterning may be used to bind paragraph to paragraph. "Dire" in 1. 624 actually (and not at all unusually) provides full rhyme for "Fire" in 612; though the lines are distant from one another, the rhymed sounds are traced through so many of the intervening lines, particularly at line end, that the rhyme has its effect, if only subliminally. It may not be an advantage to us, necessarily, to be actively conscious of all the rhyme in *PL*. Milton seems not to have wanted to call our attention to it. That it is there is beyond question. One would scarcely describe its sound, perhaps, as "the jingling sound of like endings," and that phrase is usually taken to refer to couplet rhyme, the rhyme Cowley used (for example) in writing the *Davideis*.

    Sometimes, as in *PL* 1. 183–91, Milton uses end rhyme ("tend"–"offend"; "there" –"repair"–"despare") to give decisive form to a scene-ending verse paragraph, much as Elizabethan and Jacobean playwrights had used couplet rhyme in otherwise blank verse to signal the end of a scene; often, as above, Milton uses rhyme in *PL* and *PR* to provide a continuity between paragraph and paragraph—perhaps a little as the *chiave* provided for Italian poets a connection between otherwise

separate groups of lines (with independent rhyme structures) within the *canzone*. It should be noted that end rhyme of the kinds described occurs in Milton's blank verse from the very beginning : thus *Mask* 4 and 6 rhyme, as do 13 ("key" pronounced as Milton pronounced it), 18, 22 and 36, and as do 31 and 45 (thus completing unification of the first two movements of the opening "tirade"); rhyme resumes at once with 46/47–52/53; and so on. In the opening monody of *SA* we may note the rhyme in 12–23, 32–38, 52–76, 53–59, 55–58–66, 63–67, 71–93–98–99, 80–87, 89–102, and 97–106. It is idle to suppose that patterns of this kind are accidental, or unavoidable; they are neither. We are not perhaps accustomed to the use Milton makes of rhyme in his "blank" verse; we are not accustomed to apprehend structures of such magnitude. But they are in keeping with what Joseph A. Wittreich, Jr., has shown us about the "unrhymed" lines of *Lyc* (in "Milton's 'Destin'd Urn' : the Art of *Lycidas*," *Publications of the Modern Language Association* 84 : 60–70); and they are very much in keeping with Milton's need to give us a sense of the basic unity of long passages of verse that must not seem to be chain-stitched together, line by line. Every great poem trains its own readers. By the end of *PL* we have been trained in such a way that we feel the absolute inevitability of the simple final lines,

They hand in hand with wandring steps and
    slow,
Through *Eden* took thir solitarie way,
                (12. 648–49)

whether or not we are actually *conscious* of the fact that "slow" and "way" have been prepared by "know" at the end of 12. 599, "array" at the end of 12. 627, and—principally—Eve's haunting lines

In mee is no delay; with thee to goe,
Is to stay here; without thee here to stay,
Is to go hence unwilling. . . .
                (12. 615–17)

That *PL* should end on rhymes for "go" and "stay" is not, surely, without meaning, not without effect; nor is this use of rhyme one we have always, and automatically, understood.

The metrical unit in Milton's blank verse is, then, as we should expect, the ten-syllable or five-foot line; but as his purposes lead him, Milton defines for us rhythmic sequences now smaller than the line, now larger, syntactical groups now identical with the line, now other. With sound patterning he unifies single lines, parts of contiguous lines, clusters of lines, successions quasi-stanzaic. He constructs, and gives individual character to, verse paragraphs short and long; unobtrusively he relates verse paragraphs to one another so that their individuality may not have an effect too great, may not stop the flow of the narrative. He trains us at last to respond to formal gestures of the greatest amplitude, patterns larger, it may be, than any other English poet has ever devised.

It should not be necessary to say that *PR* displays the devices that have been illustrated in *PL*, but displays them in characteristic ways, and on an appropriate scale. Even in *PL* a honeyed smoothness, an excess of sound patterning, a kind of persistent formal ostentation, is at times associated with Satan's hypocrisies and self-deceptions; *PR* 3.204–26, however genuinely moving we may (for our sins) find it, may be examined in this light. But *PR* is a plainer poem than *PL*; its rhythms are shorter; its syntax is more straightforward; its periods do not, on the whole, require the sustaining that heightens and lends formal control to the long periods of *PL*. There is rhyme in *PR*; see, for example, 4. 421–26, 427–37, 461–65, 470–78, 475–87, 476–98–511, 504–14, 530–38, et cetera. There are fine sound progressions; see the "fell"–"fall"–"foil" of 4. 562–71, and the end-of-line sequence "worlds" – "work" – "mankind" – "meek"– ("refresht") – "unobserv'd" – "return'd" of the last lines of the poem. But the barer and subtler harmonies of, for example, *PR* 1. 497–502 better represent, perhaps, what is individual in the excellence of the poem's form :

> He added not; and Satan bowing low
> His gray dissimulation, disappear'd
> Into thin Air diffus'd: for now began
> Night with her sullen wing to double-shade
> The Desert, Fowls in thir clay nests were couch't;
> And now wild Beasts came forth the woods to roam.

But of course we should expect a perceptible if moderate difference between the verse of the "diffuse" epic and that of the "brief model" (*RCG* 3 : 237), as between that of epic and that of drama. "I mean not here the prosody of a verse . . . but that sublime Art which . . . teaches what the laws are of a true *Epic* Poem, what of a *Dramatic*, what of a *Lyric*, what Decorum is, which is the grand master-piece to observe. This would . . . shew . . . what religious, what glorious and magnificent use might be made of Poetry both in divine and humane things" (*Educ* 4 : 286). Alas that we have not all hit on "the prosody of a verse . . . among the rudiments of Grammar." We can at least allow our ears to be educated by that English grand master of the "grand master-piece" which readers as well as writers must in the end know how to observe. [EW]

BLANK VERSE, CONTROVERSY OVER. John Dryden's* *Essay on Dramatic Verse* (1668) is the best known document recording the controversy over rhyme and blank verse* in the second half of the seventeenth century. The merits of rhyme had been argued by Dryden and his brother-in-law Sir Robert Howard* before the publication of the *Essay*, with Howard championing blank verse. The issue continued to be discussed between them and others well after this date. It is probably highly significant, therefore, that *PL* did not include the statement on "The Verse" in its first three issues of 1667–1668, but that it was added to the fourth issue in 1668. Howard, a friend of Milton, may have been influential in eliciting Milton's defense of unrhymed verse, particularly since the poem must have fueled the controversy with in longer Works especially, but the Invention of a barbarous Age, to set off wretched matter and lame Meeter. . . ." To Milton the "neglect" of rhyme may seem a defect to "vulgar Readers," but the use of rhyme is "troublesom and modern bondage." All of this did not sit well with Thomas Rymer, who, in *The Tragedies of the Last Age* (1678), proposed that "With the remaining *Tragedies* I shall also send you some reflections on that *Paradise lost* of *Miltons,* which some are pleas'd to call a Poem, and asserts *Rime* against the slender Sophistry wherewith he attaques it . . ." (p. 143). In the succeeding years the half-sentence struck many people, who referred to this promise that was never kept. For example, Thomas Shipman commented on Milton's error in using blank verse, but since Rymer was going to discuss the matter fully, he would not go into it further; see *Henry the Third of France, Stabb'd by a Fryer* (1678), Preface, pp. [A4v–*1r]. Dryden in his preface to the translations of Juvenal (1693) wrote: "But I will not take Mr. Rymer's work out of his hands: he has promised the world a critique on that author; wherein, though he will not allow his poem for heroic, I hope he will grant us, that his thoughts are elevated, his words sounding . . . ," and he continues, "Neither will I justify Milton for his blank verse, though I may excuse him, by the example of Hannibal Caro, and other Italians, who have used it; for whatever causes he alleges for the abolishing of rhyme, (which I have not now the leisure to examine,) his own particular reason is plainly this, that rhyme was not his talent; he had neither the ease of doing it, nor the graces of it; which is manifest in his *Juvenilia,* or verses written in his youth, where his rhyme is always constrained and forced, and comes hardly from him, at an age when the soul is most pliant, and the passion of love makes almost every man a rhymer, though not a poet . . ." (p. viii). There was also Samuel Wesley*, who wrote himself in rhyme: "And for his blank Verse, I'm of a different mind from most others, and

think they rather excuse him uncorrectness than the contraries; for I find its easier to run into it, in that sort of Verse, than in Rhyming Works where the thought is oftner turned; whereas here the Fancy flows on, without check or controul"; see "The Preface, Being an Essay on Heroic Poetry," *The Life of Our Blessed Lord and Saviour Jesus Christ* (1697), p. 24. Andrew Marvell* commends Milton and seems to cast aspersions on Dryden in his poem on the epic; but he himself wrote in rhyming couplets. Nathaniel Lee calls the verse "rude" and "rough" when praising Dryden's *State of Innocence* (1677; written ca. 1674) in rhyming couplets; but his *The Rival Queens* (1677) is in blank verse and has an imitative passage in Act 4 (see p. 44).

Perhaps the earliest champion of Milton's verse form was Wentworth Dillon, Earl of Roscommon, whose second edition of *An Essay on Translated Verse* (1685), lines 377–403, praises the poem in blank verse in an otherwise rhymed poem, with a marginal note, "An Essay on blanc verse out of the 6th Book of *Paradise Lost.*" Too little attention has been given the criticism of John Dennis*, who is strong in his approval of Milton's blank verse, although he does not denigrate rhyme, in "The Preface," *The Passion of Byblis* (1692). To Addison* Milton "Unfetter'd in majestick numbers walks," although his own "An Account of the Greatest English Poets" (1694) is in rhyme.

The controversy continued through the eighteenth century with critics like William Benson in *Letters Concerning Poetical Translation, and Virgil's and Milton's Arts and Verse* (1739); Edward Manwaring in *Of Harmony and Numbers, in Latin and English Prose, and in English Poetry* (1744); John Mason in *An Essay on the Power and Harmony of Prosaic Numbers* (1749); and Henry Home, Lord Kames in *Elements of Criticism* (1762). Mason charged that "If the antient Poetry was too lax in its Numbers, the modern is certainly too strict, the just Medium between these two Extreams seems to be that which *Milton* hath chosen for his Poem . . ." (p. 47). For Kames, "Our verse is extremely cramped by rhyme; and the peculiar advantage of blank verse is, that it is at liberty to attend the imagination in its boldest flights" (p. 128). Rather typically for the period the anonymous *Milton's Sublimity Asserted: In a Poem. Occasion'd by a late Celebrated Piece, Entituled, Cyder, a Poem; In Blank Verse, By Philo-Milton* (1709) proclaims :

in moving Numbers, he excites
The Vig'rous Soul to the sublimest Thoughts.

Sneyd Davies's "Rhapsody to Milton" (written February 1740) echoes the sentiment :

For O! great Pattern to succeeding Times!
Dost thou not smile indignant, to behold
The tinkling modern fetter'd, yet well pleas'd
Dance to the tiresome Musick of his Chains;
While all *Parnassus* rings the silly Chime.

Many poets wrote in "Miltonicks" or "in the style of Milton," by which was meant blank verse; for example, the anonymous poems, *Lucifer's Defeat: or, The Mantle-Chimney. A Miltonic* (London, 1729), and "A Panegyric on a Louse, in the Style of Milton," *London Magazine* 18 (October 1749) : 474.

The major critical antagonist to Milton's versification during the eighteenth century was Samuel Johnson*, whose four articles in *The Rambler* (nos. 86, 88, 90, 94; 1751) oppose the form but praise the content and result. Some of these ideas are repeated in *The Life of Milton* (1779), where Johnson concludes : "I cannot prevail on myself to wish that Milton had been a rhymer, for I cannot wish his work to be other than it is; yet, like other heroes, he is to be admired rather than imitated. He that thinks himself capable of astonishing, may write blank verse; but those that hope only to please, must condescend to rhyme." [JTS]

BLINDNESS, MILTON'S. Until he completely lost his sight, Milton appears to have suffered throughout his life from some kind of visual distress, perhaps inherited from his mother. He himself blamed the trouble on youthful bookishness; his enemies saw it as punishment inflicted upon him by God for his evil ways. Consciousness of this unflattering interpretation probably led Milton to the several autobiographical* accounts that he wrote about his blindness. Critics have generally interpreted the blind Samson, for instance, as being in some sense a self-portrait.

According to his most objective and detailed statement, made in a letter to Leonard Philaras* and dated September 28, 1654, he had "felt my sight getting weak and dull" about ten years earlier. He suffered from a general malaise, and his eyes hurt whenever he read anything. Physical exercise seemed to offer some help, but "a kind of iris" seemed to cut off candlelight. In a short time he lost all vision in his left eye, and his right one grew weaker. The disappearance of any surviving handwriting, even signatures, led J. M. French to conclude that his vision failed totally about the end of February 1652. In the same letter Milton reported that "the darkness which is perpetually before me, by night as well as by day, seems always nearer to a whitish than to a blackish, and such that, when the eye rolls itself, there is admitted, as through a small chink, a certain little trifle of light."

Although they are at best only guesses, several modern diagnoses of Milton's illness have been advanced : detachment of the retina, a cyst, and glaucoma, of which the last seems most persuasive. An interesting feature of one type of glaucoma is that it appears to be associated with a certain type of personality : one who is excitable, a perfectionist with sometimes difficult interpersonal relationships. Acute attacks of glaucoma in such individuals may be precipitated by emotional stress. It may then not be accidental that Milton's blindness in his left eye (around 1644) occurred at the same time as attacks upon him that resulted from the publication of his divorce pamphlets, and that his total blindness overcame him not long after he had written his answer in *1Def* to Salmasius's* attack upon him.

Whatever the cause, there is no reason to question the fact that Milton had experienced a terrible blow, one that was to influence to some degree almost everything that he wrote during the rest of his life. *Sonn* 19 is a statement of part of his mental adjustment to blindness; *Sonn* 22, to Cyriack Skinner*, expressed his response to total blindness three years after the event. Other testimony in his poetry appears in the last sonnet, and in his prayers in *PL* for inner illumination. [WBH]

BLOUNT, CHARLES: *see* ADAPTATIONS, LITERARY.

BOCCACCIO, GIOVANNI. Milton's only explicit reference to the works of Boccaccio (1313–1375) appears in *CB* under the category *Rex* (18 : 174). Milton's interest in Boccaccio's *Life of Dante,* from which he quoted, was limited to the fact that the statement "that the authority of a king does not depend upon the popes" was deleted from later editions (Yale *Prose* 1 : 438).

Probable uses of the *Genealogia Deorum* reveal Milton's further knowledge of Boccaccio's writings. His *Genealogy of the Gods,* "the most massive and most erudite" of his works, is a mythological encyclopedia. Milton assumes that his readers are acquainted with such mythology* when he relates how Satan, on plunging into the Abyss, sees there the pavilion of Chaos with Night, Orcus, Ades, "and the dreaded name of Demogorgon" (*PL* 2. 959–67). Other echoes of the same tradition may be seen in *El* 6 : 71; *Idea* 4; *SA* 971–74; and *QNov* 141. Though he may have learned the genealogy of Chaos from Hesiod* (see *PL* 2. 895–903), he may still have been indebted to Boccaccio's work for the idea of the Infernal Council. [RMa]

BOCCALINI, TRAIANO (1556–1613), an Italian satirist and political theorist, best known for his *Ragguagli di Parnaso,*

a work cited twice in Milton's *CB* 18: 191). Along with works by Berni*, Tassoni*, Boccaccio*, and Villani*, the *Ragguagli* comprised part of Milton's independent study of Italian during the years 1642–1645. This very popular work, found in many English and foreign-language editions, contains several hundred satirical news letters purportedly sent from Parnassus, where Apollo acts as an arbiter in all sorts of causes. Milton, consulting the fifth edition (Venice, 1630), paraphrased Boccalini's criticism of the study of law and alluded to the decree that would prevent lawyers from going to the New World, a regulation that would ensure a peaceful, nonlitigious life for the natives. Though more popular, the *Ragguagli* is perhaps not so mature a work as Boccalini's *Commentarii sopra Cornelio Tacito,* a series of comments on Tacitus* that provided a base for his criticism of then-contemporary government. This work was in part printed posthumously and much of it remains in manuscript. [RMa]

BODIN, JEAN (1530–1596), political economist, was a councillor to Henry III but, as a delegate to the States General elected by the Vermandois, he successfully opposed the King's attempt to sell royal property and go to war with the Protestants. As a result, Bodin's political career was destroyed. Milton alludes to his position in *CB,* citing it to show that representatives may be instructed to take certain public positions as Bodin did for his constituents.

Bodin's most important book is *De Republica,* an argument favoring exercise of absolute power as necessary for effective government, its only limits being divine or natural law. Milton certainly read the book, for he cites it in *CB* (18 : 156) as favoring divorce* (for incompatibility). His only other reference is in *RCG,* where he cites Bodin, "the famous French writer," as asserting that government will "flourish in vertu and piety when the church does not exercise a jurisdictive power." [ILD]

BODMER, JOHANN JAKOB (1698–1783) seems to have become enthusiastic about *PL* before he secured a copy of it. He had read French translations of Addison's* *Spectator* papers in praise of Milton and the poem. In an early issue of *Discourse der Mahlern,* a journal that he and Johann Jakob Breitinger, a fellow Swiss, had started in 1721 in order to "build better artistic taste, to teach new moral ideas, to drive out the false, and to encourage the natural," Bodmer spoke highly of *PL*. In 1724 he finished his first translation*, called *Verlust des Paradieses,* which was not published, however, until 1732. This prose translation was in "Schweizerdeutsch"; in 1742 Bodmer published another translation in high German. Finally, in 1780, appeared a translation which, Bodmer said wittily, was neither Swiss German nor high German, but poetry.

No ambivalence appears in Bodmer's regard for Milton, whom Bodmer regarded as the very model of the ideal citizen, the advocate of domestic, civil, and religious freedom. Not just his historical research and citizen's activities, but also his returning often in his own literary works to an imagined period of innocence, when nature and man were at one, testify to Bodmer's high regard for Milton as a person and as an artist.

In that term *artist* lies one major difference between Bodmer and Gottsched*: Bodmer, and his friend Breitinger, were the first critics in the German speech area who looked upon poetry as an art. In their *Critische Dichtung* (1740), most of which Breitinger wrote, they place poetry in two kingdoms—the actual world and the nonmaterial. The poet, with a kind of creative act, sees the unseeable and presents it as if it were real. This they called "painting," speaking in pictures. The poet raises reality to the height of the unreal, making it strange and wonderful, through the medium of a special, almost sacred language. This turning of the unreal into pictures, and the real into wonder, Bodmer thought he had found not only in *PL* but also in medieval chivalric

poems. In 1748 he edited *Parzifal* and the *Nibelungenlied,* in 1758 his *Sammlung der Minnesänger.*

The second major difference between the opponents lay in their differing interpretations of imitation of nature. Bodmer and Breitinger held that true poetry is the imitation of nature, not only in her real (phenomenal) aspects but also in the possible. "The poet describes not only what has actually happened, but also what, in altered circumstances, could have happened and the consequences therefrom." Gottsched thought only of empirical possibility, the Swiss of logical possibility. They thought too of poetic as well as historical truth, thereby opening immeasurably the borders of poetry's realm.

Gottsched and Bodmer were alike in their desire to better the taste of the German reading public. In his essay "Abhandlung von dem Wunderbaren," Bodmer took the public to task for their failure to appreciate *PL*. They lacked the necessary free spirit. The scanty success of the poem, he said, is no fault of Milton's but must be ascribed to the incapability of readers and critics. Milton had used the freedom that poetry allows, "for his intention was not to write a metaphysical treatise of nature and of invisible spirits, but to capture the imagination with inventive and instructive representations. Therefore he gave those invisible spirits visible, bodily forms, without which they otherwise could not be understood" (Sigmund von Lempicki, *Geschichte der Deutschen Literaturwissenschaft bis zum Ende des 18. Jahrhunderts* [1968], p. 263).

The Bodmer-Gottsched controversy had far deeper implications than perhaps at first appear. Most literary centers in Germany, from the seventeenth century on, were Protestant, and very often Pietistic, so that there already existed antirationalist sentiment. Gottsched had made many enemies by his authoritarianism. Writers who sided with the Swiss, then, were likely to have mixed motives. Immanuel Pyra (1715–1744) read Bodmer and Breitinger's *Critische Dichtkunst* in

1736, then wrote "The Temple of True Poetic Art," five unrhymed Alexandrine songs, in which True Poetry escorts the poet on a trip through her realm, explaining in terms drawn from the Swiss, the false and true. Pyra also fought Gottsched in a weekly called *Gedanken der unsichtbaren Gesellschaft,* and finally wrote a direct attack, "Resolved, That the Gottsched Group are destroying Taste." In this last, he praised both Milton and Albrecht Haller, Swiss poet of *The Alps,* a long poem dealing with the lives and folkways of the Alpine farmers, shepherds, and hunters. Poetry, for Pyra, is in the service of the highest, holiest thought; it is a pietistic art. Milton and the humanist Hieronymus Vida* are Pyra's trustworthy authorities. Klopstock* is his follower.

Gotthold Ephraim Lessing, ever on the side of broad tolerance, was perhaps the most important figure to be engaged in the controversy. Though interested primarily in drama, he analyzed the classical ideas advanced by Gottsched and the objections voiced by the liberal Hamburg school and decided for the latter. He called Gottsched's ideal a "phantom" and later denied that Gottsched had rendered any service to the German theater. (Gottsched had called him a "patriotic dung-carrier.")

Johann Andreas Fabricius, of the Hamburg school, defended poetic freedom against "the unoriginal charges of malcontented language teachers." A living language, he said, cannot be bound by rules, either in speaking or in writing. And Christian Friedrich Weichman declared that since taste is manifold, it is folly to say that one preference is correct and another not. Many persons hold that French poetry is merely rhymed prose, he said, tasteless as clear water soup, which is useful and has a pure flavor though it has no strength. [MM]

BOEHME, JAKOB (1575–1624), German shoemaker who as a result of mystical experiences of divine illumination published voluminously on the subject in the last twelve years of his life. His writings are extremely difficult, owing in part to his employment of Paracelsian terminology.

Although Milton never mentions him, the two men have some ideas in common: creation of the universe *ex deo,* emphasis upon the divine will, an angelology of good and evil spirits, a Son* of God who represents light and wisdom. Margaret Bailey argued for strong direct influence (*Milton and Jakob Boehme* [1914]), going so far as to assert that "Milton penetrated into 'the Teutonic philosophy' beneath the veil of language that obscured its meaning, and became one of the first to share Boehme's true *Weltanschauung.*" Few critics today would agree, for the two writers are more probably expressing independently the Neoplatonic* tradition of the period. Significant differences must be noticed: Boehme's God is neither good nor evil but contains the elements of both. His Godhead has both good and evil wills, and it reveals itself in seven nature spirits. Such conceptions are totally alien to Milton. In the 1640s and later a number of English groups became interested in Boehme's system, but there is no evidence that Milton ever joined them. Eventually the movement amalgamated with the Quakers*. [WBH]

BOETHIUS: *see* ETERNITY AND TIME.

BOIARDO, MATTEO MARIA (1441–1494). Milton's references to the *Orlando Innamorato* of Boiardo occur primarily in *CB* (18 : 142, 145–46, 174, 188). On the one hand, Francisco Berni's* name is associated with these citations, and since they can be found in Berni's *rifacimento* it is tempting to think that Milton preferred the Tuscan's version of the poem. On the other hand, Milton included two lines to which he attached Boiardo's name, indicating that he was perhaps quoting a copy given him in 1642 (French, *Life Records,* 2 : 68, 87). This book was the *rifacimento* of Lodovico Domenicini (Venice, 1608).

Milton alluded to the action of the poem in both *PL* and *PR.* Beyond using a number of place names common to *Orlando Innamorato*, he named the heroine, Angelica, and the antagonists, Orlando and Agricane (*PR* 3. 338–44). The battle of the angels (*PL* 6. 354–62) is an echo of the comic battle between devils and Saracans in Boiardo. A passage in *PR* reflects his recollection of a battle between Orlando and Agricane (*PR* 3. 338–43).

Orlando was incomplete at the time of Boiardo's death, but the third book of nine cantos appeared in 1495, after other printings of the first two books. Generally, the poem was not much in vogue after the appearance of Berni's *rifacimento*. The tone of Boiardo's poem with its spontaneity and "vernal freshness" has now more appeal than Berni's rather smooth but expressionless recasting. Neither version enjoyed much popularity after the beginning of the seventeenth century. [RMa]

BOLD, MATTHEW: *see* TRANSLATIONS OF MILTON'S WORKS.

BONMATTHEI, BENEDETTTO: *see* ACCADEMIA DEGLI SVOGLIATI.

BOOKSELLERS: *see* PUBLISHERS.

BOWDOIN, JAMES: *see* INFLUENCE IN AMERICA, MILTON'S.

BOYD, HENRY: *see* TODD, HENRY JOHN.

BOYLE, KATHERINE: *see* RANELAGH, LADY KATHERINE.

BRACKENRIDGE, HUGH HENRY: *see* INFLUENCE IN AMERICA, MILTON'S.

BRADSHAW FAMILY: *see* BIOGRAPHY.

BRADSHAW, JOHN (1607–1659) served as judge at the trial of Charles I* and was president of the Council of State*. Milton apparently first met Bradshaw when the poet employed him as his attorney in the suit brought against him by Sir Robert Pye in February 1647. Later,

Milton, serving as Secretary for Foreign Tongues*, must have worked closely with Bradshaw, who may have been the "private acquaintance" who recommended him to that position. Milton wrote a letter (*Epistol* 43) to Bradshaw on February 21, 1653, introducing Andrew Marvell* for the position of assistant to the Secretary (which Philip Meadows*, not Marvell, originally received). In *2Def* Milton defends Bradshaw, that "incorrupt judge" and "friend of my own," and praises him highly. And when Emeric Bigot* requested that Milton check some references for him, the poet borrowed material from Bradshaw's library. At Bradshaw's death, Milton received a bequest of £10. Parker suggests that perhaps Milton and Bradshaw were distantly related. [WM]

BRAMHALL, JOHN: *see* ANTAGONISTS.

BRANTHWAIT, MICHAEL. Sir Henry Wotton* gave Milton a letter of introduction to his friend Michael Branthwait, formerly an agent at Venice and tutor to the son of John, first Viscount Scudamore* (the English Ambassador to Paris). Branthwait was to help Milton plan his Italian journey*, and probably gave the young poet several letters of introduction to various Italian families. [WM]

BREAD STREET: *see* BIOGRAPHY.

BRIDGES, ROBERT SEYMOUR (1844–1930), English poet and critic. Born into a well-to-do family, he was educated at Eton and at Corpus Christi, Oxford, where he became friends with a coeval at Balliol, Gerard Manley Hopkins*. The Oxford Movement, then flourishing there, left Bridges essentially untouched. Besides extensive travel on the Continent, he studied medicine and was admitted to practice, a career that he followed for a few years.

His real interests, however, lay with literature. In 1873 he published his first poems, which even then exhibited prosodical experiments, especially in quantitative verse—not so radical perhaps or successful as the accentual work of his friend Hopkins, with whom he carried on an extensive correspondence and whose poetry he first brought to public attention, long after its author's death. Toward the end of the century he wrote a number of closet dramas and a narrative poem *Eros and Psyche,* and compiled the Yattenden Hymnal, named for the village where he lived and serving to repopularize many of the songs of the earlier English church.

The rector of the region was H. C. Beeching, who in 1887 edited the first book of *PL,* to which Bridges contributed an introductory essay, "On the Elements of Milton's Blank Verse*." Two years later the poet published an extension of his theories of Milton's verse as it fitted *PR* and *SA,* and in 1901 his full-fledged *Milton's Prosody* appeared, expounding prosodic theories that he somewhat revised several times before his death. Written in rather a fussy style, the book argues that Milton's mature prosody is based on a scansion of five theoretical iambic feet into which natural English stresses intrude to produce a line in which the syllable counts for more than the foot: "Milton came to scan his verses in one way, and to read them in another" (*Milton's Prosody,* 1921 ed., p. 35). To achieve the decasyllabic reading, Bridges argued for elaborate employment of synaloepha—elision—between adjacent vowels or through *l, n,* and *r,* which to some degree does reflect actual English pronunciation. The book was vigorously attacked, especially by George Saintsbury in his *History of English Prosody* (1908–1910), but Bridges's theories have proved fruitful, the most important key to an understanding of Milton's verse techniques.

He was named poet laureate in 1913, to the regret of the followers of the popular Kipling, and continued his experiments, applying his discoveries about Milton's prosody to his own poetry, including the "Neo-Miltonic Syllabics" of *New Verse* (1925) and the *Testament of Beauty* (published on his 85th birthday), written in the "Miltonic" manner though in twelve-syllable lines. He directed that this long poem be published only as a whole; the result in an age dominated by anthologies has been to make it almost unknown although it is one of the important poems of this century. [WBH]

BRIDGEWATER, EARL OF: *see* EGERTON FAMILY.

BRIDGEWATER MANUSCRIPT. Also known as the Ashbridge MS and the Ellesmere MS, the Bridgewater Manuscript of *Mask* is preserved in Bridgewater House, London, the possession of the family for whom the masque was written. It was first discussed by Thomas Warton* in his edition of the minor poems in 1791, and first published by Henry J. Todd* in his edition of the masque in 1798. It is given in facsimile by Harris F. Fletcher in vol. 1 of *John Milton's Complete Poetical Works Reproduced in Photographic Facsimile* (1943). Fletcher's transcription, given with slight correction by John S. Diekhoff in *A Maske at Ludlow* (1968), is frequently inaccurate.

The manuscript, of twenty quarter sheets (pp. 2 and 40 being blank), is in a professional scribe's hand throughout, although a few directions have been erroneously assigned to Henry Lawes*. The ascription on the title page, "Author Jo: Milton," is in the hand of Thomas Egerton*, who played the Second Brother in the masque. Names of speakers are generally written in red ink; there is a ruled line in red ink in the left margin of each page. Rather than the 1023 lines of the printed text the manuscript presents 908 lines. Omitted are lines 188–90, 195b–225, 357–65, 632–37, 679–87, 697–700, 737–55, 779b–806a, 847, 984–87, 997, 1000–11; lines 733–34 are combined into one; and eleven lines appear that are not in the printed edition. Lines 357–65 and 779b–806a do not appear in *TM;* the first passage was once attached on a pasted scrap of paper, now lost. Lines 679–87, 948–87, 997, 1000–11 were all added later to *TM,* and the eleven unprinted lines are found in the basic transcription there. The scribe, therefore, seems to have cut only lines 188–90, 195b–225, 632–37, 697–700, 737–55, perhaps on specific directions, and to have erred in omitting line 847 and in combining lines 733–34.

The major change in the text of *BrM* is that lines 976–83, 988–95, 995A, 996, 998–99 are transferred to the beginning of the masque as a kind of prologue. Differences between the printed version of *Mask* and that in *BrM* can be accounted for by examination of the development of the text in *TM* and as the result of slips by the scribe, except for directions, which are sometimes variant.

The suggestion that the cuts in *BrM* resulted from its being the stage copy for the first production involving the Egerton children is uninformed. First, some of the supposed cuts, as enumerated above, simply did not exist in *TM* at the time that the state of the text of *BrM* indicates it was produced. Second, the lines that were cut came from the Spirit's lines (632–37) and Comus's (737–55) as well as the Lady's (188–90, 195b–225, 697–700). Third, only Comus's lines might be considered unacceptable for a younger audience, and the Lady's lines 195b–225 should have been retained for their moral content and uplift. There seems no reason to conclude that the cuts were made to accommodate young performers.

The date of the manuscript is debated. Formerly it was believed that the manuscript represented the first performance of the masque and it was thus dated 1634. However, textual analysis has indicated that it was transcribed while the version in *TM* was being written. Lines added to the basic transcription of the masque in *TM* and found in *BrM* show the use of the Italian "e," which Milton began to employ around November 1637 (*see* HANDWRITING, MILTON'S). The poem in *TM* was further revised after the version given in the *BrM* was transcribed, and it was published in 1637/38. Thus *BrM* seems to be dated in late 1637/38 or seems to derive from a copy transcribed then. Besides, the title page of *BrM* indicates the date of the first performance and therefore seems to postdate that performance. [JTS]

BRIEF HISTORY OF MOSCOVIA, A.

The exact time when Milton wrote *Mosc* has never been established. It was published posthumously in 1682. According to his own testimony he had undertaken the project "many years since." The "Advertisement" adds that he composed the piece "before he lost his sight" and that "sometime before his death [he] dispos'd of it to be printed. But it being small, the Bookseller hop'd to have procured some other suitable Piece of the same Author's to have been joyn'd with it, or else it had been publish'd 'ere now." There is a great probability that Milton actually wrote *Mosc* in the 1640s, perhaps in connection with the tutoring he was doing at that time. In 1648 Theodore Haak* told Samuel Hartlib* that "Milton is . . . writing . . . an Epitome of all Purchas* Volumes," which is identified with *Mosc*. The context suggests that the epitome has already been accomplished. At any rate the work is clearly what he hoped to make it, "a Pattern or Example" of what he thought a geography should be. "The study of Geography is both profitable and delightfull," he wrote in his Preface. And in *Educ* he advises the pupil "to learn in any modern Author, the use of the Globes, and all the Maps; first with the old names, and then with the new."

He is quite explicit about his intention. He finds that most geographers have "miss'd their proportions" by including extraneous details. When they do treat manners, they are apt to dwell on absurd superstitions, ceremonies, quaint habits, "and other petty Circumstances little to the purpose. Whereby that which is usefull, and onely worth observation, in such a wood of words, is either overslip't, or soon forgotten." His whole aim is to correct those faults, "to render others more cautious hereafter." Why he should have concentrated on Russia is another question. It was probably because, as he says, it was "first discovered by *English* Voi-

"and other petty Circumstances little to the purpose. Whereby that which is usefull, and onely worth observation, in such a wood of words, is either overslip't, or soon forgotten." His whole aim is to correct those faults, "to render others more cautious hereafter." Why he should have concentrated on Russia is another question. It was probably because, as he says, it was "first discovered by *English* Voiages." In other words, Milton's nationalism plays its part in the choice. Here as elsewhere he insists that he will reproduce only what has been "observ'd at several times by *Eye-witnesses* [italics added] so that old errors may be corrected by those "who describe the Countreys in their way far otherwise than our common Geographers." And the accounts Milton depends on are the narratives of England's own intrepid seafarers, Willoughby, Chancellor, and Jenkinson, those pioneers who opened up England's trade with Russia and whose accounts appear in the great collections of Hakluyt and Purchas.

Mosc is divided into five chapters. The first opens with the boundaries of the "Empire of Moscovia," proceeds to describe its great cities and rivers, next the government and armed forces, finally the religious, marriage, burial, and traveling habits. It is a model of logical orderliness. Chapter 2 is devoted to an account of regions to the northeast such as "Samoedia" and Siberia, which came under the Russian rule. The third chapter describes other countries to eastward, countries reaching to the very walls of Cathay, by which Milton professes himself to have been fascinated. The next chapter, in the manner of geographies of that time, provides a background of history by giving a brief account of the successive rulers. And the final chapter shows just what were the English connections with the vast eastern empire between 1553 and 1604. It is here that he speaks proudly of Willoughby and Chancellor and Jenkinson.

Characteristically Milton acknowledged his sources, Hakluyt and Purchas, mainly the former, even going to the extent of listing in the margins the exact pages from which he derived his material, exceptional to his usual practice of citing authorities in the text. The reader gets insight into the poet's mind by observing what he chose to omit and what to emphasize. Throughout, he stresses the *human* element. Next, his fine craftsmanship is shown in his fusion of two or more narratives. Nowhere can we observe better the operation of his sensitive mind recognizing likeness of material and so interweaving details from various sources that the result seems at once more full-bodied and concise. The special circumstances underlying the Willoughby-Chancellor expedition to Russia in some measure regulated Milton's story of that noble venture (10 : 364–67). Chancellor, the chief pilot, tells most of it, but there were some tragic developments, which Willoughby alone knew. Milton therefore uses the former as basis for his account but resorts to Willoughby for points of which Chancellor was ignorant; the result is a history complete in many details such as is found in no single voyager. The London preparations are all taken from the chief pilot. But the ship's course is copied from the admiral's log; from it Milton gets such geographic information as *"Aegelands," "Lofoot,"* and *"Seinam."* The calling together of Willoughby's captains for final instructions, however, is told from the point of view of Chancellor, who was himself one of those captains. At the time of writing Chancellor still did not know the fate of poor Willoughby, from whom a storm had separated him; and Milton therefore transfers to the latter's account and tells of his putting into Arzina in Lapland, of his desperately sending out contact parties in three directions, and of his perishing miserably "in bleak Arzina's road." Details of the death itself Milton took from a letter of Henry Lane, an agent of the Muscovy company. And now, with Willoughby dead, Milton returns at last to Chancellor and follows him out to the end. He had broken off just as the pilot major has uttered a fervent prayer for the safety of his emperor to King James. But then he turns back twelve pages and summons an incident that makes the beginning of Vasily's rule especially dramatic; the new czar was elected, "having not long before been at the Block for reporting to have seen the true *Demetrius* dead and buried." A later grafting illustrates the same quality. In telling about an upstart, Michael Pheodorowich, Milton consistently follows one section of his original. But then he transplants from the story of Michael's predecessor, Vasily, a telling incident wherein the latter consulted the sooth-sayers about the succession and, being duly warned against a man named Michael, had three aspirants of that name put to death, only to see this other unsuspected Michael, a mere axe-bearer in his household, succeed to the throne. Here was not merely drama but irony as well.

In some ways *Mosc* is a work thoroughly typical of Milton. He makes every effort to be objective but, given a mind as strong as his, preoccupations creep through. The voyager praised Russian subjects for their fealty to the czar: "Oh that our sturdie rebels were had in the like subjection to knowe their duety towarde their Princes." That passage finds no place in Milton's digest. On the other hand, though he shared with many of his countrymen a somewhat low opinion of Russia and the Russians, he pointed out elements that were right. He could not help admiring the hardiness of the Russian soldier; perhaps he was thinking of the lily-livered back home. He was duly impressed with the fact that in Russia "no man [was] forc'd to Religion." Furthermore, "wives are very obedient" and a man need not stay married to a woman who has proved her unfitness. When he dwells on the czar's being tyrannous, exacting in his taxes, Milton may well have King Charles* in mind. Democratic principles were seen to flourish even in darkest Russia; a mere butcher, brave enough to inveigh against corruption in high office, was able to rise till he became a councillor of state.

There are other ways in which *Mosc*

may be regarded as characteristic of Milton. It is, for instance, phenomenally accurate; in an age when orthographic rules were notoriously lenient, he spells complicated Russian names just as his sources do. Moreover, the human interest is forever present. Finally, the little geography exhibits his self-restraint, his sense of balance, and his concision, in other words his classicism. [RRC]

BRIEF NOTES UPON A LATE SERMON, Milton's response to a tactless sermon entitled, *The Fear of God and the King* (based on Prov. 24 : 21), preached by Matthew Griffith on March 25, 1660, which attacked both Independents* and the Presbyterians*, and called for the immediate restoration of Charles II*. When printed on March 31, the sermon was dedicated to General Monck*, a fact that proved embarrassing to the general since he was not yet ready to declare himself for Charles. Accordingly the Council ordered Griffith's imprisonment. Milton's response, *BN*, printed in early April without publisher's or printer's name, centered only on the theological issues. One expects more, but Milton fails to deal with the real issues of April 1660. Perhaps his faith in Monck, who had not acted as Milton earlier advised in *Way*, was thoroughly shaken. Milton probably hoped to stem the rising Royalist sentiment by playing on Griffith's impulsiveness and tactlessness, but the hope must have been faint. The poet in turn was answered by Roger L'Estrange* in *No Blind Guides* (dated April 20, 1660), headed by the motto: "If the blind lead the blind, both shall fall into the ditch." [WM]

BROMPTON, JOHN: *see* TWYSDEN, SIR ROGER.

BROWNE, WILLIAM: *see* MARGINALIA.

BUCER, MARTIN, also spelled Butzer (1491–1551), a first-generation Reformation leader of Strasbourg and Alsace, who attempted to mediate between Luther* and Zwingli*. Bucer served as adviser to

Calvin* and was called to England by Archbishop Cranmer to help revise the English liturgy. At Cambridge he wrote his masterwork, *De Regno Christi* (Basle, 1557), a portion of which Milton "epitomiz'd" in *Bucer*. Milton called him "the pastor of Nations," "the Apostle of our Church," and "that elect Instrument of Reformation."

Bucer was born in Sélèstat, Alsace, November 11, 1491, and educated as a Dominican. He entered the monastery at Heidelberg in 1517, where he came under the influence of Humanism*, learned Greek, read Plato*, and admired Erasmus*. When Luther disputed the Ninety-five Theses in 1518, Bucer turned toward Protestantism. After a struggle, he obtained release from his monastic vows in 1521, and, like Luther, married a nun. He began preaching Lutheran doctrines in Wissembourg, was excommunicated, and in 1524 became the first Evangelical preacher installed at Strasbourg, where he brought about many reforms in worship. With Bucer's help, Jacob Sturm (d. 1553) reformed Christian education from Kindergarten through Hochschule, and a new university was established. Bucer successfully opposed both Romanists and Anabaptists* in Strasbourg. On February 21, 1529, mass was abolished. Strasbourg had become a Protestant theocracy and international refuge for reformers, with Martin Bucer as foremost preacher and spokesman.

In 1531 Bucer was among the theologians whom Henry VIII asked for an opinion on his plan to divorce Catherine of Aragon. Like Luther, Bucer said no, but suggested bigamy as a solution since polygamy* is not contrary to divine law. In 1538 the Landgrave Philip of Hesse did avail himself of bigamy. Political pressures forced Bucer, then reluctant, to condone the arrangement.

After the Smalkald War (1546–1547), Emperor Charles V forced Catholic reforms upon Strasbourg. Rather than subscribe to the Interim, Bucer and his associate Paulus Fagius (d. 1549) chose exile. In October 1548, Archbishop Cranmer invited Bucer to become Regius Professor of Theology at Cambridge. Cranmer knew of Bucer's special ability in church liturgy and discipline and his support of civil authority. He asked Bucer for help on the (Second) Prayer Book of Edward VI (1552). In the Vestment Controversy, Bucer was asked to defend traditional usages against the Puritans. While at Cambridge, Bucer also strengthened English Humanism by initiating a correspondence between Roger Ascham* and Jacob Sturm. Bucer died at Cambridge on March 1, 1551. During the reign of Mary, he was condemned as a heretic, exhumed, and burned. Elizabeth restored his name to its place of honor.

Bucer's greatest achievement in England was the completion of *De Regno Christi*, published posthumously in 1557 and again in 1577 in a folio edition of works, lectures, and letters entitled *Scripta Anglicana*, edited by Conrad Hubert. In *De Regno Christi* Bucer advises King Edward on social and ecclesiastical reforms needed for establishing Christ's kingdom in England. Book 1 concerns the duties of ministers to teach doctrine, administer sacraments, and discipline the congregation. Book 2 unfolds the duty of Edward as sovereign to reform religious education, observance of the Sabbath, the poor laws, and particularly the laws on marriage* and divorce*. Edward is advised to institute truly Christian laws, legalizing divorce for spiritual causes as well as physical, since the morality of the commonwealth ("respublica Christiana") is rooted in wholesome family relations. Appealing to the primitive church, the Fathers, the Scriptures, and natural law as incorporated in Roman civil law, Bucer contends in 2 : 22–47 that Christian marriages are civil rather than ecclesiastical and may be dissolved when the spiritual solaces of matrimony are frustrated.

According to Milton, it was about three months after he published the second edition of *DDD* (i.e., ca. April or May, 1644) that *"I then first came to hear that Martin Bucer had written much concerning divorce: whom earnestly turning over, I soon perceav'd, but not without amazement, in the same opinion, confirm'd with the same reasons which in that publisht book without the help or imitation of any precedent Writer, I had labour'd out, and laid together"* (4 : 13). Milton was elated to find that Bucer had anticipated the argument that Christ's words on divorce in Matthew 5 must be interpreted by comparison with other Scriptures such as Deuteronomy 24 : 1. In *Tetra* (1645) Milton includes Bucer among the "famousest" Reformed divines who support his position on civil divorce, translating a sentence from *De Regno Christi*, 2 : 49 (4: 244).

Bucer's importance was primarily as corroborator for Milton, who was convinced by *Scripta Anglicana* that his own discoveries on Christian divorce were providential. The way was again opening in England for the reforming of Reformation. [TLH]

BUCHANAN, GEORGE (1506–1582),

Scottish poet, historian, political theorist, translator, and educational reformer, educated at St. Andrews (Edinburgh) and at Paris (1520–1528). Buchanan's early mastery of the classical languages and humanistic disciplines made him a sought-after tutor for a number of French and Scottish noblemen, particularly the young James VI, later James I* of England. The elegant style of his classical tragedies (*Baptistes, Medea, Jephthes, Alcestis,* 1530–1545) and his Latin translations of the Psalms (early 1550s) won him wide recognition and several university posts on the Continent.

Always testy by nature, Buchanan was an accomplished satirist and polemicist of political and ecclesiastical abuses (*Franciscanus et Fratres,* 1536–1539) and ran afoul of the Catholic powers on several occasions in Scotland, France and Portugal. His sense of the terror of tyrannous political power, sharpened by a lengthy forced seclusion by the Inquisition in the early 1550s, became a dominant theme in his writings for the rest of his life. With this background, Elizabeth was fortunate that Buchanan was in a position to help prosecute Mary Queen of Scots in the notorious Darnley affair and to investigate the Norfolk rebellion in the late 1560s. The results of this long inquiry were published in his scurrilous pamphlet, *A Detection of the Doings of Mary, Queen of Scots,* in 1571.

Near the end of his life, Buchanan completed his two major works of history and political thought: *History of Scottish Matters* (1582) and *The Powers of the Crown in Scotland* (1579), the latter a defense of limited monarchy and the power of the people to depose tyrants. Something of Buchanan's political and educational orientation would certainly have reached Milton through his teacher, Thomas Young*, himself a product of the reforms of St. Andrews carried on by Buchanan and Andrew Melville.

Although there has been considerable commentary on the relationship between Buchanan's Latin lyrics and Milton's, not much in Milton's Latin elegiac* verse can be attributed directly to the influence of Buchanan. Milton echoes several phrases from *Maiae Calendae* in *El* 5 and *El* 7. There are a few insignificant verbal parallels between Milton's other Latin poems and Buchanan's *De Sphaera* (1586), *Psalms* (1566), and *Baptistes* (1578). Thomas Warton* found several parts of Buchanan's *Franciscanus* (1566) analogous to the description of Satan (*PL* 1. 80ff.) and some other passages in *QNov.* From remarks by Francis Peck* in *New Memoirs of John Milton* (1740), it has sometimes been thought that Milton was the author of an English rendering of the *Baptistes* that appeared in 1642. But this is patently absurd and merely an unfounded guess on Peck's part. In his prose treatises, Milton shows thorough knowledge of Buchanan's major prose works. There are two citations from the *History* in *CB*, pp. 186 and 198, dated 1639–1641 (?) and after 1652. In *Brit*, Milton refers to the *History* several times as a source for facts, on several occasions gently chastizing Buchanan for his bias in reporting several English victories over the

Scots and for some inconsistency in insisting on historical accuracy at the same time that he adds, as in the case of Arthurian legend, some speculations of his own. Milton also uses Buchanan's *History* for facts to support the justice of deposing bad kings, citing the Scottish custom of choosing clan leaders by vote and referring to the people's refusal of allegiance to Mary Queen of Scots for breaking her oath to them. Both Milton, in *Eikon,* and Buchanan, in *Powers* and *History,* cite examples of princes and prelates submitting themselves to law, notably Trajan's decree that he should be deposed by sword should he abuse his power. Although many of Buchanan's ideas in these works are close to those in *Tenure* and *Eikon,* there is, finally, not much *direct* resemblance between these works in tone and structure. Besides the sundry facts to support his own positions, what Milton found most amenable in Buchanan's works was, perhaps, his outspoken defense of liberty against tyrants. [GHS]

BUCHANAN, JAMES: *see* ADAPTATIONS.

BUCK, THOMAS: *see* PRINTERS.

BUCKINGHAM, GEORGE VILLIERS, FIRST DUKE OF (1592–1628), a favorite of James I* and Charles I*, a significant minister in their court. Buckingham, Chancellor of Cambridge (1626–1628), was assassinated by John Felton in 1628. Milton had little regard for Buckingham and accused him of poisoning King James and of being an improper and immoral guide to King Charles (*Eikon, 1Def*). [WM]

BÜRDE, SAMUEL GOTTLIEB: *see* TRANSLATIONS, POETIC.

BURNETT, GEORGE: *see* EDITIONS, PROSE.

BURNEY, EDWARD F.: *see* ILLUSTRATIONS.

BURNING OR CONFISCATION OF MILTON'S WORKS. Public burnings of *1Def* occurred in Toulouse on June 25, 1651, on an order dated June 7, and in Paris on June 26, 1651, on an order dated June 26. The orders are found, respectively, in the Bibliothèque Nationale, MS F. L. 602, ff. 21–22 and f. 23. Reports of the action are found in *Hollandsche Mercurius* (July 1651), p. 70; *Mercurius Politicus**, No. 56 (June 26–July 3, 1651), p. 899; and ibid., No. 57 (July 3–10, 1651), pp. 913–15. Condemnation was imposed because the tract contained impious and seditious ideas tending to destroy the monarchies established by God and because it was injurious to Royal authority. Further, a newsletter among the Thurloe* papers (Bodleian, Rawlinson MS A.9, f. 73v) prints a communiqué from Ratisbon, dated December 18, 1653, that "all the bookes of Miltonius" were to be confiscated. In England, after the Restoration, the House of Commons called for confiscation and burning of *Eikon* and *1Def,* and *A Proclamation** by Charles II* was promulgated on August 13, 1660. According to White Kennet in *A Register and Chronicle* (1728), 1 : 239, the public burning took place on August 27. There may have been additional acts in the days following; at least undated reports are given in *The Parliamentary Intelligencer* for September 3–10, p. 589, and *Mercurius Publicus* for September 6–13, p. 578 of the London edition. Two books of Milton's were also burned at Oxford in 1683, *Tenure* and *1Def*; see *The Judgment and Decree of the University of Oxford Past in Their Convocation July 21. 1683, Against certain Pernicious Books and Damnable Doctrines Destructive to the Sacred Persons of Princes, their State and Government, and of all Humane Society* (1683), heresies nos. 3 and 26. Richard Baron* reported from John Swale, a bookseller, that "*Many High-Church Priests and Doctors*" of Leeds, during the eighteenth century, sought to destroy Milton's prose works, most notably *Eikon* and *1Def;* see his edition of *Eikon* (1756), Preface, p. iv. [JTS]

BURNS, ROBERT (1756–1796), the Scottish poet, shows no direct influence from Milton in his verse, but he does mention Milton once in his poems and twelve times in his letters, most significantly with references to Satan, "my favorite hero." He wrote in 1787 that he purchased a copy of Milton "in order to study the sentiments—the dauntless magnanimity, the intrepid, unyielding independence, the desperate daring, and noble defiance of hardship, in that great personage, Satan." [WM]

BURTON, ROBERT (1577–1640), the younger son of a Leicestershire family, was vicar of St. Thomas's in Oxford. Admitted as a student of Christ Church, Oxford, in 1599, he lived there the rest of his life. His Latin comedy, *Philosophaster*, not printed till 1862, was performed at Christ Church in 1618. Aside from Latin poems for many Oxford anthologies, his only work published during his lifetime was the enormously popular *Anatomy of Melancholy*, written, says Burton, to relieve his own acute despondency. First printed in 1621, it was altered and enlarged by the author in five more editions, the last one posthumous (1651). Frequently digressing, garnished with satire, and drawing on more than a thousand authorities—the majority of them obscure—the *Anatomy* was long regarded as a curious collection of antiquated lore; more recent opinion considers it also as a serious study of the causes, symptoms, and cure of psychological depression and as anticipating the findings and the approach of modern psychoanalysis (see Bergen Evans, *The Psychiatry of Robert Burton* [1944]).

Many of Burton's notions on such topics as the humours*, the fabric of the heavens, the nature of spirits, and the psychology of love* were so commonplace that their occurrence in Milton's work, occasionally noted by the poet's editors, argues no proof of influence. Several scholars have pointed to closer similarities. George Whiting (*Milton's Literary Milieu* [1939]) found parallels in the *Anatomy* for the catalogue of fallen angels (*PL* 1. 376–521) and the golden chain from heaven (*PL* 2. 1051–52); W. J. Grace (*Studies in Philology* 52 : 578–91) points to verbal echoes of Burton's Limbo in the Paradise of Fools* (*PL* 3. 422–97) and gives Burton's comment on Rome's doctrine of reward and punishment ("two battering Cannons and principle Engines") as a possible source of the "two-handed engine" in *Lyc*; J. B. Leishman (*Milton's Minor Poems* [1969]) traces line 28 of *L'Al* ("Nods, and Becks, and Wreathed Smiles") to Burton's translation of a passage from Musaeus's *Hero and Leander*.

In 1785, Thomas Warton gave Burton's "Abstract of Melancholy," a poem included in the 1628 edition, as a source for *L'Al* and *IlP*. W. J. Grace ("Notes") argues that Milton owes to Burton's poem the distinction between "loathed" and "divinest" Melancholy, which leads to religious contemplation. Leishman (*Minor Poems*) denies that the "Abstract" makes such a distinction and finds Milton's debt to Burton on this point unproved. [JRM]

BYRON, GEORGE GORDON, LORD: *see* INFLUENCE ON THE LITERATURE OF NINETEENTH-CENTURY ENGLAND, MILTON'S.

CONTRIBUTORS TO VOLUME 1

AA   Arthur Axelrad. California State University, Long Beach, Calif. 90840.
ACL   Albert C. Labriola. Duquesne University, Pittsburgs, Pa. 15219.
ALT   Amy Lee Turner. 833 S. Kennerly Ave., Tyler, Texas 75701.
CAP   C. A. Patrides. University of York, Heslington, England.
CH   Calvin Huckabay. Houston Baptist College, Houston, Texas 77036.
ERG   E. R. Gregory. University of Toledo, Toledo, Ohio 43606.
ETM   Elizabeth T. McLaughlin. Bucknell University, Lewisburg, Pa. 17837.
EW   Edward Weismiller. George Washington University, Washington, D.C. 20052
GHS   Gerald H. Snare. Tulane University, New Orleans, La. 70118.
ILD   Ivar Lou Duncan. 3627 Valley Vista Road, Nashville, Tenn. 37205.
JAW   Joseph A. Wittreich, Jr. University of Maryland, College Park, Md. 20742
JCB   Jackson C. Boswell. University of the District of Columbia, Washington, D.C. 20001.
JD   James Dale. McMaster University, Hamilton, Ontario, Canada.
JGD   John G. Demaray. University of Kentucky, Lexington, Ky. 40506.
JGT   James G. Taaffe, Case Western Reserve University, Cleveland, Ohio 41106.
JHS   James H. Sims. University of Southern Mississippi, Hattiesburg, Miss. 39401.
JMS   John M. Steadman. Huntington Library and Art Gallery, San Marino, Calif. 91108.
JRK   John R. Knott, Jr. University of Michigan, Ann Arbor, Mich. 48104.
JRM   John R. Mulder. Drew University, Madison, N.J. 07940.
JTS   John T. Shawcross. City University of New York, N.Y., N.Y. 10036.
JWH   Jack W. Herring. Baylor University, Waco, Texas 75703.
MF   Michael Fixler. Tufts University, Boston, Mass. 02155.
MLD   Michael L. Donnelly, Kansas State University, Manhattan, Kansas 66502.
MM   Marian E. Musgrave. Miami University, Oxford, Ohio 45056.
PAF   Peter A. Fiore. O.F.M. Siena College, Loudonville, N.Y. 12211.
PEB   Purvis E. Boyette. Tulane University, New Orleans, La. 70118.

PGH   Patrick G. Hogan. University of Houston, Houston, Texas 77004.

PMZ   Paul M. Zall. California State University, Los Angeles, Calif. 90032.

PRS   Paul R. Sellin. University of California, Los Angeles, Calif. 90024.

RCF   Roy C. Flannagan. Ohio University, Athens, Ohio 45701.

RF   Robert Fox. St. Francis' College, Brooklyn, N.Y. 11201.

RHW   Robert H. West. University of Georgia, Athens, Ga. 30602.

RMa   Rosemary Masek. University of Nevada, Las Vegas, Nev. 89109.

RMF   Roland Mushat Frye. University of Pennsylvania, Philadelphia, Pa. 19104.

RRC   Robert R. Cawley. Late of Princeton University, Princeton, N.J. 08540.

RS   Reed Stock. Utah State University, Logan, Utah 84321.

SEF   Stanley E. Fish. The Johns Hopkins University, Baltimore, Md. 21218.

SW   Susanne Woods. Brown University, Providence, R.I. 02912.

TAC   Thomas A. Carnicelli. University of New Hampshire, Durham, N.H. 03824.

TLH   Theodore L. Huguelet. Western Carolina University, Cullowhee, N.C. 28723.

VRM   Virginia R. Mollenkott. William Paterson College, Wayne, N.J. 07470.

WBH   William B. Hunter, Jr. University of Houston, Houston, Texas 77004.

WJO   Walter J. Ong, S.J. St. Louis University, St. Louis, Mo. 63103.

WM   Willis Monie. P.O. Box 105, Hartwick, N.Y. 13348.